Themes of Peace in Renaissance Poetry

Cephisodotus, *Eirene*, fragment of a marble copy, Metropolitan Museum of Art, New York. (Photograph courtesy of the Museum)

Themes of Peace in Renaissance Poetry

JAMES HUTTON

EDITED BY

RITA GUERLAC

Cornell University Press

ITHACA AND LONDON

THIS BOOK HAS BEEN PUBLISHED WITH THE
AID OF A GRANT FROM THE HULL MEMORIAL
PUBLICATION FUND OF CORNELL UNIVERSITY

First published 1984 by Cornell University Press.
Published in the United Kingdom by
Cornell University Press Ltd., London.

International Standard Book Number 0-8014-1613-2
Library of Congress Catalog Card Number 84-7631
Printed in the United States of America
*Librarians: Library of Congress cataloging information
appears on the last page of the book.*

*The paper in this book is acid-free and meets the guidelines
for permanence and durability of the Committee on Production
Guidelines for Book Longevity of the Council on Library Resources.*

I'vo gridando pace, pace, pace.

Petrarch, *Canzoniere*, Italia Mia, 122

Contents

Editor's Preface

'This little book,' wrote James Hutton in a draft for a preface, 'may be said to have written itself without full intention on my part. . . . I have constantly tried to reef sails and hug the shore, avoiding wake and deep, but the subject constantly thrusts out to further implication. "Sempre si fa il mare maggiore."'

Had James Hutton published no more than his two monumental volumes on the Greek Anthology in Italy and in France and the Netherlands, his reputation would be secure and scholars of the Renaissance deep in his debt. But the books on the transmission of the Anthology in the West were merely the groundwork he considered essential for the study of Renaissance poetry, both Latin and vernacular, and its permeation by the poetry and thought of antiquity. The groundwork laid, he could turn his attention, his extraordinary scholarship, and his poetic sensibility to a single, grander theme.

He tells us that the collecting of materials for the *Anthology in France* was virtually ended in the summer of 1939, though the volume did not go to the printer until late in 1944. In the interval came the war, with its horrors on a scale mankind so far had never known. To this most pacific of men, the war inevitably called up the themes of peace as yearned for and celebrated by poets through the ages. The alluring portraits of peace in Bacchylides and Stobaeus; the haunting prayer of the imprisoned Charles d'Orléans; Molinet's bitter *Testament*; the impassioned words of Erasmus; Ronsard's high eloquence; and the succession of voices down the centuries—homely, lofty, lyrical, classical, and Judaeo-Christian—cried out to be brought together to attest the innate desire of mankind for peace. But at the same time the deep skepticism of the war-torn sixteenth century led to disturbing doubts that man could be a peaceable animal.

[9]

The book on the peace poems, as it was known to his friends, was effectively completed by 1960, but Hutton put it aside. Perhaps the reason lay, as his friend Friedrich Solmsen believed, in a growing and almost crippling perfectionism. At any rate, he continued to publish elegant articles on a wide range of subjects. His never-failing generosity to students, colleagues, and friends, whose manuscripts he perused with the same meticulous care he gave his own, consumed much of his time and energy, as did his professional activities beyond the campus. He was a founding member of the Renaissance Society of America, an adviser and referee to university presses and learned periodicals, and an important contributor to such far-reaching enterprises as P. O. Kristeller's Catalogue of Mediaeval and Renaissance Latin Translations and Commentaries.

In the summer of 1978, when I proposed to James Hutton to collect his published articles into a single volume of essays, he appeared surprised but pleased. His health was declining, and he said he was nearly resigned to being a helpless invalid. My husband and I were to spend the academic year 1978–79 in England. When I went to say good-bye I asked if he had planned any disposition of the peace poems. Would he like them sent to a younger scholar who was working along similar lines? His answer was monosyllabic: No.

That year in Cambridge, I assembled the writings that were to appear as *Essays on Renaissance Poetry*, and when I returned we worked on them together, adding three previously unpublished works. In the fall of 1980 I was able to put the page proofs into his hands. The last day I visited him he remarked that the publication of the *Essays* encouraged him to think the peace poems, too, might appear in print. The manuscript was too unwieldy for him to handle, he said, and it was unpaginated. I promised to come one day soon, spread it out on the floor, and go over it with him. And then time ran out.

James Hutton's will named three of his friends to 'take charge of all my unpublished manuscripts to do with as they think best.' Knowing how much the peace poems meant to him, I volunteered to take charge of them.

It was clear that during my year in Cambridge, Hutton had spent time on the book. The manuscript was finished, much of it retyped, with only a few teasing lacunae—'the precocious hand of Camilla Morel, then   years old.' Camilla's sole literary bequest to posterity, so far as I could ascertain, was her introductory couplet to Arnold de Pujol's poem *De pace*, but I found that her age was ten; I also tracked down such minutiae as the device of Henri II and the name of Galen's uranoscopus.

The notes, however, were a thorny thicket. It would have been fun to work on them with Hutton; without him they were a nightmare. Some were fragmentary, cryptic, mere clues. One note was peremptory: 'Search.' Another said, 'For the Middle Ages I cite at random — —.' To compound the difficulty, Hutton's library, which contained some few of the rare sixteenth-century books not in the Cornell University Library, was sold and dispersed immediately after his death. I had the good fortune to consult those books in the Réserve of the Bibliothèque Nationale in 1981, and in 1982 to visit the Bibliothèque de la Ville de Lyon.

So the notes are as nearly complete as I could make them. The rest of the book is presented just as Hutton left it. Nothing has been added (except for a few translations of Greek passages, mine in square brackets) or deleted. I have not attempted to bring references or bibliography up to date or, of course, to modernize or standardize the orthography of the French poems. The few references to works published after 1970 are enclosed in square brackets.

James Hutton's book stands on its own merits, the work of an erudite and humane scholar, touched with his own wit and grace. May it be a talisman for us in a time when the world faces dangers inconceivable when *Themes of Peace* was begun.

> Donc, Paix fille de Dieu . . . veuilles de ta grace
> A jamais nous aymer, & toute notre race.

RITA GUERLAC

Ithaca, New York

Acknowledgments

Once again Professor Hutton's friends and colleagues have helped me in preparing one of his books, and their many generous contributions are acknowledged in the footnotes. In his own Department of Classics at Cornell I wish to mention Kevin Clinton and especially Gordon M. Kirkwood. Professor Kirkwood, who has just seen Hutton's edition of Aristotle's *Poetics* through the press, has encouraged me from the start and read sections of the manuscript. As editorial assistant Martha Malamud, also of the Classics Department, has provided wise and indispensable help in completing the footnotes. I am grateful for the ready assistance of the staffs of the Cornell University Libraries, the Réserve of the Bibliothèque Nationale, and the Bibliothèque de la Ville de Lyon. My greatest debt is to James Hutton's longtime friend Professor Paul Oskar Kristeller, who very kindly read the whole typescript and saved me from numerous mistakes. Any that remain are of course my own.

R. G.

Abbreviations

Baudrier	Henri Louis Baudrier, *Bibliothèque Lyonnaise* (Lyons, 1895–1921)
Bellum	Erasmus, *Adagia, Dulce bellum inexpertis* LB 2
BHR	*Bibliothèque d'humanisme et renaissance*
BM	British Museum
BN Rés.	Bibliothèque Nationale, Réserve
Cat. Roths.	*Catalogue des livres . . . du feu M. le baron James de Rothschild* (Paris, 1884–1920)
CPI	*Carmina illustrium poetarum Italorum* (Florence, 1719–26)
DND	Cicero, *De natura deorum*
DPB	Janus Gruter, *Delitiae C. Poetarum Belgicorum* (Frankfurt, 1614)
DPG	Janus Gruter, *Delitiae C. Poetarum Gallorum* (Frankfurt, 1609)
DPI	Janus Gruter, *Delitiae CC. Poetarum Italorum* (Frankfurt, 1608)
DPS	*Delitiae C. Poetarum Scotorum* (Amsterdam, 1637)
Du Verdier	*Bibliothèque françoise*, Rigoley de Juvigny, ed. (Paris, 1772)
Exhort.	Ronsard, *Exhortation pour la Paix*
Laumonier	Ronsard, *Œuvres complètes, édition critique*, Paul Laumonier, ed. (Paris, 1937)
LB	*Desiderii Erasmi Opera Omnia*, J. Clericus, ed. (Lugduni Batavorum [Leiden], 1703–6)
Le Roux de Lincy, *Chants*	Le Roux de Lincy, *Receuil des chants historiques depuis le xiie jusqu'au xviiie siècle* (Paris, 1865)
Lovejoy-Boas	Arthur O. Lovejoy and George Boas, *Primitivism and Related Ideas in Antiquity* (Baltimore, 1935)
Migne, *PG*	J. P. Migne, *Patrologiae cursus completus, series Graeca* (Paris, 1857–94)

Abbreviations

Migne, *PL*	J. P. Migne, *Patrologiae cursus completus, series Latina* (Paris, 1844–64)
Milton, *PL*	John Milton, *Paradise Lost*
Niceron	Jean-Pierre Niceron, *Mémoires pour servir à l'histoire des hommes illustrés* . . . (Paris, 1727–38)
Ode	Ronsard, *Ode de la Paix*
Paix	Ronsard, *La Paix, au Roy*
PW	A. Pauly, G. Wissowa, and W. Kroll, *Real-Encyclopädie der klassischen Altertumswissenschaft* (Stuttgart, 1894–)
Querela	Erasmus, *Adagia, Querela pacis*, LB 2
Répertoire	Louis Petit de Julleville, *Répertoire du théâtre comique en France au moyen âge* (Paris, 1886)
RHL	*Revue d'histoire littéraire de France*
Roscher	W. H. Roscher, *Ausführliches Lexikon des Griechischen Mythologie* (Leipzig, 1884–86)
SVF	H. F. A. von Arnim, *Stoicorum Veterum Fragmenta* (Leipzig, 1903–24)

Themes of Peace in
Renaissance Poetry

Introductory

Whe know what Peace looks like. Peace is a female figure of mild countenance, clad in flowing antique garments, with a wreath of laurel or corn spikes in her hair, and bearing in her hand an olive branch or a staff, more rarely the cornucopia. She is often represented with large wings at her back, and above her head there appears a dove that may have a sprig of olive in its beak. We owe this symbol to the coinage of the Roman Empire through the revival of ancient iconology in picture books and paintings of the sixteenth and seventeenth centuries. Some of the attributes—olive branch, staff, cornucopia—carry Pax back to the Greek Eirene; the dove may have associations with Aphrodite; and the laurel and the wings were added by the Romans from Victoria, since peace and victory were inseparable to the Roman mind. In a Christian culture, however, it is likely that the wings suggest an angel rather than a goddess of peace; and the dove is a Christian, indeed a modern, addition to the picture. It first appears in a second-century catacomb fresco, and from an early period it is found in all baptisteries. With olive spray it recalls the dove of Noah, the end of cataclysm, and the reconciliation of God and man; but the dove goes deeper in the Christian tradition as the symbol of the Holy Spirit, and the Spirit is peace—indeed the Holy Spirit of Christian theology takes up the function of the Stoic Spirit in 'holding the universe together' in peaceful order; and still more definitely the position of the dove over the head of Peace suggests the Jordan baptism: Christ is Peace (Eph. 2.14).

Such symbols are the common coin of public intercourse, varying in value with the strength of the tradition. The public artist must new mint them, assembling the familiar attributes in such a way as to communicate a fresh idea suited to his historical moment—joyful, it may be, or bitter. The poets have been in exactly the same position with regard to the symbols and motifs they use, and in the Renaissance occupied it gladly. This is the more true when the poets handle subjects of public, and not merely private, emotion. The Renaissance knew that poets—witness Virgil and Horace—had always been close to kings; and an inner instinct urged every Renaissance poet to come as close to the Court as he could. His humanist education too was oriented towards public functions and was admirably adapted to the opportunities offered by the monarchical and ecclesiastical pattern of the times. What did he learn if it was not to compose *epistulae, orationes*, and *poemata*? And it never occurred to him that the last, as well as the first two genres, should not be employed on public matters. A vast amount of 'occasional' verse was written, to which the modern literary historian turns a blind eye, hurrying past it for the most part under the impression, apparently, that only love poetry is literature. But the term 'occasional verse' is modern and will interest the historian of the period that coined it. The Renaissance poet regarded the writing of such poetry as a serious part of his career, and there is probably as much 'sincerity' in it as in his sonnets; he certainly put into it a full measure of his literary skill.

The poet who set out to write on peace had at his command a much larger fund of *topoi* than the graphic artist handling the same theme. He could draw, with some limitations, on the whole literature of peace. In this literature, from antiquity to the present day, the topics tend to range themselves in accordance with whether the main intention is philosophical, rhetorical, or poetical. It is the first category that chiefly survives in modern plans and arguments for international peace; among its topics, traditional from the Hellenistic period onward, may be mentioned 'all men have the same birth and destiny,' 'the peace principle extends from the individual personality to the family, the state, the world,' 'the cohesive principle of the material universe is peace.' Christian theology here inherited much from the philosophical schools. The rhetorical strain perhaps represents the oldest peace literature, going back to the Sophists; it influenced the philosophical discussions and later borrowed freely from them, so that we shall often be justified in speaking of a 'prose tradition' including both the philosophical and the rhetorical topics. The orations of Dio and Gregory Nazianzen on behalf of peace employ philosophical and theological motifs for their rhetorical purpose, as do also the later sermons. A typical rhetorical topic, however, advanced by the Sophists, is the admonitory example of the lower animals: 'within their several kinds they live at peace, but man destroys his own kind.' In antiquity the poetical tradition is quite different and scarcely knows these topics; it is close to the symbols of graphic representation in statues and coins: for the Greek poets peace represents plenty and fruitfulness; for the Roman it is associated with the Golden Age which the poet hopes to see realized in an orderly empire. The fundamental difference is obvious: the prose writers are arguing for peace and seek topics or arguments, while the poets for the most part are celebrating peace as attained or the peace hero who has attained it.

The eclectic Renaissance poets often cross this line, sometimes advocating, sometimes celebrating peace, though basically they follow the topics of the ancient poets. The typical Renaissance peace poem, as a form, was unknown to antiquity. It is an oration, an encomium, in verse, often consciously modeled on the rules of the prose encomium; but for its substance, the beneficence of peace, it draws on the ancient poetical celebrations rather than on the hortatory writers. And yet by grace of rhetoric the topics of the latter gradually creep in. Ronsard, seizing a unique moment when peace is in sight but not yet confirmed, can write a 'deliberative' oration in verse in his *Exhortation pour la Paix*. We may find some interest in seeing how he chooses and handles his motives. And in general, there is, I think, much to be learned about Renaissance poetry in contemplating our assembly of some 150 poems, all drawing from the same fund of topics and based on a common rhetorical tradition, but adapted to the historical moment, and each seeking originality of arrangement and 'idea,' as, for example, the embodiment of the praise of peace in an eclogue—drawn perhaps from Calpurnius—a favorite form, enriched not only by allusions to Virgil but by an unexpressed parallel with the shepherds of the Nativity; or a lively narrative in allegory of how Peace is brought down from heaven to earth.

The great year, perhaps in all time, for peace poems was 1559, on the occasion of the Peace of Cateau-Cambrésis. Perhaps in part by concerted action, a remarkable number of poets brought out in small separate brochures their poetical offering on this event. It was indeed a great occasion; but it also coincided, in France, with the most mature and vigorous moment in the development of the Renaissance style of poetry. Peace poems had been written in France since the fourteenth century; humanists in Italy had set the form for the rhetorical peace poem; we shall include these in our survey, and also some later examples of the type, but everything leads up to, or away from, 1559.

I

Pax Aeterna: The Tradition

Debellare superbos / Pacisque imponere morem . . .
                                                    Aen. 6.852–53

To battle down the proud, and impose the rule of peace . . .

I t will be the special object of later sections of this essay to
relate the topics employed by the Renaissance poets to the
ancient tradition which they were reviving. We shall there call upon
the individual topics as we need them. In this section, I have ventured
to cast a perspective glance upon the tradition from which they
worked. As an outline, it does not pretend to be complete or evenly
consecutive, but only to chart successive moments in the stream of ut-
terance about peace up to the Renaissance, and thus to suggest both
the parts of the tradition upon which the poets fastened and the parts
which they abandoned.[1]

The alternation of peace and war forms a fundamental contrast in
the experience of humanity, both states being rooted in the nature of
man, as the mediaeval psychologists noted, yet both 'coming upon'

[1]For the ancient period, complete and penetrating studies will be found in the well-
known book of Harald Fuchs, *Augustin und der antike Friedensgedanke* (Neue Philolo-
gische Untersuchungen 3) (Berlin, 1926), and in Wilhelm Nestle, *Der Friedensgedanke in
der antiken Welt* [*Philologus*, Suppl. 31, Heft 1] (Leipzig, 1938), and in the earlier work of
W. E. Caldwell, *Hellenic Conceptions of Peace* (New York, 1919) (*Studies in History, Econom-
ics and Public Law*, Columbia University, vol. 84, no. 2). These are complemented by the
articles "Eirene" and "Pax" by Otto Waser and Carl Koch respectively in PW. For the
Hebrew-Christian tradition, see the bibliography in Fuchs, p. 205, n. 1, and also the ar-
ticle "Paix" in the *Dictionnaire de Théologie Catholique*. For the early Middle Ages we
have Roger Bonnaud Delamare, *L'Idée de paix à l'époque carolingienne* (Paris, 1939); but
the work on the idea of peace from the eleventh to the thirteenth centuries promised by
the same author (p. 316) has not appeared. My dependence on these works, and on oth-
ers mentioned as we proceed, is obvious, and had it not seemed desirable to provide
here a background for the Renaissance poets, I would gladly have substituted for this
chapter a reference to them.

him as though they were external and objective events or even hostile and benevolent personalities. War, as the more forceful and noticeable, and to human feeling exceptional, probably is the first to assume this personal character. In Homer, Ares or Enyalios is a divinity and 'real,' while the state of peace does not appear in personified form. No doubt is left that 'impetuous Ares' is a hateful power, and a text is provided for later advocates of peace in the words Zeus addresses to him (*Il.* 5.890): 'Most hateful to me art thou of all gods who hold Olympus.' The representation on the Shield of Achilles (*Il.* 18. 490–540) of the city at war and the city at peace as an epitome of the world witness to a refined sense of imagery on the part of this poet of the warlike epos, and in the city at peace he graphically portrays the association of peace with plenty which the *Odyssey* also assumes: πλοῦτος δὲ καὶ εἰρήνη ἅλις ἔστω (and let them have prosperity and peace in abundance [Lattimore]) (24.486), and which was in fact the fundamental Greek reaction to the idea of peace. Nevertheless, Peace also appears early in personalized form, and we may emphasize here at once that throughout the Western tradition peace is never regarded as the mere absence of war, but as a positive and effective idea, productive of benefits deserving of praise, as fundamental to life and prior to war, which is waged only for its sake. Such an attitude seems clearly implied in Hesiod's *Theogony* (901–3), where Peace (Eirene) first appears in divine form as one of the three Horai, Dike, Eunomia, and Eirene, daughters of Zeus and Themis.[2] Though Horai or Seasons, they are, as their names and parentage indicate, the apotheosis primarily of political and human virtues, not powers of nature. They keep human affairs in order (ὡρεύουσι 'explaining' Ὥρας); and their very association amounts to the statement that, under Zeus, justice, lawfulness, and peace are interdependent and interactive. This is indeed the statement of *Works and Days* 228, where we are told that those who do justice (δίκη) to citizen and foreigner alike see their city flourish, 'and Peace nurse of children is in their land, nor does far-seeing Zeus ever decree for them a cruel war.' 'Nurse of children' (κουροτρόφος) became a standard epithet for Eirene.[3] In *Works and Days* also, peace evidently is assumed to have been the condition of the men of the Golden Age, who dwelt in quiet (ἥσυχοι

[2]The 'Daughters of God,' sometimes four in number, sometimes three, is a theme that runs through peace poems of every period.

[3]Other references to Eirene with epithets: *Lyr. adesp.* in Stobaeus 1.5.10–12 (Herbert Weir Smyth, *Greek Melic Poets* [London, 1900], p. 147); στεφανοφόρον Εἰρήναν [Garland-bearing Peace], plus Smyth note, p. 427, on Horai in art and literature; Anonymous, *Hymn to the Curetes*, 1.40, φιλόλβος Εἰρήνα [Peace, lover of gladness], J. V. Powell, *Collectanea Alexandrina* (Oxford, 1925), p. 161.

119), and it is only the third, brazen, generation who cared for Ares (145–46) and perished thereby. Later writers on peace would make much of this implication.

The association of peace and justice is an obvious (and certainly important) political observation (the Christian centuries will more often quote Isaiah than Hesiod, 'Justitiae opus pax'; and Pindar, in an ode full of 'justice,' refines on his predecessor in making Peace ('Ησυχία) the daughter of Dike: 'Kindly Hesychia, daughter of Dike, who makest cities great, holding the master keys of councils and of wars' (*Pyth.* 8.1–4). We note in passing that a stray fragment of one of Pindar's hyporchemes gave to Erasmus the occasion of one of the most famous of peace manifestos: Γλνκὺ δὲ πολέμος ἀπείροισιν, *Dulce bellum inexpertis.*[4]

The Horai often appear separately, and Eirene, like Dike and Eunomia, has a life of her own, sometimes, such is the Greek facility of personification, seeming to be created afresh from political experience.[5] Such an Eirene, great in her own right, is celebrated in a paean of Bacchylides which will occupy us on a later page (below, Ch. V). A famous poem in antiquity, it is echoed by Euripides and still quoted by Plutarch, and gave to the tradition a much-repeated epithet for Peace 'deep in wealth' (βαθύμλουτος) and an image—the cobwebbed armor—that has never died. Upon the conclusion of peace treaties a paean was regularly sung (Xenophon *Hell.* 7.4.36, Arr. 7.11), but we cannot assume that Bacchylides' paean was composed for such an occasion, nor indeed that the whole poem was dedicated to the subject of peace.[6] The goddess of Peace always remained something of an allegory, yet was not altogether without a cult, at least in Athens, where she may have been regarded as an aspect of Athena.[7] We hear of an altar erected to her after Cimon's victory at the Eurymedon in 465 B.C., and of a festival of Eirene inaugurated on the occasion of the

---

[4]*Pindari carmina, cum fragmentis*, Bruno Snell, ed. (Leipzig, 1971–75), fragm. 110. Erasmus actually begins with the proverbial form of the thought, Γλνκὺς ἀπείρῳ πόλεμος, E. L. Leutsch, *Corpus Paroemiographorum Graecorum*, 2.20 (Diogenianus 2.16) (Hildesheim, 1958); Eustathius (*Commentary on Homer's Iliad*, 841.33); he had the fragment of Pindar from Stobaeus 50.3, as his text shows. It first appeared in the 1515 edition.

[5]It is perhaps better to put the matter in this way than to say outright that the later Eirene has nothing to do with the Horai (Waser, "Eirene" in PW). The association could always be resumed, and the cornucopia regularly attributed to the later Eirene belongs to the Horai: Roscher, art. "Eirene."

[6]In a new fragment of Aeschylus (?) *Oxyrhynchus papyrus* 20.33 (No. 2256.8) Peace is apparently praised for increasing the beauty of households and creating a rivalry of wealth, and is associated with agriculture.

[7]See Waser, "Eirene" in PW, quoting Ernst Curtius, *Gesammelte Abhandlungen* (Berlin, 1894), 11.190 ('vielleicht wie Nike, nur eine Seite der Athena').

Peace of Callias (445 B.C.), and later of various offerings to her by generals in the fourth century.

The Peloponnesian War gave an impetus to the discussion of peace, and we must regret the loss of the utterances of the Sophists on this subject, since they influenced later discussion and were in the background of Aristophanes' peace plays. Yet Aristophanes' idea of peace is inevitably equivalent to the image that the collective Greek unconscious formed of the matter. Peace the daughter of justice is less prominent than Peace the bringer of agricultural plenty, of revived trade, of revels and marriages. This is the 'Ionian' Eirene of the Shield of Achilles and of Bacchylides.[8] It about sums up the meaning of peace in Aristophanes' *Acharnians*, where Dicaeopolis, having made a separate treaty with Sparta, enjoys the fruits of foreign trade and spends his time in revels while others still suffer the hardships of war. Similar ideas were expressed in the same poet's *Farmers* (Ch. V below) and in his *Freighters*.[9] In the *Peace* the goddess herself occupies the center of the play, though she appears only as a mute figure. Hellas is destroying herself with wars, and hence the visionary Trygaeus flies up to heaven on a beetle to appeal to Zeus; but he learns from Hermes that the gods in disgust have withdrawn higher up and have left War in their place. War has cast Peace into a deep pit. With the help of the chorus of farmers, Trygaeus draws her out and flies with her and her two attendants, Harvest and Games, back to Athens. Trygaeus, and indeed all Athens, is in love with Eirene. A sacrifice follows, with prayers for resumption of trade; agricultural abundance is realized; and the play ends with the marriage song of Trygaeus wedding Harvest. The same idea of peace as accompanied by agricultural abundance, but shaded to the private repose of country life, persists in the New Comedy; compare the fragments of Philemon's *Pyrrhus* quoted below, Chapter V.

This simple but deeply felt concept of peace found visible representation in a famous bronze statue attributed to the elder Cephisodotus, erected on the Athenian Areopagus in 375 B.C., perhaps for the victory of Timotheus at Leucas. It may be said to have fixed the image of Peace for later antiquity. Reproduced in many copies, some of which remain, Cephisodotus' Eirene was adopted, with modifications, by the Roman imperial coinage under Hadrian and the Antonines (one example appears in B. V. Head, *Historia numorum* [Oxford,

[8]And of *Homeric Epigram* 15: 'Open, ye doors, for great Ploutos will enter in, and with Ploutos blooming Euphrosyne and goodly Eirene.'
[9]See Weinreich's notes to *Aristophanes: Sämtliche Komödien*, Band I, trans. Ludwig Seeger, introduction by Otto Weinreich, (Zurich, 1952), pp. lix–lx.

1887], p. 327). Eirene is shown in long chiton with diploia (a double cloak), her right hand resting on a scepter and cornucopia, while she looks down at the infant Ploutos, who sits on her left arm and with his own left hand grasps the cornucopia.[10] The only Greek coin representing Eirene before the Roman period is a silver piece of Epizephyrian Locri of the fourth century; it shows the goddess seated on a square cippus holding a caduceus (Head, p. 86, Fig. 58).

The more thoughtful discussions of the Sophists are, as we have said, lost to us, but there can be little doubt that their topics for this subject greatly influenced the later tradition.[11] Prodicus, either in his discourse *On Agriculture* or in his *Horai*, seems to have elaborated the topic of peace and agriculture; Antiphon in his Περὶ Ὁμονοίας explored the idea of friendship in various relations from the family to the state; Gorgias in his *Epitaphios* apparently advised the Greeks to make peace among themselves and turn a common front to the barbarian, and he further developed this idea in his *Olympicus*, which seems to have contained a set comparison of war and peace presented in sharp antitheses in his most brilliant manner.[12] These discussions mainly turned on peace among the Greek states or within the state. Yet even the idea of universal peace was mooted, as seems clear from a fragment of Antiphon's *Truth*, which announces the principle that all men are created equal in nature.

The Justice sought in Plato's *Republic* might be regarded as equivalent to Peace in the state and in the individual soul—an enlargement on Hesiod's Dike-Eunomia-Eirene; and the Empedoclean 'Friendship' attributed to the universe in the *Timaeus* as another term for cosmic peace. This would not be amiss, but Plato himself does not make sensitive words of either *eirene* or *homonoia*, and it remained for later Platonists to employ his thought in what may be called the technical literature of peace. His ideal world is certainly in a state of peace, but he generally assumes that war—across the border at least—belongs in the experience of the bodily and material world. War arises from the body and its desires (*Phaedo* 66C), from luxury and the increase of population demanding room to live (*Republic* 372E–373E). A primitive society might have a chance of peace. According to the myth of

[10]For other representations of Eirene, see the articles 'Eirene' in PW and in the mythological lexica. The child Ploutos and the cornucopia are usually present, but similar ideas are also expressed by Eirene accompanied by Dionysus, and she is even found represented as a Bacchant. There was a notable statue of Eirene and Hestia in the Athenian prytaneum (Pausanias 1.18.3).
[11]Nestle, *Friedensgedanke*, pp. 12–28.
[12]May we compare the sharp antitheses between peace and war in Aristophanes' *Acharnians* 1097–1142?

the *Laws* (678E–679C), life immediately after the Flood was simple, 'war and faction would have died out,' and, lacking silver and gold, men lacked the motive to do wrong. And in the still earlier Age of Cronos—an ideal time that is the pattern of what good yet remains—the divine kings rendered their human flocks happy and peaceful by the gift of 'peace and reverence and lawfulness and abundant justice' (713E). The similar myth of the *Politicus* (271E) relates that in the Age of Cronos 'there was no war nor faction whatsoever.' These after Hesiod seem to be our earliest notices of the peace of the Saturnian Age. But the trait was probably traditional;[13] it became a commonplace in the course of the fourth century, having already been ridiculed by the comic poet Telecleides in his *Amphictyones*: 'I [Cronos?] shall then recount from the beginning the life that I provided for mortals: First there was peace among all things.'[14] And Dicaearchus in his Βίος Ἑλλάδος included this trait in his influential sketch of the Age of Cronos: 'And there were no wars nor feuds among them, for there existed among them no objects of competition of such value as to give any one a motive.'[15]

From Aristotle later writers tirelessly repeat the observation that 'war is made for the sake of peace' (*Pol.* 1333ᵃ35; 1334ᵃ15). The legislator should aim in all his provisions at a norm of leisure and peace; purely military states fall apart as soon as they succeed, for want of this provision. Yet temperance and courage are always necessary virtues; war nourishes them, while good fortune and peace tend to make men insolent. Dwellers in the Islands of the Blest therefore would have special need of justice and temperance; if citizens are not to become like slaves, they must find exercise in peace for the virtues that come more easily in time of war (1334ᵃ).

In a more practical context, again, Isocrates devoted himself to a theme already broached by Gorgias. Let the Greek states make peace among themselves and turn their united strength against the barbarian—under the leadership of Athens, in the *Panegyricus*, under that of Philip of Macedon, in the *Philippus*. In the course of history how often this theme has been sounded (see Ch. IV). In the oration commonly called *On the Peace*, he argues that peace is international justice and touches in passing on a familiar recommendation: 'Peace would relieve us of the turmoil of war and allow us to secure abundance,

[13]Lovejoy-Boas, Index, s.v. 'Age of Cronos'; cf. Empedocles, fragm. 128, ibid. p. 33.
[14]Theodore Koch, *Comicorum Atticorum fragmenta* (Leipzig, 1880), 1.209, Telecleides *Amphictyones* fragm. 1.11.1–2; Lovejoy-Boas, p. 40 (Lovejoy trans.).
[15]C. Müller, *Fragmenta Historicorum Graecorum* (Paris, 1848), 2.234, from Porphyry *De Abstinentia* 4.1.2; Lovejoy-Boas, p. 95 (Lovejoy trans.).

cultivating our lands and sailing the seas, and we should see the city thronged with merchants, foreigners, and resident aliens' (18–21).

The idea of the *Philippus* was realized in fact by the Macedonian kings. Alexander aimed at uniting not merely Greeks but the whole world in a mixture of peoples—a practical application of the thought of Antiphon that all men are of the same nature.[16] That all men are brothers is a presupposition of the *philanthropia* that is a leading motive of Hellenistic philosophy and literature, and, for example, the Stoic idea of the Cosmopolis was the theoretical counterpart of the tendency of the Hellenistic monarchies in the practical sphere. It is evident that many of the later commonplaces of our subject were formed in the Hellenistic period, but unluckily the literature is lost or fragmentary. The subject itself seems often to have taken up from the equally lost or fragmentary discussions of the Sophists. The Sophistic pattern of tracing the idea of peace from family unity to the unity of the state and hence to the unity of Greece and mankind now comes to be extended to the whole universe, the unity of which Empedocles and Plato had called φιλία, but which now begins to be called ἐιρήνη.[17] The idea is reflected back upon mankind in the injunction that in human affairs it is our duty to imitate the peace of the universe and its diverse but harmonious elements. Another topic common in later peace literature, and taken up by Cynic-Stoic diatribe from the Sophists, is the admonitory example of the animals, who observe peace within their several kinds.[18] The notion now also was popular that primitive tribes, outside the civilized world, live in a state of peace; and the older notion persisted that peace was the condition of the early age before Astraea was compelled to leave mankind.[19]

Interesting from a literary point of view is the speech which the historian Timaeus put into the mouth of the Syracusan Hermocrates on the occasion of negotiating a peace with Camerina. It is scornfully reported by Polybius (12.26) as unworthy even of 'the themes we hear in

[16]See 'Alexander's prayer for peace' in Arrian 7.11.9: εὔχετο δὲ τά τε ἄλλα καὶ ὁμόνιαν τε καὶ κοινωνίαν τῆς ἀρχῆς Μακεδόσι καὶ Πέρσαις [for the other good things, and for Homonoia, and for partnership in the realm between Macedonians and Persians]. See W. W. Tarn, *Alexander the Great* (Cambridge, 1948), vol. 2, app. 25 (esp. 25.6 and pp. 443ff.).

[17]References in Nestle, *Friedensgedanke*, p. 353.

[18]Ch. VIII below.

[19]The concept that distant, half-mythical peoples live in peace is old; so the Hyperboreans in Pindar, *Pyth.* 10.42: μαχᾶν ἄτερ [far from battle]: see Lovejoy-Boas, Ch. 11, and Index, s.v. 'pacifism'; cf. Nestle, *Friedensgedanke*, pp. 8, 64. The sole Hellenistic text on the peace of the Golden Race, before Astraea departed, is Aratus, *Phaen.* 96–136, but this passage was very influential.

the schools of rhetoric,' and has indeed been convincingly carried back by Wilhelm Nestle to Gorgias.[20] Nevertheless, it is just such points as Timaeus makes that delighted the Renaissance: In war sleepers are roused in the morning by the trumpet, in peace by the crowing of cocks; Heracles founded the Olympian Games and truce voluntarily, but injured others only under compulsion [from Eurystheus] (here are quoted the verses of Homer on Zeus's hatred of Ares, and Euripides, fragm. 462 [Ch. V]); war resembles sickness and peace health, for peace restores the sick, while in war the healthy perish; in peace the old are buried by the young, in war the reverse; in war there is no safety beyond the city walls, in peace safety extends to the limits of the land.

The Hellenistic philosophies aimed at an inner state of calm which we might be inclined to equate with peace, but evidence is lacking that they employed any word for 'peace' in this sense. Both the Stoic ὁμολογουμένως τῇ φύσει ζῆν [to live in harmony with Nature] and the Epicurean ἀταραξία [calmness] were rather negative concepts of a personality that has got rid of disturbing emotions. Virtually nothing is known of Chrysippus' treatise *On Concord*, but it is likely to have dealt with human relationships in the spirit of Hellenistic *philanthropia*.[21] Possibly it was the source of the common Stoic definition of Concord (ὁμόνοια) as 'an understanding of common goods.'[22] Aristotle, in accordance with earlier usage, had defined ὁμόνοια as πολιτικὴ φιλία (*Eth. Nic.* 9.6); and ὁμόνοια (*concordia*) would naturally be opposed to στάσις (*seditio*) as εἰρήνη (*pax*) to πόλεμος (*bellum*). The Hellenistic philosophers thus seem to have given a wider sense to ὁμόνοια.[23]

Highly important, though difficult to trace, is the idea of peace in the mystique of kingship as it developed in the period of the Hellenistic monarchies but which is open to our view mainly as it was applied to the Roman emperors. In the theories of kingship, the monarch, a shepherd of his people, was to imitate God on earth, and his duty, like that of Aristotle's legislator, was to aim at peace.[24] Such benefactors,

---

[20]Nestle, *Friedensgedanke*, pp. 17–18.

[21]The one surviving fragment (*SVF* von Arnim 3.353) distinguishes kinds of slaves; Chrysippus may have been going through the pattern 'households, states, and so on.

[22]*SVF* von Arnim, 3.292.

[23]On the word, see Kramer, *Quid valeat ὁμόνοια in litteris Graecis* (Dissertation, Göttingen, 1915).

[24]Dio mentions peace in connection with the good king in the *First Discourse on Kingship*. He first compares the king to a shepherd (1.13, 11.17ff.), then says that he is πολεμικός because τοῖς κάλλιστα πολεμεῖν παρεσκευασμένοις, τούτοις μάλιστα ἔξεστιν εἰρήνην ἄγειν (those who are the best prepared for war have it most in their power to live in peace; trans. J. W. Cohoon, Loeb, 1.27). He goes on to say that all kings worthy

of whom Heracles is the type, had been rewarded with apotheosis; and the heroization of Alexander the Great after his death thus represents a Greek idea. But it was possible to go farther. In Plato's *Laws*, the kings of the Age of Cronos had been divine *(daimones)*, and it is there suggested that even now rulers should be sought who have in them a remnant of divinity. Such ideas seem later to have been reinforced by similar notions from oriental sources. The Ptolemies assumed the living divinity of their predecessors the Pharaohs. The epithet Soter (savior), once awarded to Greek benefactors in a human sense, took on a supernatural sense under oriental and Egyptian influence. The savior was expected to be of divine birth—a condition now supplied to Alexander in his legend—and to be the bringer of peace to mankind. The idea was united with that of successive world periods, which itself was now a syncretism of Greek notions, such as those of Plato, with oriental ones. The savior-king would inaugurate the recurrence of the Golden Age.[25]

At Rome, the goddess Pax is hardly known before the end of the Republic, yet the whole history of Rome is bound up with the idea of peace, and the concept of peace, in the West, has remained stamped with the Roman experience.[26] In the republican period, *pax* and its very close synonym *concordia* are dominated by the idea of internal peace among the orders, with relatively less emphasis on foreign relations. And the thought of internal peace naturally also furnishes much of the content of the expression *pax Augusta* employed after the Augustan settlement had solved the problems of internal order.[27] But the nature of Rome itself more and more merged this idea in the *pax Romana* which gave Rome her mission as bringing peace to the world and is the basis of imperial propaganda. From the first, in the poets at least, Greek ideas of the savior-king were applied to the *princeps*. Virgil announces the beginning of a new world-period in the fourth *Eclogue*; sees Octavian engaged in his beneficent

---

of the title βασιλεύς have been μαθηταί τε καὶ ζηλωταί (disciples and emulators) of Zeus (1.38), who is portrayed as the ideal ruler.

[25]On the subject of this paragraph there has been a vast amount of writing; see Ulrich Höfer, art. "Soter" in Roscher; F. Dornseiff in PW; Johannes Wendland, "Zeitschrift für neutestamentliche wissenschaft," V (1904), cited in Eiliv Skard, *Zwei religiöspolitische Bergriffe, Euergetes—Concordia* (Avhandl. Norske Vidensk. Akad., Hist.-Filos. Kl., 1931, 2. [Oslo, 1932]); Otto Weinreich, *Seneca's Apocolocyntosis: Die Satire auf Tod, Himmel-und Höllenfahrt des Kaisers Claudius* (Berlin, 1923), Ch. 2, sec. 3, esp. p. 39.

[26]For a bold, but not unfair, reading of Roman history in this sense, see Laurona Waddy, *Pax Romana and World Peace* (London, 1950).

[27]In this sense the Senate had already voted a temple of Concordia Nova in the year of Julius' death (Dio Cassius, *Hist. Rom.* 44.4.5).

work—'victorque volentes per populos dat iura' (*Georgics* 4.561–62); and defines the mission of the 'Roman' as 'pacisque imponere morem,' in the *Aeneid* (6.852). With the idea of the *pax Romana*[28] the words *iura* and *mores*, as also the words *iustitia, fides, aequitas*, were intimately bound up, and the circle of association also gave a permanent stamp to *securitas, quies, tranquillitas*, and of course *concordia*.[29] St. Augustine's definition of peace as 'tranquillitas ordinis' is thoroughly Roman. It is, in fact, Cicero's phrase, or nearly, 'concordia ordinum' (*Fam.* 12.15.3).

The ideas and the symbols that center in this great principle, both drawing on Hellenistic thought and acquiring new significance, are far-reaching and complicated. In the state worship, the most notable events are the inauguration of the Ara Pacis Augustae in the Campus Martius in 9 B.C. (voted by the Senate in 13 B.C. upon the return of Augustus from three years' absence in Spain and Gaul);[30] the closing of the Temple of Janus in 29 B.C., with implications for universal

A Roman Coin. (Photo: C. H. V. Sutherland, *Coinage in Roman Imperial Policy, 31 B.C.–A.D. 68* [London: Methuen, 1951] pl. XII, verso of no. 4)

[28]Expression first found in Seneca, *De Prov.* 4.14; *Cons. ad Pol.* 15.1; *De Clem.* 1.4.2. See Stephanus, *Thesaurus Linguae Latinae*, and cf. Bonnaud Delamare, *L'Idée*, p. 10.

[29]The association of these words has been taken as fully defining the 'Roman idea of civilization'; so Paul Strack, *Untersuchungen zur römischen Reichsprägung*, 1.53ff. 136 ap. Carl Koch in PW 18.4.2432–54, and Hans Christ, *Die römische Weltherrschaft in der antiken Dichtung* (Stuttgart, 1938), p. 112. I am much indebted to this excellent work of Christ. See also W. Gernentz, *Laudes Romae* (Rostock diss., 1918). On the association of *pax* and *libertas* see Charles Wirszubski, *Libertas as a Political Idea at Rome during the Late Republic and Early Principate* (Cambridge, 1950), Ch. 4.

[30]On this occasion, the ritual is thought to have been largely borrowed from Greek ideas about Eirene (Fuchs, *Augustin*, p. 191, n. 2; Christ, *Die römische, Weltherrschaft*, p. 106). See G. Moretti, *Ara Pacis Augustae* (Rome, 1948). This was the occasion of Horace, *Carm.* 4.5.

peace;[31] and, much later, the building of the great Templum Pacis by Vespasian in A.D. 75 from the spoils of his Jewish wars.[32] More continuous evidence of the conscious propaganda for the peaceful Empire are the very numerous coins representing Pax in varying forms. Here the shadings of the idea are especially numerous and subtle, as various attributes are passed about between Pax and other related abstractions.[33] Coins of the Augustan period and a little later represent Pax in the Greek manner, with the caduceus or herald's staff—regarded by Varro as the special *signum pacis* (Gellius 10.27.3)—and with olive branch and cornucopia.[34] A persistent type of coin, beginning under Augustus and continued by Tiberius, associates Pax and Justitia.[35] A long series of coins from Alexandria extending from Augustus to Maximian shows various aspects of Peace: with the child Ploutos after Cephisodotus; usually with caduceus, also with patera and ears of corn; sometimes with olive sprig in her hair (Galba and Otho) or in her hand (Domitian and Hadrian); with corn spikes (Vespasian and later).[36] Thoroughly Roman is the coupling or identification of Pax with Victoria, an idea suggested by the laurel wreath and more explicitly by coins showing Pax with Victoria in her hand, or with spear and shield or trophies of war.[37] Coins of Trajan show Pax setting foot on the necks of the conquered (Fuchs, *Augustin*, p. 201, n.

[31]On the Temple of Janus see W. F. Otto, "Ianus" in PW, Suppl. vol. 3; also Roscher's article in his *Lexikon*.

[32]Koch in PW 18.4.2435–36. In the coins and inscriptions connected with this event, we first find the expression *Pax aeterna et perpetua* and the like, evidently with reference to the eternity of Rome. (But for a coin of Tiberius with '*Pace Aug. Perp.*' see Michael Grant, *Roman Anniversary Issues* [Cambridge, 1950], p. 39 n)

[33]See Michael Grant, "Pax Romana," in *University of Edinburgh Journal* (1949), 229ff.; also his *Roman Anniversary Issues*, Index III, s.v. 'Concordia' and 'Pax.'

[34]Koch in PW, s.v. 'Pax'; according to Koch, the earliest Roman coin with the legend *Paxs* is one of L. Aemilius Buca from the year of Caesar's assassination (head of the goddess with diadem and, on the reverse, clasped hands). Pax with caduceus, behind her a *cista mystica*, on an Augustan *aureus* of 28 B.C. (ibid.); a bronze coin of 25 B.C. with the head of Peace and legend *Pacis*, had also, significantly, a colonist in the act of ploughing (Michael Grant, *From Imperium to Auctoritas* [Cambridge, 1946], p. 281).

[35]Grant, *Roman Anniversary Issues*, p. 39: 'On these coins the figure carrying the sceptre of *Justitia* also bears the olive-branch of *Pax*.' But may the scepter not be that of Pax, or even the caduceus?

[36]B. V. Head, *Historia numorum* (Oxford, 1887), p. 721.

[37]Pax with a caduceus enclosed in a laurel wreath already on a silver coin from the Augustan era (28 B.C.) (C.H.V. Sutherland, *Coinage in Roman Imperial Policy: 31 B.C.–A.D. 68* [London, 1951], Pl. I.16), Pax with Victoria in her hand (Harold Mattingly, *Roman Coins from the Earliest Times to the Fall of the Roman Empire* [London, 1928], Pl. XLII.14). A winged Pax on the coins of Claudius (Sutherland, Pl. XII.4) is noteworthy for its syncretism: she has the wings of Victoria, the caduceus of Felicitas, the snake of Salus, and the modest gesture (raising a fold of her dress) of Pudor. Sutherland, pp. 127–28, discusses the importance of this type. Illustration, p. 29.

1). The 'pacis imponere morem' entailed the 'debellare superbos' as well as the 'parcere subiectis.' The Roman mission is bluntly stated in the legend *Mars pacifer* found on the coinage of the emperor Commodus.[38] The idea of peace is also bound up with the idea of renewal, which, brought forward for Augustus, continues to recur in the imperial coinage, often with a reference to the return of the Golden Age in the legend *aurea aetas* and the like.[39]

This last idea dominates the topic of peace as it appears in the Roman poets of the Empire. The Augustans hailed Augustus as the peace hero, destined to win apotheosis — 'hac arte Pollux et vagus Hercules / Enisus arces attigit igneas' (Horace, *Carm.* 3.3.9). And to bring peace is to usher in again the Golden Age of Saturn (revived before, or nearly so, by Numa). This concept, pervasive in Virgil and Tibullus, was passed on to later poets; Calpurnius sees the coming reign of Nero as an *aurea aetas* (diminished in the event to an *aureum quinquennium*), as later Porphyry, for example, see that of Constantine.[40] The age of Saturn was marked not only by the absence of war but by simplicity of life and by agricultural abundance. In fact, country life is our nearest realization of that golden time: 'O fortunatos nimium sua si bona norint / Agricolas, quibus ipsa procul discordibus armis / Fundit humo facilem victum iustissima terra' (Virgil, *Georg.* 2.458–60). Much emphasis was placed on bucolic/pastoral poetry, as in Virgil's *Eclogues*, Ovid's *Fasti*, and even Horace's verses in praise of his Sabine farm. And Seneca (*Phaedra* 491ff.) begins a long description of the Golden Age with the statement that the woodland life (of Hippolytus) is its equivalent: 'Non alia magis est libera . . . / vita quae priscos colat, / quam quae relictis moenibus silvas amat.' Pax and Ceres are frequent companions (Ovid, *Fasti* 1.704). With the coming of peace there will also be a revival of the virtues, and these commonly appear in the poets as the 'comites' of Pax: Fides, Honor, Pudor, Virtus, Copia (Horace, *Carm. saec.* 57ff.); Fides, Iustitia, Concordia (Petronius, *Bell. civ.* 299ff; Juvenal 1.116, and others). And in general, as the past was marked by the loss of the characteristics of the Golden Age (Virgil, *Georg.* 1.125–28), so the new time will witness their return (*Ecl.* 4). Augustus seemed to be realizing this reversal, and in a poem on his return from his sojourn in Spain and Gaul Horace (*Carm.* 4.5) hails him in terms that suggest that the Imperator is the embodiment of Pax herself.[41]

[38]Roscher 2.2425, s.v. 'Mars.'
[39]Michael Grant, *Roman History from the Coins* (Cambridge, 1958), Pl. 25.
[40]Porphyry, *Carmina*, Elsa Kluge, ed. (Leipzig, 1926), X, scholion.
[41]Appendix, below, no. 24, on the peace hero.

The utterances of the poets on peace are close to the public and even official symbolism and seldom venture upon the topics of the prose literature of peace—for example, cosmic peace or peace among the animals. Dio Chrysostom, in one of his orations (*Or.* 38.10), remarks that peace is universally praised in literature, and that, in particular, poems and philosophical discourses[42] are full of the subject. Apart from Bacchylides' paean and, in Latin, Tibullus 1.10, we know of no ancient poems specifically in praise of peace, though Timaeus quoted Homer and Euripides on this theme; and it is enough to understand Dio as referring to poetical passages and perhaps to anthologies such as we still have in Stobaeus 55. It remained for the poets of the European Renaissance to create this type of poem, uniting to some extent the ancient poetical and prose traditions.

Of the prose literature itself we have only a shadowy idea in the earlier periods. Half-rhetorical and half-philosophical in the Sophists, it took on, we may think, more philosophical topics in the Hellenistic period, but it emerges to view in the writers of the second sophistic still partly rhetorical and partly philosophical. At the Hellenistic stage it had passed into Latin in the treatise *De pace* of M. Terentius Varro, which, though itself lost, has had a continuing influence through St. Augustine. But we get our best view of this tradition in the Greek writers, particularly in Dio Chrysostom and Aelius Aristides. The consecrated topics duly appear in Dio's several orations on peace.[43] There is the example of the heavens above: 'Do you not see in the heavens as a whole, and in the divine and blessed beings that dwell therein, an order and concord and self-control which is eternal . . . ?' (*Or.* 40.35, trans. Crosby; cf. 38.11). Again: 'Do you not see also the stable, righteous, everlasting accord of the elements, as they are called —air and earth and water and fire—with what reasonableness and moderation it is their nature to continue . . . ?' (ibid.). There is the example of the animals: 'Why, birds make their nests near other birds, yet do not plot against each other nor quarrel over food and twigs; ants do not quarrel . . . not bees . . . ; cattle . . . horses . . . goats and sheep . . . pasture together; but human beings are worse than cattle and creatures of the wild' (40.40−41). In his interesting treatise on kingship (3), Dio also recurs to the comparison of health in the human body with peace within or between cities (38−39), and to the analogy between the friendship of individuals (41) or the unity of households (38) and political peace. The topic of making peace so as to present

[42]καὶ τὰ ποιήματα καὶ τὰ τῶν φιλοσόφων συγγράμματα; he also specifies histories.
[43]*Or.* 38−41, H. Lamar Crosby, trans. (Loeb), esp. 38 and 40, *To the Nicomedians on Concord with Nicaea* and *On Concord with Apamea.* Cf. Nestle, *Friedensgedanke,* pp. 48−49.

a united front to a common foe receives a contemporary turn in 38.33ff.: Be at unity with Nicaea and other cities so as to present a united front to the tyrannical Roman governor of the province (Bithynia). Dio duly repeats the commonplace that the king should imitate Zeus and bring peace to his people. Drawing on the same tradition, the second-century rhetorician Aelius Aristides, in his orations on peace, gives us topics very similar to Dio's[44]—the example of the peaceful heavens (*Or.* 23.76–77); peace like health (24.16–18); the unity of households (24.32–33). Notable from the point of view of literary form is Aristides' handling of the obligatory comparison between peace and war (ὁμόνοια and στάσις) in his Rhodian speech (24.41–44). The benefits of peace are assembled in a *bravura* passage—a device that we shall notice in the Renaissance poets[45]—for which Aristides seems to have gone to the poets rather than to the philosophers:[46]

'Tis Peace alone who stablishes the seasons that are from Zeus, alone she puts her seal on everything—in the country, bringing order and beauty through agriculture, and continually bestowing new capital with the usufruct of the old, while in the city she makes things go as we desire. Through her we have marriages in fit season, giving and taking in marriage to and from whom we wish, and the rearing and education of children follows ancestral norms; our womenfolk are safe, contracts honored, foreigners welcomed, and the gods enjoy their customary rites, their processions, choruses, and feasts; we hold the assemblies and councils which Themis, eldest of the gods, convenes; the poor have the means of livelihood, the rich the enjoyment of their possessions, the old have the care they require, the young a normal life. In a word, Peace gives all things to all, even as the light of the sun to which we owe our preservation.

Having presented Homonoia in a prose-poem, Aristides varies his procedure and gives Stasis in a verbal portrait sketched with the most forbidding features.[47]

The transformation of vast areas of ancient thought into the terms of Christianity offers a subject of absorbing interest; Themistius' *Ora-*

[44]Aelius Aristides, Bruno Keil, ed. (Berlin, 1898), *Or.* 23, *To the Cities, on Peace* (ὁμόνοια); 24, *To the Rhodians, on Peace*; and cf. 26, *To Rome.* See Nestle, *Friedensgedanke*, pp. 72–73.

[45]Below, Ch. IV. E.g., Ronsard's *Exhortation pour la Paix*, p. 95; Remy Belleau, *Chant de la Paix*, 109; Charles de Navières, *Cantique de la Paix*, 149; J. A. de Baïf, *Hymne à la paix*, 151.

[46]Compare the poetical passages in Stobaeus, below, Ch. V.

[47]Erasmus, *Bellum*, 957 F–958 A; *Querela*, 639C–E. Also 627, 633, 634 A ff.

tion 10 might offer an example. Trained for the most part in schools that embodied the ideas of pagan philosophy and literature, the Christian writers had undergone a great experience which replaced all this earthly wisdom with the Word of God embodied in the Old and New Testaments. Nevertheless, many of the assumptions of the pagan tradition lay too deep even to be noticed, and many were identifiable with the tenets of Scripture, once they or the scriptural texts were 'properly' understood. The interpenetration is therefore pervasive; yet the total result is a new orientation. This cannot but be most striking in the matter of peace, a subject of central importance both to the politically oriented thought of the Greeks and Romans and to the spiritually oriented thought of Christianity. Certain traditional concepts remain, though differently understood—for example, the reference to the peacefully ordered universe or to the unity of households. But for the Christian the all-important fact was that the awaited Prince of Peace had come. Without embarking on the vast implications of this fact, we note its effect on the interpretation of history. The view that finally prevailed—represented, for example, by Augustine and Orosius—was that the peaceful settlement of the world by Augustus was God's means of preparing the earth for the advent of the true Prince of Peace. The seductive Arian view that failed was that the Savior and the Empire arrived together and that both Christ and the Emperor were equally the instruments of God's care.[48] It was also possible to maintain that such peace as the world had enjoyed under the Empire was the effect of the advent of Christ.[49] But in any case, the peace that Christ gave was not given as the world giveth; and what transforms the Christian discussions of peace can be brought down to one principle, that, whereas the best pagan thought founded peace on justice, the Christian, not forgetting justice, founded it on love *(caritas)*.

The Greek *eirene* primarily means repose; the Latin *pax* an agreement; the Hebrew *shalom* health, and hence to the Bible is owing the Semitic greeting 'Peace!' or 'Peace be with you,' an expression that might be untimely, so that we have the proverbial rebuke of those

---

[48]Eusebius, *Demonstr. Evang.* 7.2. Eusebius showed considerable sympathy for the Arian view; along with Eusebius of Nicomedia, one of Arius' strongest supporters, he helped formulate Constantine's religious policy towards the end of his reign. Eusebius continued the generally optimistic Eastern view (based largely on the work of Origen) that Church and state could work together, while Western writers such as Tertullian, Augustine, and Orosius were more preoccupied by the opposition between the *civitas terrena* and the *civitas Dei.*

[49]Quoted by Roland Bainton in his comprehensive article, "The Early Church on War," *Harvard Theological Review*, 39 (1946), 204.

who say 'Peace, peace' when there is no peace.[50] In the Old Testament, peace is the right relationship of man to God and of man to man. It is the object of God's covenant with Israel (Num. 21.12), and atonement or reconciliation with Jehovah is ritually assured by 'peace-offerings' (OT, passim). Among men, it is the gift of God (Lev. 26.6; Num. 6.26) and is the object of prayer (Jer. 29.7), though often it is sought in vain (Jer. 8.15; Ezek. 7.25). It is the way of wisdom (Prov. 3.17): 'All her paths are peace.' It brings agricultural abundance: 'He maketh peace in thy borders, and filleth thee with the finest of wheat' (Ps. 147.14). Men are exhorted to seek peace and pursue it (Ps. 33.15; cf. 1 Pet. 3.11); it is the result or the associate of justice: 'Justitiae opus est pax' (Isa. 32.17), 'Justitia et pax osculatae sunt' (Ps. 85.11); its fruits are excellent: 'Habeto pacem, et per haec habebis fructus optimos' (Job 22.21); it is the end of the just man (Ps. 36.37), but there is no peace for the wicked (Isa. 48.22; 57.21; 59.8). In particular Isaiah, the prophet of the Prince of Peace (9.6), found memorable phrases: 'Peace, the work of justice' (32.17); had Israel been obedient, her peace would have been 'like a river' (48.18); 'How beautiful upon the mountains are the feet of him that bringeth good tidings and publisheth peace' (52.7, repeated in Nah. 1.15 and Rom. 10.15); and a time is foreseen when 'they shall beat their swords into ploughshares . . . neither shall they learn war any more' (2.4.), a verse found also in Micah 4.3 and capable of being turned the other way by Joel (3.10)—compare Virgil!—'Beat your ploughshares into swords, and your pruninghooks into spears.'

For the Christian, a higher spiritual meaning attaches to the idea of peace in the New Testament. 'Christ is our peace' (Eph. 2.14). The angels of the Nativity announce peace on earth to men of goodwill (Luke 2.14). In the mouth of Jesus, new significance lies in the old salutation 'Peace be with you' (Luke 10.5; 24.36; John 20.19). 'Have peace one with another' (Mark 9.50). Peacemakers are blessed as the children of God (Matt. 5.9), and the extreme command is 'Love thine enemies' (Luke 27); 'Resist not evil, but turn the other cheek' (Matt. 5.39). Yet, 'think not that I am come to send peace on earth; I came not to send peace but a sword' (Matt. 10.34)—a statement that the commentators are able to explain. And, finally, in parting from the Disciples: 'Peace I leave with you, my peace I give unto you; not as the world giveth' (John 14.27). The message of peace was fully absorbed by Paul, who speaks of 'the Gospel of peace' (Rom. 10.15; Eph. 6.15),

[50]For example, Jer. 6.14. On *eirene*, *pax*, and *shalom* see Fuchs, *Augustin*, pp. 205–11; Marino Barchiesi, "De 'Pax' particulari vi atque usu," in *Atti dell' Istituto Veneto di Scienze, lettere, ed arti*, 3 (1952–53), 233–55.

[35]

and 'the God of peace' (Rom. 15.33; 16.20), says 'the kingdom of God is peace' (Rom. 14.7), and regularly opens his epistle with the words: 'Grace be upon you and peace from God our father and from the Lord Jesus Christ' (1 Cor. 1.3; 2 Cor. 1.2; Gal. 1.3; Eph. 1.2; Col. 1.2). He exhorts the Hebrews: 'Follow peace with all men' (Heb. 12.14), and the Romans: 'If it be possible, . . . live at peace with all men' (Rom. 12.18), and the Thessalonians: 'Be at peace among yourselves' (1 Thess. 5.13). The fruit of the Spirit is love, joy, peace (Gal. 5.22). Melchisedek means first 'rex justitiae' and then 'rex Salem, quod est, rex pacis' (Heb. 7.2). There is a notable collocation of ends: 'sectare vero justitiam, fidem, spem, charitatem, et pacem' (2 Tim. 2.22); and a summing up in the benediction: 'The peace of God, which passeth all understanding, shall keep your hearts and minds through Christ Jesus' (Phil. 4.7). In this context the Christian peace is more an internal peace, as in the Hellenistic philosophy, than political or international peace.

Beyond the individual texts, the whole spirit of Christianity transformed and spiritualized the attitude of the believer in all relationships; and a comprehensive study of the concept of peace in the early Church would carry us far afield into such subjects as Christology, the attitude of the Christians to the state, and so on.[51] But to remain within the realm of literary expression, we note that even in such an early writer as Clement of Rome (late first century) a mingling of pagan and Christian motives—at least Clement recommends the example of the peaceful heavens—οἱ οὐρανοὶ τῇ διοικήσει αὐτοῦ σαλευόμενοι ἐν εἰρήνῃ[52] (all the heavenly bodies observe their appointed courses in peace) reaches full development. This assimilation comes with the theologians of the fourth and fifth centuries.[53] Thus three orations of Gregory Nazianzen are entitled εἰρηνικοί, De pace.[54] The first in particular offers an interesting blend of Christian attitudes with the rhetoric and topics of the school tradition. Addressed to the monks of Naziansus after dissension inadvertently occasioned by Gregory's father, it first dilates on the speaker's own reaction to the troubles, passes on to admonish the monks on the obligations of fraternal concord—this part heavily laden with passages of

[51]See Bainton, "Early Church," pp. 189–212, with citations from Christian literature and references to modern evaluations of the evidence it offers.

[52]Clement of Rome, *Epist. ad Cor.* 1.20.33; Fuchs, *Augustin*, pp. 98ff.; Bainton, "Early Church," p. 210.

[53]Pagan philosophy continued to make its own contribution, particularly in the idea of cosmic peace. We know as little of Iamblichus' treatise Περὶ Ὁμονοίας, however, as we do of Chrysippus'.

[54]*Or.* 6.22.23 (Migne, *PG* 35.721, 1132, 1152).

Scripture—and hence (Ch. 14ff.) to a recommendation of peace as an 'imitation of God and of things divine': 'Let us look to the heavens above and the earth beneath, giving ear to the divine voice, and learn the laws of Creation.' There follows an eloquent description of the concord of the universe and its parts, including the elements. He has earlier (Ch. 12) pointed to the supreme example of unity—the triune Godhead and the harmonious hosts of angels— which Christian writers were often to invoke.

Gregory has juxtaposed rather than assimilated these ideas. The full program of a Christian peace is the work of St. Augustine, the nineteenth book of whose *De civitate Dei* forms an unsurpassed treatise on this subject, deeply thought out and destined to rule the Western mind for centuries to come.[55] Peace, defined as *tranquillitas ordinis*, is the *summum bonum* and the end and perfection of the Heavenly City. In the present life there is no perfect peace, which comes only to the blessed after death (Ch. 10). The world is divided by diversity of languages, and even a world-state with a universal language would be subject to variance (Ch. 7); friendship, whether among men or between men and Spirits, offers no security (Ch. 8, 9); the individual is at variance with himself (Ch. 4). It is evil that destroys peace, and hence peace must be striven for by exercise of the moral virtues, temperance, prudence, justice, and fortitude (Ch. 4). On an international scale, a just war *(justum bellum)* may have to be waged against a wrong-doing nation in defense of the good (Ch. 7). Nevertheless, peace is the essence of the law of nature. The aim of war is peace, never the reverse, and even the ambitious aggressor aims to impose his own 'peace'; bandits have to keep peace among themselves; one powerful enough to need no friends still must keep peace in his household, or, if a solitary monster like Virgil's Cacus, must secure peace in his cave and in his own body; the wildest animals keep peace within their kinds. In fact, so long as a thing exists at all, it has some peace, and when destroyed, a cadaver for example, its elements eventually go to join the peace of the universe (Ch. 12). Peace of body, peace of soul, peace of soul and body, peace of man with God, peace among men, peace of households, of the state, of the Heavenly City, each has its definition, and peace in general is the tranquillity of order (Ch. 13).

[55] I need hardly refer again to the well-known work of Harald Fuchs on the background of Augustine's thought in this book; for a faithful and illuminating exposition of Book 19, see Kato Kiszely-Paysz, "St. Augustine on Peace," *New Scholasticism*, 18 (1944), 19–41. The following summary is also limited to this book, which gives the essence of Augustine's views; but the subject of peace comes up in many of his writings, notably cosmic peace (*Confessions*, 12–13), and these have been taken into account by Bonnaud Delamare, *L'Idée*, pp. 27–53.

The Christian, seeing through the law of nature to the law of God, possesses the secret of the good peace through his possession of faith (Chs. 4, 17, 23, 27); the pagan empire, without the faith, had no true peace (Ch. 24). The just man lives by faith (Ch. 4; Hab. 2.4). Just law is the pattern of peace based on love (Ch. 14). Right use of temporal peace will lead to immortal peace (Ch. 13), the *pax aeterna* (Ch. 14), and the Christian may live in hope of attaining it hereafter. The wicked lack the *tranquillitas ordinis* in various degrees, though never entirely—Satan himself retains some 'peace' or he could not feel pain; but for them there is in store the *summum malum* of eternal conflict.

Though Augustine's treatment of peace is by far the most important, many theologians of Christian antiquity contributed their reflections on this subject.[56] Especially noteworthy for its influence, in the West as well as in the East, is chapter 11 of the *De divinis nominibus* of the pseudo-Dionysius which stresses the universal efficacy of Peace as one of the Names and Virtues of God.[57] Early Christian liturgies are replete with expressions of peace both celestial and terrestrial.[58] The Pax or Kiss of Peace goes back to early Christian times. On the secular side, we note in passing the rhetorical phrasing of Cassiodorus, which found many echoes: 'Omni quippe regno desiderabilis debet esse tranquillitas, in qua et populi proficiunt et utilitas gentium custoditur. Haec est enim bonarum artium decora mater; haec mortalium genus reparabili successione multiplicans, facultates protendit, mores excolit, et tantarum rerum ignarus agnoscitur, qui eam minime quaesiisse sentitur.'[59] Still more important for the literary and artistic representation of Peace is the *Psychomachia* of Prudentius, which is organized around the idea of inward peace, to be gained (as in Augustine) by subduing the vices. It distinguishes, not altogether clearly, between Pax and Concordia. The principal champions of the battle are Veterum Cultura Deorum against Fides and Discordia against Concordia. The struggle between the special vices and virtues ends with the overthrow of Avaritia, whereupon Pax appears upon the scene (631); but

[56]See Bainton, "Early Church." The utterances of Hilary, Ambrose, Jerome, Cassiodorus, Gregory the Great, and Isidore of Seville are considered by Bonnaud Delamare, *L'Idée*, Ch. 2.

[57]Gregory Nazianzen, *Or. 2 de pace* (Migne, *PG* 35.500) already considers *eirene* among the Names and Virtues of Christ.

[58]Cf. Gerd Tellenbach, *Römischer und christlicher Reichgedanke in der Liturgie des frühen Mittelalters*, Sitzungsberichte der Heidelberger Akademie der Wissenschaften, 25 (June 1934), pp. 12–15. P. 13: 'Auxiliare, domine, temporibus nostris et tua nos ubique dextera protegente et religionis integritas et Romani nominis securitas reparata consistant' (quoting from the *Sacramentum Leonianum*).

[59]*Variae*, 1.1, to the Emperor Anastasius.

the war is ended only by the great duel in which Concordia, with the
help of Fides, defeats Discordia. Then Concordia and Fides mount a
tribunal and speak, Concordia praising peace (767ff.):

> Sic, quicquid gerimus mentisque et corporis actu,
> Spiritus unimodis texat compagibus unus.
> Pax plenum virtutis opus, pax summa laborum,
> Pax belli exacti pretium est pretiumque pericli;
> Sidera pace vigent, consistunt terrea pace;
> Nil placitum sine pace Deo. . . .

In commemoration of the victory they summon the Virtues to build a
temple, in which Sapientia is enthroned (804, 875).[60]

The upshot of the thought of the Fathers was to distinguish the ter-
restrial from the celestial peace, or a peace of this world (which might
be a 'bad' peace) from the true peace of heaven. The celestial peace
might exist as an inner peace in the Christian heart and so might af-
fect the political world, urging it towards the City of God. These ideas
entered deeply into the political theory of the Middle Ages, and only
too often they brought not peace but a sword, as pope or emperor as-
serted himself as defender of the peace. Charlemagne was crowned as
imperator pacificus; Louis the Pious deposed as the *perturbator pacis*. In
general, the priesthood, including the papacy, was regarded as the
custodian of inner and celestial peace, the secular power as charged
with keeping the earthly peace; but the secular power was expected to
defend the Peace of the Church, and on the other hand, the King's
Peace was recognized as at best a reflection of the celestial peace dis-
pensed (for example, through prayer) by the priesthood. There was
room here for fatal differences of emphasis as the power of main-
taining order waxed or waned. Often enough the ecclesiastical peace
of the cloister maintained itself when secular peace failed.[61] On occa-
sions when the Church and the secular arm joined forces to reduce
warfare, as in the Peace of God in the late tenth century and the
Truce of God some fifty years later, their efforts bore little fruit.

There is no dearth of writing on peace in the literature of the Mid-
dle Ages. Laws, epistles, biblical commentaries, sermons, philosophi-
cal or theological treatises, 'mirrors' of kingship, moral treatises, all

[60]Prov. 3.17: 'Her ways are ways of pleasantness, and all her paths are peace.' See
also Prudentius, *Contra Symmachum* 2.634–40; Lactantius, *Div. Inst.* 7.24, equating
peace of the Golden Age with the peace of Eden.
[61]These sentences are but a faint adumbration of the events and doctrines illuminat-
ingly studied in the work of Bonnaud Delamare.

are likely to bear upon this subject.[62] By and large, the fundamental positions are those of Augustine. Primarily, peace is discussed as one of the virtues, as already in Alcuin's *Moralia,* Ch. 6, *De pace,* and more elaborately in Hrabanus Maurus' *De Ecclesiae disciplina.*[63] Separate treatises on peace seem to be rare, and because they are we may pause briefly over one of them, the *De bono pacis,* written in Italy by a certain Bishop Rufinus apparently in the latter part of the twelfth century.[64]

The word 'Pax,' consisting of three letters and having no plural form, symbolizes the Trinity (1.1).[65] The idea of peace is divided into eight phases: 'Est enim pax Dei ad se, pax Dei ad homines, pax angelorum ad se, pax angelorum ad homines, pax diaboli ad se, pax diaboli ad homines, pax hominum ad se, pax hominum ad homines' (1.2). This is comprehensive. Book I enlarges on these topics through 'pax hominum ad se,'[66] while the much longer Book II is devoted to the all-important 'pax hominum ad homines.' This has three forms: 'pax Aegypti,' 'pax Babyloniae,' and 'pax Jerusalem.' The first is the conspiracy of evil men for evil ends, having its source in *superbia* and confirmed by *contumacia*; Jesus brought *not* (this) peace, but a sword (against it). Babylonian peace is what we commonly mean by peace in this world, relating to foreign and civil wars and to the conduct of private life. Rufinus aptly quotes Jer. 29.7: 'seek the peace of the city whither I have caused you to be carried away captives, and pray unto the Lord for it; for in the peace thereof shall ye have peace.' Babylonian peace is founded upon *justitia*—he fails to quote Isa. 32.17, 'Justitiae opus pax'—is nursed by *humanitas,* and is confirmed by *pruden-*

[62]Most of these types are already represented in the ninth-century writings studied by Bonnaud Delamare: laws (capitularies, decretals, and the like); epistles (Alcuin, Hincmar of Reims, and others), biblical commentaries (Smaragdus, Paschasius, Radbert); philosophical treatises (John the Scot, *De div. nat.* 4.26), mirrors of kingship (Jonas of Orleans, Sedulius Scotus), moral treatises (Alcuin, *Moralia,* Hrabanus Maurus, *De Eccl. disc.*). So pervasive is the theme in the later Middle Ages that it defies attribution, though mention should be made of Joachim of Flora. [See Herbert Grundmann, *Studien über J. von Fiore* (Stuttgart, 1966); also Robert Lerner, "Refreshment of the Saints," *Traditio,* 32 (1975–76), 97ff. I am indebted to Professor Robert E. Kaske for this last reference. R.G.]

[63]Migne, *PL* 101.617; 112.1236. See the 'Index de Virtutibus' in Migne, *PL* 220.585ff. (col. 644, 'De Pace').

[64]Migne, *PL* 150.1591–1638. The date (c. 1180) and the identity of Rufinus have been determined by Fuchs, who devotes the last section of his *Augustin* to this work.

[65]This is from ps.-Augustine, *De unitate sanctae Trinitatis* (Migne, *PL* 43.1210).

[66]The 'pax diaboli' means that the devil has his own, based on Luke, 11.21: 'Cum fortis armatus custodit atrium suum, in pace sunt omnia quae possedit.' The notion is not quite the same as that expressed by Erasmus later in this chapter. The 'pax hominum ad se,' or inner peace, has three forms: namely, 'of bad men' ('carnis et mundi prosperitas'), 'of good men' ('bonae conscientiae securitas'), 'of the blessed' ('rationis et sensualitatis in delectatione superiorum perfecta consensio').

tia. Here Rufinus moves into the topics of a tradition as old as the
Sophists: All men have a common origin in Adam[67] and, as made in
the image of God (2.8), a common home in the world with its varie-
gated floor and spangled ceiling. He quotes Aratus (by name) from
Acts 17.28 ('We also are his offspring'), and adds that since all men
are akin, they should keep the peace, 'quemadmodum et aves eius-
dem generis amicae sibi sunt, hostilis inter se odii discordiam nescien-
tes.' That kings should observe justice is supported by biblical pas-
sages and by the words of the 'facundissimus doctor' who writes:
'Tunc felices sunt respublicae cum aut philosophi regnant aut reges
philosophantur.' Subjects must 'render unto Caesar the things that
are Caesar's,' a command with which Virgil's 'Tu regere imperio' har-
monizes. This Babylonian *pax mundana* has three grades: 'pax orbis,'
'pax urbis,' 'pax domus'—again an ancient topic. Among the 'goods'
of peace, he notes the peaceful working of the universe, especially of
the elements (2.18); and he summarizes the goods of peace in a rhe-
torical passage such as we come to expect: 'Pax enim haec producit
rempublicam, propagat potentiam, fortificat regna, libertates nobili-
tat, condit leges, alit artes, illustrat honores, religionem fovet, implet
urbem, multiplicat sobolem, altrix est pueritiae, tutrix adolescentiae,
juventutem laetificat, canitiem condecorat senectutis.'[68] The Babylo-
nian peace is also a 'ladder' to the peace of Jerusalem. The peace of
Jerusalem or ecclesiastical peace is founded on *caritas* and confirmed
by *humilitas.* The earthly peace of the Church is not, however, perfect;
perfect peace is found only in the heavenly Jerusalem.

   We must traverse the centuries by picking out a few typical utter-
ances as we go. The School of Chartres is, as might be expected,
strong on the transcendent peace of the universe.[69] Alain de Lille, in
the *Anticlaudianus,* makes Concordia, 'mediatrix of all things,' a major

   [67]See discussion of Postel at the end of this chapter.
   [68]*De bono pacis* 2.18. Cf. Aristides, Keil, ed., *Or.* 23, 24.42; 26 on the benefits of
ὁμόνοια; Cassiodorus, *Variae* 1.1. as cited in note 59; Chrysogonus, *De pace* (Migne,
PL 347); Isidore of Seville, Appendix ad *Op. S. Isidori: De numeris* (Migne, *PL* 83.1289).
   [69]John of Salisbury's *Entheticus* has several passages that describe universal harmony
and transcendent peace: 305–9 compares philosophy to God's universal love ('divinus
omnia vincit amor' [308]); 607–10 describes the orderly structure of the natural world;
955–58 is the most relevant to the theme of peace:

> Est deus aeternus, mundus cum tempore coepit,
>   Hic manet at tempus caetera cuncta movet
> Per numeros elementa sibi contraria nectens
>   Vincit et aeterna pace vigere facit.

Alanus ab Insulis, *Anticlaudianus* 2.4, gives Concordia a lengthy speech describing her
role in holding the universe together. Abelard, *Theologia Christiana* (Migne, *PL*
178.1146–47).

character who, in Book II, delivers a long speech on cosmic peace and world harmony. In *De planctu Naturae* he associates Nature with peace and love and addresses her as the one who 'dost with the bond of peace marry heaven to earth.' In the thirteenth century, Thomas Aquinas deals with peace in the course of discussing the virtues in the *Summa Theologica* 2.2.Q.29 ('De Pace') articles 1–4, and again in his commentary on the *Divine Names* of the Areopagite (Ch. 11).[70] He chiefly relies on Dionysius and Augustine. In the *Summa* he asks (1) whether *pax* and *concordia* are the same, (2) whether all things seek peace, (3) whether peace is an effect of charity, (4) whether peace is a virtue. He replies that *pax* is a more inclusive term than *concordia*, which is properly consent of will among different individuals, whereas *pax* also implies that the individual's own desires are at one and harmonious. All things do indeed seek peace—seek without hindrance to gain what they desire, which is Augustine's *tranquillitas ordinis*; war itself is sought for peace. Both peace and concord are effects of *caritas*; the inner peace results from the love of God, the external concord from loving one's neighbor as oneself. With regard to Isaiah 32.17, 'Justitiae opus pax,' justice is the indirect cause of peace, in that it removes obstacles, but the direct cause is love. Peace therefore is not itself a virtue but the actualization of the virtue Charity. Opposed to peace, and hence to charity, are the vices, discord, contention, schism, war, quarreling, sedition (*ST* 2.2, Qs. 37–42). On war, however, Aquinas with Augustine excepts the *justum bellum*: 'Illa bella peccata non sunt quae non cupiditate aut crudelitate, sed pacis studio geruntur, ut mali coerceantur et boni subleventur.' With the Areopagite, he sees peace as the 'vis unitiva' in heaven and earth, and this is love. He traces the possibility of terrestrial peace to the individual personality and its desires and notes that this *pax terrena* can therefore never be perfect; what peace there is is the gift of God through Christ ('Pacem meam do').[71] Apart from the scholastic method, there is little here that goes beyond St. Augustine.

As a realization of love, peace like the other virtues is to be enjoined (*ST* 2.2., Q. 29, art. 4): 'Pacem habete inter vos' (Mark 9.50). It has therefore been the subject of sermons from the patristic period to the present day.[72] Bernard of Clairvaux, himself a peacemaker in the po-

---

[70]See Francis E. M. McMahon, "A Thomistic Analysis of Peace," *Thomist*, 1 (July 1939), 169–92.
[71]*Comm. on Ephesians* 2.14, in McMahon, "Analysis," p. 186 n.
[72]Leo I, *Sermo* 26.5 ('In Nativitate Domini'); *Sermo* 95.9 ('Homilia de gradibus ascensionis ad beatitudinem'). Augustine, *Sermo* 218.2 (Migne, *PL* 38.912). See Bonnaud Delamare, *L'Idée*, index, for a more complete list of Augustine's sermons on peace.

litical sphere, enjoined his congregation, *(Sermo* II, *In Annunciatione B. Mariae*, Migne, *PL* 183.389–90): 'Tunc vero seorsum pax consolans eas: Vos, inquit, nescitis quidquam, nec cogitatis. . . . Qui consilium dedit, ferat auxilium.' In the thirteenth century, the now familiar distinctions of the kinds of peace offer obvious sermon points. Jacques de Vitry, for example, makes an entire sermon out of them for the eighteenth Sunday after Pentecost.[73] The text is Isaiah 14: 'Da pacem, Domine, sustinentibus te,'[74] and the discourse ranges from 'peace with the devil' and 'with the world' (that is, its pleasures) and 'with the flesh' to 'peace with one's neighbor' and finally to 'peace with God,' the last progressing through the 'peace of reconciliation' to the 'peace of His will,' while 'peace from God' follows in three stages: 'peace of mind' ('tranquillitas conscientiae, quam peccatum mortale non remordet') 'peace of the purged conscience,' and the 'peace of eternity': 'Post pacem reconciliationis et pacem conscientiae non remordentis et pacem tranquillae et purgatae mentis, dat Dominus pacem aeternitatis, velut sabbatum ex sabbato.' Precisely the same points are made in the sermon for the twenty-third Sunday after Pentecost on a text from Jeremiah 29. 11–12: 'Dicit Dominus, Ego cogito cogitationes pacis,' where the main division is between 'bad peace' (with the world, flesh, and devil) and 'good peace.'[75]

In the sermons we are aware that the ideas of peace had been reduced to a common language and symbolism immediately recognized by all. Everyone knew that 'Jerusalem' meant 'visio pacis' (Augustine *De civ. D.* 11); and, for example, in the treatise *De claustro animae*, perhaps by Hugh of Folieto, the chapter (4.21) 'De pace quae in coelesti Hierusalem est' beginning with this etymology, goes on to 'Pacem meam do vobis,' and expands on the contrast between Christ's peace and the world's peace. A run-of-the-mill performance, as is also the chapter (5.40) 'De quadruplici pace claustrali' in an anonymous *Miscellanea*, with its succinct, not to say glib, form of the Augustinian distinctions: 'Quatuor enim sunt differentiae pacis multum necessariae religiosis. Est enim pax extra, pax inter, pax intra, pax supra. Pax extra, ad saeculum; pax inter, pax inter fratres; pax intra, ad seipsum; pax supra, ad Deum. Prima bona, secunda melior, tertia optima, quarta excellentissima.'[76]

[73]*Sermones in Epistolas et Evangelia dominicalia totius anni* (Antwerp, 1575), p. 829.
[74]*Introit* for the day, in the Ordinary of the Mass.
[75]Vitry, *Sermones*, p. 892. See Petrarch, *De remediis*, below, and Rufinus' 'pax Aegypti,' p. 40 above; also G. R. Owst, *Preaching in Medieval England* (Cambridge, 1928), pp. 22, 204–6, for English sermons *de pace*.
[76]Both treatises in the Appendix to the works of Hugh of St. Victor (Migne, *PL* 176.1159 and 177.766).

In mediaeval art, Pax is a virtue among the other virtues, and, at least until well into the thirteenth century, lives in the atmosphere of Prudentius' *Psychomachia*.[77] Thus Pax and Concordia sometimes appear together, though more often Concordia appears alone. It is to her that Prudentius gives the olive branch (*Psych.* 687), and with olive branch she is represented, for example, at Amiens.[78] Pax commonly appears as a female figure without special attributes, but in manuscript illumination often is represented in the act of kissing Justitia; for biblical peace is never far away.[79] The influence of Prudentius declined in the thirteenth century, and Pax becomes rare, though Concordia persists.[80] In cathedral sculpture, however, the virtues gradually were confined to the theological virtues, Faith, Hope, and Charity, and the cardinal virtues, Courage, Justice, Temperance, and Prudence, so that at the end of the Middle Ages one hardly expects to find either Concordia or Pax.[81]

In Chapter III we shall consider some late mediaeval poems on peace. We have already mentioned the twelfth-century poems of Alain de Lille. In the *Romance of the Rose*, Jean de Meun, relying on Alain, knows that the four elements 'se font pais de quatre anemis' (16,967 Langlois, ed. [Paris, 1924]); following Virgil, he relates the decline from the Golden Age of 'la simple gent paisible e bone' (20,124) to the hard age of Jupiter, a decline already described after Ovid, as owing to Avarice (9,493ff.). Characteristic is the discourse of Reason on the superiority of Love to Justice (5,473ff.). In the reign of Saturn, Justice held sway; but without love, Justice is too stern; if people loved one another, they would live 'paisible e quei' without kings or magistrates. This Love fled from earth with the gods when the Giants assailed them, and with Love went Law, Chastity, and Faith (5,387–92). In Dante's *Commedia*, peace usually means beatitude after death. The *pax cum diabolo* is not recognized, and there is no peace in hell;[82] Purgatory is a picture of striving toward peace; the word is significantly placed in a paraphrase of the Lord's Prayer: 'Vegna ver noi la pace del tuo regno' (*Purg.* 11.7), and though Adam lost the Earthly

---

[77]Emile Mâle, *L'Art religieux du xiiiᵉ siècle en France* (Paris, 1902), pp. 124–60; Adolf Katzenellenbogen, *Allegories of the Virtues and Vices in Mediaeval Art* (London, 1939), Index s.v. 'Concordia' and 'Pax,' and figs. 44, 45, 64.

[78]Mâle, *L'Art religieux du xiiiᵉ siècle*, fig. 62, p. 156.

[79]Sometimes Pax is represented with wings (Katzenellenbogen, *Allegories*, p. 43, n. 2, twelfth century).

[80]Mâle, *L'Art religieux du xiiiᵉ siècle*, pp. 130 and 137ff.

[81]Mâle, *L'Art religieux de la fin du moyen âge en France* (Paris, 1908), pp. 331–52. And cf. Thomas Aquinas, *ST* 2.2.29, 'Peace an actualization of charity.'

[82]The word *pace* occurs five times in the *Inferno*, without special significance. But there is justice in hell. *Inf.* 3.14 and 125; 12.133; 29.56; 30.133.

Paradise given by God as an earnest of eternal peace ('per arra d'e-
terna pace,' *Purg.* 28.93), the waters of peace still reach us from the
eternal Fountain (*Purg.* 15.131). The word becomes frequent in the
Paradiso, and characteristic phrases are: 'da essilio venne a questa pace'
(*Par.* 10.129); 'venni dal martiro a questa pace' (*Par.* 15.148);
'd'Egitto vegna in Gerusalemme, per vedere' (*Par.* 25.55); 'E'n la sua
volontade è nostra pace' (*Par.* 3.85).[83] In short, 'peace' in Dante is
the actualization of love, which is by far the more prominent word,
and in heaven the actualization is complete: 'O vita integra d'amore e
di pace!' (*Par.* 27.8).

Terrestrial peace, such as it might be, also concerned Dante, for
whom it was still bound up with the pretensions of pope and emperor.
In the *De monarchia* 1.3–4, he argues that the 'end' of civil life is the
exercise of the intellectual virtues; that prudence and wisdom are ex-
ercised by sitting still and keeping quiet; and that for the whole race to
exercise them requires universal peace: 'Unde manifestum est quod
pax universalis est optimum eorum quae ad nostram beatitudinem
ordinantur.' Hence to the shepherds was proclaimed, not riches, plea-
sures, honors, long life, health, strength, or beauty, but peace. Hence
the Savior appropriately used the salutation 'Pax vobis,' and the Disci-
ples and Paul followed this custom. This terrestrial perfection, fig-
ured by the terrestrial Paradise, is to be sought under an earthly ruler,
while for the higher spiritual beatitude of the celestial Paradise, reve-
lation is required, and this higher aspect is the province of the pope
(*Mon.* 3.16). That certainly is traditional enough.[84] A few years later,
Marsilio of Padua—perhaps linked with Dante through their com-
mon friend Albertino Mussato—pursues a similar end, but in open
hostility to the papacy. In the *Defensor pacis* he begins (1.1) with a quo-
tation from Cassiodorus (above p. 38) on the fruits of peace and ex-
pands with the usual biblical quotations: Job 22.21 ('habebis fructus
optimos'), Luke 2.14 ('In terra pax hominibus'), John 20.19 ('Pax vo-
bis'); Mark 9.50 ('pacem habeto'); Matt. 10.12 ('pax huic domi'), and
John 14.27 ('pacem relinquo vobis'). Peace is a necessary condition of
a 'sufficientiam vitae,' and its contrary (1.2) is discord; he quotes Sal-
lust: 'Concordia parvae res crescunt, discordia vero maximae dilabun-
tur' (*Jug.* 10.6).[85] The papal pretensions are the disturbers of the

[83]Translated from St. Augustine's *Confessions* 13.9: 'In bona voluntate tua pax nobis
est.' And for Egypt and Jerusalem (*visio pacis*), see discussion of Bishop Rufinus above.

[84]The concept of the whole race unanimously exercising the intellectual virtues at
least recalls the Averroistic unity of the intellect, and St. Thomas, no defender of Aver-
roes, allows it in some sense.

[85]Also a common quotation; Erasmus, *Bellum* 957E, quotes it from memory, without
mentioning Sallust.

peace. Marsilio already thinks primarily of the conditions of the Italian states, and modern students of his work do not fail to remark on the similarities between his attitude and that two hundred years later of Machiavelli, whose Prince also is to bring peace—a sort of Mars pacifer—despite the papacy.

Petrarch's reflections on political peace found immortal expression in the great canzoni *Italia mia* and *Spirito gentil*, in which he laments the torn condition of Italy or envisions a peace hero or *soter* with feet beautiful upon the seven hills of Rome. His utterance is the more fervid for keeping his eye on the hope of peace in his own time and place and extending a certain 'ignorantia' to the mediaeval distinctions in the subject, founded though they are on his own guide and mentor, Augustine. Though he goes crying 'Pace, pace,' in his time there was no peace, and he might have turned in a public sense the words he uses in a famous sonnet for the inner peace of the lover: 'Pace non trovo.'[86] And indeed it is a skeptical eye that he casts on the subject in two little dialogues between Hope and Reason in his *De remediis utriusque fortunae* (1.106–6). The first is entitled *'De spe pacis'*: 'S. Spero pacem. R. Melius est pacem servare quam sperare. S. Pacem spero. R. Spes pacis multos perdidit, sperataque paci succedens insperata calamitas incautos obruit sopitosque quos inexpertos inveniens laesisset. S. Spero pacem. R. . . . Quatuor vobiscum habitant hostes, avaritia, invidia, ira, superbia.' These 'enemies' of peace certainly are traditional, harking back perhaps to Prudentius. And of course the main theme that peace—here the hope of peace—carries the risk of 'unpreparedness' is also old (Aristotle, Vegetius). The dialogue concludes that for the stout-hearted a 'bellicosa libertas' is far better than a 'pacifica servitus.' The topic is continued in the second dialogue *'De pace et indutiis.'* Peace with Carthage was the ruin of Rome, both in *mores* and *humanitas* itself. When they laid aside their armor, the Romans laid aside their virtue, and with Pax came her *comites*, luxuria, licentia, and libido.[87] He quotes Juvenal, 'Nunc patimur longae pacis mala' (6.292), which is always cited in this argument. To make a truce with the enemy is merely to offer him time to rearm for a greater effort against you; a truce is neither peace nor war and worse than either.

[86]Since inner peace has to do with the ordering of the desires (Aquinas, above; cf. the 'bestia sanza pace' of Dante [*Inf.* 1.58]) this concept—Heine's 'Du bist die Ruh, du Friede mild'—is probably as old as amatory poetry: Sappho, 16; Ovid, *Amores* 2.18; 3.2.49–50; Tibullus 1.1, 1.10; Propertius 1.10.2–5; as is its counterpart, amatory strife ('militat omnis amans'), which is often contrasted with war (Tibullus 1.10.57–68; Secundus, *Basia*, 8, 9, and *Epithalamium*).

[87]From Sallust, *Cat.* 1–10 or fragms. 11 and 12.

These dialogues, written in 1361, do not represent Petrarch's most serious thought. That is to be found in the canzoni and in his letter to the Doge Andrea Dandolo in March 1351 (*Fam.* 11.8) urging an end to the war between Venice and Genoa. Since it is youth that precipitates wars, Petrarch is glad that Venice is ruled by a Council of Elders and that Dandolo himself is convinced that peace is more glorious than triumphs.[88] He recalls the words of the belligerent Hannibal in Livy (30.30.9): 'melior tutiorque certa pax quam sperata victoria,' but would prefer to say 'quam certa victoria.' For what is more pleasant, more happy than peace? Without it, what is life but perpetual fear? What pleasure is there in the soldier's life, nights in the open, sleep broken by bugles, one's grey head (as Virgil says) pressed by the helmet? Life is anyhow so short. Worst of all is the strife of Italian cities. Would that your enemies were Damascus or Susa, Memphis, Smyrna —anything but Genoa. You are fighting your own brothers. And the issues of war are uncertain, except that now whichever wins, one of the eyes of Italy must needs be put out.[89] Where the mediaeval preacher flanked his observations with citations from Scripture, Petrarch flanks his with citations from ancient history.[90]

Others still applied the topics of the mediaeval argument to the situation of their day. In the North, the theologian Jean Gerson (1363–1429), for example, naturally brought forward the old definitions and citations in the sermons on peace that he preached before the French king and other princes.[91] Yet basic attitudes were chang-

[88]'Nullos triumphos clariores, nulla opimiora patriae spolia referre posse, quam pacem' (*Fam.* 11.8.12, in *Opera*, Guido Martellotti et al., eds. [Milan and Naples, 1955–68]). The thought and the first three words suggest Silius Italicus 11.593–94: 'Pax una triumphis / Innumeris potior'; but—unless from a *florilegium*—Petrarch cannot very well have got them from the author.

[89]*Fam.* 11.8.15. The metaphor refers to Athens and Sparta, as Petrarch indicates, 11.8.33. [I am indebted to Professor Benjamin G. Kohl of Vassar College for this reference. R.G.]

[90]It is interesting to compare the topics of Petrarch's letter to Dandolo with those of Ronsard's *Exhortation* (below, p. 96) and many others.

[91]See *Opera*, ed. Ellies Dupin (Antwerp, 1706) Index, s.v. 'Pax.' For example, in a sermon for Easter on the text *Pax vobis* (*Opera* 3.1204), he quotes from Augustine; adds, 'Bellamus, (inquit Aristoteles in *politic.*) 'ut pacem habeamus'; and follows with biblical passages and Sallust's 'Concordia parvae res crescunt.' In a sermon on the Circumcision (2.69) he details four 'considerationes de pace,' namely, (1) 'Fines politiae ecclesiasticae et cujuslibet legis eam regulantis, est pax salutifera.' (2) 'Quaelibet in ecclesiastica hierarchia potestas in pacem salutiferam ordinatur.' (3) 'Quilibet rationis capax, obligatur secundum vocationem suam, pacem Ecclesiae salutiferam procurare. Ille orando, hic disputando, hic praedicando, hic exhortando, hic agendo, vel quolibet modo alio' (4) 'Tantum est pacis salutiferae bonum ut pro ejus adoptione neque mundanus honor, neque status, neque gradus, neque propria utilitas debeant aliquem deterrere, et nihil prorsus nisi peccatum contra legem Dei aeternam.' A sermon 'Pro pace Ecclesiae et unione Graecorum' (2.141) was preached before the king of France after the Council of

ing. The mediaeval Aristotelian would have accepted some such summary as this: All things seek peace, 'omnia pacem petunt.' The passage from nonbeing or pure potentiality to actuality is a realization of form, and for every thing its form is its peace. All things ultimately are moved to form and being by the Prime Mover through love, and the result, the total actualization, is the peace of the universe. Peace is thus the contrary of a *quies mortua* and is the proper term for complete being and the fullest activity possible. This satisfactory world-view was shaken in the fourteenth century by the nominalists and in general by the very sharp criticisms of the doctrine of forms.[92] Many persons were simply impatient of the disputes of the schools and found rest in the various lines of pietism and illumination that are characteristic of the fourteenth and fifteenth centuries—in a reconciliation or even, with the mystics, a union of the individual soul with God; in the search for inward peace. With Petrarch himself, taught by Augustine, this quest is central and has the form of the abandonment of 'science' for the care of one's own soul.[93] For the *devotio moderna*, as represented by the *Imitatio Christi*, inward peace (3.41: 'interius pacificari et stabilari . . . spiritualiter illuminari') is attained by withdrawal from human relationships (1.11)—even from friendship (3.42; cf. Augustine, *De civ. D.* 19.8); by complete humility (3.23–25); by submission to the will of God (ibid.). Such peace is 'true liberty' (3.23), but perfect peace is not of this world, and, hoping for the City above, one will ask (3.48): 'When shall there be solid peace, peace unruffled, always secure, peace within and without, peace on all sides firm?' On the other hand, Cardinal Nicholas of Cusa unites a public career, devoted with considerable success to the promotion of peace, with the pietism of the *devotio moderna*, which was the atmosphere of his youth, and with an im-

---

Pisa; another, addressed to the monarchs of Europe (2.253), urges them to unite against the enemies of Christendom: 'Opus Justitiae est pax . . . plane quia nihil aliud est pax quam ordinis tranquillitas. . . . Justitia et pax osculatae sunt'; in a sermon for Christmas on the text *Gloria in excelsis* (3.955), he apostrophizes: 'O desideratissima Pax, quo abiisti? O devoti principes et domini!' His imitation of Boethius, *De consolatione philosophiae*, includes a 'metre' on inward peace (1.179):

> Pulchra pax, summi munus optimum,
> Te voluntati (sit bonae tantum)
> Nuncius defert missus ab alto;
> Nam malae mentis qualis erit pax?

[92]See Anneliese Maier, *Zwei Grundprobleme des scholastischen Naturphilosophie* (Rome, 1951).
[93]Petrarch, *De sui ipsius et multorum ignorantia, Opera* (Basel, 1554), p. 1164; passage truncated in Martellotti, ed., but included in Hans Nachod, trans., *The Renaissance Philosophy of Man*, ed. P. O. Kristeller et al. (Chicago, 1948), p. 121; *Ascent of Mt. Ventoux* (*Fam.* 4.1, in *Opera*, ed. Martellotti, 7.842).

pressive attempt to construct a new philosophy aimed at transcending the difficulties of the schools. His problem is that of accounting for the finite world, with all its discords, in relation to God the infinite, in whom he finds the 'reconciliation of opposites' (*coincidentia oppositorum*) and the source of unity.[94] Cusanus' positions are fundamentally Platonic, and he thus anticipates what was to be—certainly on the level of literature—the prevailing outlook of the Renaissance.

Although the transcendent and universal connotations of the word 'peace' thus remained available throughout the Renaissance, the prevailing tendency set afoot by the humanists laid the emphasis on political peace among men. The humanist education trained the ruling element of the modern national state, and this by and large was its conscious aim. Its substance lay in ethical and political wisdom, and the instrument it sought to perfect was the spoken and written word. The literature it produced is apt to seem to us banal in content, too easily pleased with convenient *topoi*, and of too copious an eloquence. It closely resembles that of certain periods of antiquity, and in a long view of Western literary expression one might justifiably call the Renaissance the Third Sophistic. It is saved, however, insofar as its basis was laid in the ethical and political realities of the period, and in the best hands the richness of expression answers perfectly to a complex sense of life.

An early example of humanist rhetoric about peace is the dialogue *De pace et de bello* of the Spanish bishop Rodrigo Sánchez of Arévalo, described by Sir Geoffrey Butler, and written, according to Butler's conjecture, at the time of the Italian peace arranged by Pope Paul II in 1468.[95] The interlocutors are Platina, who speaks on behalf of peace, and Sánchez himself, who takes the side against it. In his Preface, Sánchez offers this verbal tournament in place of the armed tournaments with which the conclusion of a peace is commonly, and very inappropriately, celebrated. Platina begins with a vivid picture of the horrors of war and traces war to its source in the false standards of men—for example, historians vaunt as heroes men who are no better than murderers. In earlier times, the human person was held sacred as made in the image of God. He is barely able to admit the justifica-

---

[94]See Cusanus' *Concordantia catholica*, for union and harmony between Church and state and peace a cooperation reposing on 'concord'; *De pace fidei* for peace and unity among religions; *De docta ignorantia* for a unifying philosophy. See also E. Vansteenberghe, *Le Cardinal Nicolas de Cues* (Paris, 1920), Ch. 8, for Cusanus as 'man of peace.'

[95]Sir Geoffrey Butler, *Studies in Statecraft* (Cambridge, 1920), Ch. 1. The dialogue remains unprinted, and the following sentences depend on Butler's description and excerpts. On Sánchez see Richard S. Trane, S.J., *Rodrigo Sánchez de Arévalo, 1404–1470: Spanish Diplomat and Champion of the Papacy* (Washington, D.C., 1958).

tion of defensive warfare. Let humanity raise its eyes to heaven and contemplate the peaceful order of the universe. Consider also the animals, who keep peace within their several kinds.[96] Peace is natural—who ever prayed for war? All things seek peace—witness the phenomena of external nature, storm and calm. Peace is a divine gift—'My peace I give unto you.' Peace is the necessary condition for all the arts and industries of civilized life. Sánchez replies that discord as well as concord is found throughout nature. No created thing has peace; the animals after all fight furiously among their several kinds. War, says Aristotle, is fought for the sake of peace and hence may be said to be necessary to peace. War is indispensable for the production of the virtues, and without it the world would degenerate. He offers some etymologies—*pax* from *pactum*; *casta* from *castra*; *bella* (wars) from *bella* (beautiful). On the whole, he has not cared to make a very strong case for war.

The same humanist impulse to mark the conclusion of a peace with a literary utterance is represented a few years after Bishop Rodrigo's dialogue by the poem *De pace* of Baptista Mantuanus, which we consider below (Ch. III). The Renaissance literature of peace is rapidly accumulating.[97] Out of it we must be content here to choose two figures of contrasting character and of unequal importance, yet both representative of the mental directions of the first half of the sixteenth century. The first inevitably is Erasmus.

The summons to peace, written throughout Erasmus' works as throughout his life, is as much a part of his message as is the call to a simple, inner faith or the advocacy of 'good letters.' On a subject so important to him he was bound to lavish all the arts of rhetoric of which he was a master and which ensured that his voice would be heard in its time; but with Erasmus the rhetoric does not obscure the sincerity of his intent. His topics are always much the same, so that the lost *Antipolemus*, against Julius II in 1507, doubtless exists merged in his two principal peace writings, the adage *Dulce bellum inexpertis* (*Adagia* 4.1.1), first published in 1515, and the declamation *Querela pacis* published two years later; some of these topics indeed already

[96]I assume that Platina makes this point, since Sánchez later answers it; Butler does not mention it here.

[97]See K. von Raumer, *Ewiges Friede: Friedensrufe und Friedenspläne seit der Renaissance* (Freiburg, 1953); Leo Spitzer, "Classical and Christian Ideas of World Harmony, Prolegomena to an Interpretation of the Word 'Stimmung,'" *Traditio*, 2 (1944), 392–464; 3 (1945), 307–64, discusses world harmony and peace in Dante, Milton, and Shakespeare. See also Hutton, *Essays on Renaissance Poetry*, Rita Guerlac, ed. (Ithaca, 1980), Index s.v. Peace, theme of in Renaissance.

appear in his *Panegyric* of Philip the Fair in 1504.[98] Especially the events of the years 1514–17, namely the contest between Francis I and Charles V, brought him out on this subject, not only in the two works mentioned, but also in the adage *Scarabeus* of 1515 (*Adagia* 3.7.1.), in letters addressed to Antony of Bergen (1514) and to Leo X (1515),[99] and in his *Institutio principis Christiani* of 1516. Later utterances are his letter to Francis I (1523)[100] and his *Consultatio de bello Turcis inferendo* (1530).

We are in the full Renaissance. No longer is the keeping of the peace a matter for pope and emperor; it lies in the hands of the several European monarchs and chiefly in the greedy hands of Hapsburgs and Valois. These in their rage for aggrandizement had been cynically heedless of the desolation of Europe. The chief object therefore of Erasmus' protests and of his satire is the warmongering king, the chief object of hope a truly Christian prince. In *Dulce bellum inexpertis*, however, he gives his thought wide scope and produces a declamation reminiscent of the writers of the Second Sophistic.

Starting from the Greek proverb, Γλυκὺς ἀπείρῳ πόλεμος, (Vegetius 3.12, 'inexpertis dulcis est pugna') and Pindar, fragm. 110, he remarks in general on the deceptive attraction of things untried—court life, for example, and the love of girls—worst of which is war, and begins his formal argument with the human body, which is plainly intended for peace; wild beasts are born fully armed, man naked but endowed with speech the instrument of friendship. Against the picture of Man is set the picture of War. But not even the animals fight their own kind, while men fight worse than any beasts. Nature may well say: 'I created man for peace; he has found weapons by his own evil invention.'

How did war arise? Gradually. At first men fought the beasts in defense, then clothed themselves in their skins, then ate them, and so got

---

[98]LB 4.529. The adage *Dulce bellum* had existed in germ since the *Adagia* of 1508 as a five-line notice of the Greek proverb and a reference to Aristotle's *Rhetoric* on the rashness of youth; it became the great essay we know, of more than ten thousand words, in the edition of 1515; further changes and additions in 1523, 1526, and 1533; see the edition by Yvonne Remy and René Dunil-Marquebreucq (Brussels, 1953). On Erasmus' peace writings the work of Elise Constantinescu Bagdat, *La "Querela Pacis" d'Erasme* (Paris, 1924), remains fundamental; a good later survey by Mario Santoro, "Pace e Guerra nel Pensiero di Erasmo," in *Giornale italiano di Filologia*, 6 (1953), 334–52. On the influence of Erasmus' peace writings in France, see Hutton, "Erasmus and France: The Propaganda for Peace," in *Essays*, pp. 265–90.

[99]P. S. Allen, *Opus Epistolarum Desiderii Erasmi Rotorodami* (Oxford, 1906–47), Eps. 288 and 335.

[100]Allen, *Opus Epist.* 1400; LB 7.149ff.

used to fighting and to possessions. Possessions led to men fighting other men, until it came to nation fighting nation, the winning of empires, and fighting for mere gain. Now war is universal; even Christians fight Christians, and are praised for it from the pulpit. Yet peace is incomparably better than war. (A set comparison follows). War not only makes men wretched, but bad. The numberless disasters—earthquakes, plagues—that have overtaken mankind have only made men wretched; war makes them both wretched and guilty. Few benefit from war, all benefit from peace. The very rumor of war is grievous; war taxes make the government unpopular; the preparations are toilsome; military life is hateful; and for all its cost war brings little gain.

But how can Christians fight? War between Christian nations is fratricide and worse, for Christians are more than brothers. The teaching of Christ, the Apostles, the Fathers is against war. A visitor from another world, hearing of man's Christian destiny, would stand aghast to see the animals living peaceably in accordance with nature and man plagued with iniquity and war. How did war come to Christians? By degrees. First the Christian message was tainted by a classical education, deemed necessary to refute the learned pagans, and the love of strife grew in fighting the early heresies. Theology made the mistake of embracing Aristotle, who thought wealth a good. The reception of Roman Law favored war. But mainly, the acceptance of riches by Christians.is the root of the trouble. Now Christians fight worse than the heathen; for whereas the ancients regulated war, our soldiers proceed like bandits. The Romans had the excuse of civilizing those they conquered.

If in the Old Testament the Jews fought at God's command, they did not fight Jews but foreign enemies. Anyway, Christians do not follow all the Old Testament practices—for example, the plurality of wives. The only fighting that befits Christians is with the enemies of the Church, with avarice, wrath, ambition, the fear of death. These are our Philistines. And talk of the 'two swords,' civil and ecclesiastic, is beside the point. Arguments for the 'justum bellum' [Augustine, Aquinas] are contrary to the spirit of Christ's teaching. Self-preservation, true enough, is a law of nature, but better is the command to love our enemies. There is no true analogy between the punishment of a single criminal and the 'punishment' by war of a criminal state. In the one case the wrongdoer suffers, but in the latter it is mostly the innocent who suffer, and if anyone gains it is the guilty. Even if princely disputes were analogous to lawsuits, lawsuits are not so very admirable. Nowadays wars are mostly fought by princes for territorial gains. This amounts to herding populations about like cattle; and the gains are ephemeral, handed on tomorrow by Fortune to some one else.

I cannot approve even of our fighting the Turks. If we aim to convert them, we should display ourselves to them as true Christians. Anyway, the friars who might better be converting them prefer to swarm in royal courts. After all, the Turks are largely semi-Christians, and perhaps better Christians than many of us. If on the other hand our real aim is to plunder them, why make religion a pretext? At best these methods would only make pretended Christians of them and certainly make bad Christians of ourselves. If they were the aggressors, it might be different, but in that case we ought to fight with clean hands.

Wars among Christians arise from folly or malice. Many persons promote wars in order to seize power. Most of our 'reasons' are rationalizations concealing baser motives. A prince wins neither true glory nor real gain from war—quite the opposite. Our task is to win heaven by innocence, charity, and long-suffering. If Christ is a fable, explode the fable, if he is 'the way, the truth, and the life,' why do our reasonings so clash with his? Let princes and prelates together seek peace. This indeed is the intent of the peaceful pope Leo X, a worthy scion of the Medici who made Florence great; Julius may glory in his wars, but Leo will win true glory by bringing peace to the world.

This is the kind of writing, aimed at moving the heart, that Petrarch had desiderated in place of the cerebrations, however, scientific, of the Aristotelians;[101] it is what he and the Renaissance returned to antiquity to find.[102] If less profound, it seemed to be the method of better teachers than Aquinas. The *Bellum* was issued as a separate pamphlet many times, first in April 1517, to be followed in December by the first of many editions of the *Querela pacis*. Here, resuming the form, but not the irony, of his popular *Praise of Folly*, Erasmus makes Peace plead in her own behalf.

Men have driven me away from them, and hence I mourn, not for myself but for them. How can rational creatures act in this way? It might be expected of irrational animals, but they are peaceful. The celestial bodies move in peace; the health of the living body is peace; animals—elephants, sheep, and the rest—live in peace; plants grow in association; stones cohere; wild animals are peaceable within their kinds; even the demons in hell are united; only man wars on man, though obviously created for peace, having reason, speech, natural affection, the gift of tears, complementary capacities. The other animals are born armed, man na-

[101]*Des sui ipsius et multorum ignorantia*, in *Invective*, ed. Martellotti, pp. 714, 718–24.
[102]Major sources of the *Bellum* (See Ch. VIII, pp. 223–25, below): Ovid, *Met.* 15.75–477, but esp. 75–126; Pliny, *HN* 7, Praefatio; Lucretius, *De rer. nat.* 5.222–34; Plutarch, *De esu carn.* Minor sources: Cicero, *De fin.* 3.19, *De off.* 1.4, *De leg.* 1.6, *Ad Fam.* 6.6.5; Dio, *Or.* 40.35; Horace, *Epode* 7, *Sat.* 50; Lactantius, *De Ira* Ch. 2; Plato, *Rep.* 470–71; Plutarch, *De cohibenda ira*; Seneca, *De Ira*, Ep. 99, *De Clem.* 1.26. For a more complete list see Roland Bainton, "The *Querela Pacis* of Erasmus, Classical and Christian Sources," *Archiv für Reformationsgeschichte*, 41 (1948), 32–48. Many of the sources he cites are sources for the *Bellum* as well. See also the Remy and Dunil-Marquebreucq edition cited in note 98, which lists some sources.

ked and in need of help. Thus Nature has ordained man for peace, and one might think the common name of Man would ensure it; still more among Christians their common name. Yet I Peace can find no place, whether among commoners or kings, or among the learned, or the clergy (least of all in monasteries), or even in the breast of some one man, since this is torn by lust, anger, avarice, and ambition.

How can such men be called Christians? Consider the life of Christ, and first the terms in which Isaiah foretold his coming. [Here follows a long development, running through the Bible from 'Justitiae opus pax' to 'Pacem meam do,' and beyond to the sacraments of baptism and the eucharist, to show that the whole Christian message is that of peace; the heavenly Jerusalem means *visio pacis*.]

When life is anyway so short and fleeting, so full of perils, how can men willfully add the supreme disaster of war?

What precedes, hardly more than a third of the diatribe, is introductory to the main theme, which is the iniquity of rulers and princes in seeking war rather than peace. A few of the main topics may be noted:

Our princes make war for frivolous causes—the clause of a treaty, royal marriages—often incited by evil ecclesiastics, of whom Julius II is the type: the very Cross is made into a military standard and cross clashes with cross in battle. Peace cannot be secured by treaties and royal marriages, which lead to more wars, but by rulers acquiring a sense of responsibility to their peoples. For example, the boundaries of kingdoms should be fixed once for all; in case of war, the consent of the whole people should be secured; arbitration should be used. I speak of wars made for trifling causes; a war of defense is another matter. If there is in the human heart a fatal and necessary propensity to war, vent it on the unbelieving Turk—though Turks too, after all, are men and brothers; if charity cannot unite men, a common enemy may do so. Meanwhile, for base and selfish ends, princes mislead their peoples by promoting the common notion that foreigners are natural enemies. Surely the whole world is our fatherland; the Church is our family and our house. Kings should weigh the good of their nations as they would weigh the good of their families. Heathen emperors like Augustus and the Antonines saw their security in the people; you kings treat the people with cynical contempt. How can you expect to pass from the murder of the battlefield to the perfect peace of heaven? Come, bind discord with adamantine chains. I appeal to kings, to priests, to preachers, to bishops, nobles, all Christian men: follow the lead of Leo, Francis, Charles, Maximilian, and Henry VIII, all of whom love peace, and, since treaties, marriages, and force have failed, try the effect of kindness and goodwill. Christ will prosper what is done in his spirit.

That Erasmus' views penetrated the conscience of Europe is true, and we shall have occasion to observe examples of his influence; but there were barriers limiting this penetration in Catholic countries. In France, the Sorbonne early set its face against him, and after 1525 the rarity of editions and translations of his characteristic writings in France is notorious.[103] How his thoughts might nevertheless penetrate may be illustrated by an attractive little book, *De bello et pace opusculum*, by Josse Clichtove, the famous opponent of Lutheranism.[104] Clichtove was a Belgian, a pupil of Lefèvre d'Etaples, and in later life a canon of Chartres. This is an independent work by a man of learning and in some respects far from Erasmian, yet many chapters are little more than restatements of Erasmus' peace writings. For our purposes it is important, since the ideas expressed in the French peace poems can again and again be traced to it.[105] The earlier chapters, on peace in general and the enormity of war among Christian princes, use Erasmus' topics and content to some extent; but Clichtove comes out strongly for a crusade against the Turk,[106] defends the principle of a 'justum bellum,' and, cleaving to Augustine, defines the limits of a just war even among Christians, urging, however, that every effort be made to avert it by legations: it should not be thought an admission of inferiority to send the first embassy. Prayer to God and an honest effort to negotiate are the only practical measures he can suggest. His presentation is remarkable for the lavish use of Scripture and a generous use of classical authors, especially the poets; while among more recent writers, he constantly quotes from Mantuan, and at the end prints in full (except for the topical last lines) Mantuan's *Pro pacata Italia*, perhaps thus helping to give to this poem the prominence it enjoyed.[107] The name of Erasmus nowhere appears.[108]

[103]Among the translations by Berquin which the Sorbonne condemned was one of the *Querela*. See Margaret Mann Phillips, "Erasmus in France in the Later Sixteenth Century," *Journal of the Warburg and Courtauld Institutes*, 34 (1971), 246–61; A. Renaudet, *Etudes Erasmiennes (1521–1539)* (Geneva, 1939), Ch. 2; see also Hutton, *Essays*, pp. 285–90.

[104]*De bello et pace opusculum, Christianos principes ad sedandos bellorum tumultus et pacem componendam exhortans* (Paris: Simon Colinaeus, 1523).

[105]See Hutton, *Essays*, pp. 269–74. On the other hand, since there seems to have been only one edition, this does not rank with the more popular books of Clichtove.

[106]Ch. 12. Europe is in danger from the Turk especially because of the religious contentions created by Martin Luther. Hence (f. 28ʳ): 'Cur non expergiscimur a gravi somno . . . ut Lutherianam hanc factionem, caelo et terris bella intentantem, dissipemus, evertamus, et exterminemus antequam amplius invalescat.' Clichtove is regarded as a temperate opponent of Luther, but this chapter, taken with Chs. 15 and 20 (below, n. 108), is an announcement of the religious wars.

[107]Below, Ch. III.

[108]The contents of Clichtove's book are given here for future reference. *Praef.* Appeal to the general Christian community. 1. Peace and war contrasted. 2. Peace the

Clichtove's attitude, like Erasmus', combines the sober earnestness of the *devotio moderna* with the excitement of classical rhetoric. As we pass into the hands of another apostle of peace, Guillaume Postel, we are in another, but equally characteristic, Renaissance atmosphere, that of Neoplatonism or rather of the Cabala that Erasmus found, he said, uncongenial. Postel was a fanatic—perhaps, as the Inquisition told him, mad—but he was practical and mostly beyond rhetoric. While Erasmus addressed a letter to Francis I, Postel, it is said, went to see the king and reasoned with him. Professor of mathematics and oriental languages at the Collège de France, he took the Cabala (with its emphasis, for example, on the feminine principle) too practically, and discovered a female redeemer in a Venetian sister of charity. Nevertheless, in his apocalyptic fashion he dedicated his long life, and a stream of publications, to the cause of universal peace. From his eastern travels, his experience embraced more than Europe: Where were the representatives, he asked, of Russia, Armenia, Greece, Georgia, and Ethiopia at the Council of Trent? He had plans for the conversion of Mohammedans—they were first to be approached on common grounds, and so led forward—and was ready to be sent out to begin the work.[109] These ideas are set forth in his first major work, *De orbis terrae Concordia* (1543), in which he establishes philosophically the truths of Christianity, examines Mohammedanism and the Koran, sets forth the common human grounds civil and religious, and proposes methods for converting Muslims and Jews. This large work is sufficiently sober; his apocalyptic ideas seem to have come to him a

principle of the cosmos and its parts. 3. Peace emanates from the heavenly Jerusalem, war is brought from hell by the Erinnys. 4. Christ's message throughout is one of peace. 5. The blessings of peace (justice is done; agriculture flourishes; trade is resumed, and so on) and the horrors of war. 6. Of the three scourges, war, famine, and pestilence, war is worst, and cause of the others. 7. Christian princes should not fight one another. 8. Such a war is worse than 'civil,' it is 'fraternal.' 9. The wars of the ancient pagans were less cruel than ours. 10. Standards displaying the Cross should not be carried in battle. 11. Ecclesiastics should not incite princes to fight one another. 12. They should encourage them to fight the infidel. 13. Just grounds for war do, however, exist. 14. Wars can be waged more or less justly: at least pay your soldiers, and do not permit them to pillage their own people. 15. Just causes are defensive: to repel invasion; to suppress great crimes such as heresy and schism, if the schismatics have resorted to arms; but the repossession of territories is not clearly just, and is usually too costly, especially in lives. 16. In such cases try legations; if the holder is unjust and contumacious, war as a last resort is just. 17. The chief cause of war is our sins (greed, luxury, and the rest) which provoke the just vengeance of God. 18. God to be appeased by prayer and repentance. 19. The use of legations to treat of peace. 20. Exhortation to princes: preserve the Christian community, now divided against itself; think of the misery of your people; if you love war, go against the *hostes fidei orthodoxae*. Mantuan's poem.

[109]Postel may well have known the *De pace fidei* of Nicholas of Cusa, which approaches the conversion of Mohammedans in the same tolerant fashion.

few years later and are perhaps first expressed in his *Absconditorum a constitutione mundi clavis* of 1547.[110] What interests us, at the end of our survey, is their reflection of the Augustinian tradition of the Middle Ages, with modifications owing to Postel's time, place, and personality. Peace is of the nature of God, and His grand design for the universe is ultimately peace. Towards this end all things are progressing, though hindered by the divisions of mankind rooted in the imperfections of man's nature.[111] That is the meaning of the petition, 'Thy will be done on earth as it is in heaven':

> Que doict-on entendre et demander, disant: Soit faicte la volunté en la terre comme au ciel? C'est qu'il fault du tout et en tout et partout, que toutes choses soyent restituées . . . à celle fin que comme nous voyons le Ciel avec ses estoilles estre resglément gouverné . . . par les divines intelligences, nous en semblable forme voyons après destruictz toutes les tyrannies de ce monde, tant les spirituelles comme les temporelles, et afin que la forme et imitation du ciel soit estendue sur la terre.[112]

The general mediaeval view had been that the divine peace, so far as it was known on earth, was in the keeping of the Church, but that the empire had the duty to effect and preserve it. Whoever means to promote peace must single out the sources of social power and appeal to their guardians. Both Erasmus and Postel assume that they, simply as Christians, may take up a duty that the clergy too often neglect, and they see what is obvious that the sources of power they must approach are the monarchies, not the empire. For Postel this means the French monarchy and, as he reads the mind of God, the divine plan aims at a *pax Gallica*. If the empire had had divine sanction, this is even clearer in the case of the Gallic monarchy. Of the sons of Noah, Shem had been set apart to witness to the divine plan for the world, and his mission is inherited by the papacy, while Japheth had the duty to effect the plan, and his mission reaches through his son Gomer to Gomer's

[110]I have not seen this work and am familiar only with the *Orbis terrae Concordia*, the *Candelabri typici in Mosis tabernaculo . . . Interpretatio* (Venice, 1548), and the *Histoire mémorable des expéditions depuis le déluge, faites par les Gaulois* (Paris, 1552), and with most of what has been written about Postel. For the present purpose, the following summary is much indebted to Butler, *Statecraft*, Ch. 3, and William J. Bouwsma, *Concordia Mundi: The Career and Thought of Guillaume Postel (1510–1581)* (Cambridge, Mass., 1957).
[111]The physical universe also has elements of disunity and is in process of becoming, but will eventually attain repose (Albert Henrik de Sallengre, *Mémoires de Littérature* [The Hague, 1715], 1.32, art. 'Postel').
[112]Butler, *Statecraft*, p. 47, who does not indicate the source.

descendants the Gauls.[113] Moreover, the times are growing late. Taking the world since Adam in thousand-year periods, we are now at 1550 in the middle of the sixth period, and there will be only seven. Ours therefore is the time of final preparation.[114] It behooves the French king to put his house in order for the fulfillment of the divine scheme. But peace and war are rooted in human nature, which must also be perfected, as is about to happen. The soul of man essentially consists of *animus*, the rational part, and *anima*, the passions. The rational soul, by which we come to know our place in God's plan, was redeemed by the coming of Christ; but 'if the old Gospel preached that man's *animus* or soul was to find redemption in Christ Jesus, it was now Postel's allotted task to demonstrate that the *anima*, the "inferior part of the spirit," needed renewal also; as man's fall was due alone to the old Eve, so his restoration should be accomplished by a new Eve.'[115] These deductions were only too logical, and the practical Postel was rewarded by the discovery of this new Eve in the person of Mother Joanna in the hospital of St. John and St. Paul in Venice about 1546. She died in 1551. Postel's eventful life extended into the reign of Henri III (he died in 1581), and hence through a period of French history that might or might not seem to be a preparation for the last things. Yet, though he had given up hope of a French monarchy, he never abandoned his life's work: 'Estant donc mon general but de conduyre le monde en fondement et vray principle de la concorde, union et souveraine paix par le seul possible moyen de la Monarchie Treschrestienne.'[116]

Postel's dreams of world peace bring us to the decade 1550–60, which we have taken as the center of the peace poetry discussed below; the poets were not strangers to the apocalyptic mood of Postel. His idea, a shadow of the *pax Romana*, of peace through the preponderance of one power, has appealed to persons as unbalanced as himself. The nature of Europe, like the nature of ancient Greece, has seemed rather to require a balance of international justice such as Isocrates once spoke of. Such an idea has informed all the well-known schemes proposed since the sixteenth century, whether a league of

[113]Bouwsma, *Concordia Mundi*, pp. 220, 228, 258; Butler, *Statecraft*, p. 49.

[114]Postal, *Candelabri . . . Interpretatio* (Venice, 1548), p. 49. Since peace is a consummation, the attachment of the idea to time cycles is inevitable and constant. We have noted the connection already in the Hellenistic period and might cite subsequent examples such as Joachim of Flora and the Franciscan Joachimites (Bouwsma, *Concordia Mundi*, pp. 76–78).

[115]Butler, *Statecraft*, p. 53, without references.

[116]Ibid., p. 50.

nations as is attributed to the mysterious 'Grand Design' of Sully and sketched in the *Nouveau Cynée* (1623) of Emerich Crucé, or in the form of international law as developed by Grotius.[117]

[117]Ibid., chs. 4 and 5.

II

Pax Poetica:
A French Literary Tradition

The type of poem contemplated in this study has peace for its subject; it either advocates peace and laments its absence (*De pace ineunda*) or celebrates the advent of peace at some historical moment (*De pace inter reges inita*). The two forms may be illustrated by Ronsard's *Exhortation pour la Paix* of 1558 and his *La Paix, au Roy* of 1559. This type of poem is rare, one may say unknown, in the Middle Ages, despite the almost unbroken tradition of poetry commenting on public events. Lamentations over the ravages of war are not infrequent, but a positive celebration of peace would be hard to find.[1] In the historical poetry that flourished in the twelfth and thirteenth centuries one may indeed run across passages commending the peaceful efforts of some mediaeval potentate. A notable instance occurs in the poem *De rebus Siculis* of Pietro d'Eboli, where this humanist poet celebrates the restoration of peace by the Emperor Henry VI in 1195.[2] In Virgilian language we are assured that the Golden Age has returned—

> Sponte parit tellus, gratis honoratur aristis,
> Vomeris a nullo dente relata parit—

[1] For the types of public poetry that existed, see Charles Lenient, *La Poésie patriotique en France au moyen âge* (Paris, 1891). An early example of the lament mentioned above is the ninth-century *rhythmus* of Angilbert on the battle of Fontenay (Ernst Ludwig Dümmler, *Poetae Latini aevi Carolini* [Berlin, 1881], 2.137); cf. Lenient, Ch. 5.

[2] Ettore Rota, ed., from L.V. Muratori, *Rerum Italicarum Scriptores*, 25 vols. (Milan, 1723–51), N.S. 31 (Città di Castello, 1904), 197–98 (vv. 1505–38).

and the whole passage turns on this Saturnian theme.[3] Yet in the rare instance when a peace settlement happens to be the subject of a separate poem, as in the poem on the peace of 1177 between Frederick I and Alexander III by Castellano di Simone da Bassano (1327), we get only a historical narration.[4] What is here instanced from Latin poetry seems to be even more true of the vernaculars; peace as such is not a common subject of poetry until the latter part of the fourteenth century.

The advance of the topic at this time seems therefore to have a certain significance. It belongs to the age of nascent nationalism, of dynastic wars, and of humanism. The humanist poet, with his historical sense and instinct for the possible good of secular life, with his belief also in the power of language to affect the will,[5] was naturally impelled, amidst the dynastic wars of the period, to address himself to a growing national consciousness and indeed to a growing public of readers. The wars of Italy called forth Petrarch's great *canzoniere*; the Hundred Years' War, dragging its weary length, brought the peace theme into French poetry, where it remained, throwing out countless representatives of itself through a succession of styles, so long as the humanist view of poetry prevailed. Appropriately, the first poet to exploit the topic of peace to any extent was Eustache Deschamps (ca. 1320–ca. 1403), no Petrarch, but a temperament well fitted to the time and place—close to the Court, but bourgeois in outlook, with little interest in the gallant and chivalric poetry of the past, intensely patriotic, and open to humanist influence. Among his poems we find the following titles:[6] *Contre les Gens de guerre* (1.159); *Contre la guerre* (1.161); *Comment on obtiendra la paix* (1.162); *Il est tems de faire la paix* (1.199); *Voeux pour la paix* (1.307); *De la Paix avec les Anglais* (3.62); *Voeux pour la Paix* (4.118); *Que la paix soit rendue au monde et à l'Eglise* (5.373); *Plus de Guerres* (5.113); *Voeu pour la paix* (5.67); *Sur la réconciliation des rois de France et d'Angleterre* (6.115). Typical is the *ballade Que la Paix soit rendue au Monde et à l'Eglise*:

> O Charité, Pité, Misericorde,
> Amour de Dieu, alez au parlement,
> Montrez aux roys qu'ilz ne croient Discorde

[3]See below, Ch. VI.
[4]*Venetianae pacis inter ecclesiam et imperium Castellani Bassianensis*, Attilio Hortis, ed., in *Archeografo Triestino*, N.S. 15 (1890), 1–51.
[5]Petrarch, *De ignorantia*, in *Opera*, ed. Martellotti, pp. 1157ff.
[6]References are to *Œuvres complètes*, Le Marquis de Saint-Hilaire, ed. (Paris, 1878–1903).

Qui a voulu guerre trop longuement
Pour terre avoir, qu'on pert en un moment;
Faittes oster du conseil Convoitise
Qui a honni tout anciennement:
Reformez paix au monde et en l'Eglise.

Dittes leur bien ce que Dieux d'eulx recorde
Pour leurs pechiez, et du peuple ensement,
Et pour l'orgueil, la vie laide et orde
Que chascun veult mener generalment
Sans craindre Dieu, la paine et le tourment
Qui vient sur eulx, mais nul ne s'i advise:
Pour eschiver d'iceulx le dampnement,
Reformer paix au monde et en l'Eglise;

Ou autrement loy divine s'acorde
Que Vengence vendra soudainement
A tout son arc, son espée et sa corde,
Qui des pecheurs fera le vengement
En un conflict, si merveilleusement
Que du monde vert la pugnacion prinse.
Pour ces dames vous pri piteusement:
Reformez paix au monde et en l'Eglise.

L'envoy

Prince mondain, qu'avez gouvernement,
Terres, pays, royaumes, tenement,
La grace Dieu en ce cas vous souffise:
Ne querez plus le desheritement
L'un sur l'autre, mais pour vo sauvement
Reformez paix au monde et en l'Eglise.

As so often in *ballades*, the substance is mostly in the first stanza. The peaceful virtues, Charity, Pity, Mercy, and Love of God, are opposed to Discord.[7] War originates in the greed of kings, who are reminded that their conquests quickly pass to others—a commonplace noted above in Petrarch and repeated by Erasmus.[8] In the mediaeval manner, peace is thought of as peace of the world and peace of the Church, both of which should be guarded by kings. What the poet can invoke by way of sanctions in stanzas 2 and 3 is the threat of eternal

[7] An echo of the Daughters of God theme.
[8] Also, 'pour leurs pechiez, et du peuple ensement,' see Ronsard, 'les pechez d'un peuple ou les fautes d'un roy . . .' (*Paix*, 79).

[62]

damnation. May God's 'sufficient grace' enable them to heed his warning![9]

The most impressive poems on peace written in the fifteenth century are the *Lay de Paix* of Alain Chartier and the *Lay de Guerre* of Pierre Nesson, both inspired by the miseries of France arising from the conflict between the Duke of Burgundy, Philip the Good, and the French crown. The *Lay de Paix* was a most famous poem, of which many manuscripts remain.[10] Its author, the leading literary man of his day, a humanist, and immersed in public affairs as secretary to Charles VII, had more than one occasion for utterance on the subject of peace. The *Lay*, if written in 1424, was immediately followed by his *Epistola de detestatione belli gallici et suasione pacis*, which made him, we may say, the Erasmus of his time—unless he were to share that honor with Cusanus.[11]

The *Epistola* begins with a picture of the horrors of civil war—cities depopulated, studies abandoned, churches profaned, virgins violated, adulteries, infants dead from hunger, countryside devastated—against which is set a picture of the happy days of peace. Examples from Greek and Roman history. The war originated in excessive good fortune, love of glory, forgetfulness of God, the English invasion; it is a punishment sent by God. But Peace with broad wings flies towards us seeking a place of rest. God, Nature, and the King all urge us to be peaceful. Peace governs the movements of the heavens, and gives us an idea of Paradise. The only end and purpose of war itself is peace. More classical examples (Sabine women and so on). But peace, coming from God, requires regenerated hearts—regulated desires, submission to law and reason—that is, a virile and prudent, not an irresponsible, moral state. Only on such hearts can God's mercy operate, to bestow the 'ordered tranquillity' of souls which makes a true peace and not a feigned one. Examples of feigned peace (Marius and the like) from Roman and more recent history. Peace calls for love of the public weal, tolerance, and sound government, which is 'ordered tranquillity' under a sovereign. Alain now summons the *king* to be conciliatory; the *princes* to turn their thoughts to peace or unite

[9]Mention should be made of *Le Livre de la Paix* of Christine de Pisan, Charity Cannon Willard, ed. (The Hague, 1958). This treatise, begun after the Treaty of Auxerre (August 1412) belongs to the 'mirror-of-princes' literature and touches our theme only because its ideal prince is a 'peace hero' (below, appendix, no. 24).
[10]*Les Œuvres de maistre Alain Chartier*, André du Chesne, ed. (Paris, 1617), p. 542. See Pierre Champion, *Histoire poétique du quinzième siècle* (Paris, 1923), 1.118–20; E. J. Hoffman, *Alain Chartier: His Work and His Reputation* (New York, 1942), pp. 110–15.
[11]*Œuvres*, pp. 477–87; Champion, *Histoire poétique*, 1.110–16. Champion notes that the mss. of this work also are numerous.

against the foreign foe; the *bishops* and *clergy* to indoctrinate the princes and the people with love and truth; the *people* to obey the king and not seek political change, for peace is their nurse; and the city of *Paris* not to give itself to a foreign king or forget itself in pleasures. Finally he prays to the Virgin and the saints to seek from God on behalf of France the peace which the world cannot give.

Very similar thoughts inform the long discourse on peace which concludes Alain's *Dialogus familiaris amici et sodalis* of 1425: Peace is rooted in moral soundness, is essentially the 'ordered tranquillity of hearts,' a special gift of God and the image of the *summum bonum* on earth.[12]

The *Lay de Paix* begins with a phrase that seems to have captivated the poets of the next century:[13]

> Paix eureuse fille du Dieu des dieux,
> Engendree du throsne glorieux,
> Et transmise par le conseil des cieulx,
> Pour maintenir la terre en unité,
> Exilee de France et d'autres lieux,
> Par oultrages et discordz furieux:
> A vous Princes nez du lys precieux . . .
> Transmetz ce lay d'amour en charité
> Pour redresser voz courages en mieulx.

'Peace' is a dramatic character, speaking in her own behalf. She describes the horrors of war, 'dames en veufvages / Orphelins sans heritages,' and so on, and the joys once to be had 'Quant en France j'estoye':

> Et ne se mesloient,
> Ne ja ne parloient
> Fors de liesse et de joie.
> De gens la peuploye,
> La foi augmentoye,
> Justice y gardoye,
> Science y mettoye,
> Et tous en seureté vivoyent.
> Les marchans gaignoient,
> Nobles voyageoient,
> Clercz estudioient,

---

[12]*Œuvres*, pp. 455–76; Champion, *Histoire poétique*, 1.90–91.
[13]At least ten sixteenth-century poets cited in Ch. IV use this salutation.

Les Prestres chantoient,
Et chacun plain de monnoye. . . .

Further lamenting the present internal strife in France, she concludes
with an appeal to the princes to renounce their pride and in humility
to seek the path of concord. It is a rather flat production. Far more
lively is the *Lay de Guerre* of Alain's friend Pierre de Nesson, written in
1429.[14] It begins:

Guerre, deesse des abysmes d'enfer,
Engendrée du felon Lucifer,
Tresbuchée du trosne imperial,
Mere aux peschiez mortel et venial
Regnant en l'air sur le climat de France,
A tous subgiez de desobeissance, . . .
Hayne, rancune et malediction,
En lieu de salut et dilection!

With this address, War proceeds to proclaim to all the demons that by
command of Lucifer, given in full council of hell, they are to be active
in maintaining the infernal rule on earth: the demons below are to get
saltpeter there and those of the air to provide the thunderbolts.[15]
Alain Chartier, a dangerous enemy of War, must be driven from
Court. We demons now rule everywhere, since our father, the En-
emy, sent us to France—

Et des que Paix apparceut regner Vice,
Elle s'en fuy et emmena Justice.

My father (says War) sought me out and gave me 'foison chiens
d'Angleterre' to assist me, though France is against us, as is Justinian who
hangs so many of our friends. In order to secure our sway we must de-
stroy the Church (vv. 129–43) and the King of France (vv. 144–80), and,
by stirring up the lower classes, the Nobility (vv. 251–300), and finally
the Third Estate (vv. 301–14). Observe the scandalous erotic relation-
ship of Peace (ce putain Paix) and Justice. (Evidently War's version of
'Justitia et pax osculatae sunt'.) But War now foresees the arrival of a for-
midable opponent (vv. 385–526). Grace of God will descend and entreat
the Duke of Burgundy to be a Christian and have a will for peace ('vueil-
lez la paix'). At first the Duke will merely laugh at this; then Grace Dieu

[14]A. Piaget and E. Droz, *Pierre de Nesson et ses œuvres* (Paris, 1925).
[15]An early example of a motive—creation of firearms—that is common in Renais-
sance literature; Jean Marot, *Oraison, Œuvres* (Paris, 1723), pp. 49–50; Erasmus, *Que-
rela* 634A, and Ronsard, *Exhort.* 82–83, 120, 128.

will make him weep. He will repent. He will pray. And the followers of Lucifer and War ('Toutes noz gens, murtriers, larrons, pillars') will then flee. Though cast in the future tense, the dramatized psychology of this crisis of the poem is effective enough. War foresees the bonfires and other celebrations of peace that 'tous les bons' will turn to, and

> Accolant l'ung l'autre per bonne amour,
> Chanter, dancer, criant jusques au jour:
> 'Nous avons paix! Dieu en soit loué.'

That will be a sad state of things for War, who conntinues to describe the hateful characteristics of peace, cursing them as well as Jesus and Mary (vv. 592–696).

Developments that may seem tiresome to the uninitiated modern reader gain interest when we see that the poet is making imaginative use of the master ideas of his time, such as peace and divine grace; but even at first glance it is obvious that Nesson has raised the whole temperature of his poem over that of Chartier, for example, by the genial application of irony.

Peace, for obvious reasons, seems to have been much in the minds of the poets of the early fifteenth century—as something long lost or something to be hoped for. The following *lay* from the *Fortunes et Adversitez* (1432) of Jean Regnier runs like an enlargement of the verses of Chartier quoted above:[16]

> Quant en France paix aviez,
> Clergié, moult aysë estiez,
> Car parmy ses beaulx moustiers,
> > Vous alliez
> > Et disiez
> > Voz psaultiers,
> Sagement vous conteniez.
> Les prestres messes chantoient
> Ou leur voulenté faisoient,
> Ceulx qui a l'escolle estoient

---

[16]Regnier, *Fortunes et Adversitez*, E. Droz, ed. (Paris 1923), vv. 1994–2038. Compare an earlier *lay* (vv. 1905–24):

> Paix est de tous biens tresoriere,
> Paix est de joye la portiere,
> Paix est de doulceur grenetiere,
> Paix est de gracë aulmosniere
> > Non usuriere. . . .

> Apprenoient
> Et lysoient
> Ou preschoient;
> Les sciences que acqueriez,
> A grant honneur vous menoient.
> Princes belle court tenoient
> Ou toutes gens recevoient,
> Les estranges festioient,
> Ils dansoient
> Et chantoient,
> Et rioient
> Et souventes fois joustoient
> Sur palefrois et destriers,
> Et dessus ses grans coursiers
> Faulcons avoient faulconniers,
> Espreviers,
> Et lamiers,
> Et levriers,
> Chiens courans et gros limiers,
> Dont souvent deduit avoient
> Chevaliers et escuyers.
> Marchans, bien vous mainteniez,
> Quant en paix vous conteniez,
> Vous portiez
> Voz deniers,
> Et alliez
> Seurement ou vous vouliez,
> Toutes gens a vous venoient.
> Les laboureux labouroient,
> Ilz couppoient
> Et rompoient
> Acertoient
> Les boys et les arrachoient,
> Tant labouroient voulentiers
> Certes, pas assez n'avoient.

Monks, priests, schoolmen, princes, merchants, laborers—all enjoyed peace in the good old days. The list is not unlike that of Alain Chartier,[17] but the pattern, whether set by him or not, seems to be the common form of 'invention' for peace poems in this period.[18] Doubtless it is 'natural,' and suggested by the facts; it remains, subordinated to other topics, in the Renaissance poems. Charles d'Orlé-

[17]The editor, p. xxviii, makes the comparison.
[18]So Nesson (above) runs through the Church, royalty, nobles, and Third Estate, and cf. Alain's *Epistola*; also Erasmus, *Querela*.

[67]

ans, who from his English captivity (1415–40) looks forward to peace to come, organizes his prayer for peace on the same pattern—only for laborers he substitutes lovers:[19]

> Priez pour paix, doulce Vierge Marie,
> Royne des cieulx, et du monde maistresse,
> Faictes prier, par vostre courtoisie,
> Saints et sainctes, et prenez vostre adresse
> Vers vostre fils, requerrant sa haultesse
> Qu'il lui plaise son peuple regarder
> Que de son sang a voulu racheter,
> En deboutant guerre qui tout desvoye;
> De prieres ne vous vueilliez lasser,
> Priez pour paix, le vray tresor de joye.
>
> Priez, prelaz et gens de saincte vie,
> Religieux, ne dormez en peresse,
> Priez, maistres et tous suivans clergie,
> Car par guerre fault que l'estude cesse;
> Moustiers destruiz sont sans qu'on les redresse,
> Le service de Dieu vous fault laisser,
> Quant ne povez en repos demourer;
> Priez si fort que briefment Dieu vous oye,
> L'Eglise voult à ce vous ordonner;
> Priez pour paix, le vray tresor de joye.
>
> Priez, princes qui avez seigneurie,
> Roys, ducs, contes, barons plains de noblesse,
> Gentilz hommes avec chevalerie,
> Car meschans gens surmontent gentillesse;
> En leurs mains ont toute vostre richesse,
> Debatz les font en hault estat monter,
> Vous le povez chascun jour veoir au clair
> Et sont riches de voz biens et monnoye
> Dont vous deussiez le peuple supporter;
> Priez pour paix, le vray tresor de joye.
>
> Priez, peuple qui souffrez tirannie,
> Car voz seigneurs sont en telle foiblesse
> Qu'ilz ne pevent vous garder par maistrie,
> Ne vous aider en vostre grant destresse;
> Loyaux marchans, la selle si vous blesse
> Fort sur le dos, chascun vous vient presser

---

[19]*Poésies complètes*, Charles d'Héricault, ed. (Paris, 1896), 1.144.

Et ne povez marchandise mener,
Car vous n'avez seur passage, ne voye,
Et maint peril vous convient il passer;
Priez pour paix, le vray tresor de joye.

    Priez, galans joyeux en compaignie,
Qui despendre desirez a largesse,
Guerre vous tient la bourse desgarnie;
Priez, amans, qui voulez en liesse
Servir amours, car guerre, par rudesse,
Vous destourbe de voz dames hanter,
Qui maintesfois fait leurs vouloirs torner,
Et quant tenez le bout de la courroye,
Ung estrangier si le vous vient oster;
Priez pour paix, le vray tresor de joye.

Envoi

    Dieu Tout Puissant nous vueille conforter
Toutes choses en terre, ciel et mer,
Priez vers lui que brief en tout pourvoye,
En lui seul est de tous maulx amender;
Priez pour paix, le vray tresor de joye.

Brief note may be taken here of the Burgundian chronicler Georges Chastellain, who was active in the Courts of Philip the Good and Charles the Bold, and whose chronicle was continued by his disciple Jean Molinet. To him is ascribed the morality play *Le Consile de Basle* (1532), in which 'La Paix' figures as a personage along with 'Eglise,' 'Concile,' 'Heresie,' and 'France'—'La Paix' being greeted with high praise partly in textual quotations from St. Augustine.[20] For the Treaty of Péronne (October 14, 1468) between Louis XI and the Duke of Burgundy, Charles the Bold, Chastellain wrote a similar play *La Paix de Péronne*, which was performed before the two princes at the château of Aire.[21] This play, however, is less to our purpose than the prose *Livre de Paix* written by Chastellain in anticipation of this settlement.[22]

[20]*Œuvres*, Le baron Kervyn de Lettenhove, ed. (Brussels, 1863–66), 6.1–48; see Louis Petit de Julleville, *Répertoire du théâtre comique en France au moyen âge* (Paris, 1886), p. 46.
[21]Chastellain, *Œuvres* 7.423–52; Petit de Julleville, *Répertoire*, p. 339. 'Coeur' and 'Bouche' unite in lauding the princes for giving peace to France; the King and the Duke express their contentment with the peace and their love for each other; 'Avis' and 'Sens' conclude with good counsel and with praise for the Duke.
[22]*Œuvres*, 7.341–422.

In a dream the author sees a rich pavilion, on the four sides of which are represented four female figures flanked by two beasts. These figures are France, Reason, Nature, and Virtue, and the beasts are a cerf-volant (Burgundy) and a lion (the French crown). The king and the duke are seen to enter the pavilion, where they are confronted by another female figure, Peace, who addresses them in a speech which the author interprets at length with numerous examples from biblical and Roman history. The lady Peace suddenly divides into four ladies—Paix de Coeur, Paix de Bouche, Paix Semblant, and Paix de vray Effect. The author interprets these figures. They reassemble and the integral Peace again addresses the princes before she vanishes together with the pavilion. But the author continues to interpret the names that had appeared on the four sides of the pavilion and on the tent-pole: Humility, Satisfaction (of persons and of the claims of duty), Obligation, Prosecution (of one's honor and of the public welfare), and Trustworthiness.[23]

In view of the tendency, characteristic of the time, to endow Peace with a personality opposed to the personality of War, one might expect to meet this character more often in the morality plays than one does. Besides the two plays of Chastellain just mentioned, it seems possible to point only to a morality *Paix et Guerre* reported by the 'bourgeois de Paris' for 1449.[24] That other such interludes must have existed is suggested by the fact that plays figured in the celebrations of peace treaties.[25] Certainly a number of such plays can be mentioned for the sixteenth century.[26] In quasi-dramatic form, 'Peace' plays her part along with other abstractions in the *Vigilles de Charles VII* of Martial d'Auvergne.[27]

[23]Chastellain's poem *Le Dit de Vérité* (*Œuvres*. 6.28–42) is also concerned with peace between France and Burgundy. For the birth of Marie, the daughter of Charles the Bold, François Villon wrote *Le Dit de la naissance Marie*, in which the name of Mary is assimilated to peace—

> La paix, c'est assavoir, des riches,
> Des povres le substantement,
> Le rebours des felons et chiches!

These are traditional topics.

[24]Petit de Julleville, *Répertoire*, p. 335.

[25]Morality plays were presented to celebrate the Peace of Arras (December 23, 1482), one at the house of the Cardinal de Bourbon in Paris (ibid., p. 343), another in January 1483 at Beauvais (p. 344); in 1493 a play was presented at Béthune in celebration of the Peace of Senlis (p. 350).

[26]Petit de Julleville (ibid., pp. 309, 369–70) records mention of *Le Débat de la Paix et de la Guerre* presented in 1524 at the abbey of Saint-Bertin at Saint-Omer, and *Le Jeu de la Paix* (perhaps the same play) in 1525; in 1530 (p. 214) the *Satyre* of Roger de Collerye at Auxerre (see below, p. 83, n. 11); in 1554 (p. 90) *Paix et Guerre* by Henry du Tour; and during the religious wars (p. 81) a play *Mars et Justice*.

[27]The 'lessons' of the poem are put into the mouths of 'France,' 'Noblesse,' 'Labeur,' 'Marchandise,' 'Clergé,' 'Pitié,' 'Paix,' and 'Eglise.' Thus 'Paix':

These examples of fifteenth-century poems on peace must here suffice. In content they strike us as rather meagre in comparison with the rich fund of motives won from ancient letters by humanism in the next century. Yet they do have a background in mediaeval theology and piety that the later poems have mostly lost. In the period between, when peace is at all the subject, the poets seem to be losing the mediaeval point of view and hardly yet gaining the topics of the Renaissance tradition. Thus when Jean Molinet speaks for peace in a poem entitled *Le Temple de Mars* (1475), he is innocent both of the irony and the theology of Pierre Nesson.[28] Harassed by war, the poet repairs to the temples of various gods, and finally to that of Mars, where he sacrifices some appropriate wild beasts and notes nearby a hospital under the care of Pitié, Abstinence, and Treve. For priests Mars has 'rois, ducs, amiraux,' and the like, and at his side is seen Guerre, a 'laide chimere' engendered by Satan. The perennial *topos* of 'the horror of war' here passes under the *rhétoriqueur* style (vv. 169ff.):

> Guerre a fait main chastellet let
> Et mainte bonne ville ville
> Et gasté maint gardinet net, . . .

But 'il n'est tresor au monde que de paix' (v. 200), and from this point the poem becomes a sermon against war, the dramatic setting having served its turn. All are bidden to seek the 'lamb of peace,' and the phrase suggests to the poet a pastoral motive, taken up in v. 209: 'Qui restaurra aux povres pastoureaux / Leurs gras thoreaux et moutons despouillés?' and completed in vv. 241–42: 'Quant la vierge mere fut acouchie, / Paix fut nonchie aux pastoureaux chantans.' Like Erasmus and Ronsard later, Molinet thinks the hardships of the soldier's life might be a deterrent (vv. 257ff.): 'Que gaigniés vous a servir guerre dure / Sinon froidure, o champions hardis?' Like them, too, he thinks that Christians should forego war unless it

---

'Paix vient de Dieu, et où Dieu est Paix est;
Paix vient d'Amours, et de Justice naist.'

There follows a long historical demonstration going back to Alexander the Great and Caesar.

[28]Jean Molinet, *Faictz et dictz*, Noël Dupire, ed. (Paris, 1936), 1.65. Dupire dates the poem 'after Sept. 1475.' Cf. also (1.251) a poem addressed in 1489 to the Count of Nassau as 'Prince de paix' on the conclusion of the peace of Montils-les-Tours (Dupire, *Etude critique des manuscrits et éditions des poésies de Jean Molinet* [Paris, 1932], p. 31).

be (vv. 284–85) 'Pour rembarer ung mescreant / Ou le grant Turc, s'il nous approche.' The conclusion is to seek peace, 'Car qui s'accord a paix et a concorde / Misericorde obtient de Dieu paisible.'

A more lasting impression was made by Molinet's poem *Le Testament de la Guerre*, which again is more ironically conceived and written in racier language.[29] There are twenty-two eight-line stanzas: 'I War bequeath my soul to God if He will take it; to princes who have employed me for the ends of justice I leave prosperity, but to tyrants shame and misfortune; to great abbeys I leave ruined cloisters . . . ; to great towns ruined walls . . . ; to brave champions, loyal to their princes, honor forever; . . . to innkeepers a sack of I.O.U.'s instead of coin . . . ; to my grooms flat wallets and empty bottles . . . ; I leave poverty everywhere, and if I live I shall reign and pillage this summer as much as ever, or more: my will I make *en santé*, fearing nought but Madame Paix.' It is curious to note that this poem remained in the public consciousness so far as to be reprinted several times in the next century on suitable occasions, notably for the Peace of Cateau-Cambrésis (1559) and for the Peace of Vervins (1598).[30]

In this period there also comes forward a more popular form of peace poem, exemplified by a *ballade* for the Peace of Arras (1482) written by Guillaume Coquillart, and largely consisting of a summons to rejoice now that peace has come.[31] Coquillart, however, retains something of the theological point of view: 'Vouloir divin a produit ces ouvrages,' and 'Du ciel sont cheutes ces plaisantes images.' The refrain is graphic: 'C'est France et Flandre et la Paix entre deux,' and the suggestion is not amiss that the celebrations at Reims (Coquillart's home) may have included such a tableau. Similar poems, mostly in the form of *chansons*, run through the sixteenth century and beyond.[32]

[29]*Faictz et dictz*, 2.718.

[30]Below, pp. 118 and 166. See Dupire, *Etude critique*, p. 101. In these editions the title is *Le Testament de la Guerre qui regne à present* [or *qui a regné*] *sur la terre*. They are anonymous.

[31]Le Roux de Lincy, *Recueil de chants historiques français depuis le xiiᵉ jusqu'au xviiiᵉ siècle* (Paris, 1841–42), 1.402.

[32]Examples in *Chants* 2.122, 367, 370, 563, 565, 568; cf. below, p. 84, n. 12.

III

The Italian Humanists

The poetry of peace seems to be a French specialty, firmly implanted in French literature during the fifteenth century. Its origins appear to lie in fourteenth-century humanism. Yet in Italy during the same period the legacy of Petrarch in this field seems ready to be taken up either by the vernacular poets or by the humanist poets writing in Latin. Among the latter, topics of the peace theme appear incidentally in other contexts. Thus Guarino in a verse-epistle to Verona (May 1432) declines an invitation to return to his native city because it is wracked with war—

> Cessit honor agri, vomer conflatus in ensem . . .
> Ut strepuere tubae, iuvenes Helicona recusant,
>   Non locus aut cura est artibus ac studiis—

whereas the Duke of Ferrara provides peace, beloved of the Muses, and plenty:

> Fertilis hinc gremio decurrit copia pleno
>   Cum Iunone venit Liber et alma Ceres.[1]

These classical topics were perhaps felt to belong properly to the imperial theme where the classical poets had placed them. At least it is within this theme that we come across a rare example of a humanist peace poem in the proper sense of the term. This is a poem desiderating peace, *Pro pacanda Italia carmen*, by Guarino's pupil Janus Pan-

---

[1] Guarino Veronese, *Epistolario*, Remigio Sabbadini, ed. (Venice, 1915–19), 2.135–37.

nonius, addressed to the Emperor Frederick III on his coming to Italy in 1452 to be crowned at Rome.[2] The poem was commissioned by René d'Anjou, the Duke of Anjou, Lorraine, and Bar, and titular King of Sicily.[3] Hailing the Emperor—

> Induperatorum decus, et sublime ruentis
> Ausoniae columen, salve . . .—

the poet bids him to imitate the ancient Romans, who subdued the world, and to make Rome rise again from her ruins, but first of all to give peace to the Italian cities. Let him think that he sees Italy at his feet, bruised and disheveled, speaking through her tears: 'I was glad, O Caesar, when I heard that you were looking my way . . . give me peace, subdue Mars. . . . The civic crown was awarded for saving the life of a single citizen, what would you not win for saving whole peoples! . . . For twice a thousand years I have scarcely known any respite.' (She outlines history beginning with the Senones and Pyrrhus.) 'The young scorn the Muses and take to arms; the free arts are neglected; my fields whiten with bones; the plough is beaten into a sword; plague follows war. I had rather be destroyed by the barbarian than by these native vipers,' (She makes specific requests:

> Fac ne civilis Genuam dissensio turbet,
> Expulsas revocet pacata Bononia partes . . .)

'Grant us peace, and God will bless us with riches. Then he who trembled at the trumpet's sound will return to his fields, and the Muses will break their long silence. . . . Grant this, and your fame will endure, 'Dum volucres aer, dum pascit sydera coelum.'

The merit of bringing about the Peace of Bagnolo (1484) has been claimed by a poet—the poet, to be sure, Giovanni Pontano, being also a state secretary.[4] This settlement ended the short War of Ferrara in which Ercole d'Este had been defended against the encroachment of Venice by a league formed under the aegis of Sixtus IV and consisting of Pontano's patron the King of Naples, the Duke of Milan, and Giro-

---

[2]*Ad Im. Caes. Fridericum tertium, pro pacanda Italia, Jani Pannonii carmen*, in J. Ph. Parena, ed., *Delitiae Poetarum Hungaricorum* (Frankfurt, 1619), pp. 116–26.

[3]*Enciclopedia Italiana*, article "Giano Pannonio." Probably drawn from Giosuè Carducci, *La gioventù di L. Ariosto e la poesia Latina in Ferrara*, in Carducci, *Edizione nationale delle Opere* (Bologna, 1944), 14.59–70.

[4]*Exultatio ob factam pacem*, Carlo Maria Tallarigo, *Giovanni Pontano e i suoi tempi* (Naples, 1874), p. 216. Pontano, *De Prudentia, Opera* (Basel, 1566), 1.491: 'Ferrariensi vero in bello, quod acerrime illatum a Venetis fuerat, sic me gessi, ut mea potissimum opera in ipso belli ardore secuta pax fuerit, cum Italiae quiete et ocio.'

lamo Riario of Forlì. Though Venice was brought to sue for peace, she gained all the advantages of the treaty, partly through buying off Ferdinand and Ludovico il Moro, and the Peace of Bagnolo is chiefly important for establishing her power on the mainland and thus creating the situation that led to the League of Cambrai in 1508.[5] The Peace of Bagnolo was the occasion of one of the most influential of all Renaissance peace poems, not by Pontano but by Baptista Mantuanus.[6] It is addressed to Cardinal Oliviero Caraffa.[7]

The pope died five days after the treaty was concluded. Since Mantuan's poem cannot have been written after the death of the pope, and scarcely in the five days between the signing of the peace and that event, we may suppose it to have been prepared in advance, perhaps on the occasion of an abortive, pre-1484 peace conference.[8] To our present interest, it deserves to be read in full as an assemblage, perhaps a reservoir, of motives for the encomium of peace that the Renaissance poets, Latin and vernacular alike, were constantly rediscovering and recombining.[9]

1. Munera qui norint et sanctae commoda pacis
    Saeva velint Stygio bella sepulta lacu.

Those who know the gifts and the advantages of sacred Peace may well wish cruel wars buried in the Stygian lake.

2. Bella necant homines, faciunt sine honoribus Aras,
    Urbis et agrorum depopulantur opes.
    A pereat quisquis tam saevi criminis author
    Extitit, et nostras misit ad arma manus.
    Ferreus exultat bellis et sanguine Mavors,
    Et ciet invito bella tubasque Deo.

Wars destroy men, make altars unattended, strip the wealth from city and country. Perish the author of this evil, who has made us take up arms. It is iron Mars who exults in wars and bloodshed, and in God's despite calls up wars and trumpets.

[5]For the celebrations in Venice, see Sabellicus (Marcantonio Coccio), *Rerum Venetarum historiae* (Venice, 1487), 4.2.

[6]*Pro pacata Italia post bellum Ferrariense ad Oliverum Carafam cardinalem Neapolitanum*, in *Opera* (Antwerp, 1576).

[7]The original builder of the Quirinal Palace; died 1511 (Bartolomeo Capasso, *Le fonti della storia delle provincie napolitane* [Naples, 1902], p. 236).

[8]I find no evidence that Cardinal Caraffa had any part in the Peace of Bagnolo.

[9]I do not attempt to detect Mantuan's sources, but note that the sentence 'Gloria pace minor, minor est victoria pace / Atque aliquid peius pace triumphus habet' possibly combines Silius' 'pax una triumphis / innumeris potior' with Ovid's 'Tu ducibus bello gloria maior eris'; cf. Petrarch, above p. 47 and n. 89.

3. Nulla quies homini, nulla est sine pace voluptas:
    Nullus amor, nullum relligionis opus.

Without peace there is no rest for man, no pleasure, no love, no good of
religion.

4. Pax facit innocuos saltus nemorumque recessus.
    Tutus it, et tutas advena portat opes.
    Pax Cererem campis, et mitem collibus uvam
    Reddit, et armoso dividit arva bove.
    Gramina pace virent, per pinguis pascua laetum
    Luxuriat multa fertilitate pecus.
    Pax vehit Eoas peregrina per aequora merces:
    Et steriles ponti non sinit esse vias.

Peace makes the woodlands and the depths of the forests secure; the
stranger goes safely and safely carries his possessions. Peace restores Ce-
res to the plains and the mellow grapes to the hillsides, and ploughs the
fields with the muscular ox. The grasses in peace are green, in rich pas-
tures the happy flock revels in vast fertility. Peace brings oriental wares
through foreign seas, and does not permit the paths of the deep to be
unfertile.

5. Gestit, et ad Thyasos agili volat ardua saltu,
    Et vocat ad festos agmina longa dies.
    At tibi qui limen reseras et claudis Olympi,
    Retia qui Petri naviculamque tenes:
    Et tibi regali qui maiestate per urbes
    Ausoniae regnas Parthenopenque colis:
    Sint faciles semper divi, sint mitia vobis
    Numina, qui paci contribuistis opem.
    Vivite concordes tranquilla per ocia pacis;
    Ducite foelices mellifluosque dies.
    Et tibi sacratam vestit cui purpura frontem
    Et cui pacificum nomen oliva dedit:
    Iuppiter ad superum faciat discumbere mensas:
    Nectaris ut succos ambrosiamque bibas.
    Semper enim tibi pacis amor, tu solvere lites
    Et genus humanum conciliare soles.

She exults, and springing up nimbly flies through the air to the Bacchic
dance, summoning long processions to festal days. But to Thee, who dost
open and close the gates of Olympus, who holdest the nets and the boat
of Peter; and to Thee (Ferrante of Naples), who in regal majesty holdest
sway in the cities of Ausonia and dwellest in Naples: may the saints ever
be kind to you both, the powers above ever merciful to you who have

united in bringing help to peace. Live in harmony in the tranquil ease of peace, spend happy days flowing with honey! And to Thee (Caraffa), whose consecrated brow is dressed with purple, to whom the Olive has given its pacific name—may Jupiter grant that you recline at the tables of the gods to drink ambrosia and nectar; for yours ever is the love of peace, you habitually calm disputes and reconcile mankind.

In the decades immediately following the Peace of Bagnolo, Venice went far in realizing her ambitions on the mainland, and in 1508 her encroachments on the Papal States prompted Julius II to form against her the League of Cambrai with the Emperor Maximilian and Louis XII of France, who was now in possession of Milan. Julius excommunicated Venice, but military operations were left to Louis, who won a brilliant victory at Agnadello (May 1509) and ravaged Venetian territory. Everyone knows the upshot. Satisfied with his gains, Julius made it up with Venice, excommunicated Louis, and formed a Holy League to drive the foreigner from Italy. In 1512 the French lost Milan itself and were forced to withdraw beyond the Alps. To a Venetian it might well seem that Venetian diplomacy had been seconded by the grace of God; and to this moment and feeling belongs one of the finest of Renaissance poems, by the best of Venetian Latin poets, Andrea Navagero, who later served the Republic in important missions abroad. Navagero's eclogue *Damon* belongs to another stage of modern Latin verse, beyond the reach of honest Mantuan, and can still charm us with its Virgilian color and fragrance. On the other hand, though we understand Navagero's feelings about the expulsion of the French, his adulation of Julius II as something more than God's vicar pleases us as little as Jean Marot's idea that Julius's League of Cambrai was directly inspired by divine Peace. He calls upon the nymphs of the Naucelus to come from their green caverns and grant a song worthy of him.[10] What misery was spread abroad when the barbarian descended from the frozen Alps! The shepherds were pillaged, and the country gods forced to hide themselves. Flocks driven from the mainland found themselves strangely in the sea ['insuetaeque maris pecudes, (miserabile visu)'], cropped seaweeds, and drank salt water. From this and worse, Julius has saved us:

> Te rupes, te saxa, cavae te, MAXIME JULI,
> Convalles, nemorumque frequens iterabit imago. . . .
> Tu nostra ante Deos in vota vocaberis omnes.

[10]*Andreae Naugerii Opera Omnia*, J. A. and C. Volpi, eds. (Padua, 1718), p. 194. Navagero's Naucelus is the Noncello, a small stream near Pordenone (Friuli) where he was the guest of the Venetian general Alviano.

Damon, the poet shepherd, will build a double altar for him on the banks of the Naucelus and will hold games in his honor. Meanwhile the shepherd may feed his flocks in peace, or sing, or sport with beautiful Dione in the shade. The poem ends with an invocation of the 'great Father'; had the poet greater gifts, he would sing more worthily of Julius' triumphs, but meanwhile—

> Interea agrestis dignatus sibila cannae,
> Dexter ades nobis, et quae facis, otia serva.

Indifferent to the occasion of this poem, but admirers of its art, the French poets of the Pléiade imitated it again and again.

The peace poem, which enjoyed so particular a florescence during the sixteenth century in France, seems to have been less intensively cultivated in other lands. We end our survey, then, as we began it, with a Latin poem from Italy in the humanist tradition: Virginio Cesarini's *Ad Gregorium XV Pont. Max. bellicos Italiae tumultus pacantem*, referring to events of 1623.[11] Cesarini, a friend of Galileo and Chiabrera, was called by Cardinal Bellarmin the 'Pico della Mirandola' of his age for his precocious attainments and was about to receive high ecclesiastical preferment when he died in 1624 at the age of twenty-nine. His poem, which is a good summary of the humanist *topoi*, has to do with the troubles of the Valtellina that occupied the last months of the life of Gregory XV. The district was a frontier between Protestant and Catholic, and also between the powers of Spain-Austria and France, Savoy, and Venice. After the massacre of the Protestants in 1620 (see Milton's sonnet 'On the Late Massacher in Piemont') the Spanish and Austrians occupied the strongholds, and the other powers prepared for war. In 1623 Gregory sent the papal troops under his brother Orazio Ludovisi, and the fortresses were peaceably yielded to him at the end of May. We must assume that Cesarini's poem was written at that moment, since the Pope died on July 8.

> Put down your arms, belligerent manhood, leave the camp of war, ye captains of the Cenomani [Valtellina]; the Roman Father forbids war. Triumphs once more return to the Capitol, but without bloodshed, for the Rhetians, though undefeated, have felt the strength of Latin law; the Adda flows peacefully into the Po, and the horrors of war are averted. Gregory has done this, and peace reigns, thanks to the greatest of kings. O Peace, kindly offspring of Heaven, glide in your chariot over the banks

[11]*CPI* 3.7–11. Cesarini's poems were first published in the *Septem illustrium virorum poemata* (Antwerp, 1662).

of the Po, accompanied by Fides, Cornucopia, Ceres, Bacchus. . . . Thou returnest Justice to her throne. . . . Merchants traverse the peaceful seas. . . . O mortal race, when death comes so soon, why hasten it with war? . . . Lions spare their kind, hyaena devours not hyaena. . . . But if you must fight, spare your native land; Thrace and the Bosporus cry for Western aid, as does the Holy Sepulchre in Palestine . . . and Greece loaded with chains. Before I die, may I see Rome celebrating a Hellespontine triumph over the Arab religion. This is what Gregory's piety and generosity demand; and God shaking his aegis above the towers of the Vatican seems to call to arms. A victory over the Turk would inspire me to sing of Gregory in more than Stentor's voice, and I would win immortality, Phoebus willing.

IV

Pax Mundana:
Sixteenth-Century France

Period of the Italian Wars

The campaign of the League of Cambrai is the subject of a long poem, *Le Voyage de Venise*, by Jean Marot, which, though anything but a peace poem, yet pretends to be so on the principle of *Mars pacifer* and the *justum bellum*.[1]

> When by the will of the gods Mars had made his son Louis XII triumphant, there was rejoicing in heaven. In the midst of it four ladies appeared before the celestial Court (the four daughters of God)—Eureuse Paix, Justice, Verité, and dame Misericorde, 'mère de Paix, nourrice de Concorde'—and Peace speaks for them all. She marvels at the long reign of Wars on earth, so complete that infants in their mothers' wombs fear to be born, churches are destroyed, nuns ravished, cities demolished, and so on, and asks now to have her turn in power. Since the time of Augustus, 1,508 years ago, the world has seen only feigned, not true peace; for this one must love Truth and Justice. But now in the Gallic region she has seen a king—'Chef belliqueux plain de misericorde'—a lover of peace who has renewed the Age of Saturn. She would go down and dwell with him. The gods agree, and send 'leur fille Paix' to earth where she mourns over the ruined cities, especially Rome, but progressing to Venice is affronted by five ugly chimaeras: Trahyson, Injustice, Rapine, Usure, and their mother Avarice. Hastily departing for France, she there sees her sister Justice on a golden throne, with Justice's eldest daughter Dame Police [Eunomia] beside her, and in great glory our mother Eglise Catholique with Foy and Devotion.

[1] *Œuvres de Jean Marot* (Paris, 1723), 47–171.

Puis regarda par boys, villes, et champs,
En seureté marcher loyaulx marchans,
Laboureurs vit repaistre en leurs maisons,
Sans craincte ou peur, plus fiers que gentilz homs;
Plus les piloyent Cordeliers, Moynes, Carmes
Que avanturiers, francs archiers, ny gensdarmes;
Semblablement sur menuës herbettes,
Vit Pastoureaux garder leur brebiettes,
Rien plus que loups ne leur menoient la guerre,
Car seurs estoient des hommes de la terre.

Rejoicing over a king who has carried war into foreign parts and left his own people in peace, she flies to Cambrai and is nobly entertained by pope, kings, emperor, and princes. She tells them that, sent to establish universal peace, she has found all Christendom ready for her, but has been repulsed by the five monsters of Venice. At once they resolve to drive out these 'chiens d'enfer' and to put Venice under the power of Justice and Verité. Peace flies up into the air and leaves them to accomplish this end.

In the air she remains; for Marot, after the *rhétoriqueur* manner, having set this brilliant façade before his poem, proceeds with his business, the Venetian campaign, and ends with the celebrations of victory in Milan.[2]

Julius II died at the beginning of 1513, and his successor Leo X, in contrast with him, bent his efforts towards a general European peace; a treaty between France and Venice was promptly concluded.[3] Louis XII lived for another year; when he died on New Year's Day 1515, the fortunes of France passed into the hands of the man in every way qualified to ruin them. By summer Francis I was on his way to Italy and in September was in possession of Milan.[4] But he set his sights on

[2]Another poem on the League of Cambrai deserves mention: Nicaise Ladam, *La Paix faicte à Chambray entre lempereur et le très crestien roy de France avec leurs aliez, imprimé à Paris pour Philipot Le Cocq demourant à Chambray*. The one known copy, described in the *Cat. Roths.* 1.489, is there dated 1508, as also in the reprint by A. Dinaux in *Archives du Nord de la France et du Midi de la Belgique* (Valenciennes, 1854) [BN Rés. Ye. 4512], 3.3.487−510; but Gustave Brunet, *Dictionnaire des ouvrages anonymes* (Paris, 1889), *Suppl.* 2.129, supplies 1529. It consists of five poetical pieces. Ladam, a Fleming, was a partisan of the Emperor.

[3]To this occasion has been assigned a *balade* published by Anatole de Montaiglon, *Recueil de poésies françaises des xve et xvie siècles* (Paris 1865) 6.90; '*S'ensuyt le traicté de la paix, avec une belle balade*,' which gives full credit to Leo.

[4]Poems on this event in LeRoux de Lincy, *Chants* 2.53−67. I note in passing the Peace of Brussels (December 4, 1516) between Venice, Francis, and the Emperor, for which was published a poem: *Questa e la pace da dio mandata, quale da tutti era molto bramata* (n.p., 1516) (*Cat. Roths.* 1.1048). Besides this poem in ten octaves with a refrain, the volume contains a sonnet, a *Dialogo di vilani*, and a *Capitolo di virtu in laude di Venetia*.

higher things, and the remainder of his reign was occupied by the long and disastrous struggle with Charles V. We pass over several peace settlements of this time, noting only the peace concluded between Francis and Henry VIII of England, October 1518, as the occasion of an oration by Erasmus' friend Richard Pace, then English secretary of state, in which, as might be expected, the influence of Erasmus' *Bellum* and *Querela* is much in evidence.[5]

Pace is embarrassed at speaking before such an august assembly, and especially before the king, who is famous for his learning and success in literary controversy. But there is no greater matter than the establishment of perpetual peace. On this he quotes Sallust, 'Discordia res magnae'; St. Paul; the opening of Isocrates' *De Pace*; Silius Italicus, 'Pax optima rerum'; and notes that the whole teaching of Christ was concerned with peace.[6] He draws a picture of war, and with it contrasts peace as the source of all good things.[7] Peace among Christian kings is most necessary now when the Turk is daily advancing: awake, princes, your house is afire! Who could better lead a movement against the Turk than these two great kings? He praises Henry VIII for his personal prowess and his resources for war, despite which advantages he has preferred peace, as Francis also has done in asking the hand of Henry's daughter for his heir. The Emperor too has shown a disposition for peace.[8] Pace compliments Cardinal Wolsey and the papal legate, who were present. The day is auspicious for union (*foederi*), for the faith, and for peace. Let him be cursed who violates the treaty. Let the kings keep the peace vowed before venerable witnesses in holy St. Paul's; and may God further what is here done.[9]

The first part of Francis' struggle with Charles V ended with the disaster of Pavia (1525) and Francis' captivity in Madrid. The treaty of Madrid was no occasion for rejoicing in France; once again free,

[5]Published in 1518 in Latin both in London and in Paris, and in French in Paris: *Oratio Richardi Pacei in pace nuperrime composita et foedere percusso*, . . . (London, R. Pynson) [BM C33 B. 39]; same title (Paris: Jean Gourmont) [BM 596.e.35]; *Oraison en la louange de la paix*, . . . (Paris: Jean Gourmont) [BM G 6119 (2)]. The oration or sermon was pronounced in St. Paul's on Sunday, October 3, on the occasion of Henry's taking the oath confirming the peace. The subtitle is *oratio nuptialis*, since it anticipates the proxy marriage on the fifth of the newly born Dauphin and the two-year-old Mary. The magnificent ceremonies attending this peace in London and later in Paris are described by J. S. Brewer, *The Reign of Henry VIII* (London, 1884), 1.197–206.

[6]Erasmus, *Bellum* 959F–960C; 970A.

[7]*Bellum* 957E–F; Pace reverse the order, describing peace first; *Querela* 642C–D. The *Querela* had been out for less than a year.

[8]A reference to the Truce of Brussels, August 13, 1516, between Maximilian, Francis, and the Venetian Republic.

[9]Compare Anon., *Exhortation de Paix* . . . (Lyons: Gilbert de Villiers, 1520), Du Verdier, 1.561, in prose.

Francis repudiated it, and the wars went on. At the end of 1528 the king's mother, Louise of Savoy, entered into negotiations with the emperor's aunt, Margaret of Austria, and they succeeded in patching up a peace, known to history as the Paix des Dames, at Cambrai in August of the next year. From the imperial side, we have on this treaty an elegy by the amatory poet Joannes Secundus of the Hague: *De pace Cameraci facta inter Carolum Imperatorem et Franciscum Galliae regem, anno 1529:*[10]

> En rata magnanimo cum Caesare foedera Gallo,
> En per foemineas foedera pacta manus!

So beginning, he proceeds to call for celebrations, consigning War and War's followers—Furiae, Bellona, Discordia, Ira—to the shades below, and welcoming Peace and her train—Fides, Plutus, and especially Amor. He banishes Poverty and other woes and calls for the beating of swords into ploughshares, the replacing of helmets by garlands, and wars and wounds with the wars and wounds of love:

> Bella lascivis nocturna movete puellis,
> Figite et optato vulnera grata loco.

Thus the poem falls into two halves, each ending on Secundus' tonic chord of love. He concludes with an allusion to the date, a numerary acrostic in which the numeral letters taken one by one add up to 1529:

> LUX sIMUL aC feLIx aUgUstI qUInta refULsit
> ProdIIt & popULIs paX bona Longa tULIt.

   The Paix des Dames was an important treaty but could bring no final settlement between Charles and Francis.[11] The French king im-

[10]Secundus, *Elegiae* 2.8. To the year 1529 belongs a motet by Maistre Jean sung at the conclusion of the peace between Charles V and Clement VII, December 1529, at Bologna (E. E. Lowinsky, "Newly Discovered Sixteenth Century Manuscript," *Journal of the American Musicological Society*, 3 [1950], 182). See also Clément Marot, *De la Paix traicté à Cambray* (1529) in *Oeuvres diverses*, C. A. Mayer, ed. (London, 1966), p. 183.

[11]The Paix des Dames was also the occasion of a *Satyre pour les habitans d'Auxerre* by Roger de Collerye (publ. 1536), a morality play in which 'Peuple François' and 'Joyeuseté' converse together and with a 'Vigneron,' 'Jenin ma Fluste' (who comes from Court), and 'Bon Temps' (who comes from England); *Œuvres*, Charles d'Héricault, ed. (Paris, 1855), pp. 1–19. See Petit de Julleville, *Répertoire*, pp. 412–16. The simple historical background of this piece has been curiously misunderstood through an assumption that the occasion was an unknown entry of Queen Eleonore into Auxerre (in 1529 she had not so much as entered France). The queen mentioned (*Œuvres*, p. 6) surely is the Queen mother Louise of Savoy, and the peace is associated with her and

mediately prepared for another war, astonishing Europe in 1534 by making an alliance with the Turk. In 1536 Charles invaded the south of France, but was driven back by the scorched-earth measures of Montmorency. A truce made in 1537 was followed in June 1538, by a meeting of Pope, Emperor, and King at Nice (though Francis and Charles would not see each other), and finally in July by the more successful conference of Aigues-Mortes, which went off like a love-fest. The truce then concluded was felt to be firm, and there was universal rejoicing in France. Popular songs celebrated the event. Nine of these *chansons*—an unusually large number—are preserved for us in a collection published in 1542.[12] Besides the religious note natural to the occasion of peace—the call for praise and prayer to God—two themes stand out in these verses. One is the belief that Queen Eleonore was chiefly to be credited with reconciling her brother (Charles V) and her husband—in several poems she speaks directly. The other is a perennial theme in all peace poetry—rejoicing that the world is set free for international trade:

> Marchantz de France et de Bretagne,
> Allez tous sur mer hardiment,
> En Portugal et en Espaigne. . . .

One chanson sketches the course of events;[13] another gloats over the gifts—'emeraudes et beaulx rubis,'—presented by Charles to the royal ladies of France;[14] the author of a third boasts that he was present at Aigues-Mortes and brought the good news from Provence to France.[15]

For the earlier meeting at Nice, Clément Marot had hopefully contributed his *Cantique de la Chrestienté sur la venue de l'empereur et du roy au voyage de Nice*, a simple poem urging, in ritual manner, the two monarchs to approach and bring down Peace from heaven whither

with the two royal children, without mention of the king, since the ransom of the princes was the basis of the treaty. The arrival of 'Bon Temps' from England has also been variously interpreted, but is perhaps only an allusion to the resumption of trade with that country, the source of good times.

[12]*Sensuyt plusieurs belles chansons nouvelles* (Paris, 1542); reprinted by A. Percheron (Geneva, 1867). I depend on Emile Picot, "Chants historiques français du xvie siècle," *RHL*, 3 (1896), 389–400, and on Le Roux de Lincy, *Chants*, 1842, 2.118–24.

[13]Le Roux de Lincy, *Chants*, 2.120, (Picot, "Chants historiques," No. 101).

[14]Picot, "Chants historiques," No. 102 (p. 399).

[15]Le Roux de Lincy, *Chants*, 2.118 (Picot, "Chants historiques," No. 100). Picot identifies this 'très noble adventurier, / Le quel est naquy de Grenoble' with one Jehan Lescot, author of two earlier ballads.

she has withdrawn. Peace will be better than victories. Let them have pity on their subjects, both humble and noble; for Mars has destroyed and will destroy many noble men.[16]

More elaborate, and in fact more impressive, is the poem that Marot's literary enemy François Sagon seems to have published on the occasion of Aigues-Mortes: *Le chant de la Paix en France, chanté par les trois Estatz*.[17] It begins in rhetorical style with Proposition and Narration; and the Acteur calls in turn upon Church, Nobility, and Labor to sing of Peace, as each then does in long passages of irregular verse. The whole ends with a *rondeau final* and a couple of quatrains.

Proposition

Paix? Que diray ie apres tant de latins?
Que dira lon, quand ung de ces matins
Chascun orra la muse Sagontine
Chanter de Paix? *(Invocation poeticque)*
O fontaine argentine,
Lieu de Phoebus, . . .

Narration

Le ciel haultain, de la paix amoureux,
Chassant de Mars le regne rigoureux, . . .
En ces bas lieux a lasché son Mercure, . . .
Pour annoncer le regne de la paix.

The Church rejoices that services will now be assured; and instances the pacific Solomon building the Temple, David's prophecy of Christ, and the angels of the Nativity:

---

[16]The truce of Aigues-Mortes is the theme in Marot's verses *A la royne de Hongrie, venue en France*, and he has two poems on the subsequent visit of Charles V to Paris in 1540 (*Œuvres complètes*, Pierre Jannet, ed. [Paris, 1884], 2.110–11). Indeed this last event was widely celebrated in verse; see René Macé, *Les Voyage de Charles V par la France* (Paris, 1879), with 'bibliography of printed pieces relating to the festivities, etc.' Also an eclogue of Jean Boiceau de la Borderie, *Le Vol de l'Aigle en France* (1540) in which there appear two shepherds, 'Paix' and 'France' (Alice Hulubei, *Répertoire des èglogues en France au XVIe siècle* [Paris, 1939], p. 14).

[17]I say 'seems to have published,' since no one since Du Verdier apparently has seen this edition: '*Le Chant de la paix en France, chanté par les trois Estatz*, imprimé à Paris, in 8°, par Denys Janot, 1538'; but a notice so precise deserves our confidence. The first edition known to me is that of Jean André (Paris, 1544) [BN Rés. Ye. 3701]. The title page is anonymous, but Sagon's authorship is assured by the words 'la muse Sagontine' in vol. 3 of the poem, and by his motto *Vela de quoy* following the *rondeau final* (sig. Biiii). See also Hutton, *Essays*, pp. 311–19.

Les Anges ont bien (soubz grace)
Pris l'audace,
Chanter paix quant Dieu fut né. . . .

(These topics suffice to show that Sagon is following Erasmus' *Querela*.) The Nobility, bidden by the Acteur to sing of the Lamb of peace, rejoice that the king will now be obeyed, since the king for his part will take cognizance of the people's complaints; the Nobility will protect merchants and others from robbers, and in turn will be defended by their vassals; their children will be instructed in letters and in virtue. In calling upon Labor, the Acteur says that the people have been so harassed by war as to be brought close to suicide. They chant at some length, happy that 'pillerye est estaincte,' and summoning woods, gardens, birds, shepherds, and villagers to join in the song: justice will be done to the guilty; merchants will travel freely; taxes will be lowered; there will be employment in building châteaux and fine houses in the towns.

Still more elaborate is the poem produced for this event by the Flemish Latin poet Corneille de Schryver (Graphaeus; Scribonius) of Antwerp: *Pacis inter Carolum V Imp. C. A. et Franciscum I Regem Christ. ad Aquas Mortuas initae Descriptio*.[18] De Schryver is a *rhétoriqueur* writing in Latin, which he writes well and with vigor. His poem reflects the sumptuous pageants for which Flanders was famous and has a special interest in exploiting the symbolism of peace.

After an address to the Emperor and a verse *argumentum*, the poet invites the world to rejoice in the new peace and gives an elaborate account of the change of heart experienced by the two monarchs [cf. Nesson, above, p. 65]. God is thus enabled to send Peace down to Aigues-Mortes, accompanied by the Savior, and she is welcomed by Charles and Francis, whom the poet acclaims as peace heroes. The triumphal procession moves forward, led by Concordia, Fides, and like figures, with the last of whom, the nine Muses, the poet holds a dialogue. Now comes Peace in her chariot, and after her the captives, Mars and his *comites*, Discordia, Furiae, and others, while the rear is brought up by rejoicing men— farmers, merchants, artisans, and many others. They halt before a temple of Parian marble, in which are the altars of Pax and Concordia. Gloria, Honos, and Decor descend the steps to welcome Peace, and Gloria conducts her together with the Emperor and the King to the temple door. At this moment the bound prisoners are led into the opposite square, and Amor as executioner lops off the head of Discordia with the

[18]Published at Antwerp in 1540 by J. Coccius, together with a *Gratulatio* on Charles's passage through France in that year. On Schryver (1482–1558), see J. Roulez in the *Biographie Nationale de Belgique*, and Allen, *Opus Epist.*, Ep. 2114. My references are to *DPG* 2.479–523.

sword of Justice. This done, Peace, holding Charles with her right hand and Francis with her left, ascends into the temple to give thanks to God. The poet bids all Antwerp to go home and celebrate with songs and drinking, as he will himself do, little as he cares for drink; and afterwards to erect permanent memorials of the occasion. These are to be a triumphal arch; pyramids inscribed with the titles of Peace, Caesar, and the King, witnessing to their treaty to root out war and give *libertas* and *quies* to weary mortals; three marble statues of the same personages; and two colossi on which images of the two monarchs shall stand facing the Turks with threatening swords. Round these statues let us hold annual games and observances, and let our descendants maintain them forever.

Though Charles V had been fêted in Paris as an honored guest on the first of January 1540, by June the rift between him and the French king had opened again, and in the following years their relations went from bad to worse. In 1543 the Emperor entered into an alliance with Henry VIII of England, and in 1544 they planned a joint attack on France. But Charles's financial difficulties altered his plans, and he made a separate peace with France, signed on September 18 and known as the treaty of Crépy. François Sagon's printer seized the moment to bring out, probably for the second time, his poem *Le Chant de la Paix*,[19] though Sagon was probably dead by August 29, 1544. Freshly written for the occasion was Gilles Corrozet's *Le Retour de la Paix*, a poem whose fortunes were to become entangled with Sagon's.[20] Destined to reappear with the return of peace on several occasions in the course of the century, it may have been the pattern, or the germ, of a number of later peace poems.[21] Written in stanzas

[19]At the end of this 1544 edition: 'Nouvellement imprimé à Paris sur le vingtiesme iour de Septembre 1544.' Since peace was concluded on the eighteenth, this was quick work, and suggests that the poem already existed, that is, was already printed in 1538 as Du Verdier says. To be sure, Corrozet's *Retour de la Paix* was ready on the twenty-second, but it is a relatively simple performance and was printed by Corrozet himself. Other poems celebrating the treaty of Crépy were the *Oraison de Mars* of Claude Colet (Paris, 1554, 1548); and Cornelius Crocus, *Ode sacra . . .* (a translation of Ps. 45) (Amsterdam, 1544).
[20]*Le Retour de la paix en France [sic]* (Paris, Corrozet, Sept. 22, 1544) [BN Rés. Ye. 1108], anonymous, but secured for Corrozet by his motto: *Plus que moins.* See S. M. Bouchereaux, "Recherches bibliographiques sur G. Corrozet," *Bulletin du Bibliophile* (1949), 94. For a detailed discussion of Corrozet, Sagon, and *La Resjouissance de la Paix de 1559*, see Hutton, *Essays*, pp. 311–18.
[21]Reprinted as anonymous, with the title: *Le Retour de la Paix, et du fruict provenant du benefice d'icelle, œuvre tres-utile digne de ce temps* (Lyons: B. Rigaud, 1570 [Lyons, Bibliothèque de la Ville, 314340]). This edition is not noted in Bouchereaux's catalogue. Again reprinted by Rigaud in 1577 with the original title, *Le Retour de la paix en France* [BN Rés. Ye. 4712]. That is, it was reissued for the Pacification of Saint-Germain (1570) and for the Peace of Bergerac (1577). In these reprints the topical last sixteen lines are omitted. But the most curious reprinting was that of 1559 in *La Resjouissance*, where it is amalgamated with Sagon's poem (below, p. 118).

of varying length (143 lines), without the devices of *rhétorique*, it combines classical and religious themes in due proportion:

> Tant plus ung bien est longuement caché,
> Plus est requis, attendu et cerché.
> Et quand il vint apres longueur de temps,
> Il rend les gens plus aises et contens.

What is this good so long lost to us? It is that from which all others flow, a gift of heaven beyond our deserts: a peace unfeigned and sincere. Time was when Peace dwelt on earth, everywhere, and with her Faith and Justice, Concord, Love, Truth, Government, Honor, Innocence. One might travel to foreign lands; one was not startled by the clang of arms; there were no lawsuits, no judges, no lawyers; all dwelt in friendship with no need of armies or walls.[22] Obedient to their betters, men lived in plenty even on a little, safe by night or in the woods. No gibbet was erected for malefactors. Happy days and months! But when sin born of malice brought in vice, Peace, daughter of God, withdrew to heaven; and to punish us, God sent from hell War with fire and steel in his hands. But now we see God's mercy, who has changed our 'Alas' into songs of joy, sending us Peace with the white olive in her hand. He does so, however, only on condition that we change our ways. Praise God. Peace on earth in hearts of goodwill and living faith.[23]

[22]Ovid, *Met.* 1.96–99. Corrozet is of course describing the Golden Age.

[23]Apparently to the year 1545 belong the verses published by Montaiglon under the title *Le Da pacem Du Laboureur* (*Recueil*, 9.276–80). The distress of the peasant, robbed of his animals and brought to near starvation by the wars, is expressed in twelve rough quatrains, each followed by a word or phrase of the antiphon—*Da pacem, Domine, in diebus nostris*, and so on (cf. John Julian, *Dictionary of Hymnology* [London, 1915]). Montaiglon had the date 1545 from a Soissons MS., the only printed edition he knew being in *Le Benedictus du prophète Zacharie* (Paris: D. Millot [1588]). Other editions are *Complainte et quérimonie des pauvres laboureurs fuyant la calamité des temps présents sur* Da pacem (Lyons, 1568) (Baudrier 3.253), and ibid. (Lyons, 1588) (BN Rés. Ye. 3749).

Here also may be mentioned a poem entitled *Complaincte de la Paix pardevant nostre Dieu contre les inventifs et procureurs de la Guerre* (sigs. A–Aiii[6]), of which the BN possesses a copy lacking the title page [Ye. 18891]. It begins:

> O Dieu vivant de ton regard nestrange
> Ta fille Paix, que les mortels mondains
> Veullent par guerre ainsi comme un estrange
> Abandonner, mais me donne louange
> Pour resister à leurs hazars soudains.
> Les soldarts sont prest de mettre les mains
> Dessus mon chef pour mon renom abattre,
> Qui a bon droict raison a les combatre.

There are eighteen of these eight-line stanzas. Peace is the speaker throughout, complaining of her treatment by the 'mondains,' and this fact together with the title suggests that the writer was inspired by Erasmus' *Querela*. The chief feature of the poem is an extended execration of warmongers (not from Erasmus) in part founded on

The war with England continued; a serious attempt to invade the island was defeated off the Isle of Wight, and Francis agreed to a treaty, signed at Campe near Ardres, June 8, 1546, on very unfavorable terms. There was little reason for the French poets to celebrate the Treaty of Ardres, but the French fashion of timely *placquettes* was on this occasion honored by the English antiquarian John Leland, whose *Laudatio Pacis* was published in London in August.[24]

This naively learned poem begins with the creation of the world and its inhabitants (including special mention of the dolphin for the sake of the Dauphin), not, as is obligatory in peace poems, to demonstrate the 'peace' of the cosmos, but to admonish mankind to honor the Creator. Leland hails the present peace, says he lacks the skill of Ovid and Pontano, and proceeds to the technical *laudatio*, giving, as the textbooks required, the honorable *origin* and the beneficent *acts* of Peace. She is the daughter of God and comes with her companions, Astraea, Concordia, and the rest from heaven. In witness of her beneficent acts, Leland quotes the Greek poets, Ovid, Tibullus, Silius Italicus, the Greek orator Isocrates, and an unnamed Latin orator. Leaving his witnesses, he runs through the blessings of peace in a rapid summation passage and concludes with a prayer for King Henry, Prince Edward, and the king of France.

It is amusing to uncover what Leland has done here. For the Greek poets, he has made a succinct translation of the chapter (55) 'De Pace' in Stobaeus' *Florilegium*, where all these fragments appear.[25] For the Latin poets, he has simply reproduced the section 'De pace' in Octavianus Mirandula's familiar commonplace book *Flores Illustrium Poetarum*, without so much as altering the elegiac couplets of Ovid and Tibullus to suit the hexameters of his own poem. Finally, for the summation passage on the blessings of peace, he has versified the corresponding passage of Erasmus' *Bellum*.[26] Be it said that the total effect

---

Psalm 109. There are no historical allusions, but style and orthography would suit the 1540s.

[24]ΕΓΚΩΜΙΟΝ τῆς Εἰρήνης, *Laudatio Pacis, Ioanne Lelando Antiquario autore* (London: Reginald Wolfe, 1546) [New York Public Library]; also in *Johannis Lelandi antiquarii . . . Collectanea*, Thomas Hearne, ed., 2d ed. (London, 1770), 5.69–78. See Leicester Bradner, *Musae Anglicanae* (New York, 1940), pp. 27–28. Also Hutton, *Essays*, pp. 319–29.

[25]See below, pp. 170–71.

[26]LB 2, 957E; *Bellum*, Remy and Dunil-Marquebreucq, eds., p. 44. The reference to Isocrates (vv. 224–29) is curiously vague; Isocrates was the 'patronus' of Peace, 'Quam sic a teneris dilexit gratior annis, / Virginis ut coleret praesentia numina divae.' Perhaps the reference is to *Antid.* 151; 'I do not seek office, because I love peace and tranquillity, and this mode of life suits the studies to which I have set myself from the first.' The Latin orator whose name Leland does not know says: 'Parvae res crescunt.

is novel and not unpleasing, though it is hard to forgive the intrusion of elegiacs into a hexameter poem.

To the year 1546 also belongs the fine *Hymnus pacis aeternae* of the well-known Latin poet Basilio Zanchi. Though published in Paris, the poem does not especially refer to French affairs; and since its underlying thought is that just as ancient Rome dispensed the *pax Romana*, so now we may hope that peace may stream from ecclesiastical Rome, it may refer to the Council of Trent.[27] Zanchi summons Peace from heaven, where first of all entities she looks on the face of God, and describes the benefits she will bring—agricultural plenty, freedom of trade, academic leisure—if she will but enter our hearts:

> Labere, Diva, polo, mentique illabere nostrae.

She will be welcome as the Phoenix returning from the East, and the river god Tiberinus, crowned with verdant reeds and pouring water from his urn, will rise to greet her.[28] The Romans will worship her image on the Capitol. May she look on Rome with propitious eye; and let Victory come, and Glory strew laurels while the world—the East, Spain, Germany—recognize her as their mistress, and Echo redouble from the seven hills:

> Victor, io, Romanus, io, nova signa reportat.

Concord will break the gates of war and Discord seek the pools of Cocytus. The Father Omnipotent will plunge wars in Phlegethon; for he has brought peace to earth and heaven by the blood of his only begotten Son.

Both Francis and Henry VIII died in 1547. The new king of France, Henri II, was of very different temper from his father. An ambassador quoted by Batiffol reported that in talking to him 'he

---

. . .' The hackneyed quotation from Sallust (*Jug.* 10.6) had been so long embedded in the peace literature that its origin was forgotten; Leland, like Pace, may take it from Erasmus' *Bellum*. Earlier (135–41), he quotes Aratus in Germanicus' translation.

[27] I have been unable to trace the 1546 edition, which is reported by Niceron, (41.254), who says that the poem is not included in the collective editions [1550, 1553] of Zanchi's *Poemata*. It appears, however, in *DPI*; my references are to the latter.

[28] Iam placidis Tiberinus ovans tibi surgit ab undis,
  Roranteis viridi praecinctus arundine crines;
  Urna humero in laevam, dextro subnixa fluentum
  Versa vomit repletque undis spùmantibus alveum.

Zanchi's *Hymn* echoes Lucretian phrases: 'Adventuque tuo laetanti daedala tellus. . . . Teque tuumque canat ventura in saecula nomen.' He is describing an ancient statue of a river god now in the Capitoline Museum. See H. Stuart Jones, *The Sculpture of the Museo Capitolino* (Oxford, 1912), Pl. 1. The cornucopia is broken off.

seemed rather to desire peace than to aim at the greatest victories.'[29] He hoped to have an end of the disastrous Italian adventures. With fewer literary interests perhaps than the Valois generally had, a sportsman chiefly, he had the luck to begin his reign with the beginnings of the great poetical movement of the century, the exponents of which were all committed courtiers. The first poem of any serious intent written by the young Jean-Antoine de Baïf was a peace poem intended for the King and presumably presented to him: *Sur la Paix avec les Anglois l'an mil cinq cens quaranteneuf*. We consider it in the final section of this chapter. The circumstances were the short war fought on behalf of the Guises to prevent the proposed marriage of Edward VI to their niece Mary Stuart, which ended in the French reoccupation of Boulogne and led eventually (1558) to the marriage of Mary to the Dauphin.[30] Baïf does not allude to the events, but implies a hope, founded no doubt on the king's known wishes, that Henri will be a peacemaker like the Roman Augustus. The same events and the same hopes inspired Ronsard to a far higher flight. His Pindaric *Ode de la Paix* was published, like so many of our peace poems, as a small brochure in April 1550.[31] Laumonier has seen in this poem Ronsard's final, successful stroke in recommending himself for the official designation of 'poète du roi.' In high vatidic language it views Peace, creatrix of the universe, as involved in history, and especially in the history of Francion's descendants down to the new peace hero Henri II. We return to this poem below in Chapter VII. But these poets had yet to create the taste by which they were enjoyed. We may imagine that most readers of the day found the Pindaric strophes of Ronsard less acceptable than the charming edition of Sagon's *Chant de la Paix*, which was issued for this occasion in a small format illustrated throughout with attractive vignettes.[32]

[29]Louis Batiffol, *Le siècle de la Renaissance* (Paris, 1921), p. 134. But see in Henry Lemonnier (Ernest Lavisse, *Histoire de France* [Paris, 1908–22], 5, 2.165), the diplomat Simon Renard's words: 'Le roy . . . de son naturel, est adonné à guerre et ambition.'

[30]Peace was concluded March 24, 1550 (1549 o.s.).

[31]In Ronsard's collections the title became *Ode au Roy sur la paix faicte entre luy et le roy d'Angleterre l'an 1550*, thus conforming to the usual title of peace poems.

[32]*Le Chant de la paix de France et d'Angleterre, chanté par les trois estatz, composé par l'Indigent de Sapience. Publié à Paris le samedy vingtneufiesme iour de Mars, mil cinq cens quaranteneuf, avant Pasques* (Paris, 1550) [BN Rés. p. Ye. 337]. The text is the same as that of the 1544 edition, but the orthography is modernized; Sagon's motto is omitted; the 'chant de Labeur' is printed in part in quatrains. The ten vignettes marking off the chief divisions of the poem illustrate the text—for example, one shows the noble youth receiving instruction in letters and virtue (see outline above, p. 86). Hutton, *Essays*, p. 316.

However peaceful Henri II may have been in intent, he pursued with zest the war with Charles V that he had inherited from his father, allying himself with the German princes in the Schmalkaldic War. The great event was the successful defense of Metz by the Duke of Guise, ending in the total dissolution of the Imperial forces at the beginning of 1553. To Joachim Du Bellay this seemed an opportunity for a general peace, or at least for a Latin poem proposing it:[33]

> Now at the year's end, on the calends of Janus, let the gates be closed, that the age of Saturn may return. In that age, iron was unknown, trumpets were silent; but now war rages and ruins all. Let the seeds of war perish (*Auspice Bellaio pereant sed semina belli*), and Furor that, stained with Hesperian and Gallic blood, brings death (*interitum*) to you, conquered Charles, while victorious valor prepares triumphs for Henry—a great glory but bought with too much blood. Let Christian kings unite, and let the barbarian (Turk) depart from Europe. Come, great kings and greatest Julius (III), make perpetual peace. Calm the tumult, Henry; be you first, Charles, to throw down arms.

These are not exactly the terms in which one calls for a 'paix non feinte.' Metz was, however, the beginning of the end for Charles, who abdicated in the autumn and winter of 1555–56, leaving Spain and the Netherlands to his son Philip (October 25, 1555) and the Empire to his brother Ferdinand (January 15, 1556).[34] After some difficulties, a truce of five years was signed by Henri, Charles, Philip, and Ferdinand on February 5, 1555, at Vaucelles near Cambrai. Du Bellay on this occasion, instead of addressing the European rulers in Latin, addressed only his own king in French:[35]

> Against Charles, Henri has been like a lioness defending her young, but when to the weary Emperor Peace sent her messenger Truce, more useful to him than to Henri, the latter accepted the Emperor's suggestion out of Christian piety, conquering himself, and for this godlike act his glory (together with that of his agents Montmorency and the Cardinal of Lorraine) will be engraved not in brass but in the hearts of posterity. As Henri's deeds would supply an Iliad, so too the poet might emulate Hesiod and write of Peace organizing chaos into the ordered universe, and of the Battle of Gods and Giants, and bring the tale of wars down

[33]*De Pace inter principes Christianos ineunda*, published in 1558. I use *DPG* 1.400.

[34]Some months before the Emperor's abdication (May 1555), Jacques Peletier du Mans had addressed to the Christian princes a fine *Cohortatio Pacificatoria*, which is discussed at length in Hutton, *Essays*, pp. 243–64.

[35]*Œuvres poétiques*, Henri Chamard, ed. (Paris, 1908–31), 6.1–16.

through history to the time of Henri.[36] He would then describe the triumphal procession—Henri in an ivory car, captives following, and Peace with her olive branch going before; but adequate treatment of such a theme must await a poet more learned than he.[37]

Cateau-Cambrésis

The relatively short, midcentury reign of Henri II was a turning point in French, and indeed in European, history, marking the end of the Italian wars, with a shift of the center of political interest from Italy to the North, and setting the stage for the wars of religion that occupied the second half of the sixteenth century. The significance of the reign found expression in its final act, the Treaty of Cateau-Cambrésis, which, ironically, gave occasion for the tragic death of the king.

In the political sphere Henri relied heavily on the elderly Constable of France, Anne de Montmorency, whose power was thus a counterpoise to the power of the Guises represented by Francis Duke of Guise and his brother Charles Cardinal of Lorraine. Montmorency was not exactly a peaceable character, but events, his age, some political acumen, and his rivalry with the Guises constantly put his very great influence on the side of peace. In 1556, however, despite Montmorency's opposition, the Duke of Guise was able to gain royal approval for an expedition against Naples and in support of the pope against Philip II of Spain. This foolish infringement of the Truce of Vaucelles can only be explained by the ambition of Guise furthered by the sinister influence of the pope's nephew, Cardinal Carlo Caraffa, who had arrived at the French Court as legate for Paul IV in

[36]This may well allude to Ronsard's *Ode de la Paix* of 1550; while what follows recalls Virgil, *Georg.* 3.10ff.

[37]Active in the negotiations leading up to Vaucelles was Reginald Pole as papal legate. His *Discorso di pace* was published in Italian and in a Latin translation by J. Pholius (Rome, 1555) (the Italian undated). It was several times reprinted (see BM Cat.). I use *Discorso intorno alle cose della guerra, con una Oratione della pace* (Nell' Academia Venetiana, 1558) [New York Public Library], in which only the *Oratione* is Pole's work. Commissioned by the pope to reconcile Charles and Henry, he chiefly addresses Charles, reminding him of his personal good fortune ('Your father was not even a king'). Peace must be placed above personal interests and must be founded on a 'congiuntione della volontà.' Pray to God; study earlier treaties to see where they were defective. By their dissensions, Charles and Henry are playing into the hands of the Turk and neglecting the difficult religious problem in Europe. They have so impoverished their subjects that these sometimes would prefer the Turks themselves. A king who wantonly engages in war is personally guilty of the murders and rapes that individually occur.

June.[38] Guise crossed the Alps in December, took Milan, went to the 'defense' of Rome, and was engulfed in the morass of Caraffa intrigue. Philip meanwhile retaliated by striking from the Netherlands, with reinforcements from his English queen, Mary Tudor, and the active help of Emmanuel-Philibert, Duke of Savoy, one of the great soldiers of the day. Early in August 1557, Emmanuel-Philibert advanced to lay siege to Saint-Quentin in Picardy, the fall of which would open the road to Paris. Montmorency, hurrying to its relief, blundered, and in one of the greatest disasters ever suffered by French arms, had his army destroyed by the Duke of Savoy. Montmorency himself, Albon de Saint-André the Marshal of France, and other notable persons were taken prisoner. Saint-Quentin fell; but Philip hesitated to extend himself in a march on Paris, and Henry, gathering new forces, summoned the Duke of Guise from Italy. On his arrival, the Duke promptly executed one of the resounding military feats of the century by taking Calais, hitherto believed impregnable, by surprise attack on the unwary English (January 8, 1558). In June by another brilliant stroke he took Thionville; but in July Marshal de Thermes lost the important battle of Gravelines. Towards the end of August, the two hostile armies were drawn up facing each other in the vicinity of Amiens. The two kings arrived to place themselves at the head of their forces, and a decisive battle was awaited. (It was then that Ronsard wrote his martial *Exhortation au camp du Roy*, which was put into Latin by Jean Dorat to give it international hearing.)[39] But there was no battle. Instead, rumors of an impending peace began to circulate early in September.

Montmorency had a good deal to do with what had happened, for he was extremely anxious to get free and return to Paris, where the Guises seemed to be sweeping all before them. But in fact both kings were eager to bring the war to an end. Neither had much to gain by it, both—especially Philip—were financially embarrassed, and both were concerned about the rising religious troubles in their realms. News of the death of Charles V arrived in September, marking the end of an epoch. Plenipotentiaries were appointed to meet at the abbey of Cercamps near Cambrai—Montmorency, Saint-André, and the Cardinal of Lorraine, accompanied by Jean de Morvillier, Bishop of Orleans and l'Aubespine, secretary of State, for the French, and the Duke of Alba, William of Orange, and Granvelle (Bishop of Arras, later Cardinal) for Philip—and a truce was made on October 17.

[38]Lemmonier in Lavisse, *Histoire de France* 5.2.165.
[39]In the placing of Ronsard's poems in relation to events I follow Laumonier, 9. Introd. ix–xiv.

On the twenty-first arrived the representatives of the English queen. In the ensuing conference, which lasted for more than five months, Philip's anxiety for peace was dissembled by his agents, who pressed for all they could get, while Henry, no less anxious, secretly supported the conciliatory attitude of Montmorency against the more aggressive Cardinal of Lorraine. Indeed, the fact that two of the French commissioners were prisoners was inevitably a weakness. Much time was spent over the question of their ransoms. The important questions, however, concerned Calais and Piedmont, and that of Calais was most hotly debated. But then, on November 24 there came the news of the death on the seventeenth of Mary Tudor, and the conference was adjourned.

The year 1558 had been one of preparation for a climax of occasional poetry; a spate of poems had celebrated the taking of Calais in January, another the marriage of the Dauphin and Mary Stuart in April, still another the victory of Thionville in June.[40] In September, when it became certain that there would be peace, Ronsard led the way with his impressive *Exhortation pour la Paix*, which, in its title, marks a ready reversal of his fiery *Exhortation au camp du Roy* of a few weeks earlier.[41] Though rapidly written, the *Exhortation pour la Paix* is to be ranked with his *Ode de la Paix* of 1550 as marking the highest level that the peace poem would reach in the sixteenth century. Ripe in style, and loaded with the spoils of ancient poetry, it departs from Ronsard's usual manner in being consciously organized on a rhetorical principle; it is a declamation in verse.[42] It is a series of commonplaces, richly developed, but for the most part commonplaces of the humanist tradition, not those of the mediaeval tradition, though this, as we shall see, was far from dead. On its high level, it scarcely touches on the events that inspired it; but that is suitable enough, since in September 1558, events were only taking shape. It was the moment to call eloquently for peace, which Ronsard knew the king ardently desired. He tactfully addresses neither kings nor counselors, but Christians in

[40]V.-L. Saulnier, "Deux œuvres inconnues de Jean Sève et une édition inconnue de Baïf," *Bulletin du Bibliophile* (1949), 270–74, lists twenty-seven poems on the taking of Calais; cf. also Du Bellay, *Œuvres poétiques*, ed. Chamard 6.20 n.

[41]Laumonier, 9.x, places the publication of the *Exhort.* in September or at the beginning of October. A Latin version by the Flemish humanist François de Thoor (Thorus) was also published in 1558.

[42]For classical and other sources, see below, pp. 179, 185, and 254. For the rhetorical organization, see my article "Rhetorical Doctrine and Some Poems of Ronsard," in *Essays*, pp. 291–310. The title *Exhortation* itself marks the literary species. In this connection see also "The 'Lost' *Cohortatio Pacificatoria* of Jacques Peletier du Mans" in the same volume.

general, and the soldiers in particular, again in allusion to his recent *Exhortation au camp.*

> Christians, cease fighting your brother Christians, whom Christ ransomed with His blood and joined one to another; war is for lions, wolves, tigers, not for Christian men (1–16).
>
> Lay aside your arms (1–26). Or, if you must fight, there are the Turks, usurpers of the Holy Land, and your natural enemies; our internal wars waste thousands of lives to gain or lose a village or a castle, but Asia with all its riches is a prize that Christian soldiers ought to save from the hands of pagans (27–80).
>
> Life is short, why further shorten it? (81–86).
>
> Mother—nay, Stepmother—Earth is the cause: overburdened with mankind she induced Jupiter to relieve her by setting in motion the Theban and the Trojan wars; and subsequent history has left her little reason to complain (87–106).
>
> Nature did not make man to be a fighting animal; dragons, lions, tigresses are armed with scale and claw, but man is born naked and tender (107–22).
>
> Cursed be the man who discovered iron and forged weapons; cursed be Prometheus who brought the fire to forge them; cursed be he who discovered gold, without which iron would be harmless (123–46). Happy was the Golden Age of primitive peace; had I but lived then I should not see our rivers choked with dead horses and abandoned armor (147–63). In war cities are overthrown, laws depraved, altars and churches burnt, justice abandoned, houses sacked, the old slain, maidens violated, the poor laborer despoiled, and vice becomes virtue (163–70).
>
> Brave soldiers, instead of committing crimes like these would you not rather live surrounded by the delights of domestic life, far from the hardships of war, while the spider spins in your helmets and the bee hives in your shields—forging swords and pikes into plough-points or curving them into sickles? (171–93).
>
> Peace created the universe out of warring elements, founded cities, developed agriculture, and civilized our wild forebears, bringing them from the woods into communities (195–212). Come, O Peace, crush the wrath of kings, and in the name of the peace that Christ made between his Father and us, banish Discord from among Christian peoples (213–20).

Similar in outlook to Ronsard's *Exhortation*, but in lyric form, is the *Ode à la Paix* of Marc-Claude de Buttet.[43] Indeed its point of view is

---

[43]*Œuvres poétiques*, Bibliophile Jacob, ed. (Paris, 1880), 2.122; the text presumably is that of Buttet's *Œuvres* of 1588 and bears the title *Hymne de la Paix*. The *Ode* was published by Gabriel de Buon in 1559, but the *privilège* (see the 1880 ed. 1.xiv) is dated 1558.

even a little earlier, that of late August when it seemed that a battle was imminent,[44] but that no doubt is employed for dramatic effect. Though conducted in the unassuming manner characteristic of Buttet, the poem succeeds in fulfilling the pattern of a peace poem and in creating an impression of real concern.

Daughter of God, thou hast returned to heaven and left us in evil case; we perish in the horrors of war. See Philip and Henry assembling their armies—if they fight, Europe is lost. Descend and crumple their arms; and let Venus, Hymen, and celebrations attend you.[45] Reason with Henry and Philip and unite them; and then will Bellona descend to hell, Europe rejoice, normal life return—

> Le prestre dedans son eglise,
> Le noble l'autrui ne cherchant,
> Le marchant en sa marchandise,
> Le laboureur soit à son champ—

and abundance will follow. How shall I praise thee? As the great daughter of Themis? Rather, from thy throne close to God thou dost rule the ages; thou didst arrange the elements of the universe; thou peoplest the cities of men; barbarous Moors and Tartars adore thee. Descend, heavenly queen, in answer to our prayer.[46]

It is refreshing to turn from the literary detachment of Ronsard and Buttet to a poet who is definitely *engagé*. Michel de L'Hospital was at the height of his poetical bent in 1558, writing Latin poems on Calais, on the marriage of the Dauphin, and on Thionville. Now as the peace negotiations were getting under way, probably in October, he published a notable epistle *De pace* addressed to the Cardinal of

[44]See stanzas 6–7, especially the lines: 'Voi, voi, en la large campagne / Henri pront les armes happer, / S'opposant aux forces d'Espagne / Et près d'Amiens se camper.'

[45]The editor (2.204) here assumes an allusion to the marriage agreements for the princesses and hence a knowledge of the outcome of the negotiations; but the stanza may be no more than the obligatory topic of peace poems. In any case, marriages were in question from the beginning of the conference.

[46]Probably earlier in 1558, there appeared at Ghent Henry de Tour's *Moralité de paix et de guerre*, which had, it seems, been written in 1554, and is dedicated to Jean-François Roffier, adviser to the Duke of Savoy; see résumé in Petit de Julleville, *Répertoire*, p. 90. Soulas, though having his Desire, together with Plaisir and Richesse, from his mistress La Paix, is seduced to abandon her by Ennoyeuse Detraction, who brings him to the realm of Guerre and Pillage. There he is beaten and despoiled; his Desire leaves him; and he laments that he ever parted from La Paix. Now, however, Bon Conseil succeeds in bringing him back to the realm of La Paix, whither his Desire has gone before. La Paix repairs his losses, giving him the cloak of Toute Abondance, the hat of Bonne Assurance, and full enjoyment of his Desire.

Lorraine.[47] None of the poems we consider surpasses it in charm of style, and none equals it in diplomacy and political sense. I give a bare summary of its two hundred lines:

He would be no patriot who asked your attention for trifling verses when you are engaged in the weighty affairs of state; but allow me to warn you that you should relax and save your health for the good of your country; leave war to your two brothers. Perhaps you would like to hear news of the Court? The royal ladies and your sister-in-law Anna implore heaven for your safe return and for an armistice of peace. The people are in a confident mood. But the evil daughter of Report, beast of a hundred tongues and as many minds, who lurks about the palace, is not silent. Sometimes she reproaches you for recklessness in exposing the army without reinforcements and the city without proper defenses; again, hearing that you have taken measures for protection and that the enemy are camped at a distance, she complains that you are protracting the war in order to perpetuate your own power; and now that the city is filled with rumors of peace, she was saying that she loved the name of peace, but that it could not be negotiated on fair terms by slaves and captives.[48] She is against giving up Piedmont and leaving Italy wholly to the Spaniard, thinks it wrong to let go Calais, so lately won back to avenge the shame of Crécy, or Thionville; and says there are many places in the Ardennes that can be exchanged for Saint-Quentin and Ham; the captives should not be redeemed with territory or towns, but each should pay his own ransom, since the treasury is empty. She complains that the leaders of the state are pursuing their private quarrels, heedless of the public interest. She really is a venomous creature—none worse—when once she whets her several tongues. I remember how you used to laugh at this great beast of the palace. Still, it is well to know what is being said, if only to be able to defend oneself, and it is useful to know what faults the people find in us. Thank you for the greetings conveyed to me by another to whom you wrote. You had my first name wrong, but I don't mind that so long as I have your affectionate regard.

In publishing these views, presumably in October, L'Hospital was, no doubt, publishing the views of the Cardinal himself. Early in the

---

[47]*Ad Carolum cardinalem Lotarenum . . . de Pace* [BN Yc. 1455], no date of *privilège*; also in *Carmina* (Amsterdam, 1732) [BN Yc. 8285], p. 154; *Œuvres complètes*, P. J. S. Dufey, ed. (Paris, 1825), 3.191. See E. Dupré Lasale, *Michel de L'Hospital* (Paris, 1875), 2.120–36.

[48]Montmorency and Saint-André.

> sed agi rem conditionibus aequis
> Per servos nec posse tamen captisque minores.

The poem was clearly written after the delegates were named and the negotiations begun.

same month, probably before the *De pace,* when the delegates had been appointed, he addressed a still longer epistle to Jean de Morvillier, Bishop of Orleans, who was one of them.[49] The theme of this interesting discourse is that France is in a position, thanks to the Duke of Guise, to demand favorable terms; too high a price can be paid for peace, and an unjust peace leads only to more and worse wars. The Spaniards now see our forces and our leaders in warlike array; and it is by these that peace is made, not by one who lightly and selfishly sells himself to the enemy to gain the credit of some sort of peace though it be neither honorable nor advantageous. This was the last of L'Hospital's effusions; as he saw Montmorency's policies prevailing and backed by the king, he said no more, nor did he lift his pen to celebrate the peace in April. He did, however, contribute an epithalamium for Marguerite and the Duke of Savoy.[50]

Beside the courtly tones of L'Hospital, Ronsard, and Buttet, there might be heard a coarser voice, one only too prophetic of things to come. The fanatical, if not mentally unbalanced, Artus Désiré had also heard the rumors of peace when he published his *Articles du Traicté de la paix entre Dieu et les hommes,* the *privilège* of which is dated September 12:[51]

> En attendant quelque bonne nouvelle,
> Et que par France et Espaigne on la crie,
> J'ay composé les articles d'icelle [peace of God].

Like the Children of Israel, we have suffered long in this calamitous reign, and like them we will be delivered if we repent. A prose discourse to this intent is followed by fifty-two quatrains, each naming an abuse that must be purged away—debauchery, plurality of benefices, improper conduct of schoolmasters, and above all heresy: 'Que tout Lutherien immunde / Soit bruslé. . . . Faictes rotir sur les charbons / Predicans de faulce doctrine:'

> Prenez ceux des conventicules
> De nuict aux conciliabules,

[49]Not published at the moment; *Carm.* 1732, p. 245; *Œuvres* 3.306; résumé in Dupré Lasale, *Michel de L'Hospital,* 2.124.

[50]'Ad Margaritam, Sabaudiae Ducem,' *Œuvres,* Dufey, ed., 3.495–503.

[51]*Les Articles du Traicté de la paix entre Dieu et les hommes, articulez par Artus Desiré. A monsieur Fizes, conseiller du Roy et secretaire de ses Finances* (Paris: Pierre Gualtier, 1558) [BN Rés. Ye. 1867]. Another edition by the same publisher, 1563. In 1561 Désiré was tried and convicted of treason as the agent of a plot to call in Philip II to aid the French Catholics, but was treated leniently, perhaps as an ecclesiatic. He published some thirty tracts, said mostly to be violent denunciations of the Huguenots.

Et les mettez tous dans le feu,
Et nous aurons la paix de Dieu.[52]

In January 1559, the peace conference was moved from Cercamps to Cateau-Cambrésis, but active negotiations were resumed only on February 6. Meanwhile Philip II, rebuffed in his tentative suit of the new English queen Elizabeth, had lost interest in Calais, which in the end was given to France for eight years but on terms that assured permanent possession. From the beginning, royal marriages, the inevitable counters in the diplomatic game, had been in the background of the negotiations. It was decided that Philip should marry Henri's daughter Elizabeth, while the question of Piedmont was settled by arranging the marriage of Henri's sister Marguerite to the Duke of Savoy. Marguerite (Ronsard's patron) had reached the age of thirty-six without a husband being found for her. In the matter of territory, the treaty looked like a diplomatic defeat for the French crown; not only did it renounce forever all claim to Naples and Milan, but much of Piedmont and many of the cities gained in recent wars were relinquished. Not only the party of the Guises, but most of the persons of the time who have left memoirs, regarded the treaty with some shame as derogatory to French honor. We shall catch an apologetic note in a number of the poems. Moreover, many persons realized that the religious question loomed behind it. Nevertheless, peace was good, and there was unaffected rejoicing.

The negotiations were completed on March 27. The treaty between France and England was signed on April 2 and that between France and Spain the next day. Public proclamation of the peace was made in Paris on April 7.[53] The royal marriages were to be celebrated in Paris at the end of June.

By the king's letter, signed at Coucy, April 5, and sent to all governors of the realm, peace was proclaimed and the order given to pay thanks to God and to celebrate with *feux de joie*. Accompanying the king's letter was an instruction signed by his secretary Du Thiers on April 7, and this was the date of the official proclamation in Paris.[54]

[52]Du Verdier (ed. Rigoley de Jovigny) mentions the following book, not seen by me: M.R.B., *La Source des guerres et le moyen pour acquérir la paix* (Paris: J. Ruelle, 1558). He also (3.86) gives an excerpt of sixteen lines, 'Si le Seigneur ne bastit la maison, . . .' from which one may guess the theme to be that the source of war is sin, and repentance the means of attaining peace.

[53]Upon the signing of the treaty, a medal was struck showing France seated on a heap of arms, with a Victory at her right hand offering her a palm and a garland; the device *Optimo principi*, and in the exergue *Gallia* (Lucien Romier, *Origines politiques des guerres de religion* [Paris, 1914], 2.347).

[54]Letter and instruction *(Teneur de la publication de la paix)* are printed in Anon., *La Paix faicte entre treshaults et trespuissants princes Henry II de ce nom, treschretien Roy de*

There the *Te Deum* was sung at Notre Dame in the presence of the
court of Parlement, the prévôt des marchands, the échevins, and
others, and bonfires were lighted throughout the city. Next day, Sat-
urday, April 8, there was a great religious procession—clergy of No-
tre Dame and the Sainte Chapelle, the Parlement and other dignita-
ries—carrying the reliquary of the true Cross.[55] Elsewhere some
days elapsed before the celebrations, depending on the time it took
for the king's messengers to arrive. At La Rochelle, where the letter
came through the king of Navarre, the celebrations did not take place
until the twentieth.[56] The king's courier reached Lyons on the thir-
teenth, and there the festivities were so extravagant, and have been so
minutely described, that we must give them some attention. After all,
our poems are a kind of literary *feu de joie*, and in many cases burnt
out as quickly, having thrown their beams perhaps less far. The actual
feux, again, show invention and artistic form and instruct us on the
Renaissance idea and iconography of peace. The last of the Lyons *feux*
reveals the mind of Barthélemy Aneau; another was the work of the
painter Bernard Salomon.[57]

---

*France, et Philippe Roy d'Espagne trescatholique, les Roy et Royne d'Ecosse, Dauphin, et la
Royne d'Angleterre* (Lyons: Nicolas Edoard, 1559), *privilège* dated April 13 [Lyons,
Bibliothèque de la Ville 354287]. The instruction serves to remind us that some of
the poets' topics corresponded with reality, for example, the freedom of commerce:
'Est la paix generelle . . . pour aller, venir, . . . marchander . . . és pays uns des
autres'; and the warning to disturbers of the peace: 'Deffendant . . . à tous . . . qu'ilz
n'ayent à entreprendre atteinter ne innover aucune chose au contraire, sur peine
d'etre puniz comme infracteurs de paix.' Cf. Ronsard and Grévin below, pp. 107,
112).

[55]Summary description in anon., *Discours moral de la paix* (below p. 120). Laumon-
ier, 9.xv, n. i, refers to a MS account.

[56]Amos Barbot, *Histoire de La Rochelle* 2.148 (*Archives Historiques de La Saintonge et de
L'Aunis* [Paris, 1889], 17).

[57]The following details depend mostly on two pamphlets by Benoît Du Troncy:
*Le Discours du grand triomphe fait en la ville de Lyon, pour la paix faite et accordée entre
Henry second, Roy de France treschrestien, et Philippe Roy des Espagnes et leurs aliez* (Lyons:
J. Saugrain, 1559) [Lyons, Bibliothèque de la Ville 354288]; and *Suytte de la descrip-
tion des grands triomphes faitz à Lyon, après la publication de la paix* (Lyons: J. Saugrain,
1559) [Lyons, Bibliothèque de la Ville 354289]. I have also used two other pamphlets
that seem to have appeared a little before Du Troncy's: *La Paix faicte . . .* (above, n.
54); and *Triomphes, pompes et magnificences faicts à Lyon, pour la paix* (Paris: Fédéric Mo-
rel, 1559) [BM 1059.h.24]. The first, *La paix faicte*, gives the events of April 13; the
king's letter; Du Thiers's instruction; notice of the General Procession of April 16;
then under a new half-title, "Triomphes, pompes et magnificences faicts à Lyon," a
succinct account of the *feux* of April 16, 17, 19 (printers' *feu*). Morel's booklet is a re-
print of this last part of *La paix faicte*, with its title. The British Museum copy belonged
to François Rasse de Neux (below, n. 96). Another reprint may be *La Paix entre
treshauts et trespuissantz princes . . .* , Poiters, P. and J. Moynes, 1559 (*Catalogue de
l'histoire de France* [Paris, 1855], 1.245–46), which I have not seen. Nor have I seen the
description of the Lyons fêtes in Guillaume Paradin's *Histoire de Lyon* (Lyons, 1573).
Du Verdier records the following: *Discours sur l'esjouissance et triomphes faits pour la paix
entre les rois de France et d'Espagne . . .* (Lyons: B. Rigaud and J. Saugrain, 1559).

When the king's messenger arrived, the great bell of St. John's was rung for an hour, and the Governor Guillaume de Sauvigny, with the clergy and the officers of the city, heard the *Te Deum* sung there, while the proclamation was read in several parts of the city to the sound of trumpets. A bonfire was lighted before the city hall, and bread and wine were distributed to the crowd. Later, private bonfires were burnt throughout the city. On the following Sunday, April 16, took place the General Procession, headed by a vast number of the poor on public relief,[58] followed at an interval by the religious orders and other clergy, the king's trumpeters, and the notables. The procession began at St. John's, crossed the bridge over the Saône, and ended at the Cordeliers, where alms were distributed. In the evening the public fireworks began.

The city was brilliant with torches and fires and loud with drums, hautboys, artillery fire, and bursts of *petereaux*.[59] Three great public *feux* drew most attention: a huge pyramid on the Saône bridge, a column of Virtue at the Maison de Ville, and the Giants, Pluto, and Peace in the square of the Cordeliers. The pyramid, said to represent the tomb of Mars, was crowned with a golden ball and on a ledge carried four urns as if for the burial of military captains; near the peak were 'hieroglyphics': a morion 'swallowing up soldiers or deeds of war,' a caduceus 'representing peace,' doves with joined beaks expressing concord, and a laurel wreath.[60] The pyramid, stuffed with fagots and straw, blazed up brilliantly, uttering *petereaux* from all sides, especially from the urns, while mortars and artillery fire answered from beneath the bridge and on the riverbanks. 'You would think that Atlas had broken down, and the heavens were falling' (*La Paix faicte*). The column of Virtue before the city hall was wrapped in laurel and sustained a pelican destroying itself for its young—symbol of good city fathers who sacrifice their own fortunes for the public good.[61] It, too, was burnt. At the Cordeliers, there

[58]According to *La Paix faicte*, seven thousand; according to Du Troncy, *Discours*, more than six thousand; at the almsgiving on Monday there were more than three thousand (*La Paix faicte*). The total population was about fifty thousand (Jean Déniau, *Histoire de Lyon* [Paris, 1951]).

[59]*Petereaux* were the ordinary fireworks, probably fireballs ejected from small tubes or pipes as mortars.

[60]Du Troncy, *Discours* and *La Paix faicte* agree that the pyramid represented the sepulcher of Mars, though this is not the usual 'hieroglyphic' use of the pyramid (Natura, Anima, or Ignis). For the caduceus as an emblem of peace, see Pierio Valeriano, *Hieroglyphica* (Lyons, 1595), p. 145. Since all the emblems except the helmet express peace, one may wonder if Du Troncy read it correctly; a morion adopted as a hive by bees represents peace in Alciati's *Emblem* 177.

[61]So Du Troncy, *Discours*; *La Paix faicte* thinks it represented the goodness of princes who shed their blood for their 'petits.'

was an elaborate 'triomphe' created by the painter Bernard Salomon and erected at the expense of the German 'nation.'[62] A scaffolding, triangular in form, but seeming to be a cube when viewed from any one side, was covered with painted cloth, on which, at the bottom, was depicted the fulmination of the Giants 'after Ovid's *Metamorphoses*';[63] above this were three enormous Furies presenting firebrands, and at their feet their 'messengers' the Harpies, having children's faces, griffons' feet, and serpentine bodies. Topping all was the figure of Pluto with crown and pitchfork, riding on his dog Cerberus. High on the west side of the square, there hung a huge picture of Peace, gathering to her bosom the arms of France, Spain, England, Lorraine, Savoy, and (below) those of the chief Imperial cities. Nearby, arquebuses and light artillery were suspended *à croc* (as no longer in use). On the ground below, a pavilion was erected for ladies and the musicians, and refreshments were served. Round the square were ranged a dozen barrels painted with giants' masks. From these, when fired, there issued bursts of *petereaux*, while to mingled music and gunfire, Pluto and his scaffold went down in fireworks, notable being the firewheels and flares from his crown and pitchfork. It was as though a battle was in progress. The spectacle seemed to Benoit Du Troncy to represent the fulmination of the Giants by the gift of Peace.[64]

Sauvigny and a procession of notables visited each of these scenes, from seven o'clock in the evening, giving the word to set the fires. Soon the great houses also were ablaze with torchlights and fireworks. Paul Benedict of Lucca had a salamander fifteen feet long that emitted *petereaux* from mouth to tail, the fires meeting overhead. A boat burnt on the Saône, throwing up showers of *petereaux*. At nine o'clock, a fiery dragon shooting flames rose from the quarter of Dauphiné and fell in the Cordeliers square.[65]

Next morning, the Florentine 'nation' heard mass at the Jacobins

[62]See Marius Audin and Eugène Vial, *Dictionnaire des artistes* (Paris, 1919), 2.197. I owe this reference to the kindness of Marcel Françon. Salomon is also called 'le petit Bernard' (Ulrich Thieme and Felix Becker, *Künstler-Lexikon* [Leipzig, 1907–50]).

[63]Du Tronyc, *Discours*. Among Salomon's works is *La Metamorphose d'Ovide figurée* (Lyons: J. de Tournes, 1557) (178 wood engravings).

[64]The explanation does not account for the prominence of Pluto and the Furies. May we see in the whole arrangement of the square the statement of so many writers on peace—for example, of Erasmus and Clichtove—that war is from hell and spread by the Furies, while Peace is from heaven?

[65]Less admirable was the '*monstre*' before the royal prison of Roanne—'un posteau, garny de bois et de pailles, et à la cyme dudict posteau y avait deux chats en un cage, dequelz, quand ilz sentirent le feu, faisoit bien ouyr le chant et melodie' (*La Paix faicte*).

and distributed alms. In the evening, the great houses again put on illuminations, sometimes with artillery fire that was answered by artillery on boats in the Saône. On Wednesday the nineteenth,[66] the journeymen printers erected in the Place de Confort a colossal god Mars thirty feet high and bristling with arms. As Mars burned, there gradually emerged from within him, safe and sound, the white figure of Minerva reclining with the nine Muses on the rock Parnassus, beneath which spouted a Castalian spring of wine and water, with Pegasus just leaving it: 'demonstrating that the death of Mars is the resurrection and the life of Minerva, goddess of wisdom and the liberal arts.'[67] So it was, sighs Du Troncy, in the days of good King Francis.

That might seem celebrations enough; but the Lyonnais having got hold of a good thing were loath to let it go.[68] On the next Sunday (April 23), there were great *feux* on the Saône and in the Place de Rohanne, while a wealthy member of the German 'nation,' Christofle Neictar, put on illuminations, with artillery fire, at his new house at Fourvière, surpassing all that had gone before. He repeated them on Monday, though held up by rain until ten at night; and on Tuesday again, when his brilliant revelries lasted from seven in the evening till dawn of the next day. On Sunday, April 30, the parish of St. George produced a dragon followed by four riders representing the Church, Peace, St. George, and Labor; and the dragon was burnt on a boat in the Saône in the presence of Sauvigny and immense crowds. 'Peace on earth is won by Labor and Arms, and the Church shares its benefits.' On Thursday of that week (May 4), the harbor guards launched a boat in the form of a great whale with a dome on top filled with guards; it was dazzlingly illuminated and emitted *petereaux*. Evidently one of the most successful shows, it was repeated on Sunday near the bridge. The din of artillery, drums,

[66]*La Paix faicte*; Du Troncy says Thursday (the twentieth).
[67]*La Paix faicte*; Du Troncy makes it clear that Minerva and Parnassus were between the legs of the colossus, doubtless concealed by the armor.
[68]What follows is from Du Troncy's *Suytte*. There is an odd confusion here. The *Discours* ends with the printers' *feu*; at the beginning of the *Suyette*, Du Troncy says he will take up from the *triomphes* of M. Nectair [sic], 'where I left off,' and proceeds with the *feux* of April 30 and May 4, 14, and 15, ending with tapering typography on p. 16. But p. 17 begins anew with a complaint that the printers had been so slow with the *Discours* that another description had appeared first, and Du Troncy had hardly been persuaded not to withdraw his manuscript. Nevertheless, he will now continue from the printers' *feu*, 'where I left off,' and he proceeds to describe the *triomphes* of M. Neictar [sic]. This evidently was intended to be an appendix to the *Discours* and not to the *Suytte*.
At the end of the *Suytte*, some verses entitled *Vray régime de santé* (extracted by Baudrier 4.327) are an imitation of Martial 10.47: 'Vitam quae faciant beatiorem . . .'

trumpets, and hautboys made Du Troncy think of Salmoneus. A week later, May 14 (Whitsunday), there were several *triomphes*. That in the Place Saint-Esprit took the form of a large *pomme* covered with pine cones and filled with *petereaux*. Within it was a white dove (the Holy Spirit) attached to the escutcheon of France. On ledges round about were four female statues: Faith holding out a *coronne celeste* and a heart; Hope holding a vine branch and a sun; Charity embracing two infants; and Concord having in one hand a scepter with a stork perched on it, and in the other two crows and an olive branch. Du Troncy read: Concord between princes, inspired by the Holy Ghost and the three theological Virtues.[69] The *pomme* burst asunder in fireworks, with such a concussion as to rock the houses nearby and deafen the spectators. Du Troncy was reminded of the cataracts of the Nile. Meanwhile the dove was seen to rise and sink at intervals, moving its wings realistically.

Most of the river shows had taken place on the placid Saône. The last, on Monday, May 15, rounding out a month of pageantry, was set in the rapid waters of the Rhone. This was Barthélemy Aneau's Hippopotamus, displayed by the dwellers in the Rue Neuve. The hippopotamus, 'according to Aristotle, Aelian, Pliny, Horapollo, and Pierius,' has 'the body and whinny of a horse, cloven hooves like an ox, two large curving tusks like a boar, and the tail of a fish.'[70] Unjust and incestuous, it is the symbol of extreme wickedness, 'as the learned Budé tells us at the beginning of the *Pandects*.'[71] One vessel, shaped like this creature, was ridden by Proteus ('a demon of storms') and symbolized War by land and sea. A second vessel simulated a Dolphin, and on it stood a lady with an olive branch, repre-

[69]Faith's crown is presumably the Christian's reward; the heart is a common symbol of concord (Valeriano, *Hieroglyphica*, p. 319.) For the vine branch and sun, Valeriano offers several possibilities; perhaps 'fertility' and 'the year,' but more likely 'the believer' ('I am the vine, ye are the branches') and God or Christ (the sun). A stork regularly symbolizes filial piety and gratitude, 'whence the sceptre of the gods has a stork for its chief adornment' (*The Hieroglyphics of Horapollo* 1.55, George Boas, trans. [New York, 1950]); Valeriano, *Hieroglyphica*, 17.157; Alciati, *Emb.* 30. Perhaps loyal gratitude to the king is the thought here. Two crows are a symbol of concord; Alciati, *Emb.* 38, *Concordiae symbolum* says they appear on the scepter of kings to show that princes stand or fall by the accord of their people. In *Horapollo* 1.8, 9; 2.40, two crows are the hieroglyphic for marriage (also a possible meaning for Cateau-Cambrésis), as they are in Valeriano, p. 191.

[70]Du Troncy's description of the '*cheval fluvial*' agrees verbally with that of Valeriano, *Hieroglyphica* 29.270, *De fluviali equo*, except for the tail *(apri cauda)*. See also Horapollo 1.56.

[71]Guillaume Budé, *Annotationes in Pandectas, Opera* (Basle, 1552), 3. (Gregg Press facs., 1967, p. 17). Horapollo and Valeriano also recognize that the hippopotamus signifies impiety.

senting Peace.[72] A third vessel, having the form of a Lion, carried a man dressed in ostrich plumes 'which in hieroglyphics symbolize Justice.'[73] He also carried sword and balances. And 'sur le dernier dudict lyon' was a nest of halcyons, constructed of vine branches and wheat spikes, signifying that in peace there is plenty.[74] The Hippopotamus was in the center, keeping the Dolphin and the Lion apart. About seven in the evening, it was set afire and burnt, Proteus and all, with such fury that Du Troncy thought it might dry up the Rhone. The remains floated away on the swift current, and War being thus banished, the Lion and the Dolphin drew together, shooting flames from their throats. As they met, the lady Peace passed over from the Dolphin to the Lion, and Peace and Justice kissed one another. In fact, improving on the Psalmist, they ended the allegory by performing a dance.

Gay it was, on the surface hopeful; and it chills the heart to think what different scenes Lyons was soon to exhibit. Just two years after his Peace and Justice had embraced, Barthélemy Aneau, mistaken for a Protestant, would be murdered in the Corpus Christi riots; and there was worse to come. Cateau-Cambrésis was a *triomphe* fraught with more than *petereaux*.

From the practical poems we turn to the verbal ones.

Probably at the time when the peace was proclaimed, Ronsard published two poetical pamphlets, *La Paix, au Roy*, and *Chant de*

[72]The dolphin is a suitable bearer of Peace because it is 'philanthropos' and 'addresse l'ancre des navigans en tormente' during storms. Aneau may have had in mind Alciati, *Emb.* 143, which expresses this idea. If so, he may also have intended the moral of the emblem, that the good prince, like dolphin and anchor, procures the safety of his subjects. Du Troncy says the dolphin also alluded to the adjacent Dauphiné.

[73]The lion is well illustrated by Valeriano, *Hieroglyphica*, 1 (p. 12), Leo: *Justitiae cultus*, based on a Roman coin showing Justitia on one side and on the other a female figure leaning upon a lion, with the legend *Leonis humilitas*. For the ostrich plumes, see Horapollo 2.118: 'When they wish to indicate a man who distributes justice equally to all, they draw an ostrich wing; for the ostrich has its wings more equally balanced than any other bird.' Valeriano, *Hieroglyphica*, 25 (p. 230) says the same.

[74]The halcyons' nest is surely derived directly from Alciati, *Emb.* 178, *Ex pace ubertas*, which pictures the nest made *ex spicis* and *palmite vitis*. Alciati's moral is that the year will be bountiful if the king imitates this bird of peace. Note that the dolphin and the halcyons draw the rough waters of the Rhone into the 'hieroglyphic.' Very likely the lion, king of beasts, and the dolphin also allude to Henri II and the Dauphin (who was associated with the Peace of Cateau): King and Dauphin, bringing peace and justice, have, like the dolphin and the halcyons, secured safety and prosperity in the rough waters of 1559. Perhaps further if the dolphin glances at the Dauphiné, the lion suggests Lyons. Du Troncy says, however, that the lion was turned towards the part of the city that looks towards Savoy, as though he was at least thinking of Philippe Emmanuel.

liesse, au Roy. Of the two, the *Chant de liesse* is a relatively slight af-
fair, obviously struck off at the moment; in sprightly rhythm it con-
trasts the present scenes of rejoicing with the gloomy scenes of war
and felicitates the king on his children, his sister, and having the ser-
vices of the Guises and Montmorency. The poem *La Paix* is a more
serious work, a companion piece to the *Exhortation pour la Paix*,
which it resembles in conscious rhetorical construction and in the
commonplaces it exploits. These handy commonplaces gave the
Renaissance poet some of the advantages of an *improvvisatore*, and it
would not have been impossible for Ronsard to write *La Paix* (9,280
lines) between the moment when the peace was concluded (March
27) and the day it was proclaimed (April 7).[75] At the same time, *La
Paix* is closer to events—which had now crystallized—than the *Ex-
hortation* had been:

A future historian will record that Henri has been continuously at
war since he came to the throne, and, though sometimes beaten, has
won great advantages. Now let him cherish the peace made for him by
the Cardinal and Montmorency. Of this peace the poet will relate mar-
vels; and he tells of the ordering of the universe out of chaos, and the
chaining of Discord. When the sins of a people or the faults of a king
violate law and justice, God looses Discord upon them (description of
the horrors of war); but when, brought low, they acknowledge their
sins, He again sends Peace (description of the blessings of peace).
Therefore, Sire, be content with your empire. Since your hair is turning
grey,[76] attend to your royal household, wife and children; build your
Louvre; read a book; enjoy the chase; for glory is fleeting. Embrace
Peace, which is better than subduing Spain and England, and embrace
the Cardinal and Montmorency, who have made peace to your honor
and advantage. O Peace, daughter of God, banish war to infidel lands;
curse him who breaks your bond; bless him who maintains it; and grant
that Henri be virtuous and lend his mind to things of importance, imi-
tating his father in the love of knowledge.[77]

[75]Laumonier (9.xiii) assumed that Ronsard was with the Court at Villers-Cotteret
when the peace was concluded and would learn the news at once. But we do not know
the day on which *La Paix* was published. The appearance of the *Chant de liesse* in a
separate *plaquette* suggests to me that Ronsard had nothing else ready on April 7 and
that therefore the *Chant* was published immediately and *La Paix* followed some days
later. See below, n. 76. Printed with *La Paix* was a *Bienvenue* for Montmorency's final
return about April 1, lauding him as the peacebringer.

[76]Henri was forty years old on March 31. Here Ronsard emphasizes his age,
whereas in the *Chant de liesse* 107−8 he minifies it: 'De sur ton chef encor n'est retour-
née / De l'age tien la quatrieme année'; cf. Laumonier, 9.xv.

[77]The last lines seem to support Laumonier's suggestion that in 'lire dans un livre'
(226) there may be a 'conseil déguisé.' Writers of the time were open in expressing
regret for the days of King Francis; even Du Troncy makes the point (above, p. 104).

Following the pattern of a deliberative declamation, this poem begins with a *captatio benevolentiae*, states a 'proposition,' offers proofs, and ends with a recapitulation in the form of a prayer. Ronsard is trying to 'persuade' the king to accept and abide by the peace (which he knew very well that Henri had desired). When the poem appeared in April, this 'persuasion' was really a consolation; it is hinted that the king does not like the peace any better than others do, but the poet urges him to accept it, since peace is good in itself. Nothing could be more courtly, both putting the king in a good light and deferring to the opinion of the Guises whose favor Ronsard was doing all he could to attract at this time.[78]

Du Bellay seems to have found it harder to rejoice in the peace of Cateau-Cambrésis. His quatrains addressed to the various personages seem formal and dry, while those entitled *Sur la Paix et sur les mariages* rather wearily repeat points from his earlier poem on the truce of 1555: The kings deserve the name of Augustuses; their deeds will be engraved in hearts rather than in marble; they have 'conquered themselves'; and (rather better) the fruit of the laurel is bitter, but the fruit of the olive is sweet.[79]

Marc-Claude de Buttet admired and imitated Ronsard, and in turn had his approval; it is curious to note therefore that just as his *Ode* follows in lyric form the motivation of Ronsard's rhetorical *Exhortation*, another ode, addressed to the king and written just after the signing of the treaty, similarly parallels Ronsard's poem *La Paix*.[80] Like *La Paix* it celebrates at length Henri's prowess in war, with the gaining of Boulogne and Calais, but prefers him as a hero of peace:

> Car qui donte soi-mesme, et commande à son ire,
> Est bien un plus grand roi et plus digne d'empire
> Qu'un qui massacre tout et par flamme et par sang—

Yet Henri's daily program included some reading (Batiffol, p. 119), and Ronsard's list of injunctions otherwise names things that Henry enjoyed. As a member of the Court Ronsard would know. At all events, Henri's *bindings* are said to surpass those of all other French kings (Louis Michon, *La Reliure française* [Paris, 1951], pp. 61–73).

[78]The difficulties that Laumonier (9.xii–xiii) makes about the composition of this poem seem to me mostly illusory, being based on his gratuitous notion that its persuasive character might reflect a moment, say in February, when Henri may have been wavering about making further concessions. Ronsard, we may be sure, would never have written such a poem on such an occasion. The explanation offered above surely does more justice to his tact as a Court poet.

[79]Cf. Juvenal 6.180, 'plus aloë quam mellis habent.' Du Bellay's poem was published in 1559. See 'L'imprimeur au lecteur' in *Œuvres françoises de Joachim Du Bellay*, Charles Marty-Laveaux, ed., Pléiade (Paris, 1948), 2.464. His *Discours* of 1555 was also republished in 1559.

[80]*Œuvres poétiques* 2.3. This poem seems not to have been published at the time.

a commonplace that recalls Du Bellay and Jacques Peletier du Mans. Like Ronsard again, Buttet was close to Marguerite de Valois, being officially her 'mathematician and secretary,' and moreover he was a Savoyard. His *Epithalame aux nosses de . . . Emanuel Philibert . . . et de Marguerite de France* seems to have been published (by Robert Estienne) in advance of the marriage, probably in June.[81]

It was now also, doubtless in April, that André Wechel published Remy Belleau's *Chant pastoral de la Paix*, though its carefully wrought style and the paucity of topical allusion suggest that Belleau had been preparing it before the actual proclamation of the peace. It consists of a hymn to Peace for which a dramatic pastoral setting is devised, and excels in its touches of picturesque imagery.

The shepherds, Bellin (Belleau) and Thoinet (Antoine de Baïf) are lamenting the miseries of the war, when Perot (Ronsard) appears upon the scene bringing glad news of peace. Thereupon Thoinet sings as a prayer ('Estendant les deux bras, alloit ainsi priant') the 'Chant de la Paix' proper:

> Ie te salue, ô Paix fille de Dieu,
> Fille de Dieu, tu sois la bien venue,
> La belle Astrée et Themis la chenue
> Sont maintenant de retour en ce lieu,

continuing to exalt Peace as the creator of the universe from chaos and as the *summum bonum* of mankind on earth. All nature flourishes on her return. Commerce is resumed:

> C'est toy, c'est toy qui fais parler les ports
> Divers langage . . .

Discord and War are chained; law prevails; peace promotes marriages, love, all pleasures. The harvester reposes—

> Le moissonneur par toy librement dort
> Dans sa moisson, la main sur la faucille.

Let empty helmets be covered with cobwebs and armor turned into ploughshares. Let any rancor that remains be spurned away to Thrace and to the Turks. Up, shepherds! engrave Peace on the trees, make annual sacrifice to Pan. Thoinet himself will fashion two altars of turf for the two who have saved us by virtues and eloquence [the Cardinal] and by the wisdom of age [Montmorency]. There he will yearly sing a song

[81]Ibid. 1.135; also an ode, ibid. 2.12.

of blessing. The *chant* ended, Perot has the last word, complimenting the song and drawing attention to the fall of evening.

The end is adapted directly from Virgil, but the Virgilian tonality throughout is doubly distilled, since as a whole the poem is founded on Navagero's *Damon*.[82] We may note the propriety of placing the announcement of the peace in the mouth of Perot-Ronsard, in allusion surely to Ronsard's *Exhortation* and general leadership in the poetry of Cateau-Cambrésis, and the equal propriety of giving the central song to Thoinet-Baïf, since Baïf's peace poem of 1550 was famous. The *Chant pastoral de la Paix* was Belleau's first essay in the bucolic form that we associate with his name, and hence it later took its place at the beginning of his *Bergerie*, with such slight modifications (for its historical references are few) as would shift the intention from the Spanish war and Henri II to the civil wars and Charles IX.[83]

[82]Above, pp. 77–78. The dependence on Navagero was pointed out by Sándor Eckhardt (*Remy Belleau* [Budapest, 1917], p. 127), who further suggests that the details of the *chant* proper are inspired by Secundus' *De pace Cameraci*. The coincidence of commonplaces hardly proves this second point, as our wider view of the Renaissance peace poems shows; but Eckhardt is among the few who have noted the existence of the type ('Le genre de l'hymne à la Paix avait . . . une famille étendue dans la poésie néo-Latine,' p. 129). The verbal parallels between Belleau and Ronsard are cited by Marcel Raymond (*L'Influence de Ronsard sur la poésie française* [Paris, 1927] 1.176–77); '*Chant*, Je te salue, ô Paix fille de Dieu, Fille de Dieu tu sois la bienvenue . . . ;' Ronsard, *Ode*, 'Je te salue, heureuse Paix / Je te salue et resalue'; Belleau, *Avant-entree du Roi* (1559), '. . . et que *l'araigne ourdisse* / Sa fine trame es vides *morions*: / Que des brassarts et des corps de cuirasse / Le fer s'allonge *en la pointe d'un soc* . . .' Ronsard (1559, a few weeks before Belleau), *Exhort.* 'Au croc vos *morryons* pour jamais soyent liez / Autour desquelz *l'araigne* enfillant de ses piedz / Y *ourdisse* ses retz . . . / Reforgez pour jamais le bout de vostre estoc / Le bout de vostre pique *en la pointe d'un soc*.'

[83]The first edition of the *Bergerie* (1565) included from the *Chant pastoral* only the first part of the introductory dialogue on the miseries of the time, spoken by Francin and Charlot instead of Bellin and Thoinet, and this was followed by an *Ode à la Paix* which later became the *Ode à la Royne pour la Paix*. The whole eclogue reappeared in the definitive *Bergerie* of 1572, with speakers Bellot and Tenot to go with Perot, and the *Ode à la Royne* at the end as a second hymn to peace. The variations in the *Chant pastoral* between 1559 and 1572, as recorded by Charles Marty-Laveaux (*Œuvres poétiques de Remy Belleau* [Paris, 1878], 1.342–45), show that, from a historical point of view, it was only necessary to omit a passage referring to the Spanish soldiery; to alter 'ces deux roys' to 'ce grand Roy des François'; and—the principal change—to rededicate the two altars. In 1559 the first altar was for the Cardinal of Lorraine ('à cellui dont les vertus . . . et la faconde ont rendu. . . . Du tout bonheur nos terres heretieres') and for Montmorency ('à celuy dont la sage viellesse,' and so on). In 1572 the first altar is given to Charles IX ('L'un à ce Roy'), and the second 'à celuy dont la sage *jeunesse*, / Le meur conseil, la vaillance et le bras / A du haut ciel tiré ceste déesse'—a description probably intended for the young and active leader of the Catholic party, the Duke of Anjou. The peace thus celebrated in 1572 therefore was probably the Pacification of Saint-Germain of August 8, 1570. Since the *Ode à la Royne* remained textually unaltered from the edition of 1565, Charles IX is curiously

Jacques Béreau of Poitou also chose the new bucolic form to celebrate the peace of Cateau-Cambrésis, influenced in this choice no doubt by Belleau. His poem only appeared in his *Eglogues* of 1565: *Eglogue X, De la paix publiée au moys d'avril, l'an mil cinq cens cinquante et neuf, entre les trespuissans Henry et Philippe, roys de France et d'Espagne*.[84] It has a great deal of charm. Beginning with a long but pleasing invocation of the pastoral Muses, Béreau touches on most of the topics of the *laudatio pacis*—shepherds, laborers, merchants free from care, justice administered, armor gathering dust—always returning to the delights of Nature, and ends with an unusually long expansion on the services and 'meure sagesse' of Montmorency, to whose glory the poet proposes to build an altar surmounted with a marble statue of the hero. The influence of Belleau is evident, and Béreau has woven into his texture reminiscences of other poets ancient and modern.[85]

Among the poems just described, only those of Ronsard and Belleau's eclogue seem to have appeared soon after the proclamation of the peace. Others described below were published, or at least ready, at this time, as the dates of their *privilèges* suggest. But these are not poems by poets of Ronsard's immediate circle. Neither Dorat nor Estienne Jodelle produced anything for Cateau-Cambrésis, nor, it seems, did Baïf.[86] To be sure, Du Bellay's *Discours au Roy . . . trefve de 1555* was republished by Morel in 1559. Yet Jacques Grévin, whose *Chant de Ioie de la Paix* has the earliest possible *privilège* (April 8),[87] appears to know that this circle is preparing something and has already published something on the peace; for 'brigade' in the following lines can hardly fail to refer to the 'Brigade':

> Et suivant la troupe heureuse,
> La brigade industrieuse
> Favorite d'Apolon,
> Qui ia gaillarde s'appreste

---

younger ('tendre jeunesse') in it than in the rehandled eclogue ('dont les vertus entiers / Et la vaillance').

[84]*Œuvres poétiques*, J. Hovyn de Tranchère and R. Guyet, eds. (Paris, 1884), p. 83.

[85]Cf. appendix below. See also Hulubei, *L'Eglogue en France*, pp. 441–42. The mention of Montmorency alone, without the Cardinal of Lorraine, may betray a rehandling of the eclogue before publication in 1565. Other poems by Béreau on the events of 1562–63 will be mentioned below.

[86]See below, pp. 151–53. Jodelle wrote an *Epithalame* for the marriage of Marguerite and the Duke of Savoy in June.

[87]*Chant de Ioie de la Paix faicte entre le Roi de France Henri II et Philippe Roi d'Espagne* (Paris: Martin l'Homme, 1559) [BN Rés Yf. 2958]. *L'Olympe de Jacques Grévin . . . ensemble les autres euvres politiques . . .* (Paris: R. Estienne, 1560) [BN Rés. Yf. 2958].

> A descrire la conqueste
> De la PAIX sur Mars felon:
> Et qui a ia la nouvelle
> De la celeste pucelle
> Par la douceur de ses vers
> Annoncée à l'univers,
>
> Ie viens d'une humble caresse
> Saluer ceste déesse.

Grévin's knowledge was at first hand; before his poem there stands a sonnet to him by Nicolas Denisot. What he says is that the 'brigade' is getting ready to describe the peace and has already announced it. This may well mean that on April 8 or soon after, only Ronsard's *Chant de liesse* had appeared, but that Grévin knew of Ronsard's *La Paix* and perhaps Belleau's eclogue as in preparation. The title, length, and lyric character of Grévin's *Chant de Ioie* make it the exact parallel of Ronsard's *Chant de liesse*.

The poem begins with a long sentence running through three stanzas:

Had we defeated Spain or Flanders us, the victorious side would not have won such honor as both now win, for it is less glorious to conquer a foe than to gain a friend. Following the 'brigade,' Grévin, who has sung of war,[88] will weave laurels for the altar of peace: her cornucopia will banish poverty. There follows a series of contrasts between peace and war, somewhat like those in Ronsard's *Chant de liesse*.[89] Next comes an elaborate passage (sta. 21–26) putting a curse on the foes of peace and blessing her friends.[90] And the poem ends with a prayer to Peace, in which, as throughout, Grévin pleasingly maintains his individual note as a love poet:[91]

[88]Presumably a reference to his *Regretz de Charles d'Austriche* of 1558.

[89]Verbally one may compare the anaphora, 'Au lieu de donner bataille . . . Au lieu de croiser les picques,' with Ronsard: 'Quel plaisir est-ce . . . Quel plaisir est-ce. . . .'

[90]Most of the parallels between Grévin's poem and Ronsard's *La Paix*, offered by Lucien Pinvert, *Jacques Grévin* (Paris, 1899), p. 212, and by Marcel Raymond, *Bibliographie critique de Ronsard* (Paris, 1927), p. 82, to suggest that Grévin was influenced by this poem, are unconvincing, being commonplaces of peace poetry and not verbal parallels; but the execration of the warmonger, though a commonplace, is less usual in peace poetry and appears in Ronsard's *La Paix* 263–68. Grévin may have seen *La Paix*, but it is at least equally possible that what appears as a passing touch in Ronsard's poem but is impressively developed in Grévin's may have been suggested to Ronsard by Grévin and not vice versa. Ronsard, however, echoes Ps. 109: 'Que ses enfans banis puissent mourir de faim': 'Let his children be vagabonds and beg their bread.'

[91]The *Chant de Ioie* was included in Grevin's *Olympe* of the next year (above, n. 87), with some alterations; e.g., he makes the reference in sta. 26, 'ceux qui l'ont moien-

> Faiz entre Espagne et la France
> Un si ferme aliance
> Que Mars n'y puisse glisser:
> Faiz aussi PAIX bien heureuse
> Qu'OLIMPE ma rigoureuse,
> Qui tient ma vie en langueur,
> Mette fin à sa rigeur.

One of the more interesting literary figures of the time, and one unfairly neglected by modern scholarship, is Guillaume Des Autels, the valued friend of Ronsard, and in his own words 'ung non mauvais poëte.'[92] Known since 1550 as a sonneteer and love poet, he came forward, after some years' silence, as a political poet with two pamphlets on the peace of 1559. The first, a *Remonstrance au Peuple françoys*, was published by Wechel in Paris, presumably in April or even earlier.[93] The consolatory note that we detect in Ronsard's *La Paix* and elsewhere here sounds as an outright defense of the king against criticism that the author, a follower of the Guises, evidently thought was to be expected in the circumstances. He celebrates monarchy as the best form of government, the French kings as the only existing descendants of the gods, and Henri as putting aside his own advantage to make peace for the good of France (f.6ᵛ):

> Quelle condition, peuple (comme tu sçais)
> A refusé ton Roy, pour te donner la Paix?
> Combien il a voulu, pour à tes vœux complaire,
> Quitter de son bon droict? que n'a il voulu faire?

The *Remonstrance* is followed by an *Eloge de la Paix à Pierre de Ronsard*, an *Eloge de la Trefve à Joachim du Bellay*, and an *Eloge de la Guerre à Estienne Jodelle*. The first hopes that the princes may be moved by Ronsard's *Exhortation pour la Paix* and tells how Des Autels has seen portrayed on an antique shield the blessings of peace that

---

née,' explicit for Montmorency and 'les princes Lorrains' (Prinvert, *Jacques Grévin*, p. 212). Grévin followed up his *Chant de Ioie* with a *Pastorale* for the royal marriages in June (Paris: Martin l'Homme, 1559).

[92]Hans Hartmann, *Guillaume des Autels (1529–1582?), ein französischer Dichter und Humanist* (Zurich, 1907); *Influence*, 1.81–90. A modern edition of Des Autels's poems would be welcome [Margaret L. M. Young, *Guillaume des Autelz: A Study of his Life and Works* (Geneva, 1961)].

[93]*Remonstrance au peuple françoys de son devoir en ce temps, envers la majesté du roy. A laquelle sont adioustez troys Eloges, De la paix, De la trefve, De la guerre* (Paris: Wechel, 1559) [BN Rés. Ye. 982].

will be enjoyed if Celt and Iberian once come to terms.[94] The *Praise of Truce* begins by noting that the truce of 1555 that Du Bellay had sung of while in Rome at the papal court had been lost to France through the necessity of going to the pope's assistance;[95] but Truce now comes again, and Des Autels will praise her. As Mars was resting briefly from the Battle of the Gods and the Titans, he was visited by Venus, who subsequently bore him a daughter Truce. The remarkable resemblance of Truce to Peace was at once observed by the Graces, yet in fact she has much of her father in her, as is shown in the way she spends her time, largely in preparations for war. In Jodelle's narrative of the *Inscriptions* for his unlucky masque intended to celebrate the taking of Calais, he declares that he always had wished to be a soldier. Alluding to that, Des Autels dedicates his *Praise of War* to him. He dreams that, guided by Apollo, he sails to Machyme, the island city of Bellona, and views the sights; but his praise is really vituperation, and he leaves the subject to Jodelle, to resume for his own part 'Les immortels labeurs des Grecz et des Rommains.'

Des Autels's second, and more important, publication on the peace of Cateau, *La Paix venue du ciel*, did not appear until July, and then was issued by Plantin in Antwerp.[96] In the interval the poet had betaken himself to Flanders, where he thought he now saw

---

[94]Note the future tense. Raymond, *Bibliographie*, p. 56, thinks that Des Autels probably refers to Ronsard's poem *La Paix*; but *La Paix* views the peace as concluded, while Des Autels seems to refer to a poem that *may yet* induce the kings to make peace, and this would naturally be the *Exhortation*. (To be sure, the *Exhortation* was addressed to soldiers, not princes, but see its final invocation to Peace.) Des Autels says (f.8ᵛ):

> Veullent les Dieux, Ronsard, que les Princes, qui lisent
> Maintefois tes beaux vers, et à bon droict les prisent,
> En lisant ceux, lesquels nagueres tu as faictz
> Pour leurs cœurs endurciz inciter à la Paix,
> Ayent par tes raisons aussi douces que sages
> Et si tost et si bien amolly leurs courages,
> Qu'ayans de leurs subiectz, et d'eux mesmes pitié,
> Ilz changent leur querelle en constante amitié.

This is also the view of Laumonier, 10.349. Of the several poetical 'shields' available for imitation, Des Autels had the originality to choose Hesiod's *Shield of Heracles*, thus giving a somewhat novel turn to his praises of peace. See below, p. 178.

[95]Above, p. 92.

[96]*La Paix venue du ciel, dediée à Monseigneur l'Evesque d'Arras. Avec le Tombeau de l'Empereur Charles V Cesar, tousiours Auguste, dedié et présenté à la Majesté du Roy son fils* (Antwerp: Plantin, 1559); *privilège* dated Brussels, July 13, 1559. I use a microfilm of Paris, BN Rés. p. Ye. 389. This copy has the owner's inscription, 'François Rasse des Neus, chirurgien à Paris,' on whom see Pierre de Nolhac, *Ronsard et l'humanisme* (Paris, 1921), p. 249. The *privilège* covers Des Autels's *Encomium Galliae Belgicae*, which was also published by Plantin at this time.

hope of realizing his ambitions at the Court of Philip II; for Article 18 of the treaty had given his native Charolois to Philip, who was therefore now his king; and besides, the king's adviser, Antoine Perrenot, Bishop of Arras, was his countryman.[97] The poem is dedicated to the Bishop, who is earnestly requested to commend the poet to the king. The point of time assumed is that of the signing of the treaty, and the narrative relates to the conference; there is no allusion to subsequent events, and it is easy to imagine that the poem was originally composed before Des Autels went to Brussels.[98]

Peace, who was with us before, has come again. Formerly the god of Wealth spread his bounty abroad in France and Flanders; but all was ruined by the avarice and sins of men. So long as the three daughters of Jupiter and Themis, 'Bonne Loy et Iustice et la Paix florissante,' held sway, the gods still visited mankind, but when man sowed the earth with crimes, Justice fled to her father's throne and induced him to punish them 'pour leurs propres pechez ou pour ceus de leurs princes.'[99] Yet God is still open to prayer if a just remnant can be found. Now Ate stirs up contention, and Peace also departs to her father's side, while Allecto, rising from hell, secretly slips a serpent from her hair into the bosom of Europe. If the poet had a hundred tongues he could not describe the horrors of war, which would have continued still longer had not * Henri and Philip, the just remnant, been imbued with faith, and the limping Prayers gone up to entreat Jupiter's mercy. Conciliated by the Prayers, and by the saints Madeleine and Clothilde, Jupiter bids Peace return to earth, taking with her her sister Astraea, the Graces, Concord, Amalthea, and two Hymenaei. But Peace cannot descend to earth without assistance. Mercury is instructed to attach to her ivory car six golden chains, and to place their other ends in the hands of six mortals—the Cardinal of Lorraine, Montmorency, Saint-André, the Bishop of Arras, the Prince of Orange, and the Duke of Alba. A large part of the poem is occupied by Mercury's travels—over the Apennines and Rome

[97]Hartmann, *Des Autels*, pp. 100–101. Des Autels's hopes were not fulfilled; there is no evidence that the Bishop paid any attention to him, or that the *Tombeau* of Charles V, published with the *Paix*, made any impression; he returned to Paris before the end of the year. Hartmann imagines that he was already in the Netherlands when the treaty was being negotiated and that he may even have been secretary to one of the plenipotentiaries or have represented the interests of the Charolois at the conference; but he offers no evidence.

[98]In view of his attachment to the Guises, it may possibly be significant that Mercury, with God's commands, comes first to the Cardinal of Lorraine and the French delegates.

[99]Compare Ronsard in a corresponding development (*La Paix* 79): 'Quand les pechez d'un peuple, ou les fautes d'un Roy . . .'; but see also below, p. 176. (Des Autels is translating Hesiod in the verse, but see also Ronsard, *Hymne de la Justice*, Laumonier 8.58–59.)

('qui par ung titre double / Se dict Royne du monde, et n'est que le trouble'), to Paris ('qui seul pourroit faire ung monde entierement'), where he hands the end of a chain to the Cardinal, thence to Granvelle, Alba, and William of Orange in Philip's camp, and finally to Montmorency in prison at Audenare, and Saint-André at Breda. He departs, and

> Les deputez soigneus à leur œuvre entrepris
> Suent tous en tirant ce beau char de haut pris.

So Peace is brought to earth. And who are these two? They are the Hymenaei, who will unite Spain with France and France with Savoy.* The poem ends with an invocation to Peace and an appeal to peoples and kings to cherish her and her sisters, for so long as Bonne Loy and Justice are present, the world will have La Paix as well.[100]

For Jean Sève of Lyons,[101] the peace of Cateau-Cambrésis seemed to be entirely the work of the Cardinal of Lorraine; neither Montmorency nor any of the other delegates is so much as mentioned in his long poem *La Ruine et trébuchement de Mars*.[102] Indeed the point of view of this poem is rather the beginning of the negotiations in 1558 than their completion in 1559, though the outcome is known and the poem probably was not published until the peace was proclaimed. The 'invention' is in *rhétoriqueur* style, and though Astraea and her companion abstractions are reminiscent of Hesiod and Aratus, their drama is played out on the plot of the mediaeval 'Daughters of God.'

[100]This description of Des Autels's poem between the asterisks is included in Hutton, *Essays*, pp. 230–31.
[101]A cousin of Maurice Scève; he became prior of Montrottier in this year 1559 and died in 1560; see V.-L. Saulnier, "Deux œuvres" 265–79, with references. The present poem, addressed to the Cardinal of Lorraine, is represented by its author as in a measure the counterpart of the poem he had published in 1558 celebrating the taking of Calais by the Cardinal's brother, *Discours des louanges . . .*, a book brought to light by Saulnier. It is referred to at the beginning of *La Ruine* and again in the last lines of the poem.
[102]*La Ruine et trebuchement de Mars dieu des guerres aux enfers et de Discorde, pour la paix receüe entre les Princes Chrestiens, par Jean Seve Lyonnoys* (Lyons: J. Saugrain, 1559) [Versailles, Bibliothèque Municipale]. Neither the title page nor the volume itself justifies the addition: *avec le discours du grand triumphe . . .*, as given, for example, by Saulnier, "Deux œuvres," p. 266. These words seem to designate Du Troncy's pamphlet *Le Discours* (above, n. 57), and their addition is perhaps due to the error of some early bibliographer. The pages are numbered; on p. 2 a sonnet in monorhyme, *Les furies de Mars . . . et les graces d'Astree deesse de Paix*; pp. 3–18, *La Ruine* in 470 verses; pp. 19–21, *A Astree deesse de Paix, chant royal* in ten six-line stanzas; p. 22, a sonnet *A Monseigneur le duc de Guyse*. Each item is followed by the motto: *In utrumque paratus*. There is no *privilège*.

After complimenting the Cardinal and the Duke of Guise, Sève begins his narration: The Golden Age knew neither iron nor the god Mars; both are the offspring of Jupiter and Juno, who realized that mankind would deserve such means of chastisement. As soon as born, Mars flew to hell, where he was armed with iron and, by the counsel of the infernal deities, married to Discord. At the head of these same deities, he came to earth bringing War, Plague, and Famine, with the intention of overthrowing Jupiter and taking his place. Jupiter crushes Mars' followers, but spares his son, and Mars continues to stir up strife—for example, he induces his wife to throw the golden apple and start the Trojan War. Astraea and her sister Justice warn mankind against giving in to Mars, but their warning is unheeded, and at last they take flight to their father Jupiter and by their accusations rouse his wrath against men.[103] Jupiter calls the gods to assembly and declares his intention of destroying mankind. At this point, his daughter Clementia pleads for them, but her prayers would have been unavailing if Themis had not taken her part. Themis reminds Jupiter of the secret she alone shares with him. It gives her assurance

> De voir un iour florir en paix la race humaine:
> Le destin fera naistre un grand Henry en France. . . .
> Ce bon Roy cherira de sa race un bon Prince,
> Qui sera Cardinal. . . .

At the birth of Charles of Lorraine, Justice will descend to dwell in his body, and though Mars will rage yet a while, Astraea also will eventually come to him and move him to make peace between the kings of France and Spain. The remainder of the poem shows the fulfillment of this prophecy. The Cardinal gets Henri's leave to go to Flanders and negotiate a peace. Peace is made. The Cardinal seizes Mars and Discord and drags them bound before the two kings who promptly join with him in strangling them:

> Et pui les atachant d'une puissante corde
> Et de mille cordons et fors liens de fer,
> Les [avez] trebuchez au plus parfond d'Enfer.

[103]They are rejected by men,

> Si quelles n'oysent plus venir fair leurs plaintes
> Le cler iour, mais de nuit elles furent contraintes
> De crier par les boys d'une voix lamentable
> Du rond de l'univers la perte miserable:
> O disoyent elles, vous boys, roches, et campagnes,
> Fontaines et ruisseaux descendans des montagnes,
> Escoutez nostre voix.

This passage is perhaps founded on Aratus, *Phaenomena* 115–18: Astraea mingled little with the men of the Silver Age, 'but came from the echoing hills in the evening, alone.' Note that Peace is called Astraea by Sève throughout.

Not everyone had attuned himself to the tonality of the new poets or had forgotten the older *topoi* of the peace argument. Indeed more than one old poem was brought out anew to grace the occasion. At Lyons, Jean Saugrain published Molinet's *Le Testament de la Guerre*, without the author's name.[104] We have already mentioned the combination of Corrozet's *Retour de la Paix* and Sagon's *Chant de la Paix* to form a small volume entitled *La Resiouissance du Traicté de la Paix en France*, published in Paris by Olivier de Harsy. The *privilège* is of April 8, the *achevé d'imprimer* of April 10, and the tailoring of the two pieces to form a continuous composition suited to the occasion shows the marks of haste.[105] But even some quite new poems were styled on the old rhetorical pattern. Such is the *Colloque social* of Jean d'Aubusson de la Maison-Neuve. Of this writer, despite his well-sounding name, nothing whatever is known save what can be gleaned from his writings, and, from his epithet, *berruyer*, that his native province was Berry (region of Bourges).[106] He was, between 1556 and 1563, the author of a series of poetical publications on various events and doubtless thereby aimed at notice and preferment.[107] Presumably as soon as the peace was announced he set to work on his *Colloque social de Paix, Justice, Miséricorde et Vérité*, but only secured his *privilège* a month or so later, on May 5. The poem was printed by Martin l'Homme in Paris, and reprinted immediately by Saugrain in Lyons.[108]

[104]*Le Testament de la Guerre, qui a regné sur la terre. Avec la prophetie qui est escrite autour de la maison peinte d'or et d'azur en la rue Mercière. Ensemble deux belles chansons de la paix* (Lyons J. Saugrain, 1559) [BN Rés. Ye. 4892]. It was also published in Paris by 'Veuve de N. Buffet.' After Molinet's poem there is a 'dixain d'un citoyen de Lyon,' which announces that the prophecy of the good news of peace, written in 1555, will follow. But the Paris copy lacks both the prophecy and the two *chansons*.

[105] *La Resiouissance de la traicté de la paix en France, publiée le septiesme d'Apuril 1559* [BN Lb³¹.89]. See above, p. 87.

[106]François La Croix du Maine, *Bibliothèque françoise* (Paris, 1572), 1.41, 443; Du Verdier 2.456; Goujet, *Bibliothèque françoise* (Paris, 1741–56) 11.456; the biographical dictionaries add nothing, not even Alfred Gandilhon in the new *Dictionnaire de biographie française* (Paris, 1741–56), 4.314 (apparently an article 'Jean d'Aubusson' in a Bourges periodical *Annonces Berruyères* 13 [1838], cited by Gandilhon, offered nothing substantial).

[107]In 1556 the Paris publisher E. Denise printed his *Déploration* on the death of François Picard, 'doyen de Saint-Germain de Lauxerrois,' and his *Cantique* on the birth of Henri's daughter Victoire; in 1558 Martin l'Homme brought out his *Adieu des neuf Muses* on the marriage of the Dauphin and Mary Stuart, and in 1559 the poem on Cateau-Cambrésis which we notice; later in the same year *L'Excellence de trois dons celestes*, on the coronation of Francis II, was printed in Rouen (L'Oyselet and Blondel); and apart from some minor verses, his last publication was a *Cantique nubtial* for Léonor d'Orléans and Marie de Bourbon in 1563 (Paris, C. Blihart). See Catalogue of printed books of the BN and the authorities cited above, n. 106.

[108]*Colloque social de Paix, Iustice, Misericorde, et verité, pour l'heureux accord de tres Augustes, & tres magnanimes Roys, de France & d'Espaigne par Iean de la Maison-neufve, Ber-*

As allegorical figures, Justice, Mercy, and Truth (primarily religious Truth) are mediaeval rather than Renaissance associates of Peace and hark back to the Daughters of God. Their social conversation is interrupted by comments and narrative from the *Autheur*.

The *Autheur* relates that Peace, in sorrow at the wars, repaired to Mt. Olympus, and lifting her eyes to heaven prayed to her Father. In this *Oraison de Paix à Dieu son Père*, Peace regrets the Golden Age, which she describes,[109] grieves that Christian kings should fight, and begs that Henri and Philip should be united. God heard her, says the *Autheur*, and despatched Justice, Vérité, and Miséricorde to Mt. Olympus to assure her that He has united the kings. They find her there, dressed in white robes that are embroidered, not like those of Arachne with scenes of Jupiter's amours, which the author enumerates, but with the words of the Beatitudes. In the ensuing dialogue the Virtues touch on the blessings they will confer. 'Par mon moyen,' says Vérité:

> L'Eglise saincte en Iesus assemblée
> Ne sera plus d'heresie troublée. . . .
> Paix nostre seur en[110] sera l'entretien
> Pacifiant les troubles de l'eglise.

Miséricorde promises that with the cessation of God's wrath the three Estates will flourish:

> L'Eglise venerable
> Resplendira, la noblesse honorable
> Triomphera, et les loyaux marchans
> Ne craindront plus les perils et dangers
> Par l'union des hommes estrangers,
> Iuges esleus de Dieu, bien sagement
> Par équité feront leur iugement,
> Les laboureurs avec liesse immense
> Recueilleront les fruicts de leur semence.

They resolve to leave Olympus and visit the 'magnifique sejour' of the two kings, thinking first of Fontainebleau and then of Paris, where preparations are afoot for the marriage of Marguerite and the Duke of Savoy.[111] Justice remarks that they must also remain perpetually with

---

ruyer. A Paris chez Martin l'Homme . . . avec privilège (1559) [BN Rés. Ye. 1739]. For the Lyons reprint see Baudrier 4.323.

[109] See below, Ch. VI.

[110] 'Peuple chrestien.'

[111] Why is the marriage of Elizabeth and Philip not mentioned here? It is barely hinted at earlier in the poem. Doubtless the *berruyer* is especially interested in Marguerite (Duchess of Berry).

Philip, and Truth adds: 'with all princes friendly to the French,' especially the King and Queen of Navarre. Assuredly the Golden Age returns; the virtues and letters will flourish; it is time for poets to sing praises of the two monarchs, and of the Dauphin and his brothers and sisters, also of Catherine de Medici. Finally, *Paix en concluant* delivers a long discourse, attributing all to the grace of God:

> Ie recognoys la grace incomparable
> De ce grand Dieu et pere pitoyable,

and calling on the peoples to be united as the kings are, if they wish Justice, Mercy, Truth, and Peace (again the four Daughters) to remain with them; let them obey their rulers, as St. Paul teaches.[112]

The anonymous author of a *Discours moral de la paix* (235 verses) holds our attention, despite his unskilled rhymes, by his earnestness and a consciousness that beneath the rejoicing the troubles of France still remain.[113] His concession to poetical invention is to imagine that the three estates have been held in duress by Discord and are now set free by the peace:

> Discorde sceut nous saiser à la gorge,
> Nous attirant à sa puante loge
> (Comme captifz) pour noz pechez commis,
> Et s'efforçoit nous estrangler d'ennuytz.

In addressing Clergy, Nobility, and 'gens de Justice,' and in describing the plight of 'le populaire,' he discloses the harm done by Discord in tones of warning. The Church has been constrained to see 'nouveaulx esprits' leading large numbers 'soubz nouveaulx dictz'; the Nobility have allowed their soldiers to pillage the people; Magistrates have neglected to punish crimes, heedless of the cries of the people; the people themselves, the rope of Discord round their necks, have been 'batu, meurtry, bien souvent excité / A renoncer la foy tant saincte et bone,' while forced to pay triple interest on money borrowed to pay taxes *(tailles)*. Their betters being unable to help them because of Discord, the people

[112]The long poem is preceded by a sonnet by the author addressed to the two kings and is followed by one to Charles Duke of Lorraine; neither the Cardinal nor Montmorency is mentioned.

[113]*Discours moral de la paix faicte entre treshaultz, tresexcellentz, et trespuissans Princes, Henry (second du nom) treschrestien Roy de France, et Philippes Roy des Espaignes, et Françoys et Marie Roy et Royne d'Escosse, Dauphins de France, et Elizabeth Royne d'Angleterre* (Paris: Barbe Regnault, 1559) [BN Rés. Ye. 3867]. On verso of the title page is a large design of angels within a circle; at the end of the poem a king with crown and scepter. There follows a succinct account of the official celebrations in Paris.

have cried to heaven, and God has sent them the messengers of his
Grace:

> Ce grand triomphe de la sacrée descente
> De digne grace, plus que soleil luysante
> Fort estonna les Princes et leurs gens,
> Prestz à combattre, en leurs droicts defendans. . . .
> Et descendant soudain brise la corde
> Dont Chrestiens furent serfs de discorde.

We turn to glance at a group of Latin poems celebrating the same
events. It is perhaps remarkable that the more prominent Latin
poets, such as L'Hospital and Jean Dorat, remained silent. Yet the
poems about to be mentioned are not without literary and historical
interest, though their authors are obscure or unknown. They are on
the whole more outspoken than most of the French poems. Least
obscure of these writers is Elie André, who is remembered for his
Latin version of the *Anacreontea*.[114] His *Carmen de pace* was pub-
lished by Morel, presumably within a few days of the proclamation
of peace, since its tone is one of urgency and immediacy.[115] It is cu-
riously naïve and sincere, for example in its clumsy humor and in
its reference to the religious danger.

> Vernia, notable among advocates, you first brought me the news. Has
> indeed a reliable report at last reached Paris? Happy news, happy
> bearer, still happier the king, author of the peace, and his delegates!
> Why mention the king's daughters, his learned sister, and you, Cather-
> ine, blessed in your spouse, your children, . . . and not least in your hus-
> band's sister Marguerite? Her marriage, though delayed, we easily think
> not really late, since God turns it to the good of the world. No wonder if
> Pallas Athene[116] long remained unwed; her marriage is the wonder.
> And wedded to Mars! Could antiquity match that? . . . All the horrors
> of war—and then suddenly the recognition of their fault by those
> whose fault it was![117] That might mean the end of all war and be a sac-
> rifice acceptable to heaven. God, more merciful than man, has averted

[114]Elie André, a native of Bordeaux, was a philologist as well as a neo-Latin poet.
In addition to the *Anacreontea* he produced a translation, with the Greek text, of
Theodore Gaza, *Liber quartus De constructione orationis* (Paris, 1555). His Latin poems
are published in *DPG* 1.67–89.
[115]*Carmen de pace, ad Joan. Jacob. Verniam, D. Catharinae Augustae oratorem eximum*
(Paris: F. Morel, 1559) [BN Rés. m. Ye. 928]. I have not seen the original publication,
but have used the reprint in *DPG* 1.65–70. André also has (ibid.) a poem *In obitum
Gallorum regis Henrici Valesii* (N.p., n.d.).
[116]The name is regularly applied to Marguerite by the poets of the time.
[117]Reference to Henri's breaking of the Truce of Vaucelles?

the ruin of Europe. Under thy guidance, Greatest of Kings, the kings have found a peace that is worth the time and trouble it took to get it. But what is this joyful ringing of bells from Notre Dame, this shouting in the street? The window is near; I will see. O joyful sight! bonfires everywhere! It is peace, no doubt of it. Vernia, you were right. Glory to thee, heaven's King, who hast united the hearts of the kings and made one realm, one race, of the estranged peoples. Banquets replace battles; Mars weds Pallas; trumpets are hateful, lyres delightful. . . . The sun shines, birds sing more cheerily.[118] Even I, mute in the absence of peace, sing as best I can. I owe it to heaven, to my country, to the world, and to you, Henri, who with God's help have cut the Gordian knot: no peace ever was or ever shall be so difficult and desperate, but you alone overcame all obstacles. This glory is not inferior to victory in war. And now that you and your gallant son-in-law are free of war, may I soon see you crowning this glory with another. Hardly since the revered name of Christ first spread abroad has religion been so much called in question as today, when one man approves not what another approves in matters of worship. The plague daily and hourly increases, until no small revolution is now to be dreaded. Forbid this impious sin. So your two fathers would have wished; follow in their footsteps; hasten to the holy Council [Trent] without fraud or favor. But why do I foolishly urge Divinities to do their duty? Spare me, clement Deities, if I err.

An anxiety similar to that of André inspired the anonymous *Heracliti ad Democritum de pace elegia*.[119] This poem is a short sermon on the theme that there is no lasting peace without moral regeneration, and after the manner of sermons it seeks movement and interest from a figure, here that of building the Temple of Peace. The speaker is Heraclitus, the weeping philosopher.

I alone mourning in the midst of jubilation might perhaps be thought intolerable, were not the reasons of my grief so great. What reasons? I will tell. Ah, me! I fear that the grass cut down will grow green again and riot in its wonted soil. Unless the causes of war are cut away, wars

[118]   O laetam speciem! fiunt ignes quoque vulgo.
          Pax est haud dubie. verum mihi, Vernia, dixti . . .
          Mollia succedunt duris convivia pugnis.
          Mars laetos primus, Pallasque parant Hymenaeos:
          Oderunt lituos, citharis laetantur amoenis . . .
          Sol quoque tam nitida qui lustrat lampide terras.
          Ipsaeque volucres dulci nunc aëra cantu
          Permulcent . . .

cf. Rodrigo Sánchez (Butler, *Statecraft*, p. 107): 'At ubi serenum effulsit et pax est reddita terris . . . garriunt tunc aves . . .'

[119]Paris: Annet Briere, 1559. (The poem is attributed to Nicolas Chesneau [d. 1581].)

will recur. Let kings cease from ambition. . . . great ladies be modest in dress, . . . the pope's slippers be laden with less gold. Then will I confess that the *foundations* of Peace have been laid. Let judges be unbiased, lawyers cease from collusion, merchants be honest. Then I will rejoice to see rise the lasting *walls* of Peace. End the assault on truth, and put down novel doctrines; let the mysteries of faith be handled by men of pure heart, not by men of blood; let not the meaning of Scripture be discussed amid the cups (the sacred page hides them *ne vilescant*, that they may not be made common). Suppress footpads and paid assassins; restore honor to the laws. Then I will allow that a golden *roof* should be placed upon the walls of Peace. Assist the poor, the orphan, the widow. End every form of carnal lust. Let parents not be overindulgent; see that schools inculcate virtue; let schoolmasters not be greedy, and, though not altogether sparing the rod, let them remember to be men of culture and learning, not army sergeants. Let monks no longer be vagrant and impudent and gregarious. In short, let us all do the will of God. Thus when the causes of war are cut away, the pact of Peace will be firm, and her temple enduring. And on the roof I will set a cupola *(culmina)* filled with roses, where a Cock shall crow, announcing that fear is ended. Here with the cock an Eagle will consort, and the cock will not affright the Lion.[120] Garlands will I spread, and tend the temple. I will raise my head and grieve no more. Meanwhile, Democritus, blame not my weeping, if you would have me tolerate your gaiety.

One might guess that Heraclitus was a schoolmaster. Rather different reflections from his, yet not altogether different, sprang from the legal mind of Pierre Coustau, whose *Carmen de pace*, issued by the same publisher, was ready on April 12, four days after peace was proclaimed.[121] This very learned poem—if a choice vocabulary of rare words is the standard of learning—is chiefly remarkable for its arraignment of the pope as the source of all the trouble. It attains some length and proceeds in a series of elaborate 'set pieces.'

Coustau begins with a standard description of primordial chaos and its ordering into the variety of creation, in which, for example,

[120]France; the Empire; England. Note that lions proverbially fear cocks.
[121]*Petri Costalii de pace carmen* (Paris: Annet Briere, 1559) [BN Rés. 2646 microfilm]. The Epistle, to a Julianus Maester or Maestrus, is dated April 12. Coustau was a lawyer of Vienne; his legal *Adversaria*, written 1554, were printed in 1563, 1597, and (at Cologne) 1627 (Jöcher); his book of emblems, *Pegma*, was published by Bonhomme at Lyons in 1555, and in a French version by Lanteaume de Romieu, same date and publisher, and again in 1560 (Mario Praz, *Studies in Seventeenth Century Imagery* [Rome, 1954−74], 2.43). Presumably from the *Pegma* (which I have not seen) comes the generous selection of Coustau's epigrams in the *DPG* 1.817−32.

Visus est extemplo super aequora caerula delphin
Chrysophris, coracinus, elops, acipenser et umbra.

The creation was intended for the enjoyment of mankind; but Bellona brought back chaos with the horrors of war (a second set piece).[122] Yet after war, peace again returns. So, Henri, the beginnings of your reign lapped us in peace, you closed the doors of Janus; but the papacy foiled you. First Julius (III) attacked you and laid siege to friendly Parma.[123] Then there was peace; but in the midst of it came you, Caraffa,[124] and forced the French to take up arms, moved neither by the sanctity of oaths nor of religion nor by our perjury in breaking the peace [of Vaucelles].[125] If a local Italian army threatens Rome, you bring out Decretals, Nephews,[126] Excommunication, and call up the fiends of hell, instead of using your authority to promote peace. But you have plenty of temporal resources of your own, if you are bent on war. So, Duke of Guise, there was new work for you; you had to cross the Alps, . . . and hence many woes, including the carnage of Saint-Quentin. But you, Henri, have now recalled the angry peoples to glorious peace. At leisure, you delight in manly sports, good for training up a martial youth (set piece on sports). But there remain things to do: Reform by law the morals of the clergy; put down legal chicane; fill the Parlement with public-spirited men. Then the British,[127] Dutch, Germans will obey you, Spain, Colchis, and the Ister bring you gifts. Again the French soldier will visit Jerusalem and return with Palestinian palms for his home orchard. The Fates will give you Greek triumphs and a Byzantine Empire. Now that you have peace and an ally, who would dare attack you? Now that heaven is appeased and Christ your defender, sacred prophecy forbids us to be doubtful of your future conquests.

[122]This is reminiscent of Leland in 1546.
[123]Julius broke his preconclave promise to restore Parma to the Farnese. When the Farnese applied to the French for help against the Emperor, Julius sent his nephew Giambattista del Monte to cooperate with the Duke of Gonzaga in the capture of Parma. It subsequently fell to the French.
[124]Pope Paul IV, not the Cardinal.
[125]
Pax fuit: occurris pacatis Carapha rebus:
Cogis et infestas Gallos armare phalanges,
Nec iusiurandi, nec religionis honores,
Nec te nostra movent ruptae periuria pacis.

[126]Here certainly a reference to Cardinal Caraffa—

Atque execrati post saecula longa nepotes.

[127]
Tunc tibi pacati referent aulaea Britanni
Nec cupient iterum patriae sociare Caletes.

The first line, a parody of Virgil's 'Purpurea intexti tollant aulaea Britanni,' which refers to the raising of the curtain in the theater, is obscure to me. Does *aulaea referent* mean that the British wool trade with France will be resumed?

Up from Bordeaux came a long Latin poem *De pace* by Arnold de Pujol, professor of law at the university.[128] It seems to have been sent with the commendations of the protonotary Christofle de Foix de Candale to Jean Morel, and was prepared for the press by the tutor to Morel's children, the humanist Charles Utenhove. In an introductory poem, Utenhove says that Morel approved of it, Du Bellay liked what he had seen of it, probably L'Hospital and the great Lancelot de Carle will not scorn it, and 'if I know you, Ronsard, and your teacher [Dorat], you too will perhaps uphold its readability.' 'It is something new when good verses, and so many of them, come from one who has been for twenty years professor of law at Bordeaux.' Utenhove admits that he has corrected the poem considerably.[129] If there are some reservations here, the poem was clearly sent into the world from the bosom of Morel's circle, and on the title page itself the elderly Bordeaux professor might feel himself honored with a couplet from the precocious hand of Camilla Morel, then ten years old.[130]

[128]*Arnoldi Puiolii I.U.D. in academia Burdigalensi de Pace nuper inter Henricum Galliae, Philippum Hispaniae, Reges inita, carmen longe eruditissimum.* (Paris: Martinus Juvenis, 1559) [BN Rés. Yc. 1646], microfilm. A 'M. de Pujol' was regent of the University in 1553 (*Archives historiques du département de la Gironde* 45.304). The contents of the booklet are as follows: (1) Utenhove to Chr. de Foix; (2) *De Pace*; (3) to Vido Brissac (by Pujol?); (4) to Jean Morel by Utenhove; (5) prose apology by Utenhove.

[129] Carmina missa tui, bis terque quaterque, Poetae,
  Ceu bona, Candali, lecta fuere mihi;
 Iudicioque meo, doctique probata Morelli, . . .
 Bellaio pars visa placet: fatearis oportet
  Nec tibi [Du Bellay] Musarum displicuisse Duci. . . .
 Spe nisi decipior, Lopitalis et illa probabit. . . .
 Nec ea despiciet, mihi crede, poemata Carlus
  Lancea cui nomen Lotos et ipsa dedit. . . .
 Si bene te novi, Ronsarde, tuumque magistrum,
  Te quoque forsan erunt vindice digna legi.
 Bis duo Burdigalae leges per lustra professo
  Quo bona proveniant carmina totque novum est.
 Non ego me vitiis, si quae notha dextera fudit,
  Inficior medicas applicuisse manus.

In a prose notice at the end of the little book, Utenhove again craves indulgence for such faults as yet remain.

[130] Carmina Minciadae si quis fastidit, et huius
  Spernat: si quis amat, vatis et huius amet.
       Camilla Morella

Of Camilla, Du Bellay wrote, after praising her faciliity in Latin, Greek, and Hebrew, 'Ronsardus queat invidere ut ipse' (*Joachimii Bellaii Poematum libri quattuor* [Paris, 1558]):

  Et vix (quod stupeas) videt Camilla
  Videt vix decimam Camilla messem.

Camilla intimates that whoever loves Virgil should love Pujol, and we suspect her of no irony, though Pujol relies so heavily on tags and epithets from the Roman poets that in reading his verses we are often in effect reading Virgil's. That degree of imitation would hardly be censured in the sixteenth century as it would be now. On the whole, the poem makes a good impression, though too long; it excels in virtuosity and variety of motives rather than in ingenuity in the total plan.

Once heavenly Peace held sway on earth, and all was well, particularly in the provision of agricultural plenty—

> Pax leges et iura dabat, tunc pinguia durus
> Arva (metus expers) tauris sulcebat arator
> Laetus et extremos cantabat vinitor antes. . . .

But Bellona or Enyo, jealous of the honor accorded to Pax, induced her sisters Wrath and Guile to join her in driving peace from the world, and accordingly they invade the several nations of Europe, while Enyo herself goes to rouse Mars in his northern fastness. Pax together with her companions Clementia, cana Fides, and Concordia take refuge in heaven. The horrors of war follow,[131] and Neptune, annoyed by the sea battles, rises up to tell the gods of the sea of the iniquities of men, who, worse than beasts, destroy their own kind. Heedless of the fate of Salmoneus, they have now invented firearms. If they disturb him again, he threatens to overwhelm them. Meanwhile wars continue to rage from generation to generation. A farmer complains of the destruction of his crops and warns of the famine and plague that will follow. The rare survivor well may ask what good came of founding cities; life was better in the age of Saturn; walls brought sorrow to Priam and to Romulus and Remus. Mother Earth takes up the tale and deplores man's search of her vitals for silver, gold and iron; Prometheus ought never to have brought fire to men.[132] The poem now reaches its climax in suppliant pleas to Jupiter by Italy, Spain, and France, each detailing her former felicity and present woes, and promising worship if Jove will save her. Moved by their prayers, he tells the assembly of the gods that he assents and has appointed as his instruments Montmorency, the Car-

[131] Including, among internal dissensions, the Reformation:

> In se tum fidei discors Alemania dignas
> Convertit, sic Fama, manus, Latiique recusat
> Pontificis prorsus leges et iura subire,
> Incertoque parum constans errore vagatur.

[132] Though this is a commonplace, compare the development in Ronsard's *Exhortation* 123–46.

dinal of Lorraine, and Saint-André.[133] The pact will be confirmed by
the marriages of Isabella (Elizabeth) and Marguerite—

Et procul exactis bello bellique furore
De caelo aeternam faciam descendere Pacem.

Rhetorically located, the poems we have been considering belong
to the *genus demonstrativum* insofar as they praise the peace and the
peacegivers, but this intention tends to be crossed by that of offering
political advice, which brings some of them—the three Latin poems,
for example, and Ronsard's *Exhortation* and *La Paix*—well within the
genus deliberativum. Since they are poems, however, or at all events
written in verse, it is questionable whether the writers were con-
scious of these distinctions.[134] As a basis of comparison, we have
two prose orations belonging to the same flight of publications as the
poems and distinctly deliberative in motive.

Guillaume Aubert is known to literary history chiefly as the friend
of Joachim Du Bellay, on whose death (1560) he published an
Elégie, and whose posthumous *Œuvres* he edited in 1569. He con-
tributed to the *Tumulus* of Jean Brinon (1554), and with Ronsard,
Baïf, and Jean Nicot, is one or the speakers in the *Dialogues* (1557)
of Guy de Bruès.[135] Originally from Poitiers, he was making a
fairly successful career at the bar in Paris, but aspired to employ-
ment by the King and succeeded through powerful friends in being
presented to Henri II precisely, it seems, in this winter or spring of
1559. He was probably about twenty-five years old.[136] Clearly the
Oraison de la Paix (*privilège* of May 10) was published with the aim of
advancing a career that was nicely ripening, and the circumstance
adds interest to some of its points. Unluckily for Aubert, the King's
death postponed these hopes, and it was not until 1588 that he got a
royal appointment.[137]

[133]Evidently Jupiter does not regard Philip's commissioners as his instruments.
[134]See "Rhetorical Doctrine and Some Poems of Ronsard," Hutton, *Essays*, pp.
291–310.
[135]Nolhac, *Ronsard et l'humanisme*, pp. 169, 249, 318.
[136]The best account of Aubert is that of Gustave Fagniez, "Mémorial . . . de
Mc Guillaume Aubert," *Mémoire de la société de l'histoire de Paris*, 36 (1909), 47–56.
Aubert himself says (in 1585) that he was twenty-two when the presentation took
place and implies that it was shortly before the king's death (ibid., p. 49, n. 2); but the
date c. 1534 given for his birth by the older biographers (Niceron) seems more proba-
ble than 1538. He was received *avocat* at the Parlement of Paris in 1553.
[137]For his rather numerous writings, divided between literature and law, see Fag-
niez, "Mémorial," and Niceron, 35.264. The first was a translation of the twelfth
book of *Amadis de Gaule* (1555).

Aubert's *Oraison*[138] is carefully framed in accordance with the rules of deliberative rhetoric, and the author is at pains to mark its several heads as he proceeds. In his *exordium*, he apologizes for treating a public question when he is only a pleader in the civil courts,[139] notes the universal rejoicing,[140] and proclaims that the making of peace is anything but a sign of weakness in a Christian prince, giving a contrasting picture of the (conventional) horrors of war under Charles V and Francis I and the (conventional) benefits of peace. The *propositio* of the oration follows: 'les moyens par lesquelles la Paix . . . se puisse bien garder et bien entretenir.' He rightly observes that his ensuing arguments are those of many weighty authors. The method of his *argument* is to show that there are no reasons for making war; and despite his warning, it is startling to find that from this point the oration is largely a translation of Erasmus' *Bellum*—Point 1: Nature framed man for peace and offers him the example of the peaceful elements and heavens; Point 2: God intended man for peace. Under the second point he makes a rather genial adaptation of Erasmus; instead of the latter's 'Man from Mars' standing in horror at the sight of human strife,[141] Aubert invokes one of the 'velus sauvages' of 'la France Antartique' [Brazil], instructed by Villegagnon in the Christian way of life and transported by him to the French Court at Amiens during the recent array of the armies of Christendom.[142] What would he say? 'Sont-ce

[138]*Oraison de la paix et les moyens de l'entretenir, et qu'il n'y a aucune raison suffisante pour faire prendre les armes aux princes chrestiens les uns contre les autres* (Paris: B. Prevost, 1559) [BN Lb³¹.93]. A year later, a young Finnish scholar, Martin Helsingus, published a Latin version of Aubert's oration, dedicated to John, Duke of Finland: *Oratio de pace deque eam rationibus retenendi . . . gallice conscripta et habita a G. Auberto . . . in latinum vero idioma nuper a Martino Helsingo tralata* (Paris: F. Morel, 1560); dedication dated August 1560 [BN Rés. p. X. 203]. We note that the original oration is said actually to have been delivered by Aubert.

[139]He says in effect that he is highly capable of handling the subject because he is used to the obscurities of private cases, whereas the motivations of international affairs cannot be concealed but are open and easy.

[140]'Laquelle a tellement transporté plusieurs, qu'ils seroient en danger de leurs personnes.'

[141]Above, p. 52. Martin Helsingus innocently puts back into his own Latin what Aubert has taken from the Latin of Erasmus.

[142]Villegagnon was charged by Coligny in 1555 with founding a colony; the experience ended in failure in 1558 but was celebrated in a book of André Thevet, *Singularitez de la France Antarctique* (Paris, 1558), which Aubert had been reading. See Arthur Heulhard, *Villegagnon* (Paris, 1897); Geoffroy Atkinson, *Les nouveaux horizons de la Renaissance* (Paris, 1935), pp. 120, 289, 314. Ronsard, *Complainte contre Fortune* 353–79 (Laumonier 10.33–34): 'Pauvre Villegagnon . . .' should be compared with Aubert; esp. 1.368: 'Sans proces engendrer de ce mot Tien et Mien' with 'teum et meum' in Aubert. Curiously 'Aubert,' in Bruès' *Dialogues* (2.185), addressing the animals, says, 'Vous n'avez jamais ouy ces mots *mien* et *tien*. Vous n'avez jamais pensé

là les Chrestiens desquels Villegagnon m'avoit parlé avecques tant de louanges dans les solitudes de mon païs? . . . Vraiment, Villegagnon, tu me devois bien faire charger sur les navires de ton Roy pour venir de si loin contempler toutes ces belles choses, mais à ce que ie voy tu m'as plustost envoyé vers les Chrestiens affin que ie leur servisse d'un nouveau spectacle, que pour m'y faire voir quelque bon example.'[143] If neither Nature nor God approves, are there any 'sufficient reasons' for Christian kings to go to war?[144] Aubert runs through five points (still mainly from Erasmus): Ambition of extending empire,[145] pursuits of greatness,[146] pursuit of wealth, pursuit of honor, recovery of territory. The last is a legal matter, and he proposes two basic international laws: (1) arbitration of disputes; (2) sanctions: if a ruler refuses to accept the results of arbitration, other Christian rulers will combine to dethrone him. He now makes two *concessions*: You may still fight—your vices [Erasmus]; and perhaps the Turk, as Aubert will suggest in his forthcoming work on Geoffrey of Bouillon.[147] There follows a succinct *recapitulatio* (neither Nature nor God, and so on) and a *peroratio* rendering thanks in the name of the peoples to the kings and their deputies.

The second oration is in Latin, by the well-known Platonist Louis Le Roy.[148]

Thanks to you, O kings, the peace we prayed for has come; we rejoice and anticipate the return of an ordered existence. Beginning in Rome,

---

que cecy est vostre et que cecy ne l'est pas?' The *Dialogues*, published in 1557, are represented as taking place in 1555 (*The Dialogues of Guy de Brues: A Critical Edition, with a Study in Renaissance Scepticism and Relativism*, Panos Paul Morphos [Baltimore, 1935], p. 28).

[143]*Or.*, f.10ᵛ–11ᵛ. Editors of Montaigne might well cite Aubert as anticipating him in drawing a moral lesson from Villegagnon's cannibals.

[144]With Aubert's 'raisons suffisants' compare Ronsard's 'trop de raisons' *Exhort.* 122).

[145]Now futile, he says, because all peoples are alert to defend their liberty and can always find allies.

[146]He duly cites the anecdote of Cineas and Pyrrhus; so also Le Roy below.

[147]*L'Histoire des guerres faictes par les Chrestiens contre les Turcs* [sic!] *soubs la conduicte de Godefroy duc de Buillon, pour le recouvrement de la Terre Saincte* (n.p., 1559). The BN copy [Rés. La⁹.4.A] is bound with the arms of Catherine de Medici.

[148]*Ludovici Regii Constantini oratio ad invictissimos potentissimosque principes Henricum II Franciae & Philippum Hispaniae Reges, de Pace & concordia nuper inter eos inita, & bello religionis Christianae hostibus inferendo* (Paris: F. Morel, 1559). The book was presumably published in April. After the oration, there are addresses to the Cardinal of Lorraine, Philip II, and the Duke of Savoy, the first dated 'Kal. Aprilis' and the last 'mense April.' On this work see A. Henri Becker, *Un Humaniste au xviᵉ siècle, Loys Le Roy* (Paris, 1896), pp. 42–59.

the war spread over almost all the world; you arrayed the greatest of armies, the worst was expected, when suddenly you made peace. Surely it was God's doing. Kings truly imitate God when they seek the welfare of their peoples. The history of the ancient empires proves that kings who have used vast resources for conquest have perished, and that immoderate power breeds crime. History is a vast tide controlled by Fortune as by the moon. In this ebb and flow, one man cannot establish empire over the whole world. Even were it possible, the world is only a point in space. Far better to merit the kingdom of heaven than to ruin an earthly kingdom through ambition. Kings make themselves wretched in order to be remembered by posterity, but with small chance, since posterity has too much to remember. So Cineas taught Pyrrhus. Augustus indeed gave peace to the world after Actium. And this rare felicity is also yours.

To man *humanitas* is proper, and kingdoms are established to preserve justice. Why then do we have wars? The cause is in the complexity of our nature. The body, a compound of warring elements, is principally appetite, and rebels against the mind, which itself, so Plato says, is a compound of 'the same' and 'the other.' Some like Juvenal see the causes of war in protracted peace; others in the stars, others in the wrath of God; while Lycurgus thought war and military virtue essential to preserve all we have, and peace an empty name without them.

Since childhood, I have pursued every kind of study, and especially that of Greek and Roman antiquity, in order to know what is thought about the nature of the world, of man, and of government, and to publish my findings for the benefit of others. To the same end, I have traveled widely. The sum of what I have learned is that states flourish at home and abroad when they pursue the arts of peace and war alike, neither too belligerent nor yet effeminate. As the universe is made up of four elements so united by friendship that it cannot be destroyed, so the state consists of four virtues and is saved by their union. This union is a ratio in which Fortitude and Justice are the extremes and Prudence and Temperance the means.[149] They must be mingled in due proportion. For example, Cato advised that Carthage should be destroyed, and Scipio on the other hand that it should be perserved as a bridle on Roman love of ease and luxury. When Cato's 'fortitude' overbalanced Scipio's 'prudence,' and Carthage was removed, Roman morals rapidly declined [Livy 34.43; 39.40].

We have suffered enough in our generation, which seems to have been born to offer posterity a legend of disasters. (He begins in the East

---

[149]All this, of course, is founded on Plato, *Timaeus* 32 B–D; the application to the state is already found in ps.-Artistotle *De Mundo* 396b, and in Ocellus Lucanus (O.C., *Text und Kommentar*, Richard Harder [Berlin, 1926], fragm. 1), who already compares the ἁρμονία of the cosmos with the ὁμόνοια of social life: τὸν δὲ κόσμον ἁρμονία, ταύτας δ'αἴτιος ὁ θεός· τὼς δ' οἴκως καὶ τὰς πόλιας ὁμόνοια, ταύτας δ'αἴτιος νόμος.

with Soliman's murder of his son Mustafa, and moves westward to 'Britanniae tumultus,' and so on)

But if military discipline must not be wholly given up, direct your forces against the Mohammedans. Think how far Christendom once extended and how many lands are now lost to the victorious Turk, who holds North Africa and the Balkans, and has besieged Vienna. Meanwhile, as though in answer to Mohammedan prayers, Europe is soaked in her own blood. What blindness there is in this! If you will not listen to me, hear the voice of our common mother Europe. Says she: 'I bore you, mighty Princes, to be my protectors, and for this have given you power and glory. I ask only that you collaborate in restoring my dignity and preserving my freedom. See the infidel everywhere invading my borders! Yet once my sway extended over much of Africa and Asia. What are other peoples compared with Europeans? Once the Macedonian extended his power to India; yet now I scarcely retain a trace of my former grandeur, I who in the past hundred years have made so many discoveries, even of things unknown to the ancients—new seas, new lands, new species of men, new constellations; with Spanish help I have found and conquered what amounts to a new world. But great as these things are, the moment the thought of war arises, the better arts of life fall silent, and I am wrapped in flame and rent asunder. Save me from more of this; honor the arts of peace, letters and industry; and you will be rewarded by the grateful memory of mankind.' Do but hearken to the sacred voice of Europe. Now if ever is the hour for ending discord for all time. Whatever you decide, I pray God that it may be for your own good and the good of the state.

Did the peace of Cateau-Cambrésis evoke no music from the Spanish side? There was pageantry at Brussels and music in the ordinary sense, but poems such as the French proliferated are hard to find. Significantly, one of the few poems of much elaboration seems to be Des Autels's *La Paix venue du ciel*, written in the French tradition by a French visitor.[150] From the humanist tradition, however, something could be expected, and it is possible to point to two Latin odes on the Peace, written by good poets, one by the Italian Ippolito Capilupi, the other by the Flemish poet Livin van der Beken or Laevinus Torrentius. Further search might well uncover more than these.

[150]No Spanish poems have come to my attention. This may be accidental, but if not, the difference of position might account for the lack of such writing. Latterly the war had been fought on French soil, and hence peace meant more to Frenchmen; for them the positive value of the treaty was the peace it brought, since it brought little else, while to the Spanish side it looked like a diplomatic victory. French poetry was at a moment of high vigor; the poets were public-minded; and they had a long tradition of public, and specifically peace poems to work in.

Capilupi (1511–80) was a member of a famous Mantuan family of poets and diplomats and was himself distinguished in both roles. Lifelong adherence to the imperial party earned him, just now in 1559, imprisonment by Paul IV, and later a pension from Philip II. In 1560 he became Bishop of Fano.[151] Torrentius was also eminent as humanist and diplomat and eventually became Bishop of Antwerp. He had spent five years in Rome 1552–57), where he came to know Capilupi, and though apparently in Flanders in 1559, was in Rome again in 1560. It would not be surprising if their respective Horatian odes on the Peace of Cateau—Capilupi's *De Pace inita inter Philippum et Henricum reges* in Sapphics, and Torrentius' *De Pace inter Hispaniae et Galliae reges inita* in Alcaics—were somehow connected.[152]

Capilupi takes the more impartial view. After a summons to Peace ('Alma Pax, huc ades'), he slips into an encomium of peace as already realized by the gift of the king of France and Philip ('qui tot Europae populos gubernas / Aequus, et Indos'). Now that the youthful kings, neither conquering the other, have made peace, let them join forces against the enemy of our name and faith, and so win apotheosis ('Hac iter vobis erit ad beatas / Aetheris sedes'). Torrentius is a shade less generous, and across his poem there perhaps falls the shadow of the proud victory ode, also in Alcaics, that he had written on the taking of Saint-Quentin.[153] At all events, he cannot repress a feeling that the wisdom of Pallas had attended Philip's commissioners at the conference table.

Happy Peace returns to earth. Rejoice, ye Muses! And, O Pallas, restore the peaceful arts. In war thou art fiercer than Mars, yet thy counsels abate Mars' wrath; he is ever for slaughter, but joined with him

[151]On Capilupi see Georg Kupke, "Vor Hundert Jahren," in *Quellen und Forschungen aus Italienischen Archiven und Bibliotheken* (Rome, 1899), 1.134.

[152]So far as I know, neither poem was immediately printed. Torrentius' ode appeared in his *Poemata sacra* (Antwerp: Plantin, 1572), Capilupi's in the *Capiluporum carmina* (Rome, 1590) [BN Ye. 989]. My references are, for Torrentius, to *DPB* 4.438, and for Capilupi to *CPI* 3.210. Torrentius addresses an ode to Capilupi, 'De Caesaris ad Oenipontem recessis,' *DPB* 4.410.

[153]If the two odes are companion pieces, Torrentius' peace poem would thus precede Capilupi's. The ode *In Philippi ad Fanum Quintini victoriam (DPB* 4.436) glories in the capture of the French leaders ('captiva magnorum procerum cohors') and declares that the saints rejoice in the punishment of French perfidy (the repudiation of the Truce of Vaucelles):

> Gaudentque Divi, queis pietas tua
> Fidesque cordi est, praelia fortiter
> Pugnata, et hostili solutas
> Perfidiae scelerique poenas.

thou bringest wars to the desired end of Justice. By thy favor, the better side prevailed over that of the seducer Paris; and now, if the treaty be just and agreeable to thee, let it be eternal, O Virgin, who art the wisdom and strength of the Father. Come forth from hiding, Bacchus, Ceres, Nymphs, and Satyrs, visit the sunny pastures, and make fruitful the fields so long untilled while the farmer's tools were turned into swords and bucklers, and the soldier therewith prepared impious triumphs for an unjust lord. What ills do we not endure, only to be crowned with garlands and to make the vulgar gape at titles and trophies! A great thing truly to thrust steel through the hearts of our fellow men (Erasmus), and to sever the bonds of kindness kept even by brute beasts. O Calliope, wreathe me a different crown from this; bound with which, at the table of comrades, a trouble to none, a pleasure to all, may I be empowered to sing the many blessings of peace, the many evils of war.

In Vienna, too, the Peace of Cateau-Cambrésis was greeted by at least one poetical effusion. The then Dean of the philosophical faculty of the University, Hubert Luetanus, did not publish his *Carmen elegiacum* until October, though it must have been written in the spring or early summer, since the author does not know of the death of Henri II.[154] In the Dedicatory Epistle we hear what we might expect to hear from Vienna, that peace between the Christian princes may lead to more effective measures against the Turk; but the poem itself (1,352 verses) moves on a remote mythological plane.

Venus and Juno in mutual hostility have infected with similar hostility the two Demigods who rule the earth. Jupiter, unwilling to face the goddesses alone, calls a council of the gods who have elected him to his supreme position. In their presence, he urges upon Venus and Juno the advantages of peace.[155] They shake hands, and their reconciliation is at once felt in the hearts of the kings. Venus bestows sons and daughters upon the king of France and less specific gifts on Philip; Juno, too, is bountiful; and Minerva gives both kings her gifts of wisdom. Henri gives his daughter to Philip, and his sister to the 'magnanimous Duke.' The author prays that peace may endure.

[154]*Carmen elegiacum de bello composito, et pace, quam cum Philippo Hispaniarum rege Henricus secundus Galliarum rex anno 1559 inivit. M. Huberto Luetano Noviomago autore* (Vienna: Raphael Hofhalter, 1559). The Epistle, addressed to members of the University Senate, is dated October 9, 1559. The volume contains a second *Carmen elegiacum* on the entry of the Emperor Ferdinand I into Austria after his election.

[155]The passage in praise of peace (sig. E–E2) is one of the better parts of the poem, touching on the peace that holds the world together and the effects of peace on human life; but it is stolen from Palingenius' *Zodiacus vitae* (Pierangelo Manzolli, Venice, n.d. but after 1534) 4.439–73, or only paid for by turning Palingenius' hexameters into elegiacs, whereby some lines remain unaltered—e.g., 'Nec tempestivas pluvias dimitteret aer' (see below, p. 217).

The happy ending must have struck a reader with painful irony after the events of July; and if allegory is intended to go so far, the elected Jupiter representing Ferdinand, it is certain that the Emperor remained remote from Cateau, but less certain that his distant activities determined the event.

The celebrations that followed the publication of the peace were to be continued and crowned by a series of magnificent *fêtes* which the king planned for the marriages of his daughter and his sister to take place at the end of June. And the poets, having seen their peace poems through the press, promptly turned to the composition of epithalamia.[156] The Duke of Alba, who was to represent Philip, arrived with an imposing suite and was lodged in the unfinished Louvre; the Duke of Savoy was present in person. The *fêtes* began. On June 30 Henri, himself taking part in the grand tournament of the rue Saint-Antoine, was accidentally run through the eye by the broken shaft of his opponent's lance. He lingered in the grief-stricken palace until July 10, and the night before his death the marriages were solemnized in a rapid and funereal manner in the nearby church of Saint Paul.

Period of the Religious Wars

J'ay veu guerres, debats, tantost trèves et pais.
Tantost accord promis, redéfais et refais,
Puis défais et refais; j'ay veu que sous la lune
Tout n'estoit que hazard et pendoit de Fortune.
                                        Ronsard, 1584

No allusion was made in the treaty of Cateau-Cambrésis to the problem of religion; but the silence was eloquent, for in the menace of this problem doubtless lay the ultimate motive for the suddenness of the armistice and the feeling that peace must be had at almost any price. Statesmen do not so much influence the course of events as seek an action and verbal formulation conformable to its inner move-

---

[156]Ronsard was chiefly concerned, as is natural, with the marriage of Marguerite and Emmanuel-Philibert, writing a *Discours à Mgr. le duc de Savoye* and a *Chant pastoral à Mme Marguerite duchesse de Savoye* and only a group of minor *Inscriptions* for the marriage of Philip and Elizabeth. Du Bellay wrote only briefly *Pour le Tournoy* and *Sur la Paix et sur les mariages*, with some quatrains for the personages. Both poets published their poems after the death of the king, with apologies for intruding mirth upon grief.

ment. The ending of the foreign wars was so necessary a prelude to the civil wars in France that historians used to think it was so intended; it was intended, not, however, by the men, but by the events. Everyone knew the commonplace that internal differences are likely to be put aside when danger threatens from without, and the converse was obvious, that the ending of the foreign wars would unleash the dissensions within; but now, for both kings, the internal threat was immediate and real, while the war with each other had been at most feebly motivated. Where the politicians were powerless, the poets were completely futile, and, catching at the age-old formula, could only urge the monarchs to cease fighting each other and join forces against the Turk. The first part of this advice was false or ambiguous—they shrank from naming the real peril; the second part was pathetically impractical.

Nevertheless, the impulse to give poetical expression to their feeling for the 'misères de ce temps' and in humanist fashion to draw the moral implications into line with what we call the Western tradition was honorable in the poets and may make their endless commonplaces forgivable. Of poems desiderating peace, or too soon hailing its fleeting shadow, the flow continued during the religious wars that succeeded each other through the rest of the century. We pick up a few of them here to recall that the type persisted.[157]

Francis II died fifteen months after his father (December 5, 1560). The efforts of Catherine de Medici, as regent for the ten-year-old Charles IX, to raise the throne above party engagements, and the honorable measures of tolerance sponsored by Michel de L'Hospital, now Chancellor of France, served only to reveal the weakness of the central authority. Open fighting broke out in the spring of 1562 and by autumn had engulfed the whole country. Familiar to ideological wars, mercenaries were soon on the scene, 'reîtres' and 'lansquenets' recruited in Switzerland by the Catholic party, and more successfully by the Protestant party from Germany and England. A time of decision, it tried the souls of men; yet while we may understand party loyalty, and the genuine abhorrence with which Ronsard, for one, viewed the Protestant movement, it is impossible not to deplore the violence of his *Misères de ce temps*, his *Remonstrance au peuple*, and other poems of this year. They certainly

---

[157]This section is necessarily provisional; a good many of the titles mentioned are known to me only from bibliographical sources and refer to separate publications; there probably are many peace poems included in the collective editions of the poets from 1560 to 1600 that I have at present no means of consulting. And the assumption that a peace poem published in the year of a given treaty refers to it may be rash.

did not serve the cause of peace. Other poets of the time, though equally committed, were able to rise to a note of human pity in their 'remonstrances.'[158] Yet it is possible to be too general. One is not always sure, for example, what war is the subject of a *Supplication aux Roys* by Jean Sève of Lyons.[159] It is in two parts, an *Exhortation aux roys et princes* and an *Exhortation au peuple*. In the first,

> the 'nobles princes Troyens' are admonished to cease fighting, since all are Christians and are of one blood, and to satisfy their ambitions in a crusade against the Turk: Drive Mars from your lands; it is he who incited Absolom against David, brought the Greek fleet to destroy your Trojan ancestors, and has often bathed Europe in blood. He causes mothers to weep for their sons, and wander distracted in the wilds, their hair tossing in the wind like the branches of ancient oaks, or

> > Elles semblent encor ces[160] anciennes sorcieres
> > Qui les hommes charmoyent, les forestz, les rivières.

> Do not spend your subjects' blood for the small glory of taking a city. Live in peace after the example of Christ, and he will bless you and your posterity.

In the *Exhortation* to the people, Sève strikes a still more religious note:

> > J'ay tousjours eu vouloir de chanter quelque foys
> > Un vers qui fût Chrestien.

> We must not merely pray for peace; we must repent of our sins. Our Lord says: 'I died for you, yet you scorn the pact I made for you with my Father; I will chastise you . . . will put you in the power of some foreign king.' But God is also merciful. If we put away our sins, He says: 'I will send you rains, your vines and trees will bear abundantly, you will sleep in peace, I will free your land of wolves, dragons, and lions: you shall be my people, and I will protect France from alarms.'[161]

---

[158]Poems of remonstrance continued to be published throughout the civil war period. Though they are often peace poems just as Erasmus' *Bellum* is a peace manifesto or remonstrance, I have not usually included them after 1562, but have limited my notices to poems brought out on the occasion of the peace settlements.

[159]*Supplication aux Roys et Princes Chrestiens de faire la paix entre eux et prendre les armes contre les Infidelles. Avec une exhortation au peuple Françoys d'avoir son recours à Dieu pour obtenir sa grace et sa paix.* Par Jehan Seve Lyonnais (Paris: Barbe Regnault, 1559) [BN Rés. Ye. 3031]. On Jean Sève see Saulnier, 'Deux œuvres,' 265–70.

[160]Text: *ses.*

[161]The dragons and lions are of course metaphorical *(reîtres* and *lansquenets?);* cf. Ezek. 34.25–28. Sève seems to owe something to Ronsard's poems of 1559. Com-

Perhaps the most successful of these remonstrances is the Protestant Jean de La Taille's *Remonstrance pour le Roy à tous ses subjects qui ont prins les armes.* The first published work of its author, it was continually reissued, with appropriate alterations, during the course of the civil wars.[162] The words are dramatically put into the mouth of the (at first) twelve-year-old king:

> You may think that the words of one so young can only reflect the thoughts of a child; but I am not so young that I cannot see the threat to my scepter in your civil strife. Though able to command, I prefer to entreat you to put down your arms. I begin my remonstrance with a Roman story (the belly and the members): what folly to destroy yourselves in this manner! What folly for you, the nobility, right arm of my kingdom, to destroy yourselves! The present war is worse than the wars of Caesar and Pompey or of Guelfs and Ghibellines. The demon Sedition is the cause. Daughter of *Outrecuidance* and *Trop-Presumer*, nursed by *Légèrté* and *Opiniastreté*, she was consigned to hell by the counsels of Catherine de Medici, only to send up from there her daughter *Civil War.* Before her march Envy, False Report, Calumny, Rancor, Malebouche, and Discord; behind come Ruin, Despair, Repentance. Once France was everywhere feared; now our enemies rejoice. What can the spirit of Francis I say? or that of my father Henri II who brought Peace from heaven, and took her back to heaven with him? Is this what has come of the efforts of Louis XI (in uniting France)? When I should be passing the April of my days in study and sport, you have given me only troubles and horrors. Send home your soldiers, let the spider spin in their armor. But if my tears do not soften you, be moved by the misery of the people. Worst of all your deeds is to have summoned barbarous mercenaries from Germany to pillage France. You expose my crown to the first who conquers. If you must have fighting, wait for eight years ('trois ans,' 1571); 'encore un peu,' 1580), and I will lead you against the

---

pare *Supplication* sig. 'avez vous pas bien proches / les infidelles Turcz?' and Ronsard, *Exhort.* 30–31: 'encore le Turc n'est / Si eslongné de vous'; *Suppl.* Aii[2]: 'Ou vouleut Jesuschrist de son sang precieux / Nous rechapter' and *Exhort.* 56: 'Que Christ . . . a rachetez de son sang precieux'; *Suppl.*, Aii[3]: 'Dechassez le [Mars] bien loing, et le faict abismer / Au profond des enfers, ou au creux de la mer' and *Exhort.* 24–26: 'cachez [weapons] dessoubs la terre / Loing au creux des Enfers, ou au profond de la mer . . . faites les abismer.' The chastisement and alternative mercies of God in Sève's second *Exhortation* are already sketched in Ronsard's *Paix* 132ff. Sève is not included in Raymond's *Influence.*

[162]First published by Morel in 1563, but with *privilège* of October 19, 1562. Later editions add to the title the words: '*afin de les encliner à la paix.*' There was a second edition in 1563, and an edition every year from 1567 to 1571 and again in 1580 (also in La Taille's *Œuvres* of 1572). In the *Œuvres*, René de Maulde, ed. (Paris, 1880), the text is that of 1571 with variants mostly from the first edition. Verbally La Taille owes much to Ronsard's *Misères*; cf. Raymond, *Bibliographie*, p. 102, and *Influence* 1.395, where it is noted that Ronsard in turn may later have borrowed from La Taille.

[137]

Turk in Hungary. Obscure and terrible is the destiny of God! Never was there a better peace than that (Cateau-Cambrésis) sworn by my father and sealed with his blood; but better for us had he never at the price of his life made that dismal peace ('triste Paix'). O God! extinguish Discord, and send us again thy daughter who is Peace; overlook our sins, which we confess. And redoubled curses be on those who love not peace and have seditious hearts.

Similar to La Taille's poem is the *Complainte de France* of Jacques Béreau, which is a prosopopeia not of the king, but of France herself.[163]

Once renowned beyond other nations, I am now beyond all in misery and grief; after my glorious history from Pharamond to Henri II, I see my cities desolated and my children attempting, like Nero, to destroy their mother; God sent you his daughter Peace, but you preferred vices; . . . brute beasts, more reasonably, fight only when pressed by hunger; surely Fortune rules the world; if Religion is the cause you allege, consider that war is not the way of Christ, take your differences to a council; and if you must fight, go against the Turk.

The first civil war came to an end early in the next year with the Pacification of Amboise (March 19, 1563). At this time, the Catholic party had lost its principal leader, the Duke of Guise, and also Antoine de Bourbon and the marshal Saint-André, all slain, and Montmorency again a captive, while, of the Protestant leaders, the Prince of Condé was a prisoner of the Catholics. True, the peace terms accepted by the captive Condé were anything but advantageous to the Huguenots and bore the seed of future trouble. For the moment, however, the advantage rested with the Queen Regent and the central authority. On the eve of the pacification, Jean Vauquelin de la Fresnaye published his poem *Pour la Monarchie de ce royaume contre la Division, à la Royne mère du Roy* (Paris: F. Morel, 1563), which is a transition between the remonstrances and complaints and the poems of celebration.[164] It embodies a number of traditional peace themes. A small but interesting phenomenon is a

[163]*Œuvres*, J. Hovyn de Tranchère and R. Guyet, eds. (Paris, 1884), p. 159; first published in Béreau's *Eglogues* of 1565. Cf. Eclogue VII. The *Complainte* is indebted to Ronsard's *Misères* (Raymond, *Bibliographie*, p. 25–2.6).

[164]*Poésies*, Julien Travers, ed. (Caen, 1870), 2.163. The *privilège* is of February 27, 1562 (i.e., 1563), three weeks before the Pacification was signed. The poem like that of La Taille was reprinted (by Morel) in 1567, presumably after the outbreak of the second civil war in that year, by B. Rigaud at Lyons in 1568, then again by Morel in Paris in 1570, probably in connection with the Pacification of Saint-Germain. Compare R. Garnier's *Hymne à la Monarchie* of about the same date.

pamphlet published at Lyons, entitled *Les Louanges et recommandations de la Paix, extraictes de l'Escriture saincte*. The title is slightly misleading, since the whole is made up of translations from the less controversial parts of Erasmus' *Bellum*.[165] Once again, as in Aubert's oration, Erasmus glides like a nameless ghost into the French propaganda for peace. The pamphlet was reprinted in 1568.

A small burst of poetical pamphlets greeted the pacification itself. Of some literary interest is the *Ode de la Paix* of Nicolas Renaud, which professes to be 'façonné à la mode / D'un nouveau façonneur de vers,' namely, Ronsard, and succeeds in this aim to the point of parody:

> O Apollon, Dieu de la lyre,
> Il est temps que mon arc je tire
> Pour frapper Charles de Valois.[166]

Renaud touches on a number of commonplaces: armor hung up in idleness, the horrors of war, war a chastisement for sin, and the like. At times he shoots beyond the obscurity of Ronsard's *Ode de la Paix*, as in the parentage he ascribes to Peace, whom we generally know as the 'fille de Dieu':

> Nous te saluons, fille chere
> Du chaos, et de nostre mere
> Qui tient t'enclose doucement,
> De la nature ensemencée
> L'ame dans son tout balancée
> Sur l'un et l'autre firmament.

[165]*Les louanges et Recommandations de la Paix, extraictes de l'escriture saincte, Plus est monstré que cest chose fort deshonneste, que les Chrestiens ayent guerre ensemble. Avec une Suasion à faire la Paix, au regard du grand trauail qu'il faut souffrir à mener la guerre, et des grans fraiz qu'il y faut faire* (Lyons: Jean Saugrain, 1563) [BN Lb33.], p. 96. (Baudrier, 3.256, lists a second edition, Lyons: B. Rigaud, 1568.) The first section is from *Bellum*, Remy and Dunil-Marquebreucq, eds., lines 532–72, on the peace mission of Christ; the author justifies his title by supplying the biblical references. The second section, *Est monstré . . .* , is from lines 515–32, on the unity there should be among Christians. The third section, *Suasion à faire la paix*, is from lines 481–514, miseries and expense of war and the soldier's unhappy lot. A fourth section not noticed in the title, *Que plusieurs Chrestiens au fait de guerre sont pires qu'infidelles et payens*, is from lines 712–60, on that subject.
[166]*Ode de la Paix, au Roy Charles, treschrestien Roy de France IX de ce nom*. Par N.R.P. (Lyons: Benoist Rigaud, 1563) [BN Rés. Ye. 4486]. Du Verdier identifies the author as Nicolas Renaud, and so does Raymond, *Influence* 1.385; the same style in Renaud's *Chastes Amours*. The small volume (12° of 8ff.) contains, besides the *Ode*, a sonnet, *Le combat de la Mort et d'Amour*, and a *chanson* entitled *Le Retour de la Paix en France*.

Peace is here substituted for Love born of Chaos in Ficino. The rest seems to mean: Mother Earth who holds the soul being impregnated by Nature.

More traditional is an *Esjouissance aux Chrestiens* by the academic poet Ferrand de Bez (rector of the University; principal of the Collège de Beauvais):[167]

> Astres des hauts cieulx lumières flamboiantes,
> O Phoebus radieux, ô estoilles errantes,
> Avecques moy louez ce grand Dieu tout-puissant,
> Qui envoie la paix au peuple languissant . . .

For our sins He permitted this fraternal strife to spring up among us; but like a good father, after chastising us He now lets shine on us the rays of peace.

> O poètes, cessez par voz Odes et vers
> De louer voz faulx dieux et leurs siècles divers.
> Car le siècle doré de Saturne le vieux
> Et de Nume Sabin roy ceremonieux
> Ne faut exalter de plumes mensongères.

Welcome Peace! Through you the laborer shall sow in safety. Go, merchants, to Africa, Asia, America. Let all embrace the peace sent by God, and in His name obey the law, the king, the nobility, the magistrates. Soldiers, cast away your arms, you have learned that war is not sweet.

> Las! combien d'hommes vains, pauvres et miserables
> Ont fait mourir de gens excellents et notables![168]

Our rivers have run with the blood of the slain; rape and secret murders have been perpetrated; many still lie secretly chained in prison. May God make this beginning of peace to spread. Give Him the praise. And O Lord, keep us in peace and concord.[169]

---

[167]*Esiouissance aux Chrestiens rendans grace à Dieu pour l'heureux advenement de la paix en France*, par F.D.B.P. (Lyons: Jean Saugrain, 1563) [BN Rés. Ye. 3975].

[168]An echo of Clément Marot's *Cantique de la Chrestienté*, above, p. 84.

[169]Bez seems clearly to allude to the *Bellum* of Erasmus:

> Avant de gouster la bellique secousse,
> Vous pensiez à part vous que la guerre estoit doulce.

And some of his commonplaces recall this *adagium*: compare '(Dieu a permis guerre) entre le pere et le fils, entre meres et filles, entre freres et seurs' and again 'que de sang espandu, que de fleuves coulantes / Des corps humains occis sont devenus sanglants' with Erasmus: 'undantes cruore campos, fluvios humano tinctos sanguine; fit interea nonnumquam ut frater incidat in fratrem, affinis in affinem, amicus in ami-

Jacques Béreau now followed his *Complainte* of the year before with a poem *Sur la Paix faicte entre les François*, which, however, was not published until 1565.[170] His theme, like that of Bez, is the chastisement of God upon the sins of the French.

France herself, pale and ragged, goes up to the throne of God, begging Him to send down His daughter Peace to remain forever. God pronounces an invective against the sins of men and Frenchmen as deserving of a second Flood; but He is content with the present punishment and dismisses France with a warning to live better and not to hearken to those who preach 'nouveaux songes, au lieu / De la vraie doctrine.' France returns home, bringing Peace. A curse on whoever would drive Peace away again: Prince, receive her well, punish the seditious, follow the advice of your mother and your counselors.

Passing over a slight and anonymous *Echo parlant à la Paix* (Lyons: Saugrain, 1563),[171] we take our leave of the poems of the Pacification of Amboise with Jean Passerat's *Hymne de la Paix* (Paris: G. Buon, 1563), which has the advantage of being well written.[172]

The storm is over, during which Charon's bark was overloaded; and now Mars reposes in the arms of Venus. Let us sing of Peace, by whom the doors of Janus are closed—a subject that would require a Homer or a Virgil. Before the creation of the world, the elements were in chaos until Peace assembled them and made a universe and peopled the earth with the animals [an elaborate passage] and man. Then was the Golden Age—not golden, despite the poets, for gold the father of evils was unknown, and the world was without strife. Would I had lived then! But if Peace abides with us, we shall have that same happiness once more. Alas! instead we have had the horrors of war, with the death of many noble persons—the King of Navarre, the Sieur de Randam, the Marshal, the Duke of Nevers, Montbrom son of Montmorency, the Duke of Guise. But from sorrows I revert to my hymn. God protect you, holy Peace! You founded on law the ancient cities; you prosper the universities; you scatter the fruits of autumn. Hail Peace! the common repose of men, a true peace:

cum.' But Raymond (*Bibliographie*, p. 27) may be right in ascribing these phrases to the influence of Ronsard: streams red with blood (*Exhort.* 159–63); fraternal strife (*Remonstrance* 339–40; cf. *Misères* 159–63).

[170]*Œuvres poétiques*, p. 171; published in the *Eglogues* of 1565.

[171]Described by Baudrier (4.333) as printed in the same characters as Bez's *Esjouissance*; Baudrier quotes a few lines and locates a copy at Grenoble. See also Le Roux de Lincy, *Chants* 2.588.

[172]*Poésies françaises*, Prosper Blanchemain, ed. (1880), 1.92. The poem is dedicated to the historian Alphonse Delbene, then abbé of Hautecombe.

Non une feinte Pais, non une Pais fourrée,
Mais une Pais qui soit d'éternelle durée.

The second civil war broke out in September 1567, with an unsuccessful Protestant plot to seize the royal family. It was marked by the death of Montmorency in the battle of Saint Denis and ended temporarily with the peace of Longjumeau (March 23, 1568), reestablishing the Edict of Amboise and a limited right of worship for Protestants. Michel de L'Hospital was deprived of the chancellorship. Laments over the war gave place to rather qualified rejoicing.[173] Passions had run high, as may be illustrated from the Catholic side by a *Cantique au nom du Roy* by Berenger de la Tour d'Albenas, evidently published before the peace.[174]

> After all their burning of convents and murder of monks (the young king is made to say), the Protestants dare to affirm: 'Eleus nous a l'Eternel et choisis / Et du Seigneur l'heritaige nous sommes.' 'Mais ô Dieu, fay les taire': enough hast thou chastised us; turn thy wrath now on them, and destroy them root and branch.

From the Protestant camp, as the peace was concluded, there came, from Marans near La Rochelle, a *Hymne sur le triomphe de la Paix* by one F.G.[175] The effective word here is 'triomphe.' The author believes that Peace, 'de Dieu la fille aisnee,' has driven the 'traitors' from Court, and he calls upon France to rejoice that Antichrist is fallen. The real occasion of his poem, dedicated to the reformed Church in Marans, is the repulse of some Catholic forces in a siege which he says lasted five or six days.[176] After describing the event, he again calls for rejoicing by citizens, merchants, ladies, ministers, even the birds:

[173]Examples of poetical laments: J. Passerat, *In alterum Gallorum civile bellum carmen lugubre* (Paris: G. Buon, 1568); Arnaud Sorbin, *Regrets de la France sur les misères des présens troubles de l'an mil cinq cens soixante sept* (Paris: G. Chaudière, 1568) [BN Rés. Ye. 4855]; P. Du Rosier, *Deploration de la France sur la calamité des dernières guerres civiles* (Paris: D. du Pré, 1568).

[174]Paris: D. Du Pré, 1568 [BN Rés. Ye. 1780]; 138 verses.

[175]*Hymne sur le Triomphe de la Paix, ensemble sur le Discours des guerres advenues en l'Isle de Marans, pays et gouvernement de la Rochelle, ceste presente annee mille cinqcens soixante & huit, presentee & adressee à Messieurs de l'Eglise reformee dudict Marans*, Par F.G. Le dernier iour de Mars dudict an. Psaulme cxviii . . . (n.p., 1568) (754 verses) [BN Rés. Ye. 1025]. The poem is introduced by an epistle to the reader and a verse epistle to F.G. by Jean Le Roy, citizen of Marans, who describes F.G. as being both a man of military training and 'excellente doctrine.'

[176]This obscure event was incidental to the preparations for the defense of La Rochelle. F.g. gives full credit to 'le vertueux Sauvage,' who undoubtedly is the 'David Marie, dit le Sauvage,' captain of a company from La Rochelle, in Amos Barbot's ac-

Vous tous oiseaux des taillis et forests,
Tous rossignols qui sont aux verds boccages,
Tous Perroquets et tous Linots de cage.

God has broken the Philistines, the atheists, the libertines. 'O Paix
heureuse, et de tous désirable!' There follow six pages of biblical prec-
edents (complete with marginal references) for God's saving of his peo-
ple, and an 'Imprecation' of four pages denouncing the enemy in
bloodthirsty terms—let them feed on their own 'puante chair,' and so
on. But forgive them, O Lord, for we are bound (tenus) by Matthew 5
to pray for our enemies. Let them turn from their errors, and may
happy peace sojourn among us.

Such was the 'triumph' of Longjumeau for F.G. We turn with relief
to a more important poem published the next day, April 1, in Paris.
The work of Pierre Habert, brother of the well-known poet Fran-
çois Habert, and himself a successful Court functionary, it is enti-
tled *Traicté du bien et utilité de la Paix, et des maux provenans de la
Guerre*.[177] Without claiming a high poetical merit for this perfor-
mance, we may so far dissent from a judgment passed on it in the
last century—'peu poétique et très ennuyeux'[178]—as to say that
perhaps from Habert's very inability to attain a brilliant style, he
conveys to a modern reader a sense of his sincere engagement with
his subject.

The *Traicté* has a familiar pattern—first a rhetorical comparison
of peace and war, and then a series of reflections applicable to the
present situation. In peace, taxes are lower and there are few requi-
sitions on the towns.

Justice is done; nobles, citizens, merchants, workingmen pursue their
useful vocations. In war, châteaux and towns are destroyed, villages
burnt, crops ungathered, and so on. Habert expands on the carnage of
battle—'la teste on voit ou les jambes par terre, / Ou les bras emportez
. . .' and on the terrors of a siege, rather illogically illustrated by the
harmless evacuation of Le Havre by the English. But (here he moves
into the more important part of the poem) war is necessary to defend
king and country. Yet service to the king is not enough; we must pray

---

count; at the end of February he assisted in the sack of Luçon and the removal of
the booty to Marans, 'auquel lieu la compagnie dudit capitaine Marie fut laisse en gar-
nison' (Barbot, *Histoire de La Rochelle* 2.266–67).

[177]Paris: C. Micard; the *privilège*, that is, was April 1 [BN Rés. Ye. 4138]. It was
reprinted in 1570. Also in 1568, Habert published *Le Moyen de bien regner, et de bien
maintenir la Paix*, which I have not read.

[178]E.L.N. Viollet-Le-Duc, *Bibliographic poétique* (Paris, 1843), 1.228.

God to save the king in lasting justice. Meanwhile, subjects must not take the sword into their own hands; civil war rends us all. We must maintain unity in diversity, as we see it in the human body and among the wild beasts. Let civil authorities, churchmen, and nobles all work to preserve order. It is wrong to preach war from the pulpit. Religious differences are less important than national unity; let each worship in his own way, so long as all obey the king. Merchants and citizens, do not listen to troublemakers; leave differences of conscience to God. The Turk who captures a Christian neither does him bodily harm nor forces him to renounce his religion; among us, at Avignon, Carpentras, and Rome, Jews are allowed to live in peace, and no disturbances occur. We are not obliged to answer for each others' conscience. Kings and princes, be shepherds—that means tolerant—to your flocks. Peace is the sea, fountain, wellspring of human happiness.

In writing his *Traicté*, Habert evidently kept before him both the *Dulce bellum inexpertis* and the *Querela pacis* of Erasmus, and the *De bello et pace* of Clichtove.[179] But he subordinates his sources to his own ideas and sense of urgency. A personal touch is added to his account of the quiet withdrawal of the English from Le Havre, which he ascribes to the 'benignity' of the French king; Habert was at hand as a paymaster.[180] The examples of the tolerant Turk and the unharmed Jewish communities seem to be original with him. They suit his main theme that national unity is above religious diversity:

> Que s'il y a en vous quelque division
> Seulement pour le faict de la religion,
> Ne laissez pour cela d'estre unis au reste
> Pour le deu que devez au Roy nostre bon maistre.

> Pourquoy voulons-nous donc par nostre outrecuidance
> Enquirer du prochain quelle est la conscience?

[179]Summary descriptions of the effects of peace and war (sig. Biij–Biiij) are chiefly from Erasmus *(Bellum,* 957–58); examples of Achitophel and Abiathar (sig. Diij²) probably from Clichtove *(De bello* 11, f.25ʳ), though introduced by a phrase from Erasmus *(Bellum,* 956F): 'ne mettez l'huile au feu, l'on dict souvent,' 'oleum, quod aiunt, addentes camino'.

[180]Sig. C.iij:

> Et si lon demandoit comme cela ie le sçay,
> C'est que i'ay sur les lieux de bien pres faict l'essay,
> Estant lun des Commis à faire païement
> De tous les officiers, qui servoient loyaument
> Le Roy en l'artillerie, aussi que la notice
> En ont plusiers, qui m'ont veu le service.

The withdrawal was on July 28, 1563. The English ascribed their capitulation to the plague.

Of less, or rather of no importance is an *Eclogue de deux Bergers de France* put out on this occasion by a Paris lawyer Anselme Isambert de Thouars.[181] Sirice and Criton hail the peace as from God, and discourse rather obscurely on the fighting both of 'beliers cornus' and of the shepherds themselves; but the latter have been reconciled by 'celuy là, que Dieu a couronné / Berger sur eux' (that is, the king). They sing a 'motet' on his 'nativity,' celebrating mother (Catherine de Medici) and child with overtones of doubtful taste. Isambert says that he had prepared this poem for the peace of 1563, but the second war set in before he had decided to present it, and hence he offers it now on the next available occasion. He had need to be quick, for fighting was resumed in August. The young Antoine Du Verdier, who earlier in the year had published his *Mysopolème*,[182] responded to the gathering storm with his *Antitheses de la Paix et de la Guerre, sur le bruit qui court*, dated August 4:[183]

> Quels Daimons Infernaux soufflent dedans les cœurs
> Et font sortir dehors des nouvelles erreurs?

Peace comes from God, from the heavenly Jerusalem, and Jerusalem means in French 'de paix vision,' while war comes from hell. All this first half of the poem, with the idea of antithesis itself, follows Clichtove (esp. Ch. 3; also Erasmus), carrying his biblical color and repeating his marginal references. Then like Habert, whom he may also have read, Du Verdier passes to the *moyen d'entretenir la paix*: let the king dismiss flatterers and traitors from his Court; let the clergy avoid heresy and attend to their parishes in person. 'Et toy, teste de chat, teste de girouette' (common gossips), stay at home, and do not be borne away on every wind of doctrine. You who are not niggard of human blood, go spill that of the Turk. Du Verdier expands (again after Clichtove) on the Turkish invasions of Christendom and summons the nations of Europe to 'chase these wolves,' finally issuing what must be one of the earliest calls upon the New World to come to the rescue of the Old:

[181]*Eclogue de deux Bergers de France, qui entre autres choses se reiouissent de la pacification des troubles. Dediee au Roy, et à la Royne, avecq quelques Epistres latines, et françoises, respectivement presentées à leur Maiestez, et une à Monsieur le chancellier* (Paris: D. du Pré, 1568). See Hulubei, *L'Eglogue en France*, p. 556.

[182]*Le Mysopolème, ou discours contre la guerre, pour le retour de la paix en France* (Lyons: B. Rigaud, 1568). I have not seen this poem. Du Verdier mentions it in the dedicatory epistle of his *Antitheses* and again in the poem (p. 6) in very modest terms. [It was printed with the *Antitheses* (see below) under the title 'Le mysopolème, ou discours contre la guerre dernière.' I have not found a previous printing. R. G.]

[183]*Antitheses de la paix et de la guerre, sur le bruit qui court. Avec le Moyen d'entretenir la paix, et exhortation d'aller tous ensemble contre les infideles Machometistes* (Lyons: B. Rigaud, 1568). The poem is dedicated to Guillaume de Gadaigne, who issued the *privilège*. [Lyons, Bibliothèque de la Ville, 19071].

> Et vous qui habitez toutes les terres neufves,
> De voz forces venez y faire les espreuves . . .

Feeble poetical protests were lost in the rising storm. Condé and Admiral de Coligny were again on the march.[184] A poet might make a bitter jest of it. Passerat comments in a sonnet on the coincidence that the peace of Amboise and that of Longjumeau had fallen in the month of March (Mars).[185] On both occasions he had been hopeful,

> Lorsque deux fois en cinq ans j'apperceu
> L'ombre de paix se faire voir en France,

only to have his hopes crushed by the renewal of war:

> Mais je suis sot quand je m'en esmerveille,
> Ce sont, Belot, ce sont des paix de Mars.

Still higher hopes, however, were raised by the Pacification of Saint-Germain of August 8, 1570, which marked Catherine de Medici's renewed policy of conciliating the Protestant leaders. For the moment indeed the Edict of Saint-Germain seemed to settle everything and occasioned much rejoicing. Presumably before the Pacification, Charles Sevin, Canon of Agen and a friend of J. C. Scaliger, published (in prose) a treatise entitled *Complainte de la Paix*. Though announced as 'gathered from several authors,' it is in fact a translation of Erasmus' *Querela pacis*, only lightly adapted to the times by a few alterations and by the substitution of the word 'Frenchmen' where Erasmus speaks of 'mankind.'[186] It is a striking example of the surreptitious manner in which Erasmus' peace propaganda reached the French public. Also on the eve of the Pacification of Saint-Germain, Louis Le Roy published his impressive *Exhortation pour vivre en concorde et jouir du bien de la Paix* (Paris: F. Morel,

---

[184]The poetical complaints were renewed: 'D.R.,' *Elegie ou complainte que la France fait aux François* (n.p., 1569) [BN Rés. Ye. 3953]; not seen by me.

[185]*Poésies*, Blanchemain, ed., 1.185.

[186]*Complainte de la Paix deschassée et bannie pour le iourd'hui hors du royaume de France, auquel elle souloit faire seur repos et gracieuse demeurance, recueillie de plusieurs aucteurs, par M. Charles Seuin, Chanoine d'Agen. Addressée à Iuges equitables et non suspectz* (Paris: Claude Fremy, 1570) [BN Lb.³³. 421]. At the end of the *Complainte* (which is signed C.S.) there are quotations in Latin and French: 'Pax optima rerum . . .' (Silius); 'Dulce bellum inexpertis'; 'Alta sedent semper civilis vulnera dextra' (Lucian); 'Militis est vita hominis super terram' (Job). There follows an *Oraison à Dieu pour la paix et coadunation du peuple françois* (4 pp.), which is presumably Sevin's own.

1570).[187] The Peace itself was greeted by poems old and new. Thus Pierre Habert brought out again his *Traicté* of 1568, while in Lyons Rigaud published, without the author's name, the old *Retour de la Paix* of Gilles Corrozet.[188] The revised form of Remy Belleau's *Chant pastoral* probably belongs to this occasion. In negotiating the settlement of Saint-Germain, the chief commissioners for the king were Henri de Mesmes and the Duke of Biron. Jean Passerat, who had recently formed his celebrated friendship with Mesmes, found himself able to welcome a peace made in August:[189]

> As Ulysses and Diomede saved the Grecian camp, so Mesmes with Biron has saved France after the Erinnys had thrice kindled civil war within ten years. Mesmes's eloquence has found a solution in peace which is better than victory, since victory won by the slaughter of one's own people is hateful. What reward befits the peacemaker? By your means, Mesmes, Astraea returns, War frets in chains, the Germans go home to the Rhine, swords are exchanged for sickles. . . . Let evil counselors be gone, overcome by the eloquence of Memmius, which like the club of Hercules wins him the way to Olympus.[190]

These learned strains were echoed by the voice of the people in an anonymous ballad, *Les Adieux de la Guerre civile*, which appears to have been originally composed at this time and would be repeated in years to come:[191]

> Adieu le champ, adieu les armes,
> Adieu les archers et gendarmes,
> Adieu soudines et clairons,
> Puisqu'en paix nous en retournons.

[187]Outlined by A. Henri Becker, *Loys Le Roy*, pp. 223–42.

[188]*Le Retour de la paix, et du fruict du benefice d'icelle* (Lyons: B. Rigaud, 1570). See above, p. 87, and Hutton, *Essays*, pp. 311–18. In this reprint, the impact of the religious wars is seen in at least one small detail. Where the earlier edition has 'les cueurs de bonne volonte, / De vive foy, et juste conscience,' the 1570 ed. alters to 'saine foy' (sig. A3³). This reprint bears on the title page a device representing Peace in her chariot holding an olive branch, above her the word 'Pax,' and below the motto: 'Pax olea illustris sibi Martia subiicit arma.'

[189]*In Memmii et Bironi Pacificationem.* I use *DPG* 3.82–85.

[190]Passerat later hailed Mesmes as peacemaker in poems presented to him at the beginning of 1572 and 1588 (*DPG* 3.6.49). Jean Dorat also marked the Pacification of Saint-Germain with a publication which I have not seen: *Novem Cantica de pace ad Carolum nonum Galliae regem* (Paris: in aedibus Joannis Aurati, 1570); *Cat. J. de Rothschild* 689 and 2903. The nine *cantica* are in Latin distichs, and opposite are French translations in the form of sonnets.

[191]Lyons: Gabriel Tout Blanc, 1570 (Baudrier 1.428). As printed by Le Roux de Lincy, *Chants* 2.370–74, from a *recueil* of 1580, this *chanson* consists of thirty-three stanzas.

Peace, Battista Dossi (ca. 1540), Dresden, Gemäldegalerie.
(Photograph: Alinari/Art Resource, Inc.)

At the other end of the literary scale, one of the first publications of the then Calvinist poet Charles de Navières was his ambitious *Cantique de la Paix*, issued about a month after the Edict of Saint-Germain.[192] In fifty-three six-line stanzas, it emulates, with varying success, the lyric style of Ronsard's *Ode de la Paix* of 1550.[193]

> Peace is invoked as more desired than rainfall in Libya or by Croesus on the pyre; accompanied by benevolent stars and garbed in flowing robes of crêpe, she holds in her right hand a ploughshare, and in her left a cornucopia and an oar.[194] Moving through the heavens, she creates the harmony of the spheres. At her glance, from Marseilles to Calais the mists roll away, and Frenchmen are reconciled. The poet hardly knows whether he wakes or dreams. Let the laborer return to his fields and vineyards, the merchant to the sea, the scholar to his university.[195] And may this peace endure. Rising to a higher strain, the poet invokes the Creator of the peace of the universe, who may indeed dissolve it in fire, but has now decreed that there shall be no 'fourth trouble' [civil war].[196] May He punish the warmonger with the lameness of the son of Jonathan[197] and the withered hand of Jeroboam. We have suffered enough: may thy Grace permit the King to maintain the Edict he has published.

The note of uncertainty sometimes heard in Navières's poem sounds to the point of anxiety in the harsh verses of Etienne Pasquier's *Congratulation de la Paix* (450 lines), addressed to the King:[198]

[192]*Cantique de la paix, par Ch. de Naviere. A monseigneur, monsieur le comte de Maulevrier son parein* (Paris: Maturin Prevost, 1570) [BN Rés. Ye. 1810]. The *privilège* is of September 7. Navières (b. 1544) was at this time the equerry to Robert de la Marck, Duke of Bouillon, in Sedan. The *privilège* is also for an *Art poetique françois*, tragedy *Phylandre*, and a translation of Lucan, all by Navières, none of these apparently published.

[193]Raymond, *Influence* 1.386–87. The text of the poem is preceded by a musical score, setting the first stanza. Navières was known as an amateur musician as well as poet and soldier.

[194]Agriculture and commerce.

[195]'Que l'escolier s'en retourne / En son université'—a commonplace, with the husbandman and the merchant (see appendix below), but here perhaps an echo of Passerat (above, p. 141).

[196]These obscure stanzas on cosmic peace are obviously inspired by Ronsard's *Ode*. In the verses, 'Alors que ta main paisible, / Du monde, en leur duisible / Logea les membres divers,' Raymond, who quotes them (*Influence*, p. 387), prints 'vuisible'; but 'duisible' ('proper') is correct.

[197]Mephibosheth (2 Sam. 4.4). Raymond rightly notes that the curse of the warmonger is inspired by Ronsard (*Paix* 263–68); but this does not apply to the Biblical parallels.

[198]*Au Roy, Congratulation de la paix faite par sa majesté entre ses subjectz l'unziesme jour d'Aoust 1570* (n.p., n.d.) [three copies in BN; BN Rés. Ye. 1088]; in *Œuvres* (Amsterdam, 1723), 2.913–20.

With God's help, Sire, you have transcended your youth and have produced a masterpiece of statesmanship in restoring friendship among your subjects. In civil war a king's victories are his own defeat. Civil war is a horrid monster, offspring of Mask, nursed on wind by Opinion, and growing up to throw all into confusion, the fruit of which is to open the land to the barbarian. Of civil wars, the worst are those fought over religion, in which the fanatic both 'perd gayment le corps' and 'estime en tuant faire à Dieu sacrifice.' Religious error cannot be rooted out by war. Unlike the Hebrews, who were bidden to put the Philistines, old and young, to the sword, Christ wished to prevail by the spirit alone.[199] The Church flourished so long as it was persecuted; when it won the favor of princes, it was altered, and God in wrath sent the Arian and civil strife, which gave Mohammed his chance. So in Germany, religious war has not rooted out the Lutheran error, but only opened the door to Anabaptism. The fruitless Crusades teach the same lesson, that Christianity cannot be advanced by the sword. All this, Sire, you have learned in your youth; you have learned that *réunir* by use of force is all but identical with *ruiner*, that a general bloodletting is not good medicine . . . and hence you have given us peace. . . . For a king, a stormy spring augurs a good summer—if he does not forget; and you will hereafter pluck fear from our hearts, and we shall live peacefully until God reunites us in one Church. Then we shall no longer see the unworthy promoted to religious office, and the priesthood will be restored to its ancient virtue. These, and not war, are the true means of restoring our affairs. As the Athenian [Solon], having made peace with Salamis, commanded that no one should speak to annul it, so in France be this the law: that whoever opposes this Edict of yours shall be blotted out as the enemy of king and country, be banished and eaten by vermin, and sepulchered in the belly of a wolf.[200]

Among the poems of the Bordeaux poet Pierre de Brach published in 1576, a vast Pindaric *Ode de la Paix*, in thirty-one triads, inspired by the Pacification of Saint-Germain, is clearly a conspicuous item.[201] It is also conspicuous among the peace poems that we have collected. Guillaume Colletet allowed himself to say of it that, containing more verses than Ronsard's *Ode à Michel de l'Hospital*, 'elle

[199]With the following development compare Erasmus, above, p. 52.
[200]The following is mentioned by Du Verdier (1.480): C.A.D.I.P., *Discours sur le Bannissement de la guerre, et sur l'arrivée de la Paix au royaume de France* (Lyons: J. Saugrain, 1570) (cf. Baudrier 4.344). Still another poem on the Trève de Saint-Germain is *L'Erinne*, described by L. Pertile, "Un poemetto inedito sulle guerre di religione: 'L'Erynne françoise de la France affligée' di Germain Audebert,' *BHR*, 38 (1976), 299–322.
[201]*Les Poèmes* (Bordeaux, 1576), f.102ᵛ. The *Ode de la Paix* is not included in Dezeimeris's edition of de Brach (Bordeaux, 1861).

semble quasi luy disputer aussy le prix du mérite.'[202] That *quasi* is praiseworthy, and Marcel Raymond justly notes that the lofty strain struck in the first few strophes quickly diminishes to a familiar tone more in keeping with the poet's modest powers.[203] [Rising from earth to heaven, the poet describes the 'horrible fureur de Mars,' who sows in France the terror, wrath, and disputes of Olympus; Jupiter calls himself God, yet he rules over Minerva and Ceres. There follow lamentations over war and the civil troubles of France; imprecations upon warmongers; and charming pictures of peace, its works and pleasures.] Though a Catholic, de Brach, like his friend Montaigne, had friends on both sides and is able to rise above the dissensions of the hour.

In his collective *Euvres* of 1572/3, J.-A. de Baïf included a rather elaborate *Hymne de la Paix*, dedicated to the Queen of Navarre. With this dedication, it may possibly be intended to refer to the Pacification of Saint-Germain, but there is no allusion to that event, nor is the poem very well suited to it; it appears rather to be on the marriage of Marguerite de Valois to the King of Navarre. The address, which is purely complimentary, ends abruptly at v. 28, where the hymn begins:

> Je veux louer la Paix, c'est la Paix que je chante,

and what follows is a full-blown encomium of Peace—her high parentage, the blessing she brings, the iniquity and horror of war—ending with an appeal to 'kings,' especially Christian kings—to preserve the gift of peace. Peace is the daughter of that 'Amitié' who preserves the universe of the four elements; Peace permits the arts to flourish and brings joy to our lives; but some fury or Erinnys drives men to think that war is glorious, whereas it is full of horror; true glory resides in preserving virtue and justice: therefore, Kings, since you rule over Christians and not savages or Turks, think of your Christian duty, preserve peace, and stay within your ancient boundaries.

A striking aspect of this poem is its resemblance to Ronsard's peace poems of 1558–59.[204] Indeed it is very tempting to date it

---

[202]Quoted by Dezeimeris, 2.xv.

[203]Raymond, *Influence* 2.141–42. The following summary is by Raymond, who notes the influence of Ronsard's 1559 poems and his *Misères*.

[204]Baïf, *Euvres en Rimes* (Charles Marty-Laveaux, ed. [Paris, 1881], p. 244): 'Je veux louer la Paix, c'est la Paix que je chante'; Ronsard, *Paix* 49: 'D'une si belle Paix je veux chanter merveille.' Baïf, p. 224: 'Cette belle machine / Sans la bonne amitié tomberoit en ruine'; Ronsard, *Paix* 73: 'Apres avoir par ordre arrangé la machine, / Et lié ce grand Corps d'une amitié divine.' Baïf, p. 225: 'Et le gentil Amour chaufe

close to that time and to think that it may originally have been intended as Baïf's contribution to the poetical campaign of Cateau-Cambrésis. The appeal to the kings would very well suit that occasion; for example:

> O Roys pensès à vous, et puis que Dieu vous done
> Le beau don de la Paix, chacun de vous s'adone
> A l'aimer et garder, Qui premier l'enfreindre,
> Qu'il tombe à la mercy du Roy qu'il assaudra
> Que son ennemy son païs soit la proye. . . .

As the poem now stands, this is intended generally, and 'puis que Dieu vous done / Le beau don de la Paix' must mean 'Since peace by divine ordinance is in the keeping of kings'; but the words would more naturally suit a particular occasion and mean: 'Since God has granted you [this] peace, cherish and guard it.' A similar expression was extracted from Ronsard by the peace of 1559:

> Or apres meinte guerre et meinte trefve aussi,
> Vostre grand Cardinal avecq' Montmorency
> Vous ont traitté la Paix: il faut qu'on la garde,
> Ceux qui la gardent bien, le haut Dieu les regarde,
> Et ne regarde point un Roy, de qui la main
> Tousjours trempe son glaive au pauvre sang humain.
>
> [*Paix*, 43–48]

Baïf goes on to curse the peacebreaker and bless the peaceful, as do also Ronsard and Grévin (pp. 107, 112).

Yet close as this poem is in topics and in expression to Ronsard's poems for Cateau-Cambrésis, we are not entitled to speak simply of imitation of Ronsard by Baïf. Their use of the same topics in poem after poem is more complicated than that. Here, for example, they alone, so far as I can remember, call the principle of the cosmos

---

tout de son feu'; Ronsard, *Paix* 157: 'Amour comme une flamme entre dans noz courages.' Baïf, p. 227: 'Que veux-tu conquester? . . . Ou vont les plus . . . grands Empereurs? . . . Ils ne sont plus que poudre'; Ronsard, *Paix* 229: 'Que souhaitez-vous plus? . . . Et apres vostre mort, fussiez vous Empereur, Vous ne serez plus qu'un simple laboureur.' Baïf, p. 227: 'Voir hommes et chevaux / Pesle-mesle entassez, Voir de sang les ruisseaux'; Ronsard, *Exhort.* 159–62: 'Tant de chevaux occis . . . Empescher tout le cours de Moselle.' Baïf, p. 227: 'Et quel plaisir prens-tu, race frelle chetive, / De te hater la mort, qui jamais n'est tardive?'; Ronsard, *Exhort.* 88ff.: 'Quelle fureur vous tient de vous entretuer / Et devant vostre temps aux enfers vous ruer . . . ? La mort vient assez tost, helas, sans qu'on l'avance.' Baïf, p. 227: 'Ta folle avarice / Redouble ton malheur faisant de vertu vice'; Ronsard, *Exhort.* 170: 'Et d'un vice execrable on fait une vertu.'

'amitié' in this context. Baïf did not get that from Ronsard. Where he got this and all that goes with it will be demonstrated below.[205] Did Ronsard apply to the same source, or did he borrow the expression from Baïf? Was Baïf's *Hymne à la Paix* in existence before Ronsard wrote *La Paix*?

In the years immediately following the Massacre of St. Bartholomew, there were few opportunities for celebrating peace in France. The death of Charles IX and the succession of Henri III (1574) altered nothing in the fundamental situation. One might pray for peace—Amadis Jamyn, *Prière pour la Paix, faite pour reciter en une comédie* and *A Vénus pour la Paix*[206]—but the epiphanies of the goddess herself were fleeting. At one moment, the king's younger brother, the Duke of Alençon, who courted the Huguenots, seemed the principal threat to the regime. Both he and Henri of Navarre were kept under surveillance at Court, but on September 15, 1575, Alençon made his escape and became the rallying point for a renewal of the war. The Queen Mother at once took to the road and managed to have conferences with her rebellious son at Dreux and Chambord, and following him into Poitou finally secured a truce (November 8) which was ratified on November 21 at Champigny, where Catherine occupied the chateau of the Duke of Montpensier. From November 28 until shortly after Christmas, she lingered in nearby Poitiers. Here she may have had presented to her a long *Panegyris de pace* in Latin verse composed by a young Scots visitor, Hercules Rollock, and published at Poitiers at the beginning of the new year. Hercules was the elder brother of the better-known Robert Rollock, the first Principal of Edinburgh University.[207]

After a summons to his Muse to lay aside her mourning for the wars, Rollock touches on recent events—Henri's return from Poland, his cautious policy, the departure from Paris of the 'Allenconius heros,' and his

[205]Below, pp. 257–61.

[206]*Œuvres poétiques* (Paris: Patisson, 1575), f. 67ʳ and f. 70ʳ.

[207]*Panegyris de pace in Gallia constituenda. Ad virum amplissimum Petrum Ratum, Pictaviensis provinciae praesidem. Auctore Hercule Rolloco* (Poitiers: in officina Bocherum, [1576]). The copy in the University of Edinburgh Library (of which I use a microfilm) is the only one known to me; evidently it was the author's own copy, since lines are canceled throughout and substitutions written in the margins. It came to the University among the books of William Drummond of Hawthornden. That the poem was published early in 1576 is an inference both from the contents and from the use of the word *strena* (presumably New Year's gift) in the dedicatory epigram. The *Panegyris* was not included with Rollock's other verse in the *DPS* and was unknown to the writer of the notice in the *Dict. Nat. Biog.*; but see Bradner, *Musae Anglicanae*, pp. 125, 348. A second poem *Carmen paraeneticum ad iuventutem Gallicam de bello civili* is included in the *DPS* 2.376.

success in rallying forces to his standard. Romulus might slay his brother Remus, but these two brothers were not suckled by a she-wolf. Their mother will reconcile them. Come, then, Mother of kings, convert your sons to peace and give repose to the realm that your last years may be tranquil and you may rejoice in your children. Let them keep to the natural order by which the elder reigns. Hearken to the cries of the people. If, Princes, you are moved by military ambition, glory may be won in foreign lands. Above all, guard against the intrigues of such as would protract the wars for their selfish ends; they are like the cuttle-fish that beclouds the waters to elude its pursuer. Citizens of the happy land of Poitou, receive the Queen and her train, receive the youth terrible in war, with hospitality and gifts. By a holy truce (*foedere*) they have laid in your soil the foundation (*primordia*) of peace. And you, my Muse, having essayed so high a path, having dared to appear in public and to enter the house of kings, cherish peace: if heaven is kind, I shall yet celebrate greater things.[208]

The 'Paix de Monsieur'—so called from the prominent role of Alençon—was concluded in the spring (May 8, 1576) and gave wide liberties to the Huguenots and valuable *appanages* to their leaders. The event does not seem to have been much commemorated in verse, perhaps because the poets tended to side with the fortunes of the crown; but we may mention an anonymous poem, *Advertissemens aux trois Estatz*, probably published in anticipation of the assembly of the States General in November.[209] After the old fashion, but in the new literary style, the writer addresses in turn the 'Noblesse,' the 'gens d'Eglise,' and the 'gens de la Justice et le reste du peuple,' ending with a prayer to God. As befits the moment, the terms are rather general, but the tolerant attitude is that of the 'Politiques.' To the Nobility, 'nobles estraits dela race troyenne du sang de Francion,' are presented the miseries of war and their own presumed contrition:

> J'ose dire que ceux que pensiez ennemis
> estans morts sont de vous estimez bons amis.

Woe to him who first brought the Germans into France! That man was mad who left the comforts of home to rush into battle. But if you are bent on fighting, go against the Mohammedan Turks. To the Clergy:

[208]'Ausa es / Credere te vulgi Regumque subire Penates.' The last phrase may imply that Rollock presented, or hoped to present, his poem to the queen.
[209]*Advertissemens aux trois Estatz de la France. Sur l'entretenement de la paix. Au roy treschrestien Henry III du nom, Roy de France et de Boulogne* (Paris: François Tabert, 1576) [BN Rés. Ye. 3501]; about 520 lines. At the front a short ode *Au Roy.*

differences are the basis of harmony; you must forget injuries and bless your enemies; our wars are worse than the wars of pagans. To the Third Estate: the people are a body, injury to a part injures the whole; magistrates can function properly only in peace, keeping the people 'en bride et bien posé.'[210]

The 'Paix de Monsieur,' favorable to the Protestants, only hastened the birth of the Catholic Ligue, and this in turn led to the Protestants again taking up arms in August. Another year of hostilities ended in the somewhat more balanced Peace of Bergerac (September 17, 1577). Alençon meanwhile had been reconciled with the King. In this year, presumably before the Peace of Bergerac, Philibert Bugnyon produced a poem, *De la Paix et du proffit qu'elle rapporte*, which, lacking the poetic quality of the same writer's *Erotasmes*, is one long cry for peace:[211]

> Il est temps que la Paix arrive
> En ce Royaume foudroyé.

Contrasting the states of peace and war,[212] Bugnyon comes to his main point: that Frenchmen should unite against the mercenaries who are enriching Germany with the spoils of France:

> Soldats, endossez donc vos armes,
> Et prenez vos glaives tranchans,
> Pour donner des fortes alarmes
> A ces Tudesques trop meschans.[213]

[210]Echoes of Ronsard's peace poems are especially clear in the first part; e.g., the contrast between domestic comfort and war, *Exhort.* 171ff.: 'mille chemins mortels . . . / Nous meinent . . . aux rives pallissantes, / Sans le coupable fer'; 'O vous qui bruslez / De voir sur vos dos craquer les corselets,' cf. 'ouir les armes / Craquer sur le dos de gendarmes' (*Ode* 82–83). That wars in which brother slays brother are worse than pagan is a topic of Erasmus (*Bellum* 959D) and Clichtove, *De bello* 8–9). In the preliminary ode *Au Roy*, 'la Paix augmente tout, la guerre tout descroit' is of course Sallust, but here perhaps from Erasmus' *Bellum* 957E.

[211]Lyons: B. Rigaud, 1577 [Lyons, Bibliothèque de la Ville 316540].

[212]This development seems to have been suggested by Du Verdier's *Antithèses* (above, p. 145).

[213]In 1577, probably after the Peace of Bergerac, Rigaud reprinted, again anonymously, the *Retour de la Paix en France* of Gilles Corrozet [BN Rés. Ye. 4712]. The title page bears the same device as the 1570 imprint (above, p. 87, n. 21), and this device is also used for Bugnyon's poems.

Le Roux de Lincy, *Chants* 2.367, 370, prints two *chansons* under the date 1578. One of them, *Les Adieux*, we know to be as early as 1570 (above, p. 147, n. 191). The other,

The Peace of Felix, ending the 'Guerre des Amourex,' was negotiated in the king's name by the Duke of Alençon (later the Duke of Anjou), and signed November 26, 1580. It was the occasion of a *Hymne de la Paix* by Guillaume Du Bartas.[214] In welcoming the 'sainte fille du Ciel . . . depuis vingt ans aux Gaules incognue,' Du Bartas runs lightly through the obligatory commonplaces—merchants now free to trade; legal processes restored; rejoicing with *feux de joie*; thanks to God—and comes to the immediate situation with a blessing on the King, the Duke of Alençon, and Henri of Navarre as peacemakers. He hopes that Alençon will 'pacify' the Low Countries and that the King of Navarre will regain southern Navarre from the Spaniard.[215] The *Hymne* ends with a guarded invocation, probably intended for the King of Navarre.[216]

In 1584 the death of the Duke of Anjou left only the Protestant Henri of Navarre as presumptive heir to the throne, and the Catholic Ligue hardened itself for the most desperate resistance. A not quite impossible hope was that the King of Navarre might be induced once more to change his religion, and with this end in view Catherine de Medici, old and ill as she was, braved the rigors of winter and the perils of roads infested with brigand soldiers, to visit him in the vicinity of Angoulême, where she spent two months (December 1586–January 1587). The Conference of Saint-Brice, with the accompanying truce, served only to give Henri of Navarre time to import new reinforcements from Germany; but at the beginning,

---

a pleasing dialogue between 'La Paix' and 'La France,' may refer to the Peace of Monsieur or the Peace of Bergerac—for example,

> Nous prirons tretous ensemble
> Pour la lignée des Vallois,
> Que nous tienne en assurance
> Sous l'heureuse don de la paix,
> Puisqu' ils ont fait la promesse
> Nous y maintenir.

I have not seen the *Hymne au Roy sur la Paix* of Clovis Hesteau de Nuysement in his *Œuvres poétiques* (Paris: Abel L'Angelier, 1578), f. 28 (Raymond, *Bibliographie*, p. 89).

[214]Du Bartas, *Works*, Urban T. Holmes, John C. Lyons, and Robert W. Linker, eds. (Chapel Hill, N.C., 1940), 3.487; see 1.98.104; the earliest edition known is that of Antwerp (Gaspar de la Romaine), 1582.

[215]Alençon had been offered the sovereignty of the Low Countries in September. The Spanish seizure of Spanish Navarre was an old grievance (1512), but one that Henry of Navarre hoped to avenge.

[216]
> Or Sire, en attendant
> Que j'aille ton beau nom par le monde espandant,
> Je chante le berceau de la terre nouvelle,
> Comme un doux avant-jour d'une chanson si belle.

while there seemed to be hope, a young poet of Angoulême, Paul Thomas, greeted the Queen with a Latin ode, entitled, when included in his works, *Ad Catherinam Mediceam, regum matrem, cum Pacis causa in Engolismos se contulisset anno M.D.LXXXVI.*[217] Catherine is addressed as the Cybele of France, a mother of gods, on progress through the world. The poem is a moderately clever manipulation of Horace, *Carm.* 1.2:

> Iam satis demens in acuta Martis
> Impios cives furor egit arma.[218]

After describing the horrors of civil war, the poet asks:

> Bella quis tandem lacrimosa dulci
> Pace mutabit?

And answers:

> Sancta procedes Cybele precamur
> Cui malis nostris proprium mederi.

She is invoked to bring the blessings of peace, which are enumerated, and the poem ends:

> Voce tunc omnes animoque puro,
> Gallicae numen Cybeles adorent,
> Eius et nutu sibi tanta clament
> Commoda parta.

A series of successes for the Protestants was followed by the triumph of the Ligue over Henri III, who submitted to sign the Edict

---

[217]*Poemata*, 2d ed. (Paris: C. Morel, 1627), p. 174. Thomas, born c. 1570 at Jarnac, very close to the castle of Saint-Brice, became a lawyer in Angoulême. He may at the time have been studying at Poitiers or Paris. There is nothing to show that the poem actually was presented to the queen mother, but a suitable occasion would have been the elaborate celebration of her *fête* when she paused at Saint-Maixent on November 25.

[218]
> Iam satis terris nivis atque dirae
> Grandinis misit Pater et rubente . . .
>
> Quem vocet divom populus ruentis
> Imperi rebus? . . .
>
> Cui dabit partis scelus expiandi
> Iuppiter? Tandem venias precamur . . .

of Union (of all Catholics against heretics) at Rouen on July 21, 1588, but hoped for his revenge when the States General met at Blois in September. In this year, Louis Le Roy brought out a new edition of his *Exhortation* of 1570 (Paris: J. du Puy, 1588). The Edict of Union was anticipated by an anonymous *Cantique à Dieu pour tost jouir de la paix*, printed at the end of June.[219] Avoiding more crucial issues, the writer assumes that the only enemy is the German mercenaries. Our captivity is ended, our sins have been punished; with God's help the king hopes for victory over the wicked: as the Egyptians were engulfed in the Red Sea, God will overwhelm the Germans in the Marne—

> Tu l'enveloperas dedans la profondeur
> Des Abismes de Marne, et parmy le roideur
> De son cours ondoyant on cognostra les corps
> Des ennemis de Dieu sanglants, roides et morts,
> On verra les chevaux les pistoles les armes
> (Appuy de leur vignes de farouches alarmes)
> Flotter par dessus l'eau et servir de message
> Au Roy et à Paris, de ce juste carnage.[220]

Meanwhile 'la troupe catholique' chant round the altar of God. The rather vigorous *Cantique* is followed by a prose poem, *Resjouissance de la Paix*, made up of the traditional commonplaces,[221] and this in turn by a *Hymne de la Paix*, describing in Ronsardian language the Golden Age, which the poet hopes is now returning to France.[222]

The entire literary career of Thomas Guiet, native of Berry and master baker in Paris, seems to have been concentrated within the year 1588, in the course of which he published four poetical pamphlets on public events.[223] His *Resiouissance de la Paix*, a respectable

[219]The BN copy (Rés. Ye. 3653) is without title page; at the end of the pamphlet (p. 15): 'achevé d'imprimer ce dernier iour de iuin 1588.'

[220]Perhaps an echo of the less agreeable message of the Seine in Ronsard's *Misères* 108–10: 'Et Seine qui . . . bestail . . . ravissoit, De son malheur futur Paris avertissoit' (cf. also *Exhort.* 159–62).

[221]The peasant fears no more; travelers move freely; 'les collèges . . . par cy-devant non frequentez et muets, de recheffe multiplient'; merchants . . . , artisans, and so on. Compare above, for 'les collèges,' Passerat, p. 141; Navières, p. 149, and n. 195.

[222]The Golden Age ended when the folk learned the use of the 'two metals,' 'Qu'elle becha . . . / Dans les boyaux de nostre grande mere'; cf. Ronsard, *Exhort.* 123–24: 'qui dechira la terre, / Et dedans ses boyaux le fer y alla querre,' and the following lines for the two fatal metals, iron and gold. In the fields were the flocks 'des Dieux bouquins et des gentiles Fees' (Ronsardian).

[223]All four by different Paris printers. In addition to the *Resioussance*, they are: *Advertissement faict au Roy le vingtiesme de ce mois estant a sa ville de Blois* (M. Jouin) [BN

enough performance, may perhaps be accepted as the voice of the Paris tradesman in response to the Edict of Union.[224] The poem falls into three parts: first, a summons to the four Estates to rejoice in the peace and to be united, remembering their shortcomings and trusting to conquer 'ceux qui par faulce entreprise / Ont massacré la Catholique Eglise'; second, a summons to all to welcome the king on his return to Paris; and finally, a prayer to the king reiterating the loyalty of the people and the perversity of the Huguenots. Movement is imparted to the poem throughout by the quasi-refrain of 'heureuse paix' in the first part and 'approchez-vous' in the second, while relief is sought in the second part by including in a bravura passage a summons to the animals and birds to join in the rejoicing:[225]

> Vous les oiseaux des pays plus arides,
> Et ceux aussi des maretz aquatiques,
> Degorgez vous pour ensemble chanter
> Et louer Dieu, son sainct nom exalter.
> Si les Serin et Linot en la cage
> Sont detenuz, au moins que le ramage
> Serve pourtant à leur donner plaisir,
> S'ils n'ont tousiours de chanter le loisir. . . .

Few of the more responsible literary voices seem to have been raised in praise of the Edict of Union.[226] But at Lyons, the young Pierre Matthieu, at this time a partisan of the Guises, but later well-known as the historian of Henri IV, welcomed the Union in enthusiastic verse.[227] He hails the peace as a triumph over the Huguenots. The

---

Rés. Ye. 3500]; *Convi de resjouissance au peuple de Paris sur le retour du Roy* . . . (J. de Puis) [BN Rés. Ye. 4116]; *La Harangue qui doit estre faite à l'assemblée des Etats à Blois* . . . (H. Velu) [BN Rés. Ye. 4127].

[224]*La Resiouissance de la paix, presentee aux quatre Estatz de la France, par Thomas Guiet, M. Boulanger a Paris, natif de Berry* (Paris: Jean Coqueret, 1588) [BN Rés. Ye. 4117]. The poem is dedicated to 'Monsieur Cordelle, Commissaire au Chastelet de Paris.'

[225]Compare a similar passage in the *Hymne* of the Protestant F.G. above, p. 142, and the address to 'Oyseaux' in Sagon (ed. 1550, sig. C). This development strikes a mediaeval note and perhaps in both cases echoes some older poem that escapes me.

[226]In the popular class I note *Chanson nouvelle de la Paix, par le peuple de France* (Lyons: B. Rigaud, 1588). Baudrier (3.401) quotes four lines.

[227]*Stances sur l'heureuse publication de la paix et saincte union. Avec un Hymne du mesme argument, prins de l'Erinophile du sieur de Sainct Germain d'Apchon, chevalier de l'ordre du Roy. Par Pierre Matthieu, docteur es Droicts* (Lyons: B. Rigaud, 1588) [BN Rés. Ye. 4381]. There are twenty-two eight-line stanzas. The *Hymne*, fourteen four-line stanzas, turns on the image of calm after storm. It is followed by two Latin epigrams by Matthieu, dated July 29, 1588, 'apud Fontanam amoenissimam agri Lugdunensis villam.' At the end of the volume, a Latin epigram on the Union by André Amyot.

goddess transforms our grief into joy, and happy are the old men who, after thirty years of war, have lived to see this day. The French scepter could not endure the hand of 'a Huguenot or a tyrant.' God will regard our tears and will bless our king with an heir. European kings will serve the name of Henri, the 'mignon' of Peace.

In the next year Catherine de Medici died and Henri III was assassinated; it remained for Henri of Navarre to win his throne from the Ligue and from the Spanish claimant. To the year 1590, but without direct allusion to any specific event, belongs an impressive *Hymne de la Guerre et de la Paix*, addressed to the king and published anonymously at Tours.[228] The writer pretty clearly is a Protestant, and his style, though based on Ronsard, even more strongly recalls Du Bartas:

> Vous Roy de l'univers, vous maître de tonnerre,
> Vous qui feistes de rien les cieux, l'onde et la terre,
> L'homme et les animaux,
> Qui melastes parmy les douceurs de nos vies
> Les regrets, les fureurs, les dépits, les envies,
> Les malheurs et les maux,
> Qui plantâtes l'audace au fond de nos entrailles,
> Mille dissentions, l'horreur de cent batailles,
> La vengeance et l'orgueil . . .[229]

Defying God, man is overthrown by Him and made the prey of 'les bestes les plus petites . . . cyrons . . . pouls . . . vers,' having left to him only virtue and peace, and these he rejects. With this introduction, the poem proceeds to an apostrophe of War and a eulogy of Peace, and ends with a prayer to Peace:

> Aye pitié de nous: dans les mains de nos Princes
> Remets l'authorité et toutes les Provinces
> Serves à nostre Roy,
> Affin, Paix, que par toy reflorisse la France
> Le service de Dieu, les bons et la science
> Le repos et la Foy.

The contrast of war and peace, the substance of the poem, is of course the staple of peace poetry, but very likely in this case it is a re-

---

[228]*Himne de la Guerre et de la Paix, au Roy* (Tours: Montr'oeil and Richer, 1590) [BN Rés. Ye. 544]. This anonymous *Himne* of 1590 is ascribed by A. Cioranescu in his *Bibliographie* to Philippe Le Plessis-Prévost, but he does not indicate how he knows this. For this information I am grateful to Mme Nerina Belmas Clerici in a letter to me, January 10, 1977.

[229][Marginal note by J.H.: All this is from God! R.G.]

flection of Ronsard. The writer delights in compound adjectives.[230]
His choice of commonplaces also recalls Ronsard. Thus Peace holds
in her hand the 'chain' of the elements, and the poet adds, in the
style of learned enigma, and with Hermetic overtones:

> Par toi le demi-Dieu, le docte et grand Chimiste,
> Fait germer dans son bain l'Electre trismegiste,
>   Et naistre l'or vitrin:
> Qui sert contre tous maux d'unique medicine,
> Qui sera de Sion la luizante courtine,
>   Où nous vivrons sans fin.

Perhaps this means that Nature, through Peace, creates the fifth ele-
ment.

The momentous step that alone could settle the troubles of
France, the king's abjuration of his Protestant faith, was taken in
1593, when at the Conference of Suresnes (in May) before the 'royal'
Catholics and the Catholics of the Union (of 1588), the king's inten-
tion was announced, and when on July 25 he consummated it by at-
tending mass in the cathedral of Saint-Denis. A truce of ten days,
declared in view of the conference, was extended for three months
upon the announcement of the king's resolution. Though Protes-
tants could hardly be pleased, and many Ligueurs thought the king's
conversion insincere, the majority welcomed the truce and the con-
version as the dawn of a new day. These feelings found expression
in an *Ode sur la Trefve*, which accordingly may be placed between
May and July.[231] From its four triads (strophe and antistrophe in
twelve lines, epode in ten), a few quotations will make the writer's
position clear:

> Ie te saluë ô douce Trefve,
> Unique soulas de noz maux,
> Qui avec ta douceur soüefve
> Donne relasche à noz travaux . . .

[230]E.g., *Himne*, p. 8:

> La Paix fille de Dieu, la Paix toute-sacrée
>   Et mere de bonté,
> Donne-fruits, donne-bien, donne-heur, donne-science,
> Donne-honneur, donne-vie, oste-soing, ayme France,
>   Aime-ioie et repos.

[231]I know only the two copies of this poem in the Bibliothèque Nationale, both of
which lack the title page. On the front of one (Rés. Ye. 4493) is written the date
1590, on the other (Ye. 55638) 1593; the latter date is obviously right.

> Ce n'est point une trefve inique,
> Contraire à la saincte union,
> Qui pour exalter l'heretique
> Abaisse la religion:
> C'est un courriere d'Astrée . . .
> Ainsi ô Trefve bien-heureuse,
> Tu es douce aux plus doux esprits,
> Mais aux coeurs de fureur aspris
> Tu es dure aspre et rigoureuse. . . .
> Beny soit ce Roy pacifique,
> Qui tout plein de compassion
> Donne la foy à l'heretique
> Et trefve à noz afflictions. . . .
> Beniste soit la conference,
> Benist soit le sacré Senat,
> Qui avec leur grave prudence
> Ont sauvé l'Eglise et l'Estat. . . .

There still remained the difficult task of shaking off the Spaniard—the old enemy Philip II—and of suppressing the remnant of the Ligue. Full settlement was anticipated in 1595 in an anonymous *Chant pastoral de quatre nourrissons des Muses*, which, since it ends with a 'Chant des Muses de l'université de Paris,' apparently emanated from the University.[232] It is attractively written, in a full, flowing style.

Theonot, singing to his 'chevrettes et moutons,' hints that good things are in store. He meets Epitrope and Colombin, who lament the diminishing of their flocks from the attacks of wolves and diseases. Theonot reassures them:

> L'heur vous reviendra voir, et la deesse Astrée
> Viendra bien tost icy refaire son entrée. . . .
> Dieu nous a redonné un grand PAN pour remettre
> Les troupeaux egarez en leur patis et cloistre, . . .
> Qui liberalement prodigue de sa vie, . . .
> Entrant en la forest pleine d'ombrages mouls,
> Seul dontera l'orgueil d'Espaigne et de ses lous.

Epitrope observes:

[232]*Chant pastoral de quatre nourrissons des Muses, pour l'avantvenuë d'une bonne paix, à l'honneur de Dieu, et du Roy tres chrestien* [device: angel with harp, and motto: Scripturas scrutamini] (Paris: Philippe du Pré, 1595); sixteen numbered pages [BN Rés. Ye. 3703]. The title probably does not imply that it is a joint production; the style is uniform.

[162]

Par la porte lon void entrer le vray berger,
Mais par la fenestre entre un Ligueur estranger.

As they are singing the praise of Henri, Tonon appears and reminds them of a prophetic song he once had heard sung by a disembodied voice. They sing this Song of the University Muses, to the effect that it is not always stormy weather and that under a faithful prince Justice and Peace will return. Night falls, and they prepare to return home.[233]

The same air of expectancy characterizes three *chansons* on peace that have been assigned to the years 1594–95.[234] One of them chiefly foresees an end to pillage:

Mais la trouppe est bien petite
De ce qui n'ont rien desrobé,
Soit Huguenot ou Papiste. . . .
Mais pour la fin Dieu leur pardon
Comme il fit au bon larron.

Another prays that the peace may continue and that the king be 'amateur des sainctes loix'; while the third very charmingly evokes the return of Venus and the nymphs in the springtime of peace:[235]

Voicy la saison plaisante,
Florissante,
Que la beau printemps conduict;
Voicy le soleil qui chasse
Froide glace,
Voicy l'esté qui le suit.

We pass to the final settlement in the Edict of Nantes (April 13, 1598) and the Treaty of Vervins (signed May 2, 1598).[236] The

---

[233]The situation and management of the poem recall Belleau—for example, the late entrance of Tonon parallels the late entrance of Perot in Belleau's eclogue, and the detachable *chanson* parallels his 'Chant de la Paix.' Again, the use of the name 'Pan' for the king forcibly recalls Marot's *Eglogue au Roy*, and the *impossibilia* (p. 11): 'The lamb will dwell with the wolf, and so on, before I forget Henri,' might be compared with the end of that poem. But in the absence of verbal echoes of either Belleau or Marot, these similarities may only be the result of an independent imitation of Virgil and the bucolic tradition.

[234]Le Roux de Lincy, *Chants* 2.563–70; on p. 600 the indication of a fourth *chanson* on peace.

[235]Lenient, *Poésie patriotique*, p. 235, n.2, quotes Jean Baptiste Weckerlin, *L'Ancienne chanson populaire en France* [16ᵉ et 17ᵉ siècles] (Paris, 1887), to the effect that these verses are remodeled on a *chanson* of the time of Henri III.

[236]I note, but have not seen, an extensive work by Toussain Sybille, *Le Triomphe de*

Treaty of Vervins, chiefly between the French crown and Philip II (who died four months later), ranks with that of Cateau-Cambrésis as a European settlement. The French commissioners were the minister Pomponne de Bellièvre and the Marquis of Sillery. When proclaimed on June 12, the peace brought forth poems in considerable numbers, but the voices that hailed Cateau were long silent, and those celebrating Vervins were feeble in comparison. They were often an echo. As the commissioners at Vervins read over the treaty of Cateau-Cambrésis,[237] so the poets appear to have conned the poems that Ronsard wrote for the occasion. One who was close to the event, being a native of Vervins, was Marc Lescarbot, who made his literary debut at this time and was destined to win at least a transatlantic immortality with his fascinating *Histoire de la nouvelle France*.[238] Before the proclamation of the peace, on May 14 and again on May 31, Lescarbot pronounced Latin orations before the papal legate (Alessandro Marzi de Medici, Cardinal of Florence), who was an important figure at the conference.[239] The second, which is more directly concerned with the peace, was published also in French together with a number of poems for the occasion.[240] Primarily a celebration of the internal settlement of France, it appears to give all credit to the Cardinal, and though well written displays an alarming erudition.[241] Among the general praises of peace, the speaker lingers over the topic of Discord, who will henceforth be chained, and the arrival of Astraea from heaven. These topics, now so well worn, also furnish the substance of the poems that follow the oration and are chiefly addressed to Bellièvre and Sillery.[242] The last poem, however, is addressed to Madame de

---

la Paix avec un traicté du jugement de Dieu sur l'impiété des tyrans (Lyon, T. Ancelin, 1597) [BN 8° Lb³⁵. 682].

[237]*Memoires de Bellievre et de Silleri contenant un Journal concernant la Negociation de la Paix Traitée à Vervins l'an 1598*, 2 vols. (The Hague, 1596).

[238]See *History of New France*, English trans. W. L. Grant (Publications of the Champlain Society, Vols. 1, 7, 11 [Toronto, 1907–14]); Vol. 3 also contains Lescarbot's poems *Les Muses de la Nouvelle France* and a bibliography. I have borrowed several details from the Introduction by H. P. Biggar.

[239]*Actio gratiarum pro pace . . . per Marcum Scarbotium* (Paris: F. Morel, 1598). I have not seen this volume, which, according to Biggar, contains both orations. The first is a speech of gratitude to the Cardinal for his benefactions to Vervins.

[240]*Harangues d'action de graces pour la paix, prononcée en la ville de Vervin, le dernier jour de May, 1598, . . . avec poëmes sur la paix du mesme autheur* (Paris: F. Morel, 1598) [BN 8°Lb³⁵. 732].

[241]Lescarbot starts with Ammianus Marcellinus and goes on to the *Timaeus* of Plato, Cicero's *De republica*, Plutarch, Athenaeus, Suidas, Cassiodorus, Symmachus, and others, discussing by the way the various senses of the Greek word *nomos*.

[242]A *Chant Royal* dedicated to both; an Ode and a sonnet to Bellièvre; two sonnets to Sillery; one sonnet each to France, Mme de Coucy, and the town of Vervins; a longer poem to Mme de Coucy.

Coucy, wife of the Seigneur of Vervins, and does not refer to the Treaty of Vervins, but to a local event of 1592. At that time, it appears, Madame de Coucy had arranged a truce between Vervins and the town of Capelle-en-Thiérache, to the north of it, in the Spanish Netherlands, thus facilitating trade. This is the most complete 'peace poem' of the lot, running through all the common topics; if written in 1592, it shows that Lescarbot came to his work of 1598 already well prepared.[243]

We run rapidly over some other publications of this year.[244] A decidedly inferior performance is *Le Miracle de la Paix* by J. du Nesme, published at Paris and Lyons.[245] Peace rises like a new sun over France:

> Fille du Tout-puissant, alme, riche, faconde, . . .
> Arbitre qui maintiens l'un et lautre univers,
> Sans qui, comme iadis, tout iroit à l'envers,
> Je te salue, ô Paix.

God has wrought this miracle through his instrument Henri:

> Asculape non feint, c'est toy qui a causé
> Non le recolement du corps Hippolitique,
> Mais celuy d'un Royaume en mille parts brisé.

The Theseus also and the Hercules of France, Henri without a scepter and with only a sword withstood the power of Spain. Advice is offered to Nobles, Clergy, Judges, and People: let there be no recriminations; beware of evil advisers; be tolerant (it is dreadful that altar should op-

---

[243]Agriculture will flourish; the merchant may sail in safety as far as Iceland; the artisan may pursue his tasks. Astraea, the 'fille de Dieu,' returns with her companions, Piety, Faith, and others; and may we soon see the spider weaving webs in armor and the 'instrument de Bellone' transformed to a ploughshare. For these benefits, Madame—for gathering home the people of Vervins scattered by war—we and our descendants will set aside an annual feast-day in your name.

[244]I have not seen the following three poems, listed by J. A. Taschereau, *Cat. général des manuscrits français* (Paris, 1868–1918) 1.401–2: Anon., *Poème en forme de dialogisme sur l'arrivée de la Paix*; I.M.D.L. de Tarare, *Eglogue sur l'arrivée de la Paix*; Anon., *Chant de l'Estat de la France*. Nor have I seen a poem by the Sieur de Porchères quoted by Lenient, *Poésie patriotique* 1.241, from *Les Muses ralliées* (cf. Frédéric Lachèvre, *Bibliographie des recueils collectifs de poésies du xvie siècle* [Paris, 1927], 1.279).

[245]*Le Miracle de la paix en France, au Roy tres-chrestien de France et de Navarre, Henry IIII* (Lyons: Thibaud Ancelin, 1598); (Paris, 1598) [BN Ye. 1055]. The contents are: *Au Roy* (sonnet); *A sa maiesté* (quatrain); *Le Miracle* (39 fourteen-line stanzas); *Dialogue sur les troubles passez* (20 four-line stanzas: Heraclitus and Democritus); *L'Amour et les beautez d'Astrée, Dam.* *** (130 lines, amatory); two sonnets; *Epigrammes sur la guerre et la paix* (18 of these). J. du Nesme is also the author of *La Redemption* (Paris: A. Chappelet, 1606).

pose altar); Christians cannot afford to fight one another when the Turk is on the point of adding Austria to his empire.

Still less significant is an anonymous *Elégie*, turning on the point that hearts must be cleansed of venom.[246] A decidedly archaic note is struck by another anonymous poem, *La Resiouissance du peuple de France*:[247]

> Cessez vos pleurs, humains peuples François,
> Cessez cessez d'estre en facheux esmoys.

Begone those who whisper in kings' ears; let them go fight the Turk. Rebuild the ruined towns and castles. Merchants, prepare your shops for foreign traders; and come hither, Bretons, Spaniards, English, Italians, Easterlings, Scots:

> Et vous, Auxerrois, amenez vostre vin,
> En descendans au long de ce beau Sin.

Jean des Preys, who published (or republished) this poem at Langres, did well, at the end of a century of war and peace, in issuing one more edition of Molinet's *Testament de la Guerre* and a last edition of the anonymous *Adieu aux misères de la guerre*.[248]

The Treaty of Vervins does not seem to have inspired the stronger voices. Théodore-Agrippa d'Aubigné, Jacques Davy Duperron, Jean Bertaut, and the authors of the *Satire Menippée*, remained silent. Only the young Nicolas Vauquelin among poets of repute came forward with a *Chant de louanges au Roy pour la Paix*:[249]

[246]*Elégie sur l'heureux succez de la Paix, dedié [sic] aux Dames de Lyon* (Lyons: Jonas Gautherin, 1598) [BN Rés. Ye. 3954]. The writer may have been a Savoyard, since he speaks of the peace as made between Henry, Philip, and the Duke of Savoy. The elegy is followed by a sonnet *Sur les feux de joye*, which concludes:

> Feux de Paix, et de guerre en banissant les feux,
> A nos postérieurs soyez feux de memoyre.

[247]*La Reiouissance du peuple de France, sur la publication de la Paix qui a esté le vendredy douziesme iour de Juin, 1598* (Paris: François du Chesne, 1598) [BN Ye. 5556 and Rés. Ye. 4709]; (Langres: Iehan des Preys, 1598) [BN Rés. Ye. 4709].

[248]The *Testament* is anonymous, as usual; *Le Testament de la Guerre qui a regné longtemps en la France. Avec l'epitaphe de la Guerre morte. Ensemble les feux de ioye* (Langres: Iehan des Preys, 1598) [BN Rés. Ye. 4891]. There is also a Paris imprint, which I have not seen 1894 [Rés. Ye. 4890]. The epitaph (sonnet) and the *feux de joie* (huitain) add nothing of interest. The *Adieu aux misères* (Langres: Iehan des Preys, 1598) [BN Rés. Ye. 3452] I have not seen, but assume that it is the poem noted above for 1570 and 1578.

[249]Lyons: Pillehote, 1598; reprinted in 1604 (?) and in several miscellanies under the title *Ode de la Paix*; see *Œuvres complètes*, Georges Mongrédien, ed. (Paris: Picard, 1921), p. 19.

Pax Mundana

> Henry, dieu de nostre esperance,
> Tandis que l'empire t'attend,
> Que peut faire toute la France
> Afin de te rendre content?
> De quelles couronnes de gloire,
> D'arcs de triomphe et de lauriers,
> Peut-elle marquer ta victoire,
> Qui parmy ses soupirs derniers
> Et sur les cendres reschauffées,
> Au lieu d'un sepulchre si pront,
> Luy rebastit tant de trophées,
> Et luy met cent palmes au front.

The poet is constrained to tell Henri's deeds to posterity: even if he did not reign by legal right, still by his deserts he would have to be chosen king. His worth merits altars and temples. A Hercules, he came to save, and knew both to conquer and to spare. If to establish the rule of Jupiter, destiny required a War of the Giants, France may bless her griefs that have had this happy issue; to the civil wars she owes this Neptune who sends peace over sea and land. After your victories, repose! Your name is immortal, but death claims kings and peasants alike; while living for many, live sometimes for yourself. The hand that drives the thunderbolt also takes the cup from Ganymede. Perfect glory cannot be increased; arrest fortune by maintaining peace; your fame cannot be enlarged save by enlarging the universe.

This short ode of nine twelve-line stanzas makes no pretense of rivaling the expansiveness of Ronsard's *Ode de la Paix*. There is a touch of Pindarism in the poet's claim of involvement:

> Pour moy, dans ce lieu solitaire
> Où la fortune m'a reduict,
> A la fin ie ne puis me taire;
> Ton nom me reveille la nuict,
> Et porte en moy-mesme la honte
> D'un qui cache la verité.

And, Pindarically, he sets himself to 'advise' the prince: look no farther, your glory is complete.[250] But the moderation of the style, and the distance from which the hero is viewed, are more Horatian than Pindaric:

> Que de ce iour si venerable
> On s'aille a iamais souvenant,

[250]Cf. Ronsard, *Paix*, 203–36; *Ode* 19–36, 419–36.

> Auquel cet Alcide adorable,
> Malgré le ciel le retenant,
> Vint enfin visiter la terre.[251]

The divinity of the peace hero; that he deserves altars and temples; that like the Roman triumphator he should remember that he is mortal[252]—all are of course commonplaces. That the miseries of the civil wars were the just price of present joys is a commonplace of the time:

> La France, au milieu de ses larmes,
> Benit son mal et sa douleur,
> Adorant la cause des armes
> D'ou vient l'effet de son bonheur.
> Et, bien que ses champs et ses villes
> Ayent souffert si longuement,
> Elle doit aux guerres civiles
> Sa ioie et son contentement.

The peace poem, trimmed, generalized, and mature, herewith passes from the succession of Renaissance styles into the style we associate with Malherbe.[253]

[251]Cf. Horace, *Odes* 1.2.25–52; 4.5.

[252]
> l'arrest du ciel est tel
> Pour ceux qui portent des couronnes
> Comme pour les bergers des bois.

Cf. Horace, *Odes*, 1.4.13, and, e.g., Antoine de Baïf, *Hymne*, 139–44; and Nicolas Vauquelin, above.

[253]Below, p. 276.

V

Pax Alma, Veni:
Stobaeus and Vida

ἐν τᾷ γὰρ Εὐνομία ναίει κασιγνήται τε, βάθρον πολίων ἀσφαλές
Δίκα καὶ ὁμότροφος Εἰρήνα.

Pindar, *Ol.* 13.6–7

Within her walls dwelleth Law, and her sisters, the firm-set founda-
tion of cities, even Justice and Peace. (Trans. Sir John Sandys,
Loeb)

It is a merit of the Renaissance to have begun once more
to assimilate the Greek tradition in literature into what
was necessarily in the main a Latin and vernacular tradition. In po-
etry, the process was slow and tentative, hardly beginning with the
neo-Latin poets before the latter part of the fifteenth century in
Italy, accompanying the humanist conquest of the vernacular litera-
tures in the sixteenth, and reaching its high mark in France with the
Pléiade. Even here, we honor the intention more than the deed; a
longer period of assimilation and adjustment must elapse before the
forms of epic poetry, drama, the Pindaric ode would be sustained by
a corresponding fullness of spirit. Apart from form, however, there
was a chance for the detachable literary motive in the rhetorical na-
ture of Renaissance poetry, according to which a conscious process
of 'dilation' or expansion of themes was pursued on the basis of *loci
communes*. In reading a Greek poet or, more likely, one of the recent
Latin translations, the Renaissance poet, we may imagine, would
mark such promising passages or transcribe them into his common-
place book; and he would favor such collections as the *Greek Anthol-
ogy*, conveniently arranged under topics by Planudes, and the *Flori-
legium* of Stobaeus, if he had the erudition or the luck to approach
the latter.

[169]

For the topic of Peace, surviving Greek poetry offered relatively little apart from incidental references—chiefly Aristophanes' peace plays, which were little known. Hesiod was known, at least at second hand, and we may generally count on a consciousness that Eirene is one of the Horae and the daughter of Zeus and Themis; so already in Jean Marot (above, p. 80). The most congenial source, had it been generally known, might well have been Stobaeus' chapter περὶ Εἰρήνης (*Flor.* 55), an assemblage of poetical fragments from which we may still get our best idea of the invocation of Peace by the Greek poets, with characteristic epithets and associations.[1] I translate:

55.1, Euripides, *Chresphontes* (fragm. 462) (chorus): O Peace, deep in wealth (βαθύπλουτε), fairest of the blessed gods, I am jealous of your long delay. I feared that old age and its troubles would be upon me before I saw that happy time and heard the songs of lovely choirs and garlanded Revels. Come to my city, O Queen! Avert from our houses hateful strife and maddened ire that delights in sharpened steel. 55.2, Aristophanes, *The Farmers*: O Peace, deep in wealth, and O my little oxen team, would I might cease from war, and dig and delve, and after bathing drink new wine, with a radish and a gleaming loaf at hand. 55.3, Bacchylides, *Paeans*: Peace is the mother of great blessings for mankind—of wealth and the flowers of sweet-tongued songs; that on spangled altars the thighs of cattle and of long-haired sheep flame for the gods with yellow fire, and that young men are mindful of exercises, of flutes, of revels. In ironbound shields the busy spiders have their looms, and rust subdues the pointed spear and two-edged sword. The blast of brazen trumpets is heard no more; nor are our eyelids robbed of delicious slumber that soothes the heart. The streets are thronged with lovely banquets, and hymns to the boy-loves blaze up like fires. 55.4, Euripides, *Erechtheus*: Be my spear laid up for the spider to weave its web about, and may I dwell with grizzled age in peace. May I sing, and wreathe my hoary head with garlands, hanging my Thracian shield in the pillared shrine of Athena; and let me unfold the speech of books, the famous utterance of the wise. 55.5, Philemon, *Pyrrhus*: Philosophers, I am told, inquire—and waste much time with inquiring—what the Good may be. But what it is, no one has yet made out: Virtue and Thought, they say—in fact, they say everything but what the Good is. Living on the farm and digging the earth, *I* have found it. It is peace. Dear Zeus! what a delightful and kindly goddess she is! She bestows weddings, festivals, kinship, children, friends, wealth, health,

[1]Stobaeus' *Anthologion* was first published by V. Trincavelli at Rome in 1536. Conrad Gesner produced an edition, with Latin translation in 1543, as did Grotius in 1623.

bread, wine, pleasure: if these things are lacking, the life of living men is merely death. 55.6, Euripides, *Suppliants*: When war comes to a vote among the people, nobody reckons on his own death, but turns this evil off upon another; but if death were there before their eyes in the voting, spear-mad Greece would not be facing ruin. And yet we all recognize the better of two arguments, we all know the difference between good and bad, and know how much better peace is for men than war. She is, first of all, most friendly to the Muses, she hates lamentations, she delights in children, and rejoices in wealth. Letting these goods go, we basely take up wars, and, men and cities, make other men and other cities slaves. 55.7, Aristophanes, *The Islands*: Fool, fool! It simply comes down to this: to live on your farm in the country, away from business, with your own yoke of oxen, and to hear the flocks bleating and the voice of the grapes dripping in the press, and to have for supper finches and thrushes, and not to be waiting for fish from the market, three days old, overpriced and weighed on the hand of a cheating fishmonger. 55.8, Aristophanes, *Peace* 519: O Queen, bestower of the grape, with what name shall I address you? Where can I find a thousand-gallon word? 55.9, Menander: Peace supports the farmer well even among the rocks, war ill even on the plain. 55.10, Herodotus, *History* 1.87: No one is so witless as to prefer war to peace.

These delightful expressions, redolent of Hellenic charm and sense, chime well together, though descending from high lyric through comedy to prose, and make a kind of continuous poem of which Stobaeus is the rhapsode. The *topoi* of his selection have permeated Western thought, even in altering forms—literature and peace, religion and divine service, country life and farmers, spiders and rusting armor, slumber, children, wealth, celebrations.

Such at least may have been the impression made upon the modern Latin poet, Girolamo Vida, whose hymn *To Peace*—it dawns upon us as we read—is a transposition into Horatian verse of this chapter of Stobaeus. Though rather long, it should be read beside its original:[2]

Paci

Pax alma, dulce ubique nomen gentibus
Inter Deos pulcherrima
Pulcherrimos, quam me tui expectatio
Torquet morantis ah nimis,

[2]I do not know the destination of these verses. They are included in Vida's *Poemata* of 1550 and were presumably written after the publication of Stobaeus in 1536. Possibly they were inspired by the same hopeful moment as Zanchi's *Hymnus aeternae pacis*, i.e., 1545/46.

5   Tuumne, Diva, vivus adventum amplius
        Tempus videbone aureum?
    Umquamne erit, mundum his tenebris obsitum
        Tuo ut serenes lumine?
    Quando expetentem me, Dea, spe id irrita
10   Tanto beabis munere?
    Vereor, laboriosa ne longe prius
        Vincat senectus languidum,
    Quam rursus urbes divites conviviis
        Ludisque distinerier,
15 Quam rura videam cantibus laetissimis
        Omni sonare ab angulo:
    Unisque ventorum duellis aequora
        Metuenda, non Martis dolis.
    Ut omne telum pereat, ut chalybum genus
20   Haud nominetur amplius.
    Ut regum avarities et ambitio impotens
        Sepulta sit sub aequore.
    Absente te, vix uberes alunt agri
        Numquam colonum desidem:
25 Praesente vero, nuda saxa qui colit,
        Vel dormiens bonis fluit.
    Tu grata Musis, tu in foro versantibus
        Places et urbi praesides.
    Tu merce transmarina opes parantibus
30   Voto invocaris publico.
    Te divites, te ubique pauperum greges
        Laboriosi praedicant.
    Tibi viri, tibi pudicae feminae
        Praegestientes supplicant.
35 Tui senes, tui pueri amantissimi,
        Tui omnis aetas appetens.
    Tu, si quid est mortalibus boni uspiam,
        Id una nobis comparas.
    Tu sanitatem gentibus sacram et opes,
40   Et victum, et annonam, et merum,
    Securitatem, literas, et otium,
        Et nuptias, et liberos,
    Vitamque tandem adfers, amica cantibus,
        Adversa vero luctibus.
45 Tui simul Mars hauserit pedis sonum
        Facesset hinc celerrimus.
    Simul quiescent furta, caedes, vulnera,
        Strages, ruinae, incendia:
    Totque orbitates, liberorum tot stupra,
50   Crebrique raptus virginum.

[172]

Nec audietur amplius clangor tubae,
  Viros cientis ad necem
Iuvenemque vellentis tenellae ab coniugis
  Gremio, metu inspersum genas.
55 Quae, pluraque, viri si viderent principes
  Cum bella initio cogitant,
Vel abstinerent vel quibusvis ponerent
  Mox coepta conditionibus:
Neque eos libido, neque adeo ageret gloria
60   Ut perderent caeci omnia.
Istis si ego ab malis procul tandem absiem
  Tranquillitati redditus,
Videamque pendentes acervos arduis
  Scutorum ubique postibus,
65 Araneorum fila quos obduxerint
  Nigros vetusto in pulvere,
Ensesque rursus ferreasque cuspides
  In vomerem conflarier,
Vitam haud recusem pauperem traducere
70   Fodiens agrum incurvus manu.
Saltem animus ablatis mihi his terroribus
  Quiesceret liberrimus,
Possem laborem versibus solarier
  Cinctus olea canum caput;
75 Et nocte pauculos revolverem libros
  Vel, imbre detentus, die.
O Diva largitrix bonorum una omnium,
  Quo te vocabo nomine?
Quibus te honestis efferam praeconiis?
80   Dignum unde te verbis exprimam?
Opulenta salve: iam recurre huc aurea,
  Et nos tuo vultu bea.

This poem offers us a favorable example of Renaissance imitation, paraphrase, and assimilation. Stobaeus' selections are not taken in order, but, roughly speaking, lines 1–16 are from 55.1; lines 23–26 from 55.9; lines 37–44 from 55.5 (except that 'amica cantibus / adversa vero luctibus' is from 55.6); lines 55–60 are suggested by 55.6, but not closely translated; lines 61–76 are mostly from 55.4, with traits in 70–71 from 55.2 and in 67–68 from 55.3; and, finally, lines 77–80 closely paraphrase the two lines from Aristophanes' *Peace* in 55.8. The passage from Aristophanes' *Islands* in 55.7 is left untouched, and also the prose sentence from Herodotus in 55.10. In general, Vida is closest to his source at the beginning and becomes more allusive as he proceeds.

But the tone is all Latin. Overriding everything is the metrical association of Horace's *Epodes*, particularly *Epodes* 2 and 16, which conspires with the connotations of the Latin words and idioms to carry us far into a Roman atmosphere. Certain developments are not in Stobaeus at all, but introduce motives obligatory in Renaissance peace literature. Thus lines 17–22 cite the 'avarice and ambition of kings';[3] lines 27–36 call the roll of the classes who benefit from peace, not omitting the obligatory merchant;[4] and lines 45–54 list the conventional horrors of war, which make a smooth transition into the passage from Euripides' *Suppliants*.[5] Yet on the whole, the themes are Greek; the mood and the music are Latin.

Greek Peace Poetry and Some Renaissance Poems[6]

Aristophanes' peace plays, as we have said, had little direct influence on our poets. To this statement, however, there is one notable exception in the *Paix venue du ciel* of Guillaume Des Autels, in which the climax of the action, the drawing down to earth of the goddess Peace by means of golden chains, seems to be an obvious borrowing from the corresponding climax of Aristophanes' *Eirene*. The fact is the more interesting since in general the *Eirene* has seldom been imitated in modern times.[7] But this debt to Aristophanes is far from being the whole account; for Des Autels's poem, though reminiscent of the *rhétoriqueur* style in the conduct of the narrative, at the same time stands out among the French poems on peace in the degree to which it, humanistically, exploits Greek sources. Moreover, it employs them successfully. The examples that follow do not pretend to exhaust the subject.

At the beginning of the poem,[8] the god of Wealth is introduced with features that blend Aristophanes' *Plutus* with Aristophanes' own source, Hesiod:

---

[3]See appendix, no. 21.

[4]Ibid., no. 12.

[5]See Ibid., no. 22. Line 51, 'Nec audietur amplius clangor tubae' is from Stobaeus 55.3.9: οὐδ᾽ οὐκέτι σαλπίγγων κτύπος, οὐδὲ συλᾶται μελίφρων ὕπνος. 'Tempus aureum' in line 6 is Horace, *Epode* 16, 64 (cf. Vida line 81).

[6]Much of the remaining material in this chapter has been published under the title "Classical Poetry in Renaissance Poems on Peace" in Hutton, *Essays*, pp. 225–42.

[7]See Marie Delcourt, *La tradition des comiques anciens en France avant Molière* (Paris, 1934), Ch. 2, "Aristophane." It may be that Marot was alluding to the *Eirene* in *Le Voyage de Venise*.

[8]See the outline, above, pp. 115–16.

Pax Alma, Veni

> Ce Dieu que l'on dit estre et aveugle et boyteux,
> Qui suyt les efrontez et qui fuyt les honteus,
> Qui regne sur la terre et dessus le dos large
> De la mer, que de neufs estrangeres il charge,
> Ce Dieu fils de Ceres, qui en donnant le bien,
> N'avise point à ceux qui le meritent bien,
> Versoit l'or et l'argent par tout à grandes sommes.

The blind god of Wealth, who follows the shameless and avoids the modest, is the Plutus of the beginning of Aristophanes' play (28–31, 86–91, and so on),[9] while the rest of Des Autels's description follows Hesiod, *Theogony* 969–74: 'Demeter the fair goddess bore Plutus, . . . a good deity, who goes over the land and the broad back of the sea, everywhere, and any chance person into whose hands he may fall he makes wealthy and bestows great riches upon him!

The picture of Wealth, however, is only the façade for the poem; the action will be carried out by the Hesiodic Horae:

> L'on dit que Jupiter, ayant vanqueur transmis
> Aus enfers les Titans, engendra de Themis,
> La déesse aus conseils et iugemens puissante,
> Bonne Loy et Iustice et la Paix florissante;

And the last line renders *Theogony* 902:

> Εὐνομίην τε Δίκην τε καὶ Εἰρήνην τεθαλυῖαν

As long as the three Horae ruled the world, the gods familiarly visited mankind; but the sins of men eventually drove Bonne Loy and Iustice and finally La Paix away, and all the gods departed, while man plunged into evil. For all this development, Des Autels turns, not to the brief account in Aratus 125–32, but to the fuller description of Catullus 64:

> C'est pourquoy l'on a feint que les dieux bien souvent
> Les honestes maisons hantoyent au paravant,
> Et au peuple assemblé monstroyent leur excellence;
> Et que Iupiter mesme, autrefois en presence,
> Souvent quand l'an solaire accomplissant son tour
> De ses festes avoit ramené le sainct jour,
> En son temple sacre: deignoit bien venir, voyre
> Regarder les beau jeus celebrez à sa gloire. . . .

---

[9] If *boyteux* means only stumbling from blindness, cf. *Plutus* 121: προσπταίοντα.

Mais quand les hommes ont mescongneu d'estre aymez
Du ciel, et sur la terre ont esté tant semez
De vices deshontez, et que de leur pensée
Tous ça bas d'ung accord la Iustice ont chassee, . . .
Depuis que l'on a veu les freres inhumains
Soiller du propre sang de leurs freres leurs mains,
Que du pere la mort le fils plus ne regrette, . . .
                    Les dieux ont leur griefve ire
Tournée contre nous, qui n'avons le pouvoir
D'estre plus avec eus ny clairement les voir.

Praesentes namque ante domos invisere castas
Heroum et sese mortali ostendere coetu
Caelicolae nondum spreta pietate solebant.
Saepe pater divum templo in fulgente, revisens
Annua cum festis venissent sacra diebus,
Conspexit terra centum procumbere tauros. . . .
Sed postquam tellus scelere est imbuta nefando,
Iustitiamque omnes cupida de mente fugarunt,
Perfudere manus fraterno sanguine fratres,
Destitit exstinctos natus lugere parentes, . . .
Iustificam nobis mentem avertere deorum,
Quare nec talis dignantur visere coetus
Nec se contingi patiuntur lumine claro.

Justice, thus driven from the world, repairs to the side of her fa-
ther Jupiter, and rouses him to take vengeance. For this act, Des Au-
tels turns back to Hesiod, not to the *Theogony*, but to *Works and Days*
256–62: 'There is the maiden Justice, daughter of Zeus. . . . When-
ever any one injures her by crooked speech, she at once sits down
beside Zeus Cronion and tells him of men's unrighteous heart, until
the people pay for the folly of their princes, who with evil mind turn
justice aside in crooked utterance.'

La Justice chassée, et du monde bannie, . . .
S'en va soir vers son pere, et, suyvant sa coustume,
Par une amere plaincte un courrous luy allume, . . .
L'arc de vengeance il bande alors sur les provinces
Pour leurs propres pechez ou pour ceus de leurs princes,
Qui onc mal conseillez destourne de l'endroit
Que monstroit la raison, la practique de droict.[10]

[10]Cf. Ronsard, *Hymne de la Justice*, 1555 (Laumonier 8.58–9), also from this passage
of Hesiod. See above, p. 115, n. 99).

Pax Alma, Veni

After the scourge of God's vengeance,[11] it is the turn of the Homeric Prayers to intervene and to start the reverse movement of the poem by rising to heaven to entreat His mercy:

> Filles de Jupiter, les Prières boyteuses, . . .
> Iusques avant leur pere elles sont parvenues:
> Leur habit est tout blanc, plus net que precieus,
> Leur visage est ridé, et louches sont leurs yeus.

> καὶ γάρ τε Λιταί εἰσι Διὸς κοῦραι μεγάλοιο
> χωλαί τε ῥυσαί τε παραβλῶπες τ'ὀφθαλμώ.
> [*Il.* 9.502–3]

The Prayers in Homer, however, follow slowly after swift-footed Atê in their effort to remedy the harm she has done; hence their appearance *pede claudo*, and so on. Thus they do not quite suit Des Autels's needs, but he explains that they do not move as fast in their errand of mercy as one might wish, and he dresses them in white.

In Aristophanes' *Eirene*, Trygaeus, flying to heaven in search of Peace, learns from Hermes that, the other gods having retired, War is now in charge and has cast Peace into a pit, heaping stones on her to keep her down. Trygaeus summons the men of Greece to bring spades, crowbars, and ropes, and 'pull out Peace, the darling of mankind.' In a vigorous scene, he exhorts Boeotians, Spartans, Megarians, and Athenians to pull their hardest; and at last, chiefly by the efforts of the farmers (the actual chorus), Peace is drawn forth, and with her her attendants, Harvest and Games. Apparently the scene is in heaven, and Trygaeus now simply descends to earth at the side of Peace. Des Autels takes from this only the general idea. Says Jupiter to Mercury:

> Pren ces six chains d'or, que Vulcan pour la gloire
> De son mestier forgea, et au beau char d'ivoire
> De la Paix les attache; elles de longueur ont
> Autant que de ce monde en contient tout le rond.
> Mais tant ingenieuse est leur façon menu,
> Que la subtilité en peut tromper la veuë.

[11]Des Autels has paused to explain that 'Ces fables ne sont point du tout fables legeres' and to ask indulgence of his Christian readers:

> Laissez moi recueiller des thresors poetiques,
> Et des riches presens que nous font les antiques,
> Quelque chose qui puisse entre nous avoir lieu,
> Et revienne tousiours à la gloire de Dieu.

[177]

Aristophanes' simple ropes (σχοινία) have become something not unlike the Golden Chain of Being (multiplied by six), and perhaps carry overtones of the whole Neoplatonic concept that describes the cosmic organization, dependent on the Chain of Being, as Peace.[12] As we have seen, Mercury obeys, and gives the free ends of the chains to the six chief deputies of Cateau-Cambrésis, who thus pull Peace to earth. With her come her attendants, not Harvest and Games, but Astraea and other powers who had after the time of Aristophanes found a place in the tradition.[13]

We may spare a glance for Des Autels's *Eloge de la Paix, à Pierre de Ronsard*.[14] It describes the prosperity that attends peace—the poet says: 'Tel que . . . Ie l'ay en un bouclier antique veu pourtraict,' and this shield proves to be that of the Hesiodic *Shield of Heracles*, from which Des Autels has excerpted the description of the city at peace (vv. 270–313), with some modifications. Once again he has produced a peace poem distinguished among those of the time for dwelling in Hellenic fashion on banquets, weddings, harvests, the vintage, the hunt. His reproduction is easygoing, without great responsibility to the original. Thus *Scutum* 301–4:

> And there were men treading out the grapes and others drawing off the liquor. Also there were men boxing and wrestling, and huntsmen were chasing swift hares with a leash of sharp-toothed dogs before them, they eager to catch the hares, and the hares eager to escape.

> Et tant ilz succeront ceste liqueur nouvelle
> Qu'enfin vous prendront possible entre eux querelle.
> Les gentilz hommes quoy? leur temps ilz passeront,
> Ores par la campaigne au lieuvre chasseront,
> Ou les levriers courans travailleront à prendre
> Le pouvret, qui ne peult qu'en fuyant se defendre:
> Sil s'en fuit vistement contremont, il pourra
> Eschapper la mort triste, aultrement il mourra.

Apart from sheer misconceptions (for example, 'drinking and quarreling' for 'drawing off the wine' and 'boxing and wrestling'), Des Autels introduces with 'gentilz hommes' a class distinction unknown to the original; and this form of adaptation continues in the next development, where horsemen and charioteers contending for a prize

[12]See below, p. 200.
[13]Above, p. 115.
[14]Above, pp. 113–14.

are turned into a tournament played before the eyes of ladies. And nothing in the original suggests

> Lors sera restably l'estat sainct de prestise,
> Et arrachera lon tous scismes de l'Eglise.

The chapter *De pace* of Stobaeus, Hesiod on the Horae, Aristophanes' *Peace*, and the picture of peace in the Hesiodic *Scutum* come near exhausting what survives from the Greek poetry of peace, but among Renaissance poets Vida and Des Autels are exceptional in the degree to which they avail themselves of these sources. Equally exceptional is a passage of Greek origin in Ronsard's *Exhortation* 87–102:[15]

> Ah malheureuse Terre, à grand tort on te nomme
> Et la douce nourrice et la mere de l'homme, . . .
> On dit que quelquefoys te sentant trop chargée
> D'hommes que te foulloyent, pour estre soulagée
> Du fais qui t'accabloit ton échine si fort,
> Tu prias Jupiter de te donner confort.
> Et lors il envoya la méchante Discorde
> Exciter les Thebains d'une guerre tresorde,
> Villaine, incestueuse, où l'infidelle main
> Des deux Freres versa le propre sang germain.
> Apres elle alluma la querelle Troyenne,
> Où la force d'Europe et la force Asienne
> D'un combat de dix ans sans se donner repos,
> De toy, terre marastre, ont déchargé le dos.

Though the motif is well known, it does not figure in the tradition of peace poetry; yet here it supplies a topic of that tradition, namely 'the cause of war,' and more particularly suits the rhetorical design of the *Exhortation* as describing the 'origin of war'; it came to hand from Ronsard's current studies for the *Franciade* and answered his craving for what would be, in its context, fresh and unusual.

It is, in fact—and this presumably is why it attracted Ronsard—a fragment of the early epic poem the *Cypria*. The idea is alluded to by Euripides (*Helen* 36–41; *Orestes* 1639), but the double form that Ronsard reproduces, in which *both* the Trojan and the Theban wars originated in Earth's complaint to Zeus, is found only in the *scholia* on Euripides' *Orestes* 1641 and on *Iliad* 1.5, and probably goes be-

[15]Laumonier, usually so alert in such matters, somehow passed over this rather obvious borrowing (9.20–21).

yond the poet of the *Cypria*. Without denying the possibility that Ronsard may have met with the motive in some humanist writer, we may regard it as far more likely, inasmuch as he was at this time at work on his own epic poem, that his studies extended to the *scholia* on Homer. If so, he probably knew the *scholia* in the central form given by the pseudo-Didymus, first published by Janus Lascaris (Rome, 1517), though the work of Eustathius on Homer was also available and contains an abbreviated form of the *scholium* in question. Availability was easy in a sixteenth-century edition of Homer; and one would not need to read far to reach the note on line 5. If Ronsard chanced to use the convenient Homer published by Hervagius at Basel in 1535, where the *scholia* surround the text, he would have seen it on the first page.

The *scholium* on *Iliad* 1.5 explains the phrase, 'And the plan of Zeus was being fulfilled':[16]

> Others say that Homer spoke in conformity with a historical account. According to them, Earth, burdened by the vast crowd of mankind, and these devoid of piety, requested Zeus to lighten her of the load, and Zeus promptly started the Theban War, by means of which he destroyed very many, and then later, on the advice of Momus, devised what Homer calls 'the plan of Zeus.' He could easily have destroyed all mankind with thunderbolts or floods, but Momus restrained him and suggested the mortal marriage of Thetis and the birth of a beautiful daughter [Helen], whence arose the war between the Greeks and the barbarians, with the consequent relief of Earth, for many were slain. The account is in Stasinus, author of the *Cypria*, who says: 'There was a time when the many tribes of men, wandering overland, burdened the surface of deep-bosomed Earth, seeing which Zeus took pity and in his shrewd wit bethought him to lighten all-nourishing Earth of the pressure, kindling the great discord of the Trojan War, so as to drain off the burden of slaughter; and in Troy the heroes perished, and the plan of Zeus was fulfilled.'

It is perhaps unnecessary to insist on verbal correspondences—for example, the marked succession in 'Et lors . . . Apres'; the similar fullness of expression in 'trop chargée / D'hommes qui te foulloyent' and βαρυμένην ὑπ' ἀνθρώπων πολυπληθίας; from the *Cypria* frag-

---

[16]*Scholia Graeca in Homeri Iliadem*, Hartmut Erbse, ed. (Berlin, 1969), pp. 9–10. I have abbreviated the *scholium* in translation. It also occurs in *Scholia Venetiana* A and in minor *scholia* that Ronsard would not know; see *Cypria*, fragm. 1 in Gottfried Kinkel, *Epicorum Graecorum Fragmenta* (Leipzig, 1877), pp. 20–21.

ment itself ῥιπίσσας (kindling) πολέμου μεγάλην ἔριν Ἰλιακοῖο seem to have given 'allume la querelle Troyenne.' I cannot find that the epic fragments of the *scholia* on Homer have hitherto been counted among the classical sources of Ronsard.

VI

Saturnia Regna: Roman Themes

Aurea secura cum pace renascitur aetas.

Calpurnius 1.42

The Golden Age is reborn with peace secure.

The theme of the Golden Age of primitive felicity, as one of the great commonplaces of literature from Hesiod to Milton, might in the variety of its fortunes be studied as an indicator of the *weltanschauung* of successive periods.[1] The descending series of the Hesiodic ages had, under the impulsion of the cyclical views of the universe and history, received in the Hellenistic period a new term, that of renewal and regeneration; and in this form the topic had served the poets and propagandists of the Roman Peace, nor was it entirely alien to the Christian scheme of the Earthly Paradise, the Fall, and Redemption. Certainly in no period have the poets more willingly turned to visions of the Golden Age than in the Renaissance, a period that hoped (with lessening confidence, perhaps) to be a kind of redemption, reviving the Golden Age of antiquity after the fallen Middle Ages.[2] The topic is, for instance, usually near at hand in the utopian writers. But the Renaissance had every reason to know itself to be no period of primitive peace—far from it; hopefulness passed over into nostalgia, and the theme of the Golden Age found its home chiefly in the pastoral—another revealing pre-

[1] Lovejoy-Boas, Ch. 2, pp. 23–102.

[2] Ronsard, in the *Ode à Michel L'Hospital*, thinks of the Muses as having abandoned mankind like the Horae because of the 'aveugle fureur des princes' (v. 604) in the Middle Ages, and as returning now that the Fates have created the New Man, L'Hospital, to welcome them. Laumonier (*éd. crit.* 3.152, n. 2, and *Ronsard Poète lyrique*, [Paris, 1904], pp. 226–27), observes that Ronsard changed his mind on the Middle Ages. And it is curious to reflect that the notion of the New Man is parallel to that of Alain de Lille's *Anticlaudianus*!

dilection of the time—and so rings out with special authenticity in the *Arcadia* of Sannazaro and the 'O bella età dell'oro' of the *Pastor Fido* (Act 4, sc. 9).

As a topic of peace poetry, and as a topic of the pastoral, the Golden Age was imposed by the example of the Roman poets. In the sixteenth *Epode* of Horace, written during the civil war, its characteristics are, in the Hellenistic manner, transferred to 'the ends of the earth,' namely to the Islands of the Blest.[3] Virgil's fourth *Eclogue*, a little later, more hopefully sees the Golden Age as destined to return again in relation to a peace hero. In the second *Georgic* we are to think that Italy now, and no fabled Isles of the Blest, realizes the ideal; and in the end, Horace (*Odes* 4.5) sees the return of Augustus from abroad as restoring it. And later poets of the Empire repeat the note. Calpurnius hails a new *aurea aetas* in the dawning reign of Nero; Porphyry (*Carm.* 10) salutes Constantine as *aurei saeculi restaurator*. Less politically minded, the elegists maintain an older tradition, already glanced at in Catullus 64. Tibullus draws a picture of the Golden Age of peace in constrast to the warfare of the present (1.3), and again, in a poem of unusual importance for the peace tradition (1.10), begins with this contrast between primitive peace lost in the iron age, to pass on to the quiet of country life and the general benefactions of peace. In this tradition, Ovid describes the Golden Age in his version of the Hesiodic scheme (*Met.* 1.89−113).[4] His description was destined to be far the most influential with later poets and can be traced already in the *aurea aetas* of Seneca's *Phaedra* where the happy sylvan life of Hippolytus is compared with it,[5] and also in the equally influential verses on the Golden Age in Boethius' *Consolation of Philosophy* (II, metr. 5), where the relevance is a contrast with the vanity of material goods.

In the Roman poets, the description of the Golden Age is an organized *topos*, so uniform in detail that we must suppose some Hellenistic original to lie behind it.[6] Under Saturn's reign, mankind kept

---

[3]Cf. above, p. 26 and n. 19. The attitude of Horace's sixteenth *Epode* is taken up by Ronsard in *Les Isles fortunées* of 1553 and provides a development in Belleau's *Dictamen* (*Œuvres* 1.101). Appropriate to the French civil wars, Horace's point is repeated by Passerat, *Hymne de la Paix*. But Virgil, *Georg.* 4.558ff., uses the *topos* to take away the Golden Age itself.

[4]Earlier in *Amores* 3.10.1−15, and *Ars Amatoria* 2.467−80.

[5]So also the Golden Age of the ps.-Senecan *Octavia* 405ff. is Ovidian.

[6]Of surviving examples, Aratus, *Phaenomena* 96−136, is a likely source, though it presents only one or two details: 'Not yet did mankind know hateful war or contentious dispute or battle din, but lived in simplicity; the cruel sea they left alone, and ships did not yet bring their livelihood from afar, but oxen and the plough and Justice herself, mistress of the people and dispenser of the right, furnished all things

the right without written law;[i] the pine tree was not yet cut to build ships, and no one crossed the seas;[ii] towns were open and unfortified;[iii] trumpets and swords were unknown;[iv] the earth yielded crops without ploughing;[v] men lived on acorns and on honey that dripped from the oaks;[vi] fields were divided by no boundary stones (Tibullus 1.3);[vii] gold and iron had not been dug from the earth;[viii] there were no wars.[ix] For the terms of this topic, the mediaeval poet drew upon Ovid and Boethius, the Renaissance poet mostly upon Ovid, though the other poets were open to him, or he might use an anthology like Mirandula's *Flores Poetarum*, where under the title 'De Aetatibus' he could choose expressions from a number of these sources.[7]

In the cyclical or redemptive view of history, one might expect that it would be this life of the Age of Cronos that the peace hero would come to restore. Virgil in the fourth *Eclogue*, Horace in the fifth *Ode* of Book 4, Calpurnius, complacently affirm that it is so; but with incongruities that are barely concealed by art. They must be accepted as metaphor or hyperbole.[8] No one desired a return to primitive communism and a diet of acorns—

> quelle ghiande
> le qua' fuggendo tutto 'l mondo onora.

Before Petrarch, the point was made in antiquity.[9] Against the 'soft' primitivism of the Hesiodic tradition stood the 'hard' primitivism of those who realistically saw the life of early man as 'nasty, brutish, and short.'[10] For them, the descending topic of the Hesiodic Ages

---

abundantly.' i. Aratus; Ovid, *Met.* 1.89–90. ii. Tibulllus 1.3.37ff.; Ovid, *Met.* 1.94–95; Horace's whole poem to Virgil (*Carm.* 1.3) is on the topic of primitive nonsailing. iii. Ps.-Seneca, *Octavia* 411–12. iv. Ovid, *Met.* 1.98, 99; Virgil, *Georg.* 2.539–40; Tibullus 1.10, 1–12. v. Virgil *Georg.* 1.128; Ovid *Met.* 1.101–2. vi. Tibullus 1.3.45; Ovid *Met.* 1.103–6. vii. Virgil *Georg.* 1.126; Tibullus 1.3.43–44. viii. Tibullus 1.3.47–48; Ovid *Met.* 1.138–42. ix. Dicaearchus, *Vita Graeciae*, fragm. 1 *ap.* Porphyry, *De Abstinentia* 4.1.2. Tibullus 1.3 and Ovid *Met.* 1 run all through these, or rather all these topics are found in them.

[7] For Mirandula see above p. 89, and n. 15 below.

[8] For example, Virgil is fully alive to the difficulties. In the *Georgics* he describes the Golden Age only as *taken away*. In *Eclogue* 4.31 sailing will be only because 'pauca suberunt *priscae vestigia fraudis, quae temptare Thetim ratibus,* quae *cingere muris oppida,* quae iubeant . . . *infindere sulcos;*' but in the fully developed Golden Age, none of these things: vv. 38–45: 'omnis feret omnia tellus' and 'cedet et ipse mari vector, nec nautica pinus / mutabit merces.'

[9] Petrarch *Rime.* 50, 23–24. Tibullus 2.1.38; Dicaearchus, note 6 above; Virgil *Georg.* 1.159. See Lovejoy-Boas, Index, s.v. 'Acorns,' and p. 95, n. 157.

[10] Lovejoy-Boas, 'Cultural Primitivism,' pp. 7ff., from whom the terms 'soft' and 'hard' primitivism are borrowed.

was opposed by the ascending topic of the Growth of Civilization, with its culture heroes, of whom Prometheus and Heracles are types. But the present is always a bad time; and the moral poet is tempted to reprove it by lauding the simplicity of primitive ages or savage peoples. Thus Lucretius, whose real theme is the Growth of Civilization, curiously interposes motives of the Golden Age in a wish to score points against the unsatisfactory present (*De rer. nat.* 5.925ff).[11] Another line is adopted by Virgil (*Georg.* 1.121ff.), who, taking a hint from Hesiod himself (*Erga* 140–55), declares that, after Saturn, Jupiter withdrew the traits of the Golden Age and made life hard, in order to inspire mankind to invent the arts; a point taken up and developed by Claudian (*De rapt. Pros.* 3.18–54).

A similar problem faces the Renaissance peace poets, who regularly account for the departure of Peace in a decline from the Golden Age, and just as commonly wish to end with an encomium of peace, for which the details have considerable affinity with the Growth of Civilization. In the Golden Age, there was no restraint of laws; the earth gave abundance without the plough; no one crossed the seas in ships. In peace, the laws are again in force; agriculture flourishes; the merchant may again cross the seas. There are various ways of dealing with the problem. In a long poem, the difficulty, if it is one, may be ignored; the departure of peace comes early in the narrative, the encomium of peace near the end.[12] One of the topics may be left without elaboration. Ronsard may 'adore' Henri II 'pour avoir reverdis l'age / où florissoit l'antique paix' (*Ode de la Paix* 35–36), or tell him that 'comme Auguste . . . tu as ramené l'aage d'or sur la terre' (*Chant de liesse* 14–17), without elaboration, and no questions will be asked.[13] Few will go so far as Béreau in hoping that the Golden Age is at hand:

> Quelque traces bien tost du Saturnien age
> Doibvent recommencer sous le regne puissant
> D'Henry. . . .
> Encores de leur gré produyront les campagnes

[11]So Manilius 1.

[12]Poems that combine these themes to some degree are Schryver's *Descriptio Pacis inter Carolum . . . et Franciscum . . .* ; Corrozet's *Retour de la Paix*; Buttet's *Ode de la Paix*; Ronsard's *La Paix, au Roy*; Des Autels's *La Paix venue du ciel*; J. d'Aubusson de la Maison-Neuve, *Colloque sociale . . .* ; Pujol's *De pace*; Jacques Béreau's *Sur la Paix faicte . . .* ; and Passerat's *Hymne de la Paix*.

[13]Among poets who urge the peace hero to civilize his realm we may note Ronsard, *La Paix, au Roy*; André, *Carmen de pace*; Coustau, *Carmen de pace*; Le Roy, *Oratio . . . de pace*; P. Habert, *Traicté . . . de la Paix*; Pasquier, *Congratulation de la Paix*; and Baïf, *Hymne de la Paix*.

> Le froment nourricier, encore des montagnes
> Heureux fleuves de laict et de vin couleront,
> Et les chesnes encor le roux miel sueront.

Ronsard, however, in the *Exhortation pour la Paix*, lets himself get badly caught between these two themes. In vv. 147–62, he praises the Age of Saturn:

> Qu'heureuse fut la gent qui vivoit sous Saturne,
> Quand[14] l'aise et le repos, et la paix taciturne,
> Bien long de la trompette, et bien long des soldars,
> Long du fer et de l'or, erroit de toutes pars
> Par les bois assurée, et du fruict de la terre
> En commun se paissoit sans fraude ny sans guerre.
> Helas! que n'ai-je esté vivant de ce temps là,
> Ou du temps que la Foy legère s'envolla
> Du monde vicieux, ne laissant en sa place
> Que la guerre et la mort, la fraude et la fallace.

And very shortly thereafter he praises Peace (vv. 199–212):

> La paix fonda les villes,
> La paix fertilisa les campagnes steriles,
> La paix de soubs le joug fait mugir les toreaux,
> La paix dedans les coutaux tira droit à la ligne
> Les ordres arengez de la première vigne. . . .
> Elle défouracha de nos premiers ayeux
> Les cœurs rudes et fiers, et les fist gracieux,
> Et d'un peuple vaguant es bois à la fortune,
> Dedans les grandz citez en fist une commune.

These last lines, as Laumonier notes, collide with those describing the equally happy folk who 'erroit de toutes pars / Par les bois assurée.' Ronsard is caught between the 'soft' and the 'hard' primitivism. The cause of the discrepancy may partly be that he has Tibullus' peace poems in mind; but if so, he has not noticed that Tibullus keeps the topics separate, describing the Golden Age in one poem (1.3) and the *benefacta* of Peace in the other (1.10),[15] though to be sure he begins 1.10 with some allusions to the Golden Age.

[14]Laumonier conjectures 'Dans.'

[15]However, both developments in Ronsard are mosaics. Laumonier is hardly justified in ascribing the whole of the Golden Age passage to Tibullus 1.3.35ff. Only the first line is from Tibullus 1.3.35: 'Quam bene Saturno vivebant rege'; other phrases are from Ovid: 'erroit de toutes pars / Par les bois assurée' = *Ars Am.* 2.472, 475:

The return of the Golden Age or the arrival of peace and prosperity comes about through the acts of a peace hero. He possesses the magic of power and has used it beneficently, whether out of innate goodness or inspired by the gods or the grace of God. In such a person there is something divine, and properly his final reward is heroization or apotheosis:

> Hac arte Pollux et vagus Hercules
> Enisus arces attigit igneas,
>   Quos inter Augustus recumbens
>   Purpureo bibet ore nectar.

The supreme social service merits the supreme reward, and, like Hercules, good emperors became gods. Christianity changed all that. Every good Christian has as much right as emperor or pope to look forward to heaven and immortality. Yet a distinction persists; after the twelfth century, special merit, if accompanied by evidence of supernatural power, has been acknowledged by canonization. With the grace of God, a Christian peace hero may like St. Louis reach this height; but in any case, it seems likely that he will merit Paradise. He has 'imitated God,' who is Peace.[16]

With little difficulty, therefore, the Renaissance poets were able to transfer to the peace heroes within their experience a good deal of

---

'Tum genus humanum solis errabat in agris . . . silva domus fuerat;' Ovid *Met.* 1.99–100: 'sine militis usu / mollia securae (assurée) peragebant otia gentes'; 'et du fruit de la terre / En commun se passoit' = Virgil, *Georg.* 1, 127–28: 'in medium quaerebant, ipsaque tellus / omnia liberius nullo poscente ferebat . . .'; 'la Foy . . . s'envolla,' etc. = Ovid, *Met.* 1.129–30: 'fugere pudor verumque fidesque / in quorum subiere locum fraudesque dolique insidiaeque.' Ronsard may well have had at hand a commonplace book such as Mirandula's *Flores Poetarum* and passages under the rubric 'De Aetatibus.' The passage on the benefits of peace clearly begins with an imitation of Tibullus 1.10. 45.47: 'Pax arva colat; Pax . . . duxit araturos sub juga curva boves, Pax aluit vites,' with anaphora of *pax*. But the civilizing power of La Paix is drawn from other ancient passages on the Growth of Civilization: 'Elle defaroucha de nos premiers ayeux / Les coeurs rudes et fiers' = Ovid *Ars. Am.* 2.472: 'Blanda truces animos fertur mollisse voluptas' (cf. Lucretius 5.1017ff.); and 'Et d'un peuple vaguant,' etc. = Virgil, *Aen.* 8.321–22: 'Is [Saturn!] genus indocile ac dispersum in montibus altis / Composuit legesque dedit.' Tibullus 2.1.35–86. See Kirby Flower Smith, ed., Tibullus, *Elegies* (New York, 1913), p. 400, n. 37, and cp. Tibullus 1.7.29–48; 1.3.35ff.; Ovid, *Am.* 3.10.9.; Virgil, *Georg.* 1.8 and 159. Bouwsma, *Concordia Mundi*, p. 254, points out the significance of Saturn for Postel, as representing the classical, as Noah does the biblical, world. On the importance of Saturn for the Renaissance in general, see Jean Seznec, *La Survivance des dieux antiques* (London, 1940), passim.

[16]See J. N. Figgis, *The Divine Right of Kings* (Cambridge, 1914). On 'imitating God' see Louis Le Roy, p. 130 above; also p. 199 and n. 2. [I Thank Professor Brian Tierney for the date canonization became formalized within the Church. R.G.]

what the Roman panegyrist might say about a prince of the Roman peace. Posterity may at times demur at their choices—Julius II, Henri II, Catherine de Medici, and Philip of Spain have been canonized neither by the Roman Church nor by history. There is the falseness of adulation no doubt; but the poets are praising good acts and imputing good motives, even urging upon these personages virtues that they ought to possess, and in many cases very honorably offering them as much advice as praise.[17] The rewards held out to them at all events are the same as of old—immortality in heaven and immortal fame among men. Nor, with the traditional use of Roman terms for Christian ideas—a usage carried to extremes by the humanist revival—was much difficulty felt in applying to the Christian peace hero expressions coined for a pagan emperor. Even the pious Mantuan will pray in these terms for Cardinal Caraffa:

> Iuppiter ad superum faciat discumbere mensas,
> nectaris et succos ambrosiamque bibas,

or Capilupi adapt Horace's words for Henri II and Philip of Spain:

> Hac iter vobis erit ad beatas
> Aetheris sedes superumque mensas,
> Et choro accepti ferietis altum
> Vertice Olympum.

There is no more than to wish for them the joys of heaven.

But imitation went farther than that. Throughout Renaissance literature we must be prepared to accept a convention that removes poetical expression far from Renaissance life, especially where religion is concerned, and at an interval that allegory hardly spans. This is especially true of the wonderland of pastoral, which happens also to be the realm in which the Roman poets had placed some of their most impressive utterances about *tranquillitas* and *quies* and the peacebringer. This must be the justification of Navagero's *Damon*. We may just possibly think 'saint' (taking *deus* for *divus*) when the poet addressed Julius II as 'novus deus ex alto demissus Olympo,' and declares:

> Tu nostra ante Deos in vota vocaberis omnes,

---

[17]Among our Renaissance poets at least a dozen offer advice to princes, notably Ronsard, *Paix*, 203–36; *Ode*, 19–36. Also J. Du Bellay, *De pace* . . . ; Michel L'Hospital, *De pace*; Buttet, *Ode*; Elie André, *Carmen de pace*; Jean Sève, *Supplication aux Roys*; Pasquier, *Congratulation de la Paix*; and A. du Baïf, *Hymne*.

or prays:

> Dexter ades nobis, et quae facis otia serva.

But actually the poem cannot be read in terms of the Christian sainted man. The world of Virgilian pastoral is revived in a piece, and the poem must be accepted as an extravagant expression of true feeling about the events of 1512. The grateful shepherd of Virgil's first *Eclogue* thinks in his simplicity that Octavian is a god:

> O Meliboee, deus nobis haec otia fecit:
> Namque erit ille mihi semper deus; illius aram
> Saepe tener nostris ab ovilibus imbuet agnus.

If the shepherd Virgil can see Octavian as god or hero, with his altar (*illius aram*), Navagero can do as much for Julius II (that is, Damon), and (though he has no lamb sacrificed to Julius) he compounds from his model a complete heroization, altogether antique and relevant only within the poem:

> Ipse ego bina tibi solenni altaria ritu,
> Et geminos sacra e quercu lauroque virenti
> Vicino lucos Nauceli in litore ponam.
> Hic ripa passim in molli viridante sub umbra,
> Vere novo dum floret ager, dum germinat arbos,
> Dum vario resonant volucrum nemora avia cantu,
> Annua constituam festis convivia ludis.
> Ductores pecudum hic omnes rurisque coloni
> Contendent jaculo, et rapidi certamine cursus,
> Horridaque agresti nudabunt membra palaestra.
> Ipse pecu et tenero victor donabitur haedo.
> Praeterea dulci cantabit arundine Damon
> Carmina, quae puerum docuit Sebethëïus Aegon,
> Olim quum procul hinc illis habitaret in oris.

Navagero is a strict Virgilian; every word and every phrase will be found somewhere in the text of Virgil. So too with the substance. The rather rare notion of dedicating two altars to Julius relies on the fifth *Eclogue*, where at the heroization of Daphnis two altars are assigned to him and two to Apollo.[18] For the idea of placing these al-

[18]Vv. 65–66:
> en quattuor aras:
> ecce duas tibi, Daphni, duas altaria Phoebo.

tars in the hero's sacred grove, the poet recalls the heroization of Hercules in *Aeneid* 8.271. The homely setting beside the poet's provincial stream, 'Nauceli in litore,' is from the heroization of Octavian in the third *Georgic* 13–15, where Virgil contemplates setting up a temple in his honor beside the Mincius:

> et viridi in campo templum de marmore ponam
> propter aquam, tardis ingens ubi flexibus errat
> Mincius et tenera praetexit harundine ripas.

Simply from these Virgilian passages, and not from any abstract knowledge of the rites of hero-worship, Navagero has correctly enough indicated the three important moments in the ritual—the making of an altar, the annual games, and the hymn in the hero's honor, though the last is only suggested by the statement that Damon will sing songs learned far away and long ago. That, however, is in agreement with the fifth *Eclogue*. Actually the ancient hero cult had partly the character of the cult of the gods and partly that of burial or funeral rites,[19] as is the case in the death and heroization of Daphnis in *Eclogue* 5. Navagero, of course, ignores the funereal aspect in applying the terms of *Eclogue* 5 to Julius II, justified, no doubt, by Virgil's procedure in promising this honor to the living Octavian in the third *Georgic*. Julius is addressed as still living; yet as it happened, he was dead before the poem was published.[20]

Navagero's genius favored the pastoral; he is a determined imitator of Virgil; in the Roman poets, and particularly in Virgil, peace and the peacebringer are commonly associated with rural simplicity. Were it not for these associations, one might expect a living peace hero to be celebrated rather in the terms of a Roman triumph than in those of heroization.[21] Yet none of our poets does this, and to do it would perhaps savor of arrogance. In the two poems that are built on the form of a Roman triumph, it is Peace herself who is the triumphator. In Zanchi's *Hymnus pacis aeternae*, the Romans crown her with olive, laurel, and roses; place her marble image on the Capitol, meaning to burn incense and perform customary rites before it, to maintain solemn altars and votive offerings, and to hymn her name for ages to come:

[19]Roscher, 3502.

[20]Julius died February 13. Navagero certainly knew the interpretation of *Eclogue* 5 which makes Daphnis an allegory for the dead and deified Julius Caesar.

[21]Note that in *Carm.* 4.5 Horace celebrates the living Augustus on his return from Spain as a magical peacebringer, but with no allusion to heroization.

Et septem geminis respondet collibus Echo:
Victor, io, Romanus, io, nova signa reportat.

And her captive enemies are duly put out of the way.[22] Much more elaborate is the representation of a Roman triumph in the *Pacis descriptio* of Corneille de Schryver.[23] The poem is largely occupied in describing the procession; even the fescennine verses are represented by a lively interchange between the poet and the Muses; and the chief prisoner, War, is duly executed. Here too the triumphant general is Pax, though Francis I and Charles V, the peace heroes of Aigues-Mortes, are somewhat clumsily associated with her. After the triumph, a triumphal arch, pyramids, statues of Pax, Charles, and Francis, and colossi of the two monarchs are erected, and round these images annual games and rites are to be performed.[24]

But Navagero and Virgil predominate in influence. From Navagero's *Damon* the idea of a bucolic peace poem, including the heroization of the peacebringer, came into French poetry with Remy Belleau's *Chant de la Paix* of 1559. Among other details, Belleau has adopted from Navagero the notion of two altars by the river's side, and having to celebrate two heroes of Cateau-Cambrésis, he conveniently assigns one altar to the cardinal of Lorraine and the other to Montmorency:[25]

Et quant à moy, sous les ombres mollets
De ces coudriers, pres cette eau qui jargonne
Dessus le sable, il faut que je façonne
De gazons verds deux petits autelets:
L'un à cellui dont les vertus entières
Et la faconde ont rendu pour jamais
De tout bonheur nos terres heretières
Tirant du ciel la bien-heureuse paix, . . .

[22]Above, p. 117. The chief elements of a Roman triumph were a triumphal procession, including captives, up the Via Sacra to the Capitol, the triumphator riding in a chariot and carrying the laurel, with a slave at his ear reminding him he was mortal; the exchange of obscene fescennine verses; the execution of the chief captives; arrival at the temple of Jupiter Capitolinus, where the triumphator placed the laurel on the lap of the god.

[23]Above, p. 86.

[24]The Renaissance poets seem not to be influenced by Prudentius, in whom the victory of Peace in the Battle of the Soul (*Psych.* 823ff.) is celebrated by the building of a temple after the example of Solomon (not Vespasian!). The building of the House of Peace in the anonymous *Heracliti ad Democritum elegia* (above, p. 122) is presumably founded on Prov. 9.1.

[25]Transferred in later editions to Charles IX and the Duke of Anjou; see above, p. 109, n. 82. Earlier passages in Belleau's poem are also taken from Navagero.

L'autre à celuy dont la sage vieillesse,
Le meur conseil esprouvé de nos Roys,
A du haut ciel tiré ceste déesse
Pour la loger au millieu des François.
L'autel premier d'un verdoyant lierre
Tout à l'entour aura les fronts couverts.
L'autre sera entaillé d'une pierre,
Ou tous les ans je chanteray ces vers:
'Dessous leurs pieds et la manne et le miel
Naisse tousjours,' . . .

The tone is lowered from the Virgilian grandeur of Navagero; the stream 'jargons,' altars and groves shrink to *petits autelets*, and these, as built by rustics, Belleau thinks had better be altars of turf, *de gazons verds*.[26] Later they seem somewhat grander, the one having its sides covered with ivy and the other apparently with a casing of stone—details that faintly suggest tombs.[27] The games are omitted, it is not clear why, and Toinet, the speaker, will, like Navagero's Damon, himself sing the hymn invoking over the heroes the blessings of agricultural plenty.

The concept of a peace eclogue was very likely borrowed from Belleau by Jacques Béreau for his celebration of Cateau-Cambrésis.[28] He repeats the detail of the turf-altar, but generally, ignoring Navagero, goes directly to Virgil. He has only one hero, Montmorency:

Noble Montmorency, en ferme souvenance
Du bien par toy receu, qui nous as de soufrance
Heureusement mis hors, en un val ecarté,
Joingnant mon petit Loy de longs vergnes planté
De saules et de houx, de peupliers et d'érables,
Un brave pavillon de feuillées aimables
Treillesé et couvert proprement te feray,
Et dedans un austel de gazons dresseray
Dessous lequel sera ta figure élevée
De blanc marbre, tenant en une maine l'epée,
En l'autre un olivier; et puis aux deux costez
De cest autel seront deux ronds pilliers entez,

[26]Such altars, *arae gramineae* or *caespiticiae*, are correct for country gods; cf. Horace, *Carm.* 1.19.13 and 3.8.4.
[27]Ivy and 'manne et miel' recall *Anthologia Palatina* 7.22–23, the tomb of Sophocles. Belleau seems to echo Ronsard's 'Election de son sepulcre' (Laumonier 2.101.33–40, 69–80).
[28]Above, p. 111.

Où graver je feray pour durable memoyre
De tes rares vertus et de tes faicts l'histoyre.
Les bergers à ton los, moy les guidant premier
Avecques le chef ceinct de verdissant laurier,
Tous les ans une fois sonneront mille aubades,
Diront mille chansons, feront mille gambades,
Si qu'autre ne sera mieux venu és forestz,
Qui te recongnoistront pour leur Pan desormais.

For bucolic simplicity, Béreau has transformed Virgil's marble temple into a rustic arbor. He now has both Navagero's altar (borrowed from Belleau) and Virgil's temple, which has no altar, and he places the one inside the other. But Virgil's temple contained Caesar's statue, and borrowing this for Montmorency Béreau very strangely places it upon the altar. The result—a white marble statue of the Constable, sword in one hand and olive branch in the other, standing upon an altar—may suggest that the Virgilian picture is merging into a Renaissance funerary monument, an impression that grows as the poet places two pillars *entez* (morticed) at the sides of the (turf!) altar, and inscribes them *pour durable memoyre* with the virtues and deeds of his hero. The commemorative games follow, as in Virgil and Navagero, and as in Navagero and Virgil (*Ecl.* 5), the hymn is supplied by the shepherds' songs.[29]

In Ronsard's *Bergerie* of 1565 (after the Pacification of Amboise),[30] a long passage is transcribed from Navagero's *Damon* and turned to the praise of Catherine de Medici as peacebringer.[31] The altar and the games are present but not prominent.[32] The next passage of the poem (vv. 419–510), however, is an apotheosis of the dead hero Henri II. Forests, plains, and streams

murmurent en tout lieu
Que le bon Henriot est maintenant un Dieu.

[29]These details Béreau may have independently taken from *Eclogue* 5, without knowing Navagero's adaptation. Nor is the reference to Pan in the last line necessarily an echo of 'veluti Phoebo Panique' in *Damon* 42. Nor Pan = Christ in Marot!

[30]Above, p. 138.

[31]Laumonier 13.92; dependence on Navagero was pointed out by Paul Kuhn, 'L'influence neo-latine dans les Eglogues de Ronsard,' in *RHL*, 21 (1914), 311–14.

[32]Vv. 391–93:

Tous les ans, à jours certains de festes,
Donnans repos aux champs, à nous, et à noz bestes,
Luy ferons un autel, comme à la grande Junon,
Et long temps par les bois sera chanté son nom.

And the shepherd Angelot continues:

> Sois propice à nos voeux: je te feray d'ivoire
> Et de marbre un beau temple au rivage de Loyre,
> Où au retour de l'an, aux jours longs et nouveaux,
> Je feray des combatz entre les pastouraux,
> Ordonnez tous les mois en la saison première,
> A sauter, à lutter, à franchir la carrière.
> Là sera ton Janot[33] qui chantera tes faitz,
> Tes guerres, tes cambatz, tes ennemis deffaitz.

By way of Navagero, once more, Ronsard has returned to Virgil; first to the apotheosis of Daphnis,[34] then to the temple of the third *Georgic*.[35] The season and the games are more reminiscent of Navagero.[36] The hymn or *laudatio*, enumerating the hero's *benefacta*, and to be sung by the *poeta regis*, is duly announced. Then—for Ronsard omits nothing (vv. 501–4)—

> Nous ferons en ton nom des autels tous les ans,
> De grands gazons de terre, et comme aux Aegipans,
> Aux Faunes, aux Satyrs, te ferons sacrifice.
> Ton Perrot[37] le premier chantera le service.

With more tact, and more learning, than Belleau or Béreau displayed, Ronsard has waited for the death of Henri before granting him heroization.

The visitor to the Louvre[38] who pauses among the Renaissance sculptures, Salle de Jean Goujon, after admiring Goujon's *Diane à l'Anet* and the equally familiar *Three Graces* of Germain Pilon, may

---

[33]Jean Dorat, according to Laumonier, 13.101, n. 1.
[34]*Ecl.* 5.63–66:

> Ipsae iam carmine rupes,
> ipsa sonant arbusta: 'deus, deus ille, Menalca!'
> Sis bonus o felixque tuis!

[35]Besides its place by the Loire (= Mincius), its construction of ivory and marble perhaps reflects the *sculptures* in Virgil's temple, 'ex auro solidoque elephanto' (*Georg.* 3.26).
[36]I.e., 'Vere novo dum floret ager.' It may be relevant that Henri's birthday was March 31.
[37]Ronsard. For the woodland deities compare Béreau: 'leur Pan desormés,' but here more likely from Navagero line 42, 'veluti Phoebo Panique'?
[38]This description of the tomb of Montmorency has been published, with an illustration, in 'Classical Poetry in Renaissance Poems on Peace,' Hutton, *Essays*, pp. 225–42. It has been kept here as an integral part of this chapter.

well spare a moment's attention for a monument of the following description. From a central pedestal there rises a twisted 'salomonic' column of white marble with rose-colored marble encrustations, before which stands a 'Virtue' in bronze; and this central group is flanked by two similar Virtues standing on separate marble pedestals. The column originally upheld an urn in which reposed the heart of the deceased. This is the *monument du cœur* of the Constable, Anne de Montmorency, erected in 1573 by his widow, Madeleine of Savoy, in the church of the Célestins. The monument was designed by Jean Bullant, and the bronze figures at least, and probably column and all, were executed by Barthélemy Prieur.[39]

The Virtues especially claim our interest. These draped figures are identified as Justice, Abundance, and Peace, each suitably represented, with appropriate emblems decorating the pedestals on which they stand.[40] With a certain propriety, all three figures have attributes associated with Peace. Abundance, in the center, standing before the column, extends a garland in her right hand and holds a cornucopia in her left. The emblems below consist, in the central panel, of a complicated design made up of two cornucopias, the balance of Justice, a caduceus, and two olive branches; in side panels, a gauntleted hand raises a drawn sword tipped with a laurel wreath, and on the right stands a scabbard decorated with fleurs de lys, also with wreath above (sword and scabbard being emblems of the Constable of France). Here the design is a combined hieroglyphic for Abundance, Justice, and Peace (the caduceus bespeaking Peace and Commerce).[41] On the separate pedestal to the right, the figure of

[39]See the admirable account of this monument by Francis Henry Cripps-Day, 'Le monument funéraire du cœur d'Anne de Montmorency connetable de France' in *Gazette des beaux-arts*, 18 (1928), 62–74. The present state of the monument does not represent its original form, which is better seen in the illustration from Aubin Louis Millin's *Antiquités nationales* (Paris, 1790), reproduced by Cripps-Day, p. 66. In particular, the pedestals are inadequate restorations, and the emblems (see below) have been placed beneath the wrong Virtues. The urn for the heart, and the iron grillwork connecting the pedestals (already absent from Millin's reproduction) were melted down to make cannon early in the Revolution. See also Anthony Blunt, *Art and Architecture in France, 1500–1700* (Baltimore, 1953), p. 102.

[40]That is, in the original intention as described by Cripps-Day, who reproduces the figures, pp. 67–69.

[41]The caduceus, however, is not constructed as usual of serpents entwining a *rod*, but of serpents entwining a *spade*—presumably, therefore, to be read 'Peace and Agriculture.' It is not, as usual, topped with wings, but with a rosette. I do not find the allerions seen by Cripps-Day in this design, but rather accompanying the sword and gauntlet. The central design is clearly reproduced by Cripps-Day on p. 74. On the caduceus, cf. C. Calcagnini, *De Concordia* in *Opera Aliquot* (Basel, 1544), p. 4.10: 'Non alia de causa angues in Caduceo Mercurii Herculaneo complexu iungebat antiquitas, nisi ut amicitiam concordiamque et mutuum consensum significarent. Quod symbolum

Justice, said to be a portrait of Montmorency, holds a sword in her right hand and a wheat-ear in her left. Beside her on the pedestal lie a globe and a plumed helmet. Below are again the drawn sword and empty scabbard, with Montmorency's coat of arms on the central panel between. On the left-hand pedestal, Peace, bending slightly forward, holds a torch downward, as though in act of burning a plumed helmet at her side.[42] The Constable's emblems (sword and scabbard) are represented below.[43] But the central panel, below, again bears an elaborate design: in the center, an armillary sphere, from the sides of which festoons of oak leaves hang down; under the sphere, and between the festoons, are clasped hands; under the hands, wheat sheaves; and above the sphere, a heart. These emblems may be taken to signify Cosmic Peace (the sphere) and Earthly Peace (the clasped hands) with its abundance (the sheaves), the hero's civic virtue in defense of earthly peace (oak leaves), and his enjoyment of peace in heaven (the heart above the sphere).[44] And throughout the triple monument, we appreciate how the repetition of detail binds the whole together in a thought not far removed from the Roman *Mars pacifer*.[45]

In placing this monument in the Orléans chapel of the Célestins, the Duchess of Montmorency was collaborating with Catherine de Medici in executing the last wishes of Henri II, who on his death-bed had desired that when the old Constable came to die their hearts might be buried in the same place.[46] Catherine had erected

ferentes oratores qui ad feriendum foedus ineundamque pacem proficiscebantur, caducentores dicebantur. . . .' He also has an explanation of *spicea corona* and other symbols.

[42]So Cripps-Day; but it seems not in the spirit of the monument to attribute any *dramatic* intention to the figures. The interweaving of symbols throughout the monument, and the similarity of the gesture to that of Justice, suggest that Peace may originally have presented a wheat-ear or other vegetables.

[43]So in Millin's reproduction; but this bareness seems out of balance with the other groups.

[44]Cripps-Day sees in the celestial sphere only a personal weakness on the part of Bullant for his own solar clock of 1561; but, though no doubt he was proud of his clock, it seems unlikely that he would advertise it on Montmorency's funeral monument. We know that the peaceful order of the universe is one of the great peace themes. For the clasped hands as a Roman emblem of peace, see above, p. 30, n. 34.

[45]Below each bronze figure, and above the emblems, there are black marble plaques with inscriptions traced in white proclaiming the glory of Montmorency and the nobility of his heart (produced in Baron François de Guilhermy, *Les Inscriptions de la France* [Paris, 1868], 1. 456–7). These inscriptions do not allude to the figures or to the emblems.

[46]Cripps-Day, p. 62, from A. du Chesne, *Histoire généalogique de la maison de Montmorency* (1624), p. 413. The inscriptions (see preceding note) also refer to this fact—for example, 'Cœur qui fut cœur du Roy Henry, son maître, / Roy qui voulut qu'un sepulchre commun / les enfermast.'

the *monument du cœur* of Henri in the Célestins in 1560—base by Domenico del Barbière, and the aforementioned *Three Graces* (upholding the urn) by Germain Pilon. When the Célestins church was destroyed in 1790, both monuments were substantially preserved, destined to stand together once more as they do today in the Louvre. The urns, however, were lost.[47]

The princes of the Middle Ages had also solicited human remembrance by their tombs, but generally in a different mood. These monuments of the Renaissance are devoid of any distinctive Christian symbolism—no doubt in the interest of style, but style is spirit. One would not get far in an attempt to read them as Christian allegory. Here even more than in the 'Augustan' poetry, Roman thoughts of heroization have permeated the ambience of national greatness to the point of appearing to snatch death itself from the hands of religion. Yet we should be wrong to be so absolute; Renaissance naiveté destined these monuments for no other place than a church or consecrated chapel.[48]

[47]Far more elaborate, of course, were the tomb of the Constable in the church of Saint Martin at Montmorency, and especially the Funeral Chapel at his château of Ecouen, relics of which last are preserved in this same hall of the Louvre—among them, the effigies of Montmorency and Madeleine of Savoy (reproduced in Paul Vitry, *La Sculpture de la Renaissance française au musée du Louvre* [Paris, 1936]). The tomb of Henri II and Catherine at St. Denis was executed by Pilon under the direction of Primaticcio. Prieur's Virtues on the *monument du cœur* of Montmorency are said to be variations on the corner figures of this tomb (erected in 1560), while the general idea was inspired by Primaticcio's *monument du cœur* of Francis II, now at St. Denis (Blunt, *Art and Architecture in France*, p. 112).

[48]The fashion developed rapidly; see René Schneider, *L'Art français, fin du moyen âge, renaissance* (Paris, 1928), pp. 168–69, 187: The tomb of Louis XII, though the earliest example of a 'triumphal' tomb in France, still shows a combination of Christian and pagan iconology, while the tomb of Francis I is primarily an arch of triumph.

VII

Cosmic Peace in Ronsard's
Ode de la Paix

Sidera pace vigent, consistunt terrea pace.

Prudentius, Psych. 671

It is by peace that the stars live and move, by peace earthly things stand firm. (H. J. Thomson, Loeb)

Ronsard's Pindaric *Ode de la Paix*, published in 1550 to celebrate Henri II's treaty with England, is justly reckoned among the poet's major works. It has also personal interest as marking his outdistancing of his rivals and his emergence as the acknowledged 'royal poet.'[1] Two major, and complementary, themes are developed—first, the peace of the Universe, dramatized as the creation of the world by Peace herself, and second the destiny of Francion and the establishment of peace on earth by the agency of the French monarchy. (A minor theme is the pretensions of Ronsard to be the 'poète du roi.') The poet is moving in the realm of the great commonplaces in the manner of the rhetorical poetry of his time. It might be left at that; but we may be able to revivify the poem in certain places for the modern reader if we approach it more closely.

The peace of the Universe is traditionally a philosophical and not a poetical theme; but as a commonplace of elementary philosophy it had penetrated ancient poetry to some extent, though rarely the poetry of peace, a genre little found in antiquity. Rhetoric, however, had early adopted it (above p. 26), and thence it passed to the literature of advice to princes, associated with the topic 'The prince

---

[1]Laumonier, 3.vi, implies that it does.

should imitate God.'[2] Hardly any discussion of peace from late an-
tiquity onward fails to touch on the topic, and the identification of
poetical with rhetorical topics in the Middle Ages makes it inevitable
that Renaissance peace poems should regularly include this one. In
fact the creation topic is traditional in praise of peace, since it must,
in this collocation, always have had the implication Ronsard gives it.

Yet poetry really has the prior claim to the notion, if not to the
word, for 'peace' is but a surrogate for the 'love' or 'friendship' of
the cosmos, a metaphor that can probably be traced back through
the half-poetical early philosophers to the unique position of Eros in
the cosmogony of Hesiod. From 'the old quarrel between poetry and
philosophy,' the latter emerged with many trophies from her prede-
cessor and rival, and none was more persistent than the notion of
cosmic love. The differentiated world seems to imply a prior unity,
from which it can be derived only by division or strife, yet it owes
what cohesion it has to union or love. Or perhaps strife itself works
out to a balance of opposites or a cohesive tension. Some such
thought seems to be expressed by Heraclitus' τόνος; and he is said
also to have viewed the world situation under the terms of War and
Love (Diogenes Laertius 9.7–9). But the concept under which 'love'
and 'friendship' and eventually 'peace' became traditional metaphors
was that of the four elements, with reference to the wonderful fact
that the elements, essentially so hostile to each other, are content to
join together to form the world we see. Empedocles, who may first
have fixed the elements at four, thus conceived the coming and go-
ing of the universe as dependent on the waxing and waning of the
two realities, Strife *(Neikos)* which divides, and Love *(Philotes)* which
unites. Both are essential to the differentiated world, which is de-
stroyed as either agent prevails over the other.

Most influential, of course, was the doctrine of Plato's *Timaeus.*
Here the elements are winnowed out of the All or the Recipient by
an irregular swaying which already gives them relative positions and
'some traces of themselves'; at which point they are taken by the
Demiurge, who, wishing to make a cosmos after an eternal pattern,
unites them by 'the best of bonds,' namely a geometrical proportion,
by virtue of which the cosmos possesses 'friendship' and uniting with
itself is 'indissoluble by any except the one who had bound it to-
gether' (53 A–B, 31C–32C). Later we learn that prior to this creation

[2]Cf. Erasmus, *The Education of a Christian Prince,* trans. Lester K. Born (New York,
1936). May it not be this association that brings Augustine to discuss 'the perverse imi-
tation of God' (i.e., tyranny) in the midst of his chapters on cosmic peace (*De civ. Dei*
19.12)?

the Demiurge had created the World Soul in harmonic proportion, and that this Soul fills and encloses the cosmos, uniting with it center to center (36E). Plato does not say that this constitutes a prior bond.[3] For Aristotle, the forms of the elements, like other forms, emerge from Potentiality (the *apeiron* or All) through the force of love exerted by the Unmoved Mover or God, a force mediated through the heavens, which consist of a purer fifth element, upon the world of the four elements beneath the moon; these elements perpetually pass into one another by reason of their successively common 'qualities,' for earth is dry and cold, water cold and moist, air moist and warm, fire warm and dry. Thus both 'separation' and 'union' are made dependent on the same source of motion, which is transcendent, and the world cannot be dissolved.

The world of the Stoics, on the other hand, could be dissolved. For them the present world has its being from a principle equivalent to Plato's World Soul and called by them from different points of view the Spirit *(Pneuma)*, the Reason or Word *(Logos)*, Nature *(Physis)*, or the Creative Fire *(Ekpyrosis)*, which is always immanent and material even when on occasion they call it Zeus. The Spirit is the 'bond' of the universe (δεσμός, *SVF* von Arnim, 2.458), and is constantly said to 'run throughout and maintain' the world we see. From an undifferentiated *prima materies* it evolves the world as though by germination from 'seminal reasons,' and this world consists of the four elements, or rather of their 'powers,' which are held together for the present by the Spirit, forming our 'mixed world,' a *concordia discors*; but eventually the elements, by the 'ambition' *(pleonexia)* of one of them, fire, will dissolve into fire, from which the process will begin anew. In regard to the present 'mixed' world, the Spirit is regarded as Physis or Natura, acting as a tension (τόνος *SVF* von Arnim 2.447) in graded ascent from the mere 'habit' (ἕξις) by which such things as stones cohere up to the perfect nature of the stars. This action of the Spirit could be regarded as a chain of 'causes' extending through the universe. The Platonic schools of later antiquity retained much of this Stoic point of view, but for them the One or Mind or God was transcendent, as for Aristotle, and the chain of causes became a chain of being, extending from the One by 'emanation' through Soul and eventually to matter,

---

[3]Proclus, *In Tim.*, Diehl, ed. (Leipzig, 1903), 146E and 173F; Aelius Aristides, *Or.* 43.15; Pierre Lévêque, *Aurea Catena Homeri: Une étude sur l'allégorie grecque* (*Annales littéraires de l'Université de Besançon* 27 [Paris 1959], 23–28); Le. R. P. Festugière, *La Révélation d'Hermès Trismégiste* 2 (Paris, 1949), 216–17. See Hutton, *Essays*, pp. 172–72.

drawing the four elements into existence and uniting them by a
bond or proportion as in the *Timaeus*, though the proportion was
generally thought of as a proportion among the Aristotelian 'quali-
ties.' The World Soul remained a critical point at which Mind meets
matter, and it seemed convenient to divide again and find a lower
part of the Soul, namely Physis or Natura, to deal directly with mat-
ter and form the mixed world, the two parts of the Soul being justi-
fied by the earthly and heavenly Aphrodite of the Symposium. The
world process was not pictured, as in the *Timaeus*, as having a mo-
ment of creation, but, as in Aristotle, as eternal and continuous.

Christian theology was born into the world of Platonic thought,
but was committed, like Stoicism, to a beginning and end of the
world. It was necessary only to square the philosophical inheritance
with the first chapter of Genesis. The world was created from noth-
ing by God. But the processes of creation were 'appropriated' to the
persons of the Trinity, originating in the Wisdom of the Father and
carried into actuality by the Logos-Son in collaboration with the
Spirit, who in particular divides and unites the four elements. The
various steps were disputed. Generally speaking, it was understood
that what was created *ex nihilo* was chaotic 'without form and
void'—that is, the *prima materies*—until the Spirit 'moved upon the
face of the waters' and God said, 'Let there be light,' whereupon the
elements were actualized and took their places. The resulting con-
struction is 'good,' and its duration, as in Plato, depends on the will
of the Creator but this will has determined that eventually 'heaven
and earth shall pass away.'[4]

Though Empedocles had made Strife and Love the active agents
of world organization, later tradition preferred to place the activity
in the hands of a higher power, reserving these terms for a descrip-
tion of the resulting condition. In the *Timaeus* the Demiurge unites
the elements by a 'bond' (δεσμός) by virtue of which they enjoy
'friendship' (φιλία). Since the correlative term is generally 'war' (for
example, Heraclitus' πόλεμος καὶ ἔρις), 'friendship' might be ex-
pected to have some political shading, yet in Plato's *Sophist* (252 D),
for example, the 'war' (πόλεμος) of the elements is said to end
in—marriage. The concept of a cosmic Aphrodite carries the meta-
phor in the same direction; even in Lucretius' *Prologue* political
peace is secondary to the sexual and generative power of Venus. It is
in fact difficult to find early examples of 'peace' as the correlative of

[4]See *Dictionnaire de Théologie Catholique*, vol. 5, art. 'Fin du Monde.' For the Stoic
view, see Gérard Verbeke, *L'Evolution de la doctrine du pneuma, du Stoïcisme à St.
Augustin* (Louvain, 1945), Ch. 1, pp. 11–174.

'war' among the elements, but our sources are fragmentary, and it seems likely that ὁμόνοια if not εἰρήνη was used by the Stoics for the world condition.[5] The expressions tirelessly repeated by them for the Pneuma as universal bond are συνῆκον, συνέχεσθαι, and διήκων καὶ σῴζων, running through and 'holding together' or 'saving,' and the resulting condition is *sympatheia*. The Stoics were notoriously given to synonyms, and Philodemus complains that they identified Zeus with universal Nature and with Eunomia and Dike and Homonoia and Eirene.[6] The Latin *concordia* is said to represent either *homonoia* or *sympatheia*, and *concordia* is already used by Cicero for the condition of the universe.[7] But *homonoia* is no more than a synonym for *philia*. Lucan in a passage dense with Stoic terms contrives to combine the notion of the 'bond' of the 'mixed' universe with an amalgamation of 'saving' (σῴζειν), 'concord,' and 'love' (*Bellum civ.* 4.189–81):

> Nunc ades aeterno complectens omnia nexu,
> O rerum mixtique salus, Concordia, mundi
> Et sacer orbis amor.

And it is difficult to avoid the inference that a Stoic original lies behind the common Latin description of the 'mixed' world as a *concordia discors*, a paradoxical construction of 'warring peace.'[8] Manilius, who uses this expression, also describes the union of the elements under the thoroughly Roman concept of *foedus*, a treaty.[9] Only occasionally does *pax* appear in this sense, as in the influential creation passage of Ovid (*Met.* 1.25), where, however, an explanatory *concors* is added: '(Deus et melior Natura) dissociata locis concordi pace liga-

[5]No passages in Arnim's SVF under ὁμόνοια or εἰρήνη have a cosmic reference. Eros is the *syndesmos* of the universe in Plato, *Symposium* 202 E, and Philia serves the same function in *Gorgias* 508 A (Jaeger, *Paideia* 2.188).

[6]*De Pietate* 12.79, Comperz-Diels, *Doxographi graeci* (Berlin, 1879), 545, 31ff. Possibly Philo is using Stoic language for this universal principle when he represents God as separating light from darkness 'in order that war might not prevail instead of peace' (πόλεμος ἀντ' εἰρήνης); *De opific. mundi* 29.33.

[7]*De univ.* 13: 'Mundus ipse se concordi quadam amicitia et charitate amplectitur.' Pliny, *HN* 37.59: 'Docere . . . de discordia rerum *concordia*que, quam antipathiam Graeci vocavere ac *sympatheiam*.' Dio on ὁμόνοια; *Or.* 38.11; 40.35–37; 48.14; Fuchs, *Augustin*, pp. 10ff.; Prudentius, *Psych.* 671: 'Sidera pace vigent, consistunt terrea pace.'

[8]Horace, *Epist.* 1.18.19: 'Quid velit et possit rerum *concordia discors*'; Ovid, *Met.* 1.433: 'discors concordia fetibus apta est'; Manilius 1.142: 'Sit . . . haec discordia concors'; Seneca, *Nat. Quaest.* 7.27.4: 'tota haec mundi concordia e discordibus constat.' For the Stoics see Verbeke, *L'Evolution*, Ch. 1.

[9]Manilius 1.251–2: 'Deus . . . mutuaque in cunctas dispensat foedera partes'; 3.55: 'aeterno relegatus foedere mundus' (but 3.54, *concordia*).

vit.' In later antiquity, however, *pax* and *eirene* become more common in this usage, partly perhaps under the influence of the *pax Romana* and partly from the inveterate habit of drawing lessons of conduct from the example of the orderly and peaceful heavens.[10] Dio, to be sure, in this usage, prefers *homonoia*. Indeed, perhaps it is only with the Neoplatonists and the Christian theologians that *eirene* and *pax* become the usual terms.[11] The 'bond' of the elements underlies St. Augustine's celebrated chapter on Pax (*De civ. D.* 19), and in Dionysius the Areopagite (*De div. nom.* 11) we see Eirene, as one of the Names or Virtues of God, actively holding the world together. Throughout the Middle Ages and the Renaissance the 'peace' of the universe became a familiar commonplace.[12] We may note in passing how cleverly Milton takes advantage of it when in the act of creating the *prima materies* from the tumultuous Abyss, equivalent to Plato's surging Recipient, the Logos-Son is made to utter the authentic command of the incarnate Word to the waters of Galilee (*PL* 7.216–17):

> 'Silence, ye troubled waves, and thou Deep, peace!'
> Said the omnific Word: 'your discord end!'[13]

The foregoing remarks may help us to place the creation passage of Ronsard's *Ode de la Paix* rather precisely in the tradition. Henri II is celebrated (vv. 35ff.)

> Pour avoir fait reverdir l'age,
> Où florissoit l'antique paix,

> Epode

> Laquelle osta le debat
> Du Chaos, quand la premiere

[10]On Epinomia and the use of the orderly heavens, *DND* 2.75–122, where Cicero discusses the order of the universe; *De univ.* 13; Seneca, *De otio* 4.1; *Ep. ad Luc.* 102.30–31; 66.39–40; Festugière, *Rév. d'Hermès*, Vol. 2: "Le Dieu cosmique," esp. pp. 215–18 of Ch. 7, "L'Epinomie." See also Ch. 13, "Le Témoignage de Cicéron sur la religion cosmique" for a more complete account of Cicero's views on world order.

[11]See above, Ch. I, notes 50 and 52.

[12]Above, Ch. I, pp. 37ff. and note 69. Also Jean Gerson's sermons, Cusanus, *Concordantia catholica* and *De pace fidei*, and Rodrigo Sánchez de Arévalo, *De pace et de bello*.

[13]The command is, however, anticipatory; peace is not actually achieved until the Spirit of God has separated the elements and put them in their 'places,' by infusing 'vital virtue and vital warmth.' The Spirit here, as often in Christian theology, is very close to the Stoic Pneuma or the Anima Mundi.

40

Elle assoupit le combat
Qui aveugloit la lumiere.
Elle seule oza tenter
D'effondrer le ventre large
Du grant Tout, pour enfanter
L'obscur fardeau de sa charge.
Puis demembrant l'univers
En quatre quartiers divers,
Sa main divinement sainte
Les lia de clous d'aimant,
Afin de s'aller aimant

50

D'une paisible constrainte.

Strophe 2

Adonq mélant dans ce grand monde
Sa douce force vagabonde
Le bien heura d'un dous repos,
Elle fit bas tumber la terre,
Et tournoier l'eau qui la serre
De ses bras vagues et dispos.
Du soleil alongea les yeus
En forme de fleches volantes,
Et d'ordre fit dancer aus Cieus

60

Le bal des estoilles coulantes.
Elle courba le large tour
De l'air, qui cerne tout autour
Le rond du grand parc où nous sommes,
Peuplant sa grande rondeur d'hommes
D'un mutuel acroissement:
Car partout où voloit la belle,
Les amours volloient avecq' elle
Chatouillant les cueurs doucement.

Antistrophe

Lors pour sa juste recompense

70

Le saint Monarque qui dispense
Tout en tous (duquel le sourci
En se clinant pour faire sinne
Jusque au fond croulle la racine
De la terre et du ciel aussi)
Fit soir la Paix à son costé
Dedans un throne d'excellence,
Et dans un autre il a bouté
L'horrible Dieu de violence:

[204]

De l'un les grands princes il oint,
De l'autre il les picque et les point
Tous effroiés d'ouir les armes
Craquer sur le dos des gendarmes:
De l'un jadis il honora
Les vieus peres du premier age,
Et de l'autre il aigrit la rage
Contre Ilion.

80

Creative Peace is not God, but a 'virtue' of God. She does not create *ex nihilo* nor does she create souls; she creates the physical universe, and has, so to speak, been shifted from the predicate of the statement 'the uniting of the elements gives the world peace' to be the subject and agent. The first sentence of the epode, 'laquelle osta le debat / . . . Qui aveugloit la lumiere,' is preparatory; her action begins, like that of the Logos-Son in Milton, when she causes the dim outlines of the elements to appear in Chaos or the All, the words 'obscur fardeau' being equivalent to Plato's phrase 'show some traces of themselves.'[14] She then separates the four elements distinctly and, like Plato's Demiurge, binds them in 'paisible constrainte' (almost *concordia discors*) to make the 'mixed' world, by means of her 'douce force vagabonde,' like the World Soul of the Pneuma (vagabonde = διήϰων), putting the elements in their 'places,' and thereby taking the creative step called theologically 'ornatus' by which the world we see was formed. Ronsard keeps in touch both

[14]In Plato the mere shaking of the Recipient automatically produces this all-important effect. To the Neoplatonists of the twelfth century the question of whether matter was formless or already formed at the moment of creation was of great concern. In Hugh of St. Victor, *hyle* at the time of the creation is in a primal state, neither formed matter nor absolute chaos, but *forma confusionis*. In the following days of creation *hyle* is increasingly organized, passing from *forma confusionis* to *forma dispositionis* (Hugh of St. Victor, *De Sacramentis* 1.1.2 and 4. [Migne, *PL* 176.189D]) To Hugh, Bernard Sylvestris, Thierry of Chartres, and others, the *hyle* that God created *ex nihilo* on the first day contains the qualities of the elements within it, but the intervention of divine intelligence (Nouys in the *Cosmographia*) is necessary to put them in their proper order. Bernard opens the *Cosmographia* with the following description of *forma confusionis*:

Ut quid ab aeterno primae fundamina causae,
Ingenitae lites germanaque bella fatigunt,
Quando fluit refluitque sibi contraria moles,
Fortuitis elementa modis incerta feruntur (1.1.23−26).

See Theodore Silverstein, "The Fabulous Cosmology of B.S.," *Modern Philology* 46 (1947−49), 92−116. [Now also the introduction to Peter Dronke's edition of the *Cosmographia* (Leiden, 1978), and two works by Winthrop Wetherbee: *Platonism and Poetry in the Twelfth Century* (Princeton, 1972), and *The Cosmographia of B.S.: A Translation with Introduction and Notes* (New York, 1973).]

with Ovid (*Met.* 1.5–88) and the biblical Genesis: the earth is 'le rond du grand parc,' an obvious reference to the Garden of Eden; but the work of the sixth day is for La Paix only propagation, in which she takes the role of Aphrodite accompanied by the Loves. Again like the creative Son in Milton (*PL* 7.584–88), she is rewarded with a throne at the side of God (on his right hand in the revision of 1552): as a 'virtue' of God she does not 'lapse' nor of course is it intended that she has abandoned the world after creating it. It is startling to find that God has a throne also for War or Discord ('L'horrible Dieu de violence'); we know that *Neikos* and *Philotes* were once regarded as equal principles, but can Discord be a 'virtue' of God?

Ronsard is clearly original in making Peace a creative agent, though the invention may seem easy and has precedents of a sort—at least, we may cite the *Eirene* of Dionysius the Areopagite (though *Eirene* is a sustainer rather than a creator and transcends the physical universe), and a passing claim of Concordia in Alain de Lille.[15] Examples, however, are few, perhaps because of the difficulty, if it is one, that what Peace essentially creates is herself. In thus promoting her from the predicate to be the subject of the world statement, Ronsard no doubt knew that he must give her the program of one of the traditional subjects or agents; and it is of some interest for the understanding of the poem to see whose role she is playing. For her function, an activity limited to the physical universe, there are really only two candidates, Nature and the Earthly Aphrodite.[16] Either name for this identical function could be substituted for La Paix. It is noteworthy that, while boldly creative with the elements and the external world, La Paix falls in vv. 64–65 to be merely a 'sustainer,' not creating men on earth, but merely 'peuplant sa grande rondeur d'hommes / D'un mutuel acroissement.' The same reserve may be seen elsewhere in the treatment of Nature.[17]

[15]*Anticlaudianus* 2.5: 'ni . . . pace perpetua . . . elementa ligassem, / Intestinus adhuc strepitus primordia rerum . . . concuteret.'

[16]We may rule out as unusual Endelechia, who created the world in Bernard Sylvester, *De mundi universitate*, C. S. Barach and J. Wrobel, eds. (Innsbruck, 1876), pp. 13–14. For Ronsard's understanding of *endelechia*, see Henri Busson, "Ronsard et l'Entelechie," *Mélanges d'histoire littéraire de la Renaissance offerts à Henri Chamard* (Paris, 1951), pp. 91–95.

[17]Natura is primarily a sustainer, not a creator, and so Peace should be (as in Dionysius), but it is easy to slide between these concepts. So Alain de Lille, *De planctu Naturae* (Migne, *PL* 210, 447), addresses Natura: 'O Dei proles, *genetrixque rerum*, / Vinculum mundi stabilisque nexus, / Lucifer orbis, / Pax, Amor, Virtus,' where she is identified not only with Pax but the higher principle Amor; but later (453) it becomes clear that as *Dei vicaria* she only maintains the created world by generation. Also in *Anticlaudianus* 1.5, Natura might be taken as creator. Compare Ficino's statement of the subject of the *Timaeus*: 'Universa natura, id est seminaris quaedam et vivi-

Still, the identification in the following lines of La Paix with Venus accompanied by the Amores insures that here at least Ronsard's mind glanced to the Earthly Aphrodite and presumably to Ficino's *Commentary on the Symposium*.[18] We shall find further evidence below that Ronsard actually had this work before him in writing this poem. As one would expect, his doctrine is up-to-date Renaissance Platonism.

Michael Marullus, at this time one of Ronsard's favorite authors, will furnish a parallel in his *Hymn to Venus*:[19]

> Prima de patris gremio Cythere
> Caeca Naturae miserata membra,
> Soluit antiquam minimum pigendo
> Foedere litem.
> Illa supremis spaciis removit
> Lucidum hunc ignem mediasque terras
> Arte suspendit pelagusque molles
> Inter et auras.
> Tunc et immenso micuere primum
> Signa tot caelo, et sua flamina aër
> Coepit, admirans volucrum proterva
> Praelia fratrum. . . .

The animals, too, now come into being, presumably by Cythere's power, but mankind, apparently already in being, is only fostered by her and by the Loves:

fica Virtus toti infusa mundo, animae quidem mundanae subdita, materiae vero praesidens.' *Opera* (Basel, 1576) 2.1438. On Ronsard's concept of Nature, see A.-M. Schmidt, *La Poésie scientifique en France au seizième siècle* (Paris, 1938), pp. 87, 100.
[18]Cf. *Commentary* 2.7 and 6.7–8. Sears Jayne, ed. (Columbia, Mo., 1944). As the heavenly Venus exists in the Angelic Mind and is accompanied by a Love, so the earthly Venus, accompanied by a Love, is present in the World Soul and 'is the power of generation with which the World Soul is endowed.' On the other hand, Alain de Lille (*De planctu*, Migne, *PL* 210.459) pictures the relation of Venus to Natura as a subvicariate, in which Venus is assisted by her husband Hymenaeus and her son Cupido.
[19]About eight of the divinities of Marullus' *Hymns* perform these creative functions. The attitude is that of the Orphic *Hymns* and generally of Neoplatonism and goes back to the Stoics: namely that the 'created gods' (Plato's phrase) are surrogates or Virtues of the Supreme Being. Ronsard constantly avails himself of this custom (Schmidt, *Poésie*, p. 86). For the cosmic Aphrodite, see Empedocles, fragm. D. B. 17; Lucretius 1.21; Proclus, *Hymn to Aphrodite* 15–16; and Apuleius, *Met.* 38, Rudolph Helm, ed. (Berlin, 1959), where Venus is 'rerum naturae prisca parens' and 'elementorum origo initialis.'

At virum quamvis etiam labante
Aegra plebs genu, meditari et urbes
Tactaque et iam tum sociorum amicos
    Iungere coetus,
Quos ferox inter medios Cupido
Acer it, fratrum comitante turba,
Callidus quondam petiisse certa
    Quemque sagitta.

A further suggestion may be made about the personality of La Paix. In bringing the elements to birth in vv. 41–50 she acts the part of a cosmic midwife. The birth of the world or the elements is of course one of the oldest of metaphors and is common in Platonic writers, since it is practically present in the *Timaeus* (50D) where the Recipient is likened to the mother, the 'source' to the father, and the 'intermediate nature' to the offspring. What seems remarkable in Ronsard's account is the almost Orphic violence of the procedure, all the more noticeable since the agent is Peace. She dares try 'rummaging' (*effondrer*: 'eviscerate'?) the womb of the All; she 'dismembers' (*demembrant*) the universe into four quarters, which her 'divine hand' then nails together again.[20] Is it possible that in this rough handling of the universe La Paix falls under the shadow of Boccaccio's cosmic agent Demogorgon as explained by Leone Ebreo? I quote a few sentences from the *Dialoghi d'amore*:[21]

[20]A note may be added about 'nails': 'Les lia de clous d'aimant.' Ronsard knew—as the word 'lia' perhaps indicates—that the proper Platonic metaphor is 'bond' (δεσμός), but he has unexpectedly substituted 'nails,' as Laumonier notes, from Pindar, *Pyth.* 4.71: κρατεροῖς ἀδάμαντος δῆσεν ἅλοις (which also justifies 'lia' = δῆσεν). There is probably no special significance in this substitution, but a possibility perhaps deserves to be mentioned. Plato uses similar means (γόμφοι, 'pegs'; cf. Empedocles, fragm. DK B 87) to pin together the human body, a temporary structure; and Ronsard's 'nails,' adamantine though they are, might suggest that his universe is less stable than Plato's, as in fact it is. Nails have occasionally been used in cosmic construction; at least Plutarch attaches the atmosphere to the lower region of the moon by nails (ἥλοις ἀραρὼς . . . συγγεγομφωμένος). The Areopagite uses 'bolts' (i.e., door bolts, κλείθροις) to unite the elements (*DND* Ch. 11).

[21]On Boccaccio's *Genealogia deorum gentilium libri*, Vincenzo Romano, ed. (Bari, 1951) see Jean Seznec, *La Survivance*, Book II, Ch. i. Ebreo's *Dialoghi*, Santino Caramella, ed. (Bari, 1929), p. 110; the translation is that of F. Friedberg-Seeley and Jean H. Barnes, *The Philosophy of Love* (London, 1937), pp. 124–27. Pontus de Tyard's translation was about to appear in 1551; Ronsard speaks of Leone Ebreo, *Œuvres complètes*, Blanchemain, ed. (Paris, 1857), 1.419 (Sonnet 62.9–14) and 2.331. Demogorgon = Demiourgos was understood by some at least to be the Anima Mundi; so the scholium on Statius, *Theb.* 4.516 (cod. Riccard. 842, f. 46) quoted by Carlo Landi, *Demogorgone* (Palermo, 1930), p. 41 n. 4, and repeated by Ognibono on Lucan 4.742–49, quoted by M. Castelain, "Démogorgon ou le barbarisme déifié," *Bulletin de l'association Guillaume Budé*, 36 (July 1932), 34. Boccaccio thinks he is Divine Wisdom, and Leone Ebreo seems to accept this interpretation.

The disturbance left by Demogorgon in the womb of Chaos was the ability and desire of indeterminate matter to generate distinct things. . . . The stretching forth of Demogorgon's hand to open the womb of Chaos denotes the divine power resolving to promote to distinct actuality the universal potency of Chaos. Such is the meaning of opening the pregnant womb to draw forth what was hidden therein. And they imagined this extraordinary mode of generation with the hand . . . to indicate that the first production or creation of things was not ordinary, . . . but was strangely and miraculously accomplished by an omnipotent hand [*sa main divinement sainte*?]. It is said that the first issue of Chaos was Strife, because what first issued from the first matter was the distinction of things which lay therein indistinct [*obscur fardeau*], and was made distinct at birth by the hand . . . of their father Demogorgon. This (attainment of) distinctness is called Strife because it is based on an opposition . . . between the four elements.

Strife (*Litigium* in Boccaccio) is banished, and at a second birth there emerges Pan, explained as harmony or Nature, who moves to the throne of Demogorgon. The representation is crude and does not allow for the fact that the distinction (and placing) of the elements must remain. The mutual dislike among the elements, their strife, is necessary in the maintenance of the world; but given the upper hand it will reduce all to the discord of chaos again. The harmony of these opposites is peace, and there is no peace or harmony except among opposites. Peace is a tension due to opposition; if the opposition is relaxed, there is destruction, not peace.

The Renaissance constantly toyed with this *concordia discors*; Marullus (*Hymnus amori*): 'Rerum / mutuis nectis seriem catenis / Pace rebelli;' Ronsard himself (*Exhortation pour la Paix* 198–99): 'La Paix querella au Chaos le discord'; Du Bartas, (*Sem.* 1, *Jour.* 2.62–62): 'Une semblable *guerre* [to that of the macrocosm] *tient en paix* nostre corps.' Discord is certainly the enemy of peace, but a necessary enemy. Satan must be bound, but cannot be destroyed. Thus in Ronsard's later poem *La Paix, au Roy* (1559), Peace forms the world (here strictly after Ovid), binds Discord, and mounts to the throne of God (vv. 73ff.):

> Après avoir par ordre arrangé la machine,
> Et lié ce grand Corps d'une amitié divine,
> Elle fist atacher à cent chaines de fer
> Le malheureux Discord aux abysmes d'Enfer,
> Puis au throne de Dieu, qui tout voit et dispose,
> Alla prendre sa place, où elle se repose.

[209]

But God has a use for Discord (vv. 79ff.):

> Quand les pechez d'un peuple, ou les fautes d'un Roy,
> En rompant toute honte ont violé la Loy, . . .
> Le grand Dieu tout puissant à ses Anges commande
> Descheiner le Discord, afin que destaché
> Du peuple vitieux punisse le peché.

The cosmic Discord is identified with human War. Even if this is only a play on words, the parallel with the antistrophe of the *Ode de la Paix* (vv. 69ff.) which we are considering would suggest that in the *Ode* also 'l'horrible Dieu de violence' is not only War, but cosmic Discord, and that the strange tableau of God with Peace on his right hand and War on his left is indeed intended as a, rather crude, representation of the *coincidentia oppositorum*. The threatening parenthesis ('duquel le sourci . . .') suggests that, more powerful than the nod of Zeus, God's nod will destroy the present world.[22]

The vengeance of God for 'les pechez d'un peuple, ou les fautes d'un Roy' is the conventional reason given in most of our peace poems for the unleashing of War or Discord upon mankind. In the antistrophe of the *Ode* (vv. 80–86) no such reason is assigned. War is simply an alternate 'virtue' to peace. God sends it, and sent it to Troy. That touches on the central theme of the poem: God's mysterious plan for the world. The underlying form is redemption—peace lost with the Golden Age will, by God's plan, be restored by Henri II and his successors, just as in the *Ode à Michel de L'Hospital* (1552) the theme is the redemption of poetry, lost in antiquity and to be restored by L'Hospital. It is this apocalyptic purpose that makes it appropriate for Ronsard not merely to refer to cosmic peace, as most peace poets do, but to present at the beginning a creation scene that recalls the beginning of the Bible. The poem alternates between cosmic peace and discord on the one hand and human war and peace on the other and hints that they are mysteriously conjoined.

The plan of God is now unrolled in one of those passages of national prophecy, reminiscent of Anchises' prophecy in the *Aeneid*, which Renaissance poets delighted in presenting. Upon the destruction of Troy, Cassandra, and, later in Epirus, the ghost of Hector,

---

[22]A parallel, though an incomplete one, to the concept of the antistrophe may be seen in Ovid *Fasti* 1.102–26, where Janus, 'of old called Chaos,' takes on form as the elements are separated, and now holds sway in the universe, permitting, if he will, Pax to go forth to mankind, and putting *bella* under lock and key ('sub pede bella iacent').

prophesy the founding of the French monarchy in descent from Francion. We cannot accept Laumonier's view (3.9.n) that this myth-ical part of the ode is 'très artificiellement rattaché au sujet.' In fact it is the subject. As the 'Holy Monarch' has given form to the universe through Peace, it is his plan through the French monarchy to secure peace on earth. The ghost of Hector sees in the royal line (vv. 245ff.) 'un Henri'—

> Des meilleurs le meilleur roi,
> Qui finira sa conqueste
> Es deus bords où le soleil
> S'endort et fait son reveil.

The French monarchy, like the Roman Empire (also sprung from Troy), will bring peace by its conquests, and this destiny seems on the verge of fulfillment, since Henri is endowed with the necessary virtue (vv. 30ff.):

> Des long tens tu fus honoré
> Comme seul prince decoré
> Des biens et des vertus ensemble
> Que le destin en un t'assemble,

and is restoring the Saturnian age (vv. 35 and 415−18). The peace of 1550 is perhaps but a stage on the way. It is still in order for Ron-sard, like Pindar, to admonish his hero, and the latter part of the ode turns on several topics of the 'mirror of princes' theme—wari-ness of flatterers (410) and trust in good advisers (Montmorency, 349, and Ronsard, 419ff.). One may hope, in the final verses of the poem, that the prophecy of Hector will be fulfilled under Henri and his son:

> Puisse il [Dieu] desous toi
> Donter l'Espagne affoiblie,
> Gravant bien avant ta loi
> Dans le gras champ d'Italie:
> Avienne aussi que ton fis,
> Survivant ton jour prefis,
> Borne aus Indes sa victoire
> Riche de gain et d'honneur,
> Et que je sois le sonneur
> De l'une et l'autre gloire.

To an aspiring court poet it might not seem incongruous to end an impressive poem on peace with a prayer for the defeat of Spain and the military conquest of the lands of Charles V. But from a poet who aimed at immortality one might expect something better. We may ascribe to him a consciousness that the device of Henri II, the 'most Christian' king,' was the crescent moon, with the motto: *Donec totum impleat orbem*. Is it too much to think, in view of ideas afloat at the time, that the destiny so often invoked in the poem was by implication the beginning of an era of world peace to be secured by the conquests of the French monarchy? Such ideas were associated with the name of Guillaume Postel, whose notoriety in 1550 was perhaps such that Ronsard would not openly allude to him, but whose learned vaticinations might well have appealed to the young poet.

We would not wish to push this suggestion too far. It may be noticed, however, that 1550, the year in which Ronsard's poem was published, had been cabalistically determined by Postel as the turning point in history, after which the era of peace was to be ushered in by the conquests of the French monarchy.[23] Postel had insisted, with anxiety, that the French king should prepare himself for this destiny by living a virtuous life—that is, putting himself in a state of grace—as Ronsard, rather hopefully, says that Henri has done (vv. 29–32, quoted above).[24] It occurred to Postel also to connect this destiny of the French kings with the history of Francion, though he may not have done so until after the publication of Ronsard's poem.[25] The esoteric lore of the poem is Platonic and not cabalistic, unless one were to attempt to make something of the fact that it is written in exactly five hundred lines, a number that meant much to Postel.[26] Ronsard may or may not have been personally acquainted with Postel whether before or after 1550, nor does it matter.[27] Per-

[23]See above, p. 58.

[24]Postel's views on the virtues needed by a French king are to be found in *Candelabri typici* . . . (Venice, 1548), p. 49.

[25]In those writings of Postel that I have been able to examine the story of Francion is made use of only in a publication of 1552: *L'Histoire mémorable des expéditions depuis le déluge, faites par les Gaulois* (Paris, 1552).

[26]In Postel's cabalistic works, e.g., the *Candelabri typici*, the number five hundred does not figure so prominently. Many numbers held importance for him, from the quaternion through the number six in all its manifestations. See the facsimile edition of the Venice, 1548, edition, Nieuwkoop, 1966, with Italian and French translations.

[27]Not much can be made of the taunt flung at Ronsard thirteen years later (1563) by Florent Chrestien:

> Non point pour conjurer les songes de Postel
> (Postel, ton grand amy) qui a toute remplie
> De sa grande fureur la France et l'Italie,
> Et qui a pu aussi ton esprit atiser.

haps all we can say with certainty is that ideas similar to those of the *Ode de la Paix* were current at the time, inspired in part no doubt by a wish to answer the imperial propaganda of Charles V,[28] and that Postel had notoriously carried them farther than anyone else.

In noticing the prophecies of Cassandra and the ghost of Hector we have had to consider the bearing of the poem as a whole. After these prophecies, which form the 'myth' of this Pindaric ode, the poet turns back to celebrate the return of Peace as a result of the present treaty. Peace is now appropriately praised both as social peace bringing joy to men and as cosmic peace that *sustains* (rather than creating) the world:

> O Paix heureuse,
> Tu es la garde vigoureuse
> Des peuples, et de leurs cités:
> Des roiaumes les clefs tu portes,
> Tu ouvres des villes les portes,
> Serenant leur adversités.[29]

These lines blend into a passage that at first sight seems puzzling enough:

> L'effort de ta divinité
> Commande à la necessité
> Ploiant' sous ton obeissance:
> Les bestes sentent ta puissance
> Alechés de ton dous amer:
> De l'air la vagabonde troupe
> T'obeist, et celle qui couppe
> Le plus creus ventre de la mer.

(Charles Read, "Documents . . . contre Pierre de Ronsard," *Bulletin de la Société de l'histoire du Protestantisme* [Paris, 1888], 37.643; Georges Weill, *De G. Postelli vita et indole* [Paris, 1892], p. 53).

[28]The English also were moved to counter this propaganda; see Frances A. Yates, "Queen Elizabeth as Astraea," *Journal of the Warburg and Courtauld Institutes*, 10 (1947), 27–82.

[29]To say with Laumonier (3.24 n.) flatly that these lines and the four that follow are inspired by Pindar (*Pyth.* 8.1–12) does not do justice to the 'mixed world' of the poet's style, which borrows a line here and a line there. I see only the line 'Des roiaumes les clefs tu portes' as probably from βουλᾶν τε καὶ πολέμων ἔχουσα κλαΐδες ('you hold the keys of councils and of wars'—not πολίων 'of cities!'). The invocation of 'O Paix heureuse' may, as Laumonier says, render φιλόφρων Ἀσυχία, but cf. Alain Chartier, *Lay*: 'Paix eureuse fille du Dien des dieux,' echoed down the whole line of French poems on peace. The line 'Tu ouvres des villes les portes' (not at all in Pindar) is also a commonplace of these poems.

How does Peace rule necessity? And what has that to do with the
beasts, birds, and fishes? The answer is that Peace is now endowed
with the higher power of cosmic Love, who according to Ficino
'rules before Necessity,' because his power begins in God, that of Ne-
cessity in created things.[30] And Ficino hereupon quotes from the
Orphic Hymn to Aphrodite:[31]

καὶ κρατέεις τρισσῶν μοιρῶν, γεννᾷς δὲ τὰ πάντα ὅσσα τ᾽ἐν οὐρανῷ
ἐστὶ καὶ ἐν γαίη πολυκάρπῳ ἐν πόντου τε βυθῷ.

'Thou rulest the three Fates, and dost give birth to all things that are
in heaven and in the fruitful earth and in the depth of the sea.' Fi-
cino explains that Necessity resides in the three Fates. Ronsard, as is
his custom, has seized upon this jewel from the 'divine Orpheus' to
adorn his Pindaric ode, and the borrowing assures us that he had
Ficino before him when he wrote. But La Paix is still Aphrodite with
her 'dous amer.' That the beasts 'feel her power' means, not of
course that the beasts love peace, but that they are moved to genera-
tion by the cosmic Aphrodite (γεννᾷς). But it is like Ronsard to cross
his borrowing from 'Orpheus' with the similar expression of this
theme in Lucretius 1.12ff., where also birds, beasts, and (implied)
fishes follow Aphrodite, *perculsae corda tua vi* and *capta lepore.* The
statement is from 'Orpheus,' the warmth and color from Lucretius,
though from the Greek ἐν πόντου τε βυθῷ doubtless comes 'le plus
creus ventre de la mer.' The expression ὅσσα τ᾽ἐν οὐρανῷ is wrongly
taken to refer to birds—it means the stars, as Ronsard seems to have
realized when rehandling the theme in his later poem, *La Paix, au Roy*
(177–82):

> Mais pourquoy m'amuse-je à chose si petite,
> Quand les astres du ciel, et tout ce qui habite
> D'écaille dans la mer, les grans monstres des eaux,
> Tout ce qui vit en terre, et les legers oiseaux
> Qui pendus dedans l'air sur les vens se soutiennent
> Sont tous remplis d'amour, et par luy s'entretiennent?[32]

[30]*Comm. in Symposium* 5.11. This passage appears in Hutton, *Essays*, p. 227.
[31]*Orphic Hymn.* 55.5–7. Compare Marullus, *Hymnus Amori:*

> Quid? quod antiqua superata Anance
> Suscipis mundum placidus regendum.

[32]With the preceding topic, compare Agrippa d'Aubigny's epigram *De la Paix*
(*Œuvres complètes*, E. Réaume and F. de Caussade, eds. [Paris, 1873–92]), 3.307:

> Voici une suite estrange
> D'un desordre, et ses effects:

Generation is one aspect of the upkeep of the universe, but more fundamental is the tendency of the elements, to which the *Ode* now proceeds:

> C'est toi que desus ton eschine
> Soutiens ferme cette machine,
> Medecinant chaque element
> Quand une humeur par trop abonde,
> Pour joindre les membres du monde
> D'une contrepois egallement.

What Ronsard only alludes to here, the health of the universe and the danger thereto from the possible *pleonexia* of one of the elements, is also stated at length in the passage of *La Paix, au Roy* just mentioned (183–202), where he connects it with the corruption of the air and hence with the origin of pestilence, and compares the sickness that results in the human body from a similar 'hatred' among the bodily humors. Without following up this familiar topic, we may note that Ronsard is still close to Plato's *Symposium*, if not to Ficino's commentary on it. There the physician Eryximachus says (188A): 'When the Eros that consorts with wantonness gets the upper hand in dealing with the seasons of the year, there is much damage done and wrong; for from the like are pestilences prone to come, and many other indiscriminate ills, upon beasts and plants as well.'[33] Compare *La Paix, au Roy* (191–92):

> Il gaste bleds et vins, et espand mille maux
> Sur l'homme miserable et sur les animaux.

The higher principle is Love, often identified in Christian or Aristotelian or indeed in Platonic terms as God; peace is one manifestation or representative or 'virtue' of Love and may on occasion be said to do all that Love does.[34] By a persistent metaphor, not neces-

---

> Il tire Mars, Mars Anange,
> Et cet Anange la Paix:
> La Paix, qui a pour nourrice
> La dure Necessité,
> Tire après soi la Justice,
> Et la blanche Pieté.

[33]Translation by Lane Cooper.
[34]Thus Love 'creates and sustains' like the Stoic Pneuma in Ficino (*Comm. in Symp.* 3.2): 'Amor est auctor omnium et servator.' The Areopagite's Eirene not only holds the world together, but also holds the Trinity together. Abelard (*Theologia Christiana* 1.5, Migne, *PL* 178.1133–34) and others inevitably identify the Holy Spirit as Love.

sarily in conscious allusion to the Prince of Peace as Son, Peace is constantly designated as 'la fille de Dieu.' This expression, already employed by Alain Chartier, becomes common with the Platonizing poets of the Renaissance, in whom it bears a philosophical sense, mingled, it may be, with a knowledge that in Hesiod Eirene is the daughter of Zeus.[35] The philosophical relationship allows Ronsard to draw on the doctrine of Ficino's *Commentary* for the figure of La Paix; but Ficino says nothing there about Peace. The connection between cosmic Love and Peace was, as we know, conventional, especially in the poetry of peace; but a straightforward exposition of the topic, and one that Ronsard very likely knew, deserves our particular attention. This occurs in the ever-popular *Zodiacus vitae* of Palingenius (Manzolli), the fourth book of which is a versified treatise on love and friendship.[36] The center of the subject is cosmic love and peace.

Love is divine; what God loves endures: He is 'careful of the type *(species)*' but 'careless of the single life *(corpora)*,' and thus sustains the world (439–73):[37]

> Quare qui quaerit amorem,
> Rem quaerit divinam: etenim nisi cuncta perenni
> Ipse Deum atque hominum rex prosequeretur amore,
> Deficeret mundus, pariterque elementa perirent.
> Quilibet id servat quod amat gaudetque tueri,
> At quid non amat, id nemo servare laborat.
> Idcirco rerum series aeterna manebit:
> Quippe Dei est aeternus amor, qui cuncta tuetur:
> Et licet orta cadant, species nulla atterit aetas:
> Diligit has etenim per se Deus optimus; at non
> Sic ea quae rapidae debentur corpora morti. . . .
>   Non amat ipse
> Corpora: corrumpi idcirco sinit, at species non.
> Quid figulus curat, si frangitur ista vel illa
> Olla? . . .

But the Whole stands through God's love:

[35]See above, Ch. II, n. 13. Hesiod, *Theog.* 901–3, for Eirene, Dike, and Eunomia as daughters of Zeus and Themis.
[36]Venice, n.d., but after 1534, year of the accession of Hercules II of Ferrara, to whom it is dedicated.
[37]Tennyson (*In Memoriam* 54) safely ascribes this to Natura, but Manzolli is equally safe in writing *corpora* instead of 'single life.'

Praeterea coelum,[38] tellus, aërque, fretumque
Atque ignis, demum totius machina mundi
Hoc stat et hoc durat tot iam per saecula nexu.
Nam nisi tantus amor firma compage teneret
Omnia, pugnarent vinclis elementa solutis:
Non coelum terris lucem radiosque calentes,
Nec generandarum praeberet semina rerum:
Aëra finitimum consumeret improbus ignis:
Nec tempestivas pluvias demitteret aër:
Nuda foret tellus, aequorque extingueret ignem,
Aut igni potius piscosum aresceret aequor:
Ut quondam, quum flammivomos Clymeneia proles
Non bene rexit equos, metuens coelestia monstra,
Infelixque sui renuens praecepta parentis,
Corruit in voto, sensitque incendia mundus,
Donec fulmineo praeceps dejectus ab ictu
Eridani mediis flammas extinxit in undis.

From Love is born Peace, and Manzolli, with conscious rhetoric, proceeds to a contrast of peace and war parallel to his picture of the love and possible dissidence of the universe:

Gignit Amor pacem: pax est dignissima rerum:
Omnia pace vigent et pacis tempore florent
Paci summus honos, paci est quoque summa voluptas.
Tunc tuti vivunt homines, tutusque viator
Carpit iter, nec fit saevorum praeda latronum.
Tunc apium cura et pecoris, tunc arva coluntur
Assidue et largas pariunt pro tempore fruges.
Copia tunc Cereris, tunc lac, tunc Bacchus abundat
Palladiusque liquor; tunc passim luditur, et tunc
Inflata ad thyasos invitat tibia. Soli
Oderunt pacem stulti, et certamina quaerunt.
Talia fluxerunt Saturno tempora rege:
O felix aetas ipso pretiosior auro!
At nunc (proh dolor) insano discordia motu
Omnia conturbat. . . .
                              Nunc mille colubros,
Mille faces quatiunt, toto et bacchantur in orbe
Eumenides, populosque agitant regesque superbos.
Quid iuvat, O miseri, pugnando lacescere mortem?
Nunquam sera venit. Sed dira superbia tanti
Causa mali, et vesana fames atque ardor habendi.

[38]The quintessence; Manzolli is Aristotelian.

Heu cur usque adeo, vilissima terra, superbis,
Cuius foeda brevi corrodent viscera vermes?
Quid tantum quaeris? te semper forsitan esse
Victurum credis? miser, ah miser, aspice quam sit
Incertus, velox, angustus terminus aevi.
Sufficiet brevis urna tibi parvumque sepulchrum.[39]

It has not been noticed before, I believe, that this passage of the *Zodiacus vitae* furnished Antoine de Baïf with practically the whole of his *Hymne de la Paix*. It is instructive to compare the methods of Ronsard and Baïf. Both tend to compose by commonplaces or *topoi*; but where Ronsard, perhaps recognizing the *topos* as such, fills it in with phrasing from a number of sources, a phrase from one place, a line from another, Baïf seizes upon one source and clings to it, paraphrasing often with a rather empty dilation. In the present instance, noting that Book 4 of his source is on Love and Friendship, he chooses to call the cosmic principle Friendship, and Peace 'la fille d'amitié.' He sensibly leaves aside Manzolli's ideas about God's love of species. I quote some portions of his poem for comparison with the original:

Je veux louer la Paix, c'est la Paix que je chante,
La fille d'amitié dessus tout excellente.
Amitié nourrit tout: tout vit par amitié,
Et rien ne peut mourir que par inimitié. . . .
Le *ciel*, la terre, l'air, et la mer et le feu,
Et tout le monde entier, d'un aimable neu
S'entretiennent conjoints. Cette belle machine
Sans la bonne amitié tomberoit en ruine,
Car s'ils n'estoyent liez de liaisons d'émant,
On verroit rebeller tout mutin element,
Et guerroyer l'une l'autre; et soudain toutes choses
Dans l'ancien chaos retomberoyent encloses.
Le ciel refuseroit aux terres son ardeur,
Et de ses chauds rayons la vitale tiedeur. . . .
                              La terre desertée
Ne raporteroit plus: par la mer debordée
Le chaleur s'enteindroit: ou la profonde mer
Tarie se lairroit par le feu consumer:
Comme il advint jadis, quand le fils de Clymene
L'insensé Phaethon ne peut tenir la réne

[39]"pax est dignissima' = Silius, 'pax optima rerum.' Also 'omnia pace vigent' = Prudentius. On pax, and the ravages of war, see also Palingenius, *Zodiacus* 10.263ff.; 9.964ff.

Aux chevaux soufle-feus. . . .
Et le feu qui l'ardoit dans le Pô fut eteint.
    O qu'on deût bien cherir la Paix toute divine,
La fille d'amitié sur toutes choses dine! . . .
                Lors sans peur de domage,
De meurdre et de danger le marchand fait voyage:
Alors le laboureur au labeur prend plaisir
Quand le champ non ingrat répond à son desir.
L'ennemy fourageur son bestial n'emmene,
Et pillant ne ravit le doux fruit de la péne:
Le vin est à qui fait des vignes la façon, . . .
Et Ceres et Bacchus et Pales et Pomone
Font que parmy les chams grande planté foisone. . . .
Quand Saturne fut Roy sous une saison telle
La Paix avoit son regne. . . .
    Mais humains inhumains, quelle fureur si forte
Vos esprits forcenez d'aveugle erreur transporte? . . .
Mais Erinnys comande: on obeit au vice. . . .
    Et quel plaisir prens-tu, race folle chetive,
De te hâter la mort, qui jamais n'est tardive? . . .
O de la bonne terre inutile fardeau,
(Qui dois en peu de jours geté sous le tumbeau
Aviander les vers) tu partroubles ta vie
De vaine inimitié de tant de maux suivie.
Que veux-tu conquester? Je croy tu te promés
En ce monde incertain une vie a jamés.

VIII

Peace and the
Animal Kingdom

It may be accepted as a law of inertia in the history of ideas—if it is not merely a truism—that motifs and examples tend to adhere to the arguments for which they were originally devised or for which they have at some time been notably employed. Thus among the numerous *topoi* in which the habits or alleged habits of the animals have been applied to the moral instruction of mankind, one in particular is specialized to the argument for peace. This is the assertion that animals do not attack animals of the same kind; dog does not eat dog, *canis caninam non est*, but man, to his shame, does not withhold his hand from man, *homo homini lupus*.

Such persuasive force as this observation may have, it owes to paradox. Our usual feeling is that the beasts, especially the wild beasts, represent unrestrained passion—*candida pax homines, trux decet ira feras*—and that rational man ought not stoop to fight like irrational animals. We are brought up short by the reflection that the beasts, who do not attack their kind, are apparently more rational than we. The unparadoxical admonition, not to sink to the condition of beasts, implied in the line just quoted from Ovid (*Ars Am.* 3.502), has a place in peace literature and gives the paradoxical observation its significance, but seems to be more often applied to individual conduct than to the public area of peace and war. Ovid's verse, in its context, refers to lovers' quarrels.[1] In a political context, the unfa-

---

[1] It turns up fairly often, however, in Renaissance peace literature, perhaps because it was extracted for the section 'de Bello' in Mirandula's popular florilegium *Flores Poetarum*. But Erasmus had earlier made it the text of his youthful *Oratio de pace et discordia*. It is paraphrased twice by Palingenius in reference to peace and war (*Zodiacus vitae*, 10.297, and 9.964).

vorable view of the beasts is already expressed by Hesiod, whose apologue of the Hawk and the Nightingale (*Erga* 202–12) is presented as a 'fable for princes,' while Hesiod expressly denies *dike* to the animals (276–79): It is a law of Zeus 'that fishes and beasts and winged birds should devour one another, since justice is not among them, but to men he gave justice.' And in this tradition, Plato's comparison of the tyrant to a wild beast (*Rep.* 565–66) became a fixture, especially in the large literature *de institutione principum* and *de tyranno.* Not to multiply examples,[2] we cite only Erasmus' *Institutio principis Christiani*, where after comparing the true king with the 'king' bee without a sting,[3] Erasmus turns to the tyrant:[4]

> If you want a comparison for the tyrant, take the lion, bear, wolf, or eagle, all of which live on their mangled prey, . . . unless perchance the tyrant exceeds the savageness even of these beasts. Huge snakes, panthers, lions, and all the beasts that are condemned on the charge of savageness do not rage one against the other, but beasts of like character are safe together. But the tyrant, who is a man, turns his bestial cruelty against his fellow men and fellow citizens.

Here, we must grant, the motif of the animals who do not attack their own kinds has crossed over to the argument *de tyranno* from its usual place in the argument *de pace.*[5]

The theme of the animals peaceful in their kinds has been thoroughly studied in the ancient peace literature, especially by Harald Fuchs.[6] Though rooted in proverbial wisdom, it is thought to have gained currency as a pacifist argument through the Cynic diatribe or sermon, a form of popular philosophy that can often be glimpsed in the background of Roman satire.[7] Thus in a set of iambics denouncing the horrors of civil war, Horace knows that this is one of the topics to use (*Epode* 7.11–12):

[2]Seneca, *De Clem.* 1.25.1. Aristotle, *Pol.* 1253ª35: man without political virtue 'the most unholy and savage of animals.' Molinet, *Temple de Mars* (above, p. 71).

[3]Traditional for the king; Dio, *Fourth Discourse on Kingship* (*Or.* 4.63); Seneca, *De Clem.* 1.19.3: also Pliny 11.17.52; Aristotle, *Hist. An.* 5.21, 553b, 9–10; both of these say that he has a sting but never uses it.

[4]Trans. Lester K. Born, *The Education of a Christian Prince* (New York, 1936), p. 166.

[5]Erasmus rather obviously follows Seneca, *De Clem.* 1.25.3–4: 'Quae alia vita esset, si leones ursique regnarent . . . ? Illa rationis expertia et a nobis *immanitatis crimine damnata* abstinent suis, et tuta est etiam inter feras similitudo; horum [tyrants] ne a necessariis quidem sibi rabies temperat.' On tyranny, Machiavelli, *Il Principe*, and La Boétie, *Contr' un* (*Œuvres complètes*, (Paris-Bordeaux 1892), 1–57). See also Ps.-Diogenes, *Epist.* 40.2.3255, 11–15.

[6]Fuchs, *Augustin*, Index, s.v. 'Tiere.'

[7]Ibid., pp. 107–8, with reference to G. A. Gerhard, *Phoenix von Kolophon* (Leipzig, 1909).

Neque hic lupis mos nec fuit leonibus,
Umquam nisi in dispar feris.

Here the theme appears as an isolated statement, but more often we find it in some such train of thought as we have just seen in Erasmus, or as part of a development recommending the example of the peaceful universe—the heavens, the elements, the animals—as in Dio of Prusa and Gregory Nazianzen.[8] It is in a wide context resembling this that it appears in Augustine's famous chapters on peace.[9] In an influential chapter of Pliny's *Natural History* (7, *Praef.*) to which we shall return, it is joined with the topic of the superior equipment of the animals: they are born already clothed and able to care for themselves; man is born naked, knowing only how to weep, having also woes of his own devising; the animals are good to their own kinds, lions do not fight lions, but most of man's evils come from his fellow men. In a similar context, but with distinct Stoic coloring, this topic furnishes the moral of the fifteenth *Satire* of Juvenal, and it is from this source perhaps that the Renaissance knew it best. Juvenal, describing a cannibal feast he witnessed in Upper Egypt, concludes with the reflections that the experience suggested to him. To some extent these reflections are close to Pliny. In giving us tears Nature declares that she gives us a tender heart, the best part of our sensibility; it is peculiar to man ('separat hoc nos / a grege mutorum'): 'We alone have a venerable character, and are capable of knowing divine matters and of practising and learning arts,[10] we breathe a sense that descends from heaven, which the groveling animals lack;[11] the Creator gave them life (*animas*), but to us he gave reason (*animum*) also, so that mutual affection might prompt us to seek help and give it, to gather scattered folk into a people, to leave our ancestral forests, to build houses. . . .' But now the beasts have more concord than we:

Sed iam serpentum maior concordia. Parcit
cognatis maculis similis fera. Quando leoni

[8]Above, p. 36. Gregory, however, in coming down to the animals, is more general and does not specify the peace of the kinds. This method of descending through the universe to demonstrate its 'peace' is evidently an adaptation of the Stoic method of demonstrating Providence (e.g., Cicero, *DND* 2.47–52).

[9]Above, p. 37; *De civ. Dei* 19.12: 'Ipsae enim saevissimae ferae . . . genus proprium quadam pace custodiunt, . . . cum sint pleraeque insociabiles et solivagae; non scilicet ut oves, cervi, columbae, sturni, apes, sed ut leones, vulpes, aquilae, noctuae.'

[10]Editors fail to note the paraphrase of the regular Stoic definition of *sapientia*; see Eugene F. Rice, Jr., *The Renaissance Idea of Wisdom* (Cambridge, Mass., 1959).

[11]'Cuius egent prona et terram spectantia.' Juvenal 15, 147.

fortior eripuit vitam leo? Quo nemore umquam
exspiravit aper maioris dentibus apri?
Indica tigris agit rabida cum tigride pacem
perpetuam; saevis inter se convenit ursis.
Ast homini ferrum letale incude nefanda
produxisse parum est, cum rastra et sarcula tantum
adsueti coquere, et marris ac vomere lassi
nescierint primi gladios extendere fabri. (15.159–68)

As a form of admonition the topic admits two points of emphasis, which may indeed be combined. Man ought to be peaceful because peace is a law of Nature—this is the implication when the animals are included, as by Dio, in a total view of the universe. Or man ought to be peaceful because, possessing Reason, he should be better—and not, as apparently he is, worse—than the irrational animals.

It is also, even when it appears in Horace and Juvenal, a topic of the rhetorical-philosophical tradition rather than of the poetical tradition about peace. In the Renaissance,[12] Rodrigo Sánchez (c. 1468) apparently touches upon it,[13] while Erasmus in his *Oratio de pace et discordia* (c. 1487) makes much of it, relying on Juvenal. Beginning with a verse of Ovid on the ferocity of animals, he sighs that human depravity has rendered men worse than beasts: 'Parcit lupo lupus, at saevis inter se convenit ursis,' and after this quotation from Juvenal, he paraphrases the cannibal scene to show what the human race has descended to. This animal topic suited Erasmus' declamatory style, and he gives remarkable expansion to it in his mature utterances on peace, *Dulce bellum inexpertis* and *Querela pacis*. In the *Bellum* (1515), Juvenal is no longer a chief source, but perhaps taking a hint from Pliny,[14] Erasmus improvises freely:[15]

Most of the brute beasts live at peace within their kinds,[16] and help one another. Not all wild animals indeed are fighters, but only the fiercest of them. And not even these make war as we do; dog does not eat

---

[12]I have not collected mediaeval examples of this topic. Fuchs, *Augustin*, p. 237, finds it in Rufinus (twelfth century) who, he suggests, may have had it from Gregory the Great, *Regulae Pastoralis* 3.23.

[13]Above, pp. 49–50. Butler, *Statecraft*, does not show that 'Platina' employs this argument, but Sánchez' insistence in replying to him on the fact that the animals do fight, kind against kind—'Una species aliam exagitat, leo lupum, lupus canem . . . insequitur'—suggests that he has previously introduced our topic.

[14]Below p. 246.

[15]LB 2.953–54.

[16]'In suo . . . genere . . . civiliter degunt'; Pliny, 'in suo genere probe degunt.'

dog, fierce lions do not fight each other . . .;[17] but to man no wild beast is more deadly than man.[18] When animals fight, they use their own weapons, not, as men do, arms invented beyond nature by devilish art.[19] Besides, they fight only when hunger enrages them, or when attacked, or in fear for their offspring.[20] But we—from what trifling causes we raise the tragedies of war! They fight singly, and briefly, and however bloody the fight, separate when one of them is wounded. Whoever heard of ten thousand beasts falling in battle? Some species are naturally hostile to other species, some are friendly to others; but man forever fights man. That which departs from its own nature, degenerates to the worse. Would you know how brutish and inhuman war is? Have you ever seen a lion pitted against a bear? What gaping of jaws! what roaring! The spectator trembles. But how much more abominable is the sight of men, with so many weapons, fighting men. No trace of humanity remains.

In the *Querela pacis* (1517) Erasmus varies his procedure by including the beasts, more than once, in a development on the peaceful universe similar to that of Dio or Gregory Nazianzen.[21] Peace is complaining of her treatment by mankind:[22]

If *wild beasts* thus spurned me, I should bear it more easily, . . . if I were hateful to mute cattle, I could forgive their ignorance; . . . but for shame! though there is but one animal endowed with reason and capable of divine thought,[23] but one born for kindness and concord, I could find a place sooner among the most savage beasts . . . than among men. The *celestial spheres*, various as their motions are, have kept concord for all time . . . the *elements*, though mutually repugnant, keep peace among themselves. . . . In *living bodies*, what agreement of members! what mutual defense![24] As *life* is a union of body and soul, so *health* is an agreement of humors. *Irrational animals* live at peace within

[17]'leonum inter se feritas non dimicat'; Pliny, 'leonum feritas inter se non dimicat.' 'inter venena convenit'; Juvenal, 'inter se convenit ursis' (Pliny, 'serpentum morsus non petit serpentis').

[18]'At homini nulla fera perniciosior quam homo'; Pliny, 'At Hercule homini plurima ex homine sunt mala.'

[19]'suis pugnant armis'; see below, p. 250. Compare Plutarch, *Moralia, Gryllus*, Harold Cherniss, trans. (1957) (Loeb) 12.987C–D.

[20]See Marullus below, p. 227, and n. 38; Erasmus, *Querela* 626C–627A; *Bellum* 954; Béreau, *Complainte de France*, above p. 138.

[21]LB 4.626–42. Apart from the similar method, there seems to be no connection here between Erasmus and Dio or Gregory.

[22][The first passage of the *Querela* given here is in James Hutton's translation. For the second passage he used the spirited but free translation (so far as juxtaposed material is concerned), London, 1795, attributed to V. Knox.]

[23]'divinae mentis capax'; Juvenal 15.144, 'divinorumque capaces.'

[24]'quam parata defensio mutua'; see Clichtove below; also *Bellum* 960B.

their kinds[25]—elephants in herds, sheep and swine in flocks. . . . There is friendship among *trees* and *plants*. . . . You may say that *stones* have a sense of peace: the magnet draws iron. . . . There is peace even among the most *ferocious beasts*: lions do not attack lions,[26] boars, . . . lynxes, . . . dragons, . . . wolves (spare their congeners). I add a thing still more wonderful: the *evil spirits* that broke and still break the peace between God and man, keep peace among themselves and maintain their tyranny by mutual consent.[27] But man. . . .

A few pages later, Erasmus again returns to the example of the animals:

Nature has armed lions with tooth and claw, and bulls with horns; but who ever saw them go in bodies to use their arms for mutual destruction? Who ever saw even ten lions arrayed against ten bulls in battle formation? But how often have twenty thousand Christians met an equal number in the field? . . . Beasts of the forest! your contests are at least excusable, and sometimes amiable; you fight only when driven to madness by hunger or to defend your young.

A few months after the publication of the *Querela* Erasmus' English friend Richard Pace published, in Latin and French, an *Oratio in pace nuperrime composita* (Paris: Gourmont, 1518, also London), which with other echoes of the *Querela* paraphrases this passage on the animals.[28] Under the same influence, Josse Clichtove in his *Opusculum de bello et pace* (1523) devotes a chapter to universal peace: beginning with Empedocles' Love and Strife, he proceeds through celestial bodies, the four elements, their mixture in natural bodies (*fossilium, stirpium, animantiumque*), the proper mixture constituting health; the

---

[25]'in suo quaeque genere civiliter . . . degunt'; Note 16 on the *Bellum*, above.

[26]'leonum inter ipsos feritas non dimicat'; Note 17 on *Bellum*, above.

[27]'impii spiritus,' etc. I do not know the background of this idea. It is not the same as the 'peace,' i.e., organic being, of Satan in Augustine (*De civ. Dei* 19.13) or the 'pax diaboli' of Rufinus (above, p. 40). It is repeated by Gentili (below, n. 32) and by Milton (*PL* 2.496–97):

> O shame to men! Devil with Devil damn'd
> Firm concord holds, men onely disagree
> Of Creatures rational.

(Milton continues here to denounce the making of 'cruel warres.')

[28]*Oratio*, sig. [Aiv] R°: 'Quod si ne tigrides quidem huiusmodi in se pernitiem meditentur, nonne decet ut homines ratione praediti quavis virtute feras superent beluas? Quis unquam leonem cum leone dimicantem vidit? Quis serpentem serpenti infestum esse audivit? Num saevit draco in draconem? Luporum concordia locum praebuit adagio?' Cf. *Querela*: 'Draco non saevit in draconem; luporum concordiam etiam proverbia nobilitarunt.'

coordination of the body (the hand leaps to protect the head),[29] the animals, quoting Pliny. He ends by quoting Juvenal 15.159–68 and Tibullus 1.10.1–4, 33–34. Guillaume Postel, *De orbis terrae concordia* (Basel, 1544), also echoing Juvenal and Pliny, finds that mankind, one seed from Adam, and alone of animals possessing reason and thought — 'qua una praestat beluis, Deo iungitur' — has degenerated so that 'homo homini lupus': though the other animals live at peace in their kinds, man alone has most of his woes from man. But there is hope, since the concord of the animals is forced on them by Nature, whereas man by use of Reason may further the conscious growth of justice.[30]

In short, the topic permeates peace literature, and because of its paradoxical interest is extended to almost any consideration of the animals.[31] We note its continued appearance at the end of the century in the well-known *De Jure belli* (1598) of Alberico Gentili:[32] 'There is no natural hostility of man to man. Neither is there antipathy among animals of the same species. Therefore there should be none between men. Dog does not eat dog; the devil does not trouble devils; only swan does eat swan, bees sometimes have battles, and a few other animals of the same species are at variance with each other.' These exceptions do not necessarily imply that Gentili is losing faith in the argument,[33] though no doubt it plays a diminishing role as we pass from the rhetorical writers of the Renaissance to the more philosophical writers on peace in later times. Yet even Grotius retains a trace of the topic, *De jure belli et pacis, Proleg.* 6: 'Some of the other animals to some degree moderate the pursuit of their own advantage partly in consideration of their offspring, and partly in consideration of their congeners.'[34] And in our day, in the wake of Darwinism, the argument has again shown signs of life. After the

[29]*Opusculum* f. 5[v].

[30]Pp. 66, 271.

[31]The point is not omitted in Montaigne's extended consideration of man and animal (*Essais, édition Municipale*, ed. F. Strowski [Paris, 1906], 2.12.187; this edition cited hereafter): Man has perhaps little reason to pride himself on the art of war 'comme de vray la science de nous entre-desfaire et entretuer, de ruiner et perdre nostre propre espece, il semble qu'elle n'a pas beaucoup dequoy se faire desirer aux bestes qui ne l'ont pas [he quotes Juvenal 15.160–62]. 'Mais elles n'en sont pas universellement exemptes pourtant, tesmoin les furieuses rencontres des mouches à miel' [he quotes Virgil, *Georg.* 4.67–70].

[32]*De Jure belli*, T. E. Holland, ed. (Oxford, 1877), p. 52.

[33]That swan eats swan is an old exception (Aristotle, *Hist. Animalium* 610[a]1; Pliny, *HN* 10.32). J. C. Scaliger, *Exotericae Observationes* 240 (Frankfurt, 1592), p. 737, collects a few other instances but defends the dog against Cardan, *De subtilitate* (Nuremberg, 1550), p. 228: 'Humanis carnibus maxime efferantur, & sensum supra naturam acuunt.'

[34]When Hobbes (*Leviathan* 1.13) pictures natural man as 'homo homini lupus,' Rousseau dissents in terms of the same topic: 'Quel étrange animal que celuy qui

First World War, for example, it was developed in the *Biologie des Krieges* (Zurich, 1919) of Georg Friedrich Nicolai;[35] and after the second, the biologist W. C. Allee expressed himself as follows:[36] 'One species of animal may destroy another and individuals may kill other individuals, but *group* struggles to the death between members of the same species, such as occur in human warfare, can hardly be found among nonhuman animals.'

We have limited our examples to the literature of peace because that is the natural habitat of this theme in the ancient tradition, and because if any animal comparison occurs to a modern writer on peace, it is likely to be this one. But solely, I believe, through the influence of Pliny, who employs it so notably in the wider context of the 'woes of mankind,' it commonly appears in this wider context also in Renaissance literature. In turning to some poetical expressions of the *topos*, we easily see the two lines of descent—in poems on the woes of mankind, it derives from Pliny, in poems on peace, it derives from Juvenal. The animals are good to their own species, says Pliny, 'but man, by Hercules, has most of his woes from man.' So Marullus, in an ode addressed to Janus Lascaris precisely on man's inhumanity to man, gives it this turn:[37]

> Vel pictas referas licet
> > Tigres vel Libycae immane iecur leae,
> Inter se probe obambulant:
> > Nec praedae, nisi dum pulsa ábeat fames
> Naturale malum, incubant:
> > In diversa furor scilicet omnibus.
> Soli mutua vulnera
> > Exercemus, atrox soli odium in genus.[38]

---

croiroit son bien attaché à la destruction de toute son espece' (*Etat de Guerre, Œuvres complètes* Paris, 1967, 3.611). But in the tradition, this is no answer, only a statement of fact.

[35] 1.30f. I borrow this example from Fuchs, *Augustin*, p. 237 n.

[36] *Cooperation among Animals* (New York, 1951), p. 200.

[37] *Epigrammata*, lib. IV (*Poetae tres elegantissimi* [Paris, 1582], f. 45ᵛ). There are traces here also of Horace, *Epode* 16, and of Plutarch. Other writers on peace (e.g., Clichtove) also quote Pliny.

[38] 'Nec praedae,' etc.: see under Erasmus, *Bellum*, above, p. 224. 'In diversa furor' = Horace, *Epode* 16, as above. That the beasts do not fight unless pressed by hunger appears in Jacques Béreau's *Complainte de France*, which perhaps echoes Erasmus' *Querela*:

> Les brutes qui n'ont point de raison sentiment
> L'un à l'autre ne font guerre communement,
> Si ce n'est quand la faim violente les presse,
> Qui encor ne les fait se prendre à leur expresse;
> Et vous que de raison et conseil vous vantez,
> Vous qui d'humanité le nom mesme portez,

In the same argument, it figures in the *Riso di Democrito* of Antonio Fregoso Fileremo:[39]

> La faccia di vergogna io porto tinta
>> Quando al viver mortal penso, e cognosco
>> Nostra natura de le fere vinta.
> Con più concordia stanno lor nel bosco
>> Senza lege e statuti, che i mortali
>> Nelle citate—ah viver pien di tosco! . . .
> Raro una fera è quasi mai nociva
>> A la sua specie, ahyme che fra gli humani
>> L'un frate l'altro de la vita priva.[40]

In the peace poetry, Arnold de Pujol (above, p. 126), for example, virtually transcribes Juvenal:

> O genus infelix hominum, feritate ferarum
> Naturam superans! Inter se nulla Leones
> Bella gerunt, saevis inter se convenit Ursis
> Perpetuumque ferit Tigris cum Tigride foedus,
> Nec violatur Aper maioris dentibus Apri.
> Non Aquilae, non praelia Cervi
> Inter se miscent, agitat discordia nulla
> Serpentes, sed enim caudis per mutua nexis
> Inter se placide coeunt unaque cohaerent.
> Ast hominum crudele genus discordibus armis
> In se bella gerit, nec non et foedere rupto
> In sua cognatas convertit viscera dextras.

Virginio Cesarini (above, p. 78) also echoes Juvenal:

> Par plaisir exercez l'un sur l'autre voz rages,
> Plus prodigues de sang que les bestes sauvages.

[39]*Opera nova* (Venice: Sessa, 1534), Ch. 9 of pt. 2, 'Il Pianto di Heraclito.' The *Riso di Democrito* was first published at Milan in 1506; French trans. Michel d'Amboise (Paris, 1547).

[40]Ariosto, *Orlando* 5.1, curiously turns the topic to the safety of the female from the male of the same species (as a lesson for husbands and wives):

> L'orsa con l'orso al bosco sicura erra, . . .

Machiavelli, *L'Asino d'oro* 8, 143, makes the point, presumably after Pliny:

> Non da l'un porco a l'altro porco doglia,
> L'un cervo a l'altro: solamente l'homo
> L'altr' uomo ammazza, crocifigge e spoglia.

Plutarch, *Gryllus*, 985. C. B. Gelli, *Circe* (1569), Roberto Tissoni, ed. (Bari, 1967).

Cognatis parcit maculis jejuna leonum
　　Ira, nec agnata gaudet hyaena dape. . . .
Proh pudor! humana est rabies asperrima ferri:
　　Humana indomitis saevior ira feris.

Pierre Habert (above, pp. 143ff.) employs the theme to enforce the lesson of national unity. His treatment seems to be a combination of themes from Erasmus' *Bellum*—the sequence: coordination of the body, amiability of the beasts—with passages from the *Querela*, and he has borrowed phrases from both.[41] To be sure, 'hand protects head' is only in Clichtove, but might occur to anyone as interpretation of *Querela*:

> Au corps humain qui n'est en ses membres semblable
> On voit une harmonie excellente et louable.
> Avons nous oncques veu que la guerre se face
> Entre les pieds et mains, ou du corps et la face?
> Mesmement si l'on vient a faire tort au chef,
> La main se met devant, pour garder le meschef.
> En quoy nous voions bien en cest endroit nature
> Faire grand deshonneur à mainte creature.
> Les bestes que l'on voit privées de raison
> Vivent ensemblement en chacune saison
> En paix et amour, mesme la plus cruelle
> De faire à son semblable aucun mal n'est nouvelle.
> Le Lion va chercher le Lion, ou Lionne,
> L'Elephant, l'Elephant, le Cigon, la Cigogne.
> Et generallement tout autre dissemblable
> Ont naturellement un accord amiable.
> Ie vous prie donc tous iuger quel deshonneur
> Reçoit cy le Chrestien, qui n'a point cest honneur
> D'aimer incessamment le prochain en la sorte
> Comme il voit que son Dieu sans cesser l'en exhorte.

Sometimes it seems enough only to allude to the proverbial topic.[42] So Ronsard, *Remonstrance au peuple de France* 485–88:

---

[41]Erasmus, *Bellum*, 960 B, on the unity of the Church: 'Quis vidit oculum pugnare cum manu, aut ventrem cum pede? In hoc universo rerum omnium tam dissimilium harmonia est.'

[42]Laevinus Torrentius laments that military ambition is ready to shed innocent blood, 'Et mutuae quam bruta servent / Solvere amicitiae tenorem.' Philibert Bugnyon, *De la Paix*, sig. A3[3]: 'Ne faictes guerre contre vous, / François, Chrestiens, parens, amis, / "Les loups ne font la guerre aux loups," / Vous vous tuez comme ennemis.'

> Telle fureur n'est point aux Tygres ny aux Ours,
> Qui s'entraiment l'un l'autre, et se donnent secours,
> Et pour guarder leur race en armes se remuent:
> Les François seullement se pillent et se tuent.

And doubtless examples could be multiplied down to the classical expressions of Boileau, who also paraphrases Juvenal:[43]

> Voit-on les loups brigands, comme nous inhumains,
> Pour détrousser les loups courir les grands chemins?
> Jamais, pour agrandir, voit-on dans sa manie
> Un tigre en factions partager l'Hyrcanie? . . .
> L'homme seul, l'homme seul, en sa fureur extrême
> Met un brutal honneur à s'égorger soi-même.

Meanwhile it is admitted that these kindly animals fight, often savagely enough, outside their kind.[44] But maybe there was a time, in the Golden Age or in the Garden of Eden, when they were all at peace. Perhaps that time may return. Jean Passerat, in his *Hymne de la Paix*, sees them at peace in the beginning when Peace created the world:

> Le sacre [falcon] alors paisible, et la colombe blanche,
> Se perchoient bien souvent sur une mesme branche. . . .
> La Brebis et la Poulle en ce temps n'avoient peur
> Ni du Loup ravisseur, ni du Renard trompeur.
> Les plus fiers animaux, et les plus doulces bestes,
> Dormoient flancs contre flancs, et testes dessus testes.

The same notion occurs in Spenser's *Faerie Queene* (4.8.30–31):

> But the antique age, yet in the infancie
> Of time, did live then like an innocent. . . .
> The lyon there did with the lambe consort,
> And eke the dove sate by the faulcons side,
> Ne each of other feared fraud or tort,
> But did in safe securitie abide.

---

[43]Boileau, *Satire* 8.

[44]Aristotle enumerates the antipathies of the various animals and attempts to account for them, chiefly from their habits of feeding (*Hist. An.* 9.608^{b}19–610^a. He mentions some that attack their own kind, seals for example, when food is short, and others—birds, reptiles, carnivorous animals—that prey upon certain species. See below.

No doubt it is Milton who gives this view the most emphatic expression in describing the animals around Adam and Eve before the Fall (PL 4.340–52):

> About them frisking playd
> All Beasts of th'Earth, since wilde, and of all chase
> In Wood or Wilderness, Forrest or Den;
> Sporting the Lion rampd, and in his paw
> Dandl'd the Kid; Bears, Tigers, Ounces, Pards
> Gamboll'd before them.
>   Close by the Serpent sly
> Insinuating, wove with Gordian twine
> His braided train, and of his fatal guile
> Gave proof unheeded; others on the grass
> Coucht, and now fild with pasture gazing sat.

In consequence of the Fall, among other disturbances of the universal peace, Milton duly notes (*PL* 10.707–14):

> Discord first
> Daughter of Sin, among th' irrational
> Death introduc'd through fierce antipathie;
> Beast now with Beast gan war, and Fowle with Fowle,
> And Fish with Fish; to graze the Herb all leaving,
> Devourd each other; nor stood much in awe
> Of Man, but fled him, or with count'nance grim
> Glar'd at him passing.

The warfare that continues among the animal kinds in our age of the world was interrupted, according to Ovid, by the music of Arion (*Fasti* 2.85ff.), according to Claudian, by the music of Orpheus (*De raptu Proserpinae* 2, Praef. 25–28):

> Securum blandi leporem fovere Molossi
>   vicinumque lupo praebuit agna latus
> Concordes varia ludunt cum tigride dammae;
>   Massylam cervi non timuere iubam.

It was suspended, by special dispensation, in Noah's Ark. It will be discontinued when peace is restored by the Messiah, according to the prophecy of Isaiah 11.6: 'The wolf also shall dwell with the lamb, and the leopard shall lie down with the kid; and the calf and the young lion and the fatling together.' Virgil perhaps foresees the like upon the return of the Golden Age (*Ecl.* 4.23): 'Nec magnos metuent armenta leones.' Some have imagined that Christ in the wilderness (he 'was with the wild beasts,' Mark 1.13) was another Orpheus. So Giles Fletcher,[45]

> Downe felle the Lordly Lions angrie mood,
> And he himselfe felle down, in congies lowe; . . .
> Unmindful of himselfe, to minde his Lord,
> The lamb stood gazing by the Tyger's side,
> As though between them they had made accord.

But Milton (*Paradise Regained* 1.310–13) is more cautious:

> They at his sight grew mild,
> Nor sleeping him nor waking harm'd, his walk
> The fiery serpent fled, and noxious Worm,
> The Lion and fierce Tiger glar'd aloof.

Rather unexpectedly, at the end of the twelfth century, Pietro d'Eboli declares that these blessed times have already been restored under his peace hero, the Emperor Henry VI:[46]

> Evomuit serpens virus sub fauce repostum,
> Aruit in vires mesta cicuta suas.
> Nec sonipes griphes nec oves assueta luporum
> Ora timent: ut ovis stat lupus inter oves.
> Uno fonte bibunt, eadem pascuntur et arva
> Bos, leo, grus, aquila, sus, canis, ursus, aper.[47]

The concept of the amity of the animal kinds at the beginning, here imagined by Passerat, Spenser, and Milton,[48] has no support in Hesiod's account of the Golden Generation, nor (except by infer-

---

[45]"Christ's Victory on Earth," *Christ's Victory and Triumph* (1610), 11.25–26, 33–35.
[46]*De rebus Siculis* 48, ed. Rota, p. 198.
[47]On p. 196 of Rota's volume is an illustration of the ideal peace of the Golden Age, from a MS. of Pietro: it duly pictures these creatures drinking from one fountain, with the legend 'tanta pax est tempore Augusti quod in uno fonte bibunt omnia animalia.' (Augustus refers to Henry VI.)
[48]Perhaps also by Hildebert, *De ornatu mundi* (Migne, *PL* 171.1236B), where the beasts are described as happily disporting themselves, and

> Non onus hic, non hic laqueos, non ille ruinam,
> Non hic insidias, non timet ille canem.

But despite the last phrase, what is meant is the safety of the beasts from man.

ence) in the biblical Genesis. Neither is it very prominent in the classical tradition of the Golden Age that stems from Hesiod. In the perfect existence sketched by Horace (*Epode* 16.51–52), bears do not growl round the sheepfolds, nor does the earth heave with vipers—presumably meaning that there will be no vipers, perhaps no bears. The parallel in Virgil's returning Golden Age (*Ecl.* 4.22–24) relates that 'the serpent will die,' and 'cattle will not fear lions.' It is possible to suppose that there will be no noxious animals in the Golden Age to come. Amity of the animals in the bygone Golden Age is less ambiguously implied in Virgil's account of the passage from the Saturnian Age to the Age of Jupiter (*Georg.* 1.129–30), when Jupiter 'added evil poison to the deadly serpents and bade the wolves to seek their prey,' and man entered into the hunting and fishing stage (139–42). This last trait reveals that the Hesiodic tradition is here modified by later speculation. That *man* lived at peace with the animals in the Golden Age might be inferred from his diet of acorns and honeydew; but that is another question. Empedocles declares that in that time, when Ares was no god and Cypris was queen, animals were not sacrificed, and to eat them was the worst of sins; birds and beasts were tame and friendly to man.[49] Perhaps he implies that they were also friendly to one another; but in the vegetarian tradition, of which he is our earliest witness, concern about man's 'justice' or 'injustice' to the animals does not necessarily involve ascribing *dike* to them. The only explicit statement of the amity of the animals in the Cronian Age seems to be that of Plato's *Statesman*. Here (271E) we learn that at that time the animals being 'distributed by species and flocks among inferior deities as divine shepherds, . . . no creature was wild, nor did they eat one another, and there was no war among them, nor any strife whatsoever.'[50] Human beings were able to talk with the animals and learn from them, they gossiped with them and told them stories (272C).[51] But in the Age of Zeus, men had trouble from the animals, 'since most of the beasts who were by nature unfriendly had grown fierce, and they themselves were feeble and unprotected' (274B).[52] Yet though the testi-

[49]Fragms. 128 and 130. See Ettore Bignone, *Empedocle* (Rome, 1963); John Burnet, *Early Greek Philosophy* (London, 1892), 1, 'Empedokles of Akragas.'

[50]Trans. H. N. Fowler (Loeb).

[51]This notion recurs, for the Golden Age, in Babrius, *Fabulae Aesopi*, *Proleg.* 1–13. For this and many other references I am indebted to the indispensable work of Lovejoy-Boas. For the animals in the Garden of Eden being endowed with speech, see below p. 240 and n. 74.

[52]As for the domestic animals, the tradition of the Golden Age that stems from Hesiod assumes that man already possessed them—Hesiod, *Erga* 120 (sheep); Aratus, *Phaen.* 100 (oxen); Tibullus 1.10.10 (sheep); Horace, *Epode* 16.49–51 (goats, sheep);

mony is slight, the impression has prevailed that the Golden Age implies the amity of the animals. It is mostly due, perhaps, to a trustful reading of the fourth *Eclogue* of Virgil.

Nothing is said in the Book of Genesis about the relation of the newly created animals to one another, but inferences have been drawn from the two statements that man was given dominion over them (1.26) and that the beasts (as well as men) lived on an herbaceous diet (1.30). If they fed on 'every green herb,' it may be assumed (though not with complete certainty) that they did not feed on each other.[53] Man's dominion is the chief interest of the older commentators, perhaps in part because it was already a topic of the Stoic discussions of Providence. The Stoics had had to explain why, if the world is created for man, the noxious animals exist.[54] The Christian commentator had further to explain how man, having had dominion over all the animals at the beginning, lost control of those that are now harmful. Most commentators are content to say simply that this was the result of Adam's sin.[55] But how? Some took the easy way out and said that the noxious animals were created only after the Fall as a punishment for man, as apparently (Gen. 3.18) were the noxious plants.[56] Yet it would hardly do to say that all the animals were created benign and only some of them rendered savage

Virgil, *Ecl.* 4.21, 22, 43 (goats, cattle, sheep); but as the notion of the Golden Age is crossed by the concept of a primitive age succeeded by a hunting or pastoral stage—a concept popularized by the influential *Bios Hellados* of Dicaearchus—it is denied that animals were domesticated in the first period—Tibullus 1.3.35; Ovid, *Met.* 1.124 and cf. *Fasti* 2.295–98 (Arcadians); Seneca, *Phaedra* 507–8; Ps.-Seneca, *Octavia* 420–27. Indeed Varro, in a passage in which he cites Dicaearchus, says that probably the animal first domesticated in the pastoral period was the sheep (*De Rerum Rusticarum* 2.1.3).

[53]The friendliness of the animals to man and to one another is found in the Babylonian epic; see W. F. Albright in Lovejoy-Boas, p. 424.

[54]Cicero, *DND* 2.64, 161; to provide food, and for exercise in hunting; Philo, *De Providentia* 2.56–65 (without biblical color): exercise for war and health; to inspire caution (?); venomous animals supply medicines (but venomous snakes not produced by Providence but as a 'concomitant'—e.g., some arise from putrefaction; cf. Augustine, *Gen. ad lit.* 3.14). The problem is set in Carneades' answer to Chrysippus, Porphyry *De Abstin.* 3.20.

[55]See the references in F. E. Robbins, *The Hexaemeral Literature* (Chicago, 1912), p. 5, n. 4. Hugh of St. Victor, for example, makes the interesting distinction that man lost dominion *in maximis*, e.g., lions, and *in minimis*, e.g., fleas and flies, but 'retinuit dominationem *in mediis* ad consolationem.' St. John Chrysostom (*Ad pop. Antioch. Hom.* 11.4. Migne, *PG* 49.124–25) observes that man never completely lost dominion; by his wit he can subjugate any of the animals. Yet modern biologists warn us that we do not have dominion *in minimis*; we are slaves (to use the patristic expression for this) to the insects and noxious bacteria, and it is doubtful if man has the resources to cope with them; cf. Allee, *Cooperation*, p. 200.

[56]This view is noticed but rejected by Augustine, *De Gen. contra Manich.* 1.18. Nevertheless it seems to be the opinion of Albertus Magnus, *Summa de creaturis* 4.72.8.

by the Fall. The common view was that all had their present charac-
teristics (*idiomata*) from the beginning; only man was altered; when
he lost his dominion, the naturally fierce animals became his ene-
mies, for his punishment.[57] From this point, one could rejoin the
Stoics, with an additional reason why the dangerous animals are
providentially useful.[58] They seem to assume that the animals were
mutually hostile. Augustine says without qualification that they were
created to provide food for one another.[59] Philo had already put
this clearly:[60] Man was created last; the animals, astonished at his
sudden appearance, did obeisance to him and were tamed, even the
most savage becoming submissive, 'displaying their untamed pug-
nacity one against another, but to man and man alone showing gen-
tleness and docility.' This, however, fails to take account of Genesis
1.30 on their herbaceous diet. Inferences from this verse are per-
haps most fully drawn by Gregory of Nyssa in his sermon on the
words 'Let us make man in our own image,' in which he deals with
God's explicit permission to Noah after the Flood to make use of a
diet of flesh (Gen. 9.2–6).[61] In the Garden of Eden both man and
beast (Gen. 1.29–30) were herbivorous, 'until man departed from
the command.' Man did not prey on the animals, nor the animals on
one another. 'Vultures when the animals were created did not
search the earth for cadavers, since there were no dead.' After the
Flood, Gregory thinks the same concession was made to the animals
as to man. Though few went so far as Gregory in postponing a flesh
diet until after the Flood, his influence may have helped to fix atten-
tion on Gen. 1.30 with the inference that the herbivorous animals

[57]Augustine, *De Gen. contra Manich.* 1.18; *De Gen. ad lit.* 3.15; repeated, e.g., by
Bede, *Comm. in Pent.* (Migne, *PL* 91.260A). Thomas Aquinas adopts Augustine's view,
ST 1, Q. 72: 'Homo autem ante peccatum ordinate fuisset usus rebus mundi; unde an-
imalia venenosa ei noxia non fuissent.' For the constancy of the animals' characters,
see St. Basil, *Hom. IX in Hex.* (Migne *PG* 29.182C and 192C): No extent of time makes
obsolete the *idiomata* of the animals, the natures given them at creation are constantly
renewed.
[58]With Philo, above n. 54, compare St. John Chrysostom, *Ad pop. Antioch. Hom.* 11
(Migne, *PG* 49.125C): exercise in hunting; to school us by fear, and make us cautious;
to supply useful medicines; Nemesius, *De Nat. Hom.* (Migne, *PG* 40.532A, to supply
medicine; Augustine, *De Gen. contra Manich.* 1.16: God doubtless has a use for them,
though we may not know it; Augustine himself does not know why mice and frogs
were created; but through the noxious animals we are punished, get exercise in hunt-
ing, or suffer terror so that we may lay less store on this life and look to a better one
where security is complete. Honorius Augustodunensis, *Hexaemeron* 3 (Migne, *PL*
172.258D): to punish man, and to supply useful medicines.
[59]*De Gen. ad lit.* 3.16.
[60]*De Opificio mundi* 28, 83; trans. G. H. Whitaker (Loeb).
[61]*In Script. verb. Faciamus hominem*, Orat. 2 (Migne, *PG* 44.284) = Ps.-Basil, *De
Hominis structura*, Orat. 2 (Migne, *P.G.* 30.44–45).

lived in peace.[62] So Hrabanus Maurus: 'Before the Fall, birds did not live on the plunder of weaker birds, nor did the wolf seek to ambush the sheepfolds, nor the serpent have dust for bread, but all in peace fed on the green herb and the fruits of the trees.'[63] Honorius Augustodunensis and others repeat that view.[64] For those who held that only one specimen (or pair) of each kind was created, it would be natural to think that they were at peace, since otherwise they would have been created in vain; but this notion seems not to be widely entertained by Christian commentators.[65]

Though the amity of the animals at the beginning could thus be

[62]Gregory's sermon was known certainly to Hugh of St. Victor through Bede *Hex.* 1 (Migne, *PL* 91.31–32). [See Robbins, *Hexaemeral Literature*, pp. 56ff. for more information on Gregory of Nyssa and other hexaemeral writers who followed Basil.] It or the ps.-Basil was the immediate source of Tasso, *Il Mondo creato*, sest. giorn. 1824ff., as the commentators note (see G. Petrocchi, ed. [Florence, 1951], p. 269):

> Ne tinto ancor si avea l'artiglio e i denti
> L'affamato leone, o il lupo, o l'orso:
> Ne l'avoltoio allor da corpo estinto
> Cercava il cibo, perche morto ancora
> Non era alcuno, . . .

[63]*Comm. in Gen.* 1.8 (Migne, *PL* 107.462). The phrase 'nec lupus insidias explorabat ovilia circum' from Virgil, *Georg.* 3.537, probably shows that Hrabanus associates the classical Golden Age with this idea. (In Virgil it is an effect of the plague!)

[64]*Hexaemeron* 3 (Migne *PL* 172.258): Hildebert, n. 48 above. Claude-Louis Montagne, *Tractatus de opere sex dierum* (1732), though he regards it as a question *parvi momenti* whether the animals would have been mutually hostile if Adam had not sinned, nevertheless suggests that they were provided with an herbaceous diet to remove all cruelty from the happy state of Eden and that they rose against each other when Adam rebelled; but Montagne is more interested in refuting Descartes on the animal-machine (Migne, *Theologiae Cursus Completus* (Paris, 1837–45) 7.1328).

[65]Hrabanus Maurus, *Comm. in Gen.* (Migne, *PL* 107) 461: 'in singulis generibus non singula sed plura creavit,' in contrast to man. The question was also raised with regard to the 'coats of skins' with which in Gen. 3.21 God clothes the embarrassed Adam and Eve. Some solved it, according to the Syrian Moses bar Kepha, *De Paradiso* 1 (Migne, *PG* 111. 572–74), by declaring that God created these skins *ex nihilo* for the occasion; others, including Bar Kepha himself, concluded that the animals had already increased and multiplied. Theodoret's opinion is that the question where God got these skins is impertinent (Migne, *PG* 80.139). Calvin (*Comm. in Gen.* 2.21) objects to making God a tailor ('quasi fuerit Deus pellifex aut minister ad vestes consuendas') and thinks He only inspired Adam and Eve themselves to kill some animals, as they might do since they had dominion over them. Milton faces the problem in *PL* 10.213–18, giving the act to the Son, and thus obviating (though perhaps acknowledging) Calvin's scruple, and suggesting what may be a novel origin for the skin coats—that all animals may in the beginning have cast their skins like snakes:

> He disdain'd not to begin
> Thenceforth the form of servant to assume,
> As when he wash'd his servants' feet, so now
> As Father of his Family he clad
> Thir nakedness with Skins of Beasts, or slain
> Or as the Snake with youthful Coat repaid.

[236]

inferred from Gen. 1.30, the notion would seem to gain life and color from Isaiah 11.6–8. But here, too, all was not smooth. Lactantius indeed appears to take Isaiah's words literally of the time to come, remarking on the error of the classical poets who placed the amity of the beasts in a past Saturnian Age, when Isaiah meant only the future.[66] But in fact, at least at the first coming of Christ, wolves had not dwelt with lambs; and in consequence of this scruple, the view that prevailed was that Isaiah was not to be taken literally here, but only allegorically. Jerome has a long and interesting comment: Jews and Judaizing Christians make the mistake of taking this passage literally of the last days; but such material felicity would be unworthy of the majesty of the Lord; only virtue is good—or will they restore for us the Saturnian Age of the poets' fables, when wolves and lambs will feed together, and streams flow with honey-wine, and sweetest honey drip from the leaves of trees, and everywhere will be fountains of milk?[67] No, the wolf is Paul, who harassed the Church but dwelt with a lamb when he was baptized by Ananias; or we may understand it of the Church, in which all manner of unlike persons, rich and poor, kings and commons, are united. Jerome's interpretation, itself dependent on Greek sources, seems to have dominated the later tradition.[68]

With Jerome's strictures in mind, we turn with some interest to a Jewish commentary on Isaiah. In that of David Kimchi (twelfth century), which is comprehensive, we read that it was a recognized interpretation of Isaiah 11.6 that in the days of the Messiah the natures of the beasts would revert to what they had been in the beginning of Creation and in Noah's Ark.[69] For since on those occasions there existed only one pair of each kind, it would have been ruinous if the lion had eaten the lamb. At the beginning they fed on the herbs of the field (Gen. 1.30) until the beasts to be eaten had multiplied. Thereafter they ate flesh. (The Fall apparently was not involved.) The view favored by Kimchi himself, however, is that the

---

[66]*Div. Inst.* 7.24.

[67]*Comm. in Isaiam,* 4.11 (Migne, *PG* 24.147).

[68]Cf. Haymon, *Comm. in Isa.* in Migne, *PL* 116. 780; Albertus Magnus, *Postilla super Isa.*; Dionysius Cartusianus (*Enarr. in Isa.* in *Opera* [Cologne, 1899], 8.422) says that the Jews relied on Isaiah's prophecy, taken literally, to prove that Jesus was not the Messiah. Wolfgang Musculus, *In Gen. Comm.* (Basel, 1600), p. 41, says that dominion over all the animals was restored to us by Christ, but that we have not yet realized this fact.

[69]Kimchi, *Comm. on Isaiah.* 11.6, in Louis Finkelstein, ed., *The Commentary of David Kimchi on Isaiah* (New York, 1926), 75–77. I am much indebted to my colleague Isaac Rabinowitz for translating Kimchi's comment for me and for many helpful suggestions.

beasts will not change their characters in the days of the Messiah. They will still devour each other, but because of the goodness of the people of that time, they will do no hurt in Israel, neither to the Israelites nor to their possessions. They will either cease from the land (Ezek. 34.25; also Lev. 26.6) or if they pass through the land they will do no hurt (Hos. 2.18). Besides the historical interpretation, Kimchi recognizes several allegorical meanings: that the noxious beasts represent wicked oppressors; and that the cow and the bear lying down together (Isa. 11.7) signify that the whole activity of the soul will be occupied with the service of God.

Whereas the Roman Catholic commentaries seem to follow St. Jerome, it is interesting to see how near Calvin's comment on this passage draws to Kimchi. Calvin indeed makes it clear that the moral and anagogical sense is basic: Christ forms the various natures of his followers according to his own heavenly spirit.

> And yet, says Calvin, the prophet's words have a wider reference. It is as though he were promising the blessed reparation of the world. For he describes the order as it was in the beginning, before through man's defection there befell that sad and unhappy alteration under which we groan. For whence came the truculence of the beasts, whereby the stronger are impelled in horrible onset to ravine, tear, and devour? As suredly there would be no strife among God's creatures if they had remained in their first and unimpaired origins. Therefore the fact that they rage one against another, and that the weak need protection from the strong, is a sign of the ἀταξία that springs from the sin (*vitio*) of man. Since, then, Christ came to abolish the curse and reconcile the world to God, it is not irrelevant to attribute to him the renewal of the perfect state, as though the prophets were saying that the golden age would come again, in which, before the fall of man and the shock and ruin that followed it, perfect felicity reigned. So in Hosea (2.18) God says: 'I will make a covenant with the beasts of the field,' . . . as much as to say that . . . all the corruptions sprung from the sin of man shall cease. . . . The chief point is that Christ will come to take away all offences from the world and to restore the earth . . . to its pristine splendor. Hence Isaiah says that 'the lion shall eat straw like the ox': because if the pollution of sin had not defiled the world, no animal would have been given over to sanguinary prey, but the fruits of the earth would suffice for all, as was divinely prescribed. But though Isaiah says that there will be agreement between wild beasts and tame, so that the blessing of God may be strong and shine forth, yet he chiefly means that in the people of Christ there will be no effect of injury, no ferocity or inhumanity.[70]

[70]*Opera*, Wilhelm Baum, Edouard Kunitz, and Edouard Reuss, eds. (Brunswick, 1893–1900), 35.241–42.

It is not surprising that a Protestant theologian should draw so close to the Hebrew comment. Milton's notion of the ἀταξία of the world has been referred, with reason, to the Calvinist poet Du Bartas, who also includes in it the enmity of the beasts.[71] But Milton, who was a Protestant theologian as well as a poet, knew the topic, which he includes in his *De Doctrina Christiana*, apart from Du Bartas.[72] He treats it much more fully: Du Bartas indeed omits to show the previous amity of the animals, which Milton makes so striking. Milton knew Kimchi and, of course, Calvin, and it is not difficult to suppose that he had read one or the other or both on so important a passage as Isaiah 11.6. In the poem, he bases himself on Gen. 1.30, insisting on the first herbaceous diet.[73] Though the animals are at peace, the description of 'the serpent sly' suggests that Milton thought of the noxious animals as already possessing their characters, but having no occasion to show them before the Fall; and this is borne out by *PL* 7.497–98: (the serpent) 'to thee / not noxious, but obedient to thy call.' The serpent might be an exception, but the identity of names (given by Adam) with natures seems to ensure that all the animals' *idiomata* existed from the first: 'And thou thir Natures know'st, and gav'st them names' (*PL* 7.493). In a trait that recalls Plato's *Statesman*, but that no doubt is a generalization of the serpent's talk with Eve, Adam is able to converse with the animals and learn from them (*PL* 8.372–74):

[71]G. C. Taylor, *Milton's Use of Du Bartas* (Cambridge, Mass., 1934), pp. 107–9; cf. p. 22. Du Bartas, *Sepmaine 2, Les Furies* 57–78:

> Depuis, le loup en veut à la brebis tremblante,
> Le seul vol du milan le poulet espouvente. . . .

Later (vv. 179ff.) Du Bartas describes our loss of dominion over the noxious animals, great and small:

> Le farouche taureau, le cheval courageux,
> Des dents, du front cornu, des pieds nous font la guerre,
> Marris de voir marcher tels tyrans sur la terre:
> Et n'y a mouscherons qui hardi contre nous
> Ne descoche les traicts de son petit courrous.

The anonymous *Himne de la Guerre et de la paix* of 1590 makes this point (above, p. 160).

[72]*De Doct. Chr.* 1.13. In the disorder created by Adam's sin, 'even the beasts are not exempt.' He cites Gen. 3.14; 6.7; and Exod. 11.5—i.e., the serpent 'cursed above all cattle, and above every beast of the field' (hence all cursed in some degree?); 'And the Lord said, I will destroy . . . both man and beast, and the creeping thing, and the fowls of the air, for it repenteth me that I have made them;' 'And all the firstborn of the land of Egypt shall die . . . and all the firstborn of the beasts.'

[73]In *PL* 5.350–51 and 10.711 quoted above, and in 7.404, where the fishes 'graze the Seaweed thir pasture.' Perhaps it is barely pertinent to quote Aristotle, *Hist. An.* 608[b]30: 'One may go so far as to say that if there were no lack or stint of food, then those animals that are afraid of man or are wild by nature would be tame and familiar with him, and in like manner with one another' (trans. D'Arcy W. Thompson in *Basic Works of Aristotle*, Richard McKeon, ed. [New York, 1941]).

> Know'st thou not
> Thir language and thir ways, they also know
> And reason not contemptibly.[74]

After the Fall, the Age of Cronos is over, and the 'law of Zeus' obtains, whereby 'fishes and beasts and winged fowl devour one another.'[75]

In the passage quoted above from *Paradise Regained*, Milton abides by the scruple that led to an allegorical interpretation of Isaiah 11.6; the animals retain their *idiomata*, but as in Kimchi, 'do no harm.' They are, however, affected by Christ's presence, much as the lions are by Daniel or the viper by St. Paul (Acts 28.3–6)—examples regularly adduced by commentators on the Hexaemeron such as Nemesius, Migne, *PG* 40.5326. Milton even insists that postlapsarian conditions still obtained; the serpent fled (cf. Gen. 3.15), and perhaps by an intentional echo the lion and the tiger 'glar'd aloof,' as after Adam's sin (*PL* 10.714) the beasts 'glar'd at his passing.' It is not yet time for the lion to dwell with the lamb.[76]

The other passages we have quoted require less comment. Passerat was, like Milton, a man of learning, but his *Hymne de la Paix* is a relatively casual performance in which reminiscences of Genesis, Plato's *Timaeus*, and Ovid are freely mingled.[77] He no doubt knew

[74]Compare the *Book of Jubilees, or the Little Genesis*, 3.28–29 (trans. Robert Henry Charles [London, 1902]), p. 27: 'And in that day of the Fall was closed the mouth of all beasts, and of cattle, and of birds, and of whatever walks and of whatever moves, so that they could no longer speak; for they had spoken one with another. . . . And He sent out of the Garden of Eden all flesh that was in the Garden of Eden, and it was scattered according to its kinds.' Milton does not record the closing of the mouths of the beasts; but he shows the eagle and the lion driving the more timid birds and beasts 'direct to th' Eastern Gate,' and presumably forth from the Garden (*PL* 11.181–90). [Milton's use of *Jubilees* as of *Apocalypsis Mosis* and *Vita Adae et Evae* has been examined by J. M. Evans, *Paradise Lost and the Genesis Tradition* (Oxford, 1968); Adam's naming of the animals, and so on is also discussed by Evans. The editor is indebted to Professor Mary Ann Radzinowicz for this reference, in reply to a query by Mr. Hutton.]

[75]Is it ascribing too much wit to Milton to think that he may here have thought of the Hesiodic passage, and with this implication, in *PL* 10.712 (above, n. 71) 'Fowle with Fowle, / And Fish with Fish . . . Devourd each other'?

[76]Little can be added to the fine treatment of this passage in contrast with Giles Fletcher in Elizabeth M. Pope's *Paradise Regained: The Tradition and the Poem* (Baltimore, 1947), pp. 108–10. In Jean Sève's *Supplication au roys* of 1562 (above, p. 136) God's promise to the French:

> J'osteray du pais et les loups ravissantz,
> Dragons, serpins, aspicz, et lyons rougissans. . . .

occurs in a development based on Ezek. 34.25–28, and remains a promise.

[77]With Passerat (above pp. 141, 230ff.), 'Le sacre . . . et la colombe blanche / Se perchoient . . . sur une mesme branche,' perhaps compare Ovid, *Fasti* 2.89–90:

> Et sine lite loquax cum Palladis alita cornix
> sedit, et accipitri iuncta columba fuit.

the tradition that the animals were at peace in the Garden of Eden, but as he goes on to identify the time of Creation with the Golden Age he forgets Genesis so far as to say:

> Les serpents tortillés, les Dragons empennés,
> Du sang Gorgonien n'estoient encores nés.

Though Spenser's phrase 'the lion and the lamb' probably echoes 'the wolf and the lamb' of Isaiah, his 'antique age' is more likely to be the Golden Age than the Garden of Eden. Indeed it is close to Ovid's *'vetus* illa *aetas*, cui fecimus *aurea* nomen' of *Met.* 15.98ff.:

> Tunc et aves tutae movere per aëra pennas,
> et lepus impavidus mediis erravit in arvis; . . .
> Cuncta sine insidiis *nullamque timentia fraudem*
> plenaque pacis erant. [ne each of other fearèd fraud—Spenser]

As for Pietro d'Eboli, we shall not be far wrong if we understand his lines allegorically in the sense in which the commentators took Isaiah 11.6: the dissidents of the empire who have been at strife have come together in Church and state. He concludes: 'Unus sol, unus pastor, et una fides.'[78]

According to one line of ancient thought, the origin of war lay in man's first rupture with the beasts and his 'injustice' towards them. When, either to defend himself against savage animals (as was his right), or for the purpose of killing them for food or skins (probably unjust), he invented deadly weapons, it was not long before he turned these weapons upon his fellow men. So Tibullus (1.10.1−5):

> Qui fuit horrendos primus qui protulit enses?
>   quam ferus et vere ferreus ille fuit!
> tum caedes hominum generi, tum proelia nata,
>   tum brevior dirae mortis aperta via est.
> an nihil ille miser meruit, nos ad mala nostra
>   vertimus, in saevas quod dedit ille feras?

Dicaearchus, in his *Life of Greece*, seems to have seen this transition from an economic point of view. In the primitive 'gathering' stage,

---

[78]Compare Jerome (Migne, *PG* 24.148B): 'Leo quoque prius ferocissimus, et ovis, et vitulus pariter morabuntur. Quod quotidie cernimus in Ecclesia, divites et pauperes, potentes et humiles, reges atque privatos pariter commorari.' Theodoret (Migne, *PG* 81.315): Isaiah's prophecy is fulfilled in the Church, where all conditions of men 'partake of the same communion table, hear the same sermons, use the same font.'

there was no private property to be a cause of contention, and there was no war, but in the pastoral stage men gained superfluous property, taming some animals and attacking others (for food and skins?); and 'together with the injustice done to the animals, there came in war and the ambition to get the better of one another.'[79] Our knowledge of Dicaearchus' views comes from Porphyry's book on vegetarianism, and it is in a vegetarian context that this topic appears elsewhere. In the speech of the vegetarian Pythagoras in Ovid (from which we have just quoted the description of primitive peace), it is admitted that noxious animals were justly slain, 'but that does not mean that they ought to be eaten'; and the ill-advised innovation of a flesh diet inevitably led to the murder of the kindly domestic animals and the wish to involve the gods in our crime when it was imagined that they delight in bloody sacrifice.[80] Ovid alludes only by implication to the origin of war (106–7):

> primaque e caede ferarum
> incaluisse putes maculatum sanguine ferrum.

But in a closely related passage in Plutarch's vegetarian discourse, *De Esu carnium* 2 (998B), the point is made distinctly:[81]

At the beginning it was some wild and harmful animal that was eaten, then a bird or fish that had its flesh torn. And so when our murderous instincts had tasted blood and grew practiced on wild animals, they advanced to the laboring ox and the well-behaved sheep and the house-warding cock; thus little by little giving a hard edge to our insatiable appetite, we have advanced to wars and the slaughter and murder of human beings.

[79]Porphyry, *De Abstin.* 4.2 = Dicaearchus, fragm. 49, Fritz Wehrli *Dikairchos* (Basel, 1944); cf. Wehrli's commentary (*Die Schule des Aristoteles*, ibid. 1.56) and Lovejoy-Boas, pp. 93–96. The question of 'justice' to the animals turns on the question of their possession of reason; if they are reasonable beings, we do wrong to slay them for food (Plutarch. *De Sollertia animalium* 964).

[80]*Met.* 15.75–142.

[81]Trans. W. C. Helmbold (Loeb). The passage appears also, with variations, in Plutarch, *De Sollertia* 959D–E. An attempt to explain the similarity between Ovid and Plutarch by taking both back to Posidonius—Plutarch directly and Ovid through Varro—is not successful according to Johannes Haussleiter, *Der Vegetarismus in der Antike* (Berlin, 1935), pp. 58 n. 62. War and the eating of domestic animals are already coupled by Aratus as a mark of the Bronze Race, *Phaen.* 131 (quoted by Plutarch): 'They first forged the deadly sword of the brigand, and first ate the flesh of the ploughing ox.' Compare also Seneca on the Golden Age, *Epist.* 90.41 and 45: 'Arma cessabant incruentaeque humano sanguine manus odium omne in feras verterant,' but 'parcebant adhuc etiam mutis animalibus' (domestic animals?).

It was on these passages of Ovid and Plutarch that Erasmus founded a long development on the origin of war in *Dulce bellum inexpertis*, of which the following is a brief summary:[82]

> It is a matter of wonder what god, what disease, or what chance inspired the human heart to plunge the sword into another man's vitals. Men must have come to this by degrees. Primitive man, naked and without houses or ramparts, sometimes was attacked by wild beasts. It was on them that war was first declared, and he who had defended his kind against them was held to be brave and a leader. So the young men took to hunting beasts, and not content with slaying them, began wearing their skins for warmth. Next they did a thing judged impious by Pythagoras and that would be incredible to us if we did not know the force of custom—they dared to eat the cadavers, to tear the flesh with their teeth and drink the blood. The sight of a cadaver gave them sensual pleasure. They now passed from noxious beasts to attack innocent sheep, hares, and domestic oxen; no bird or fish was safe from human slaughter. Thus practiced in murder, men when in wrath began striking one another with sticks, stones, or fists. For a long time there were only single combats, in which there was some justice if the one destroyed was a monster like Cacus or Busiris. But now they began to join in groups of relations, neighbors, or friends, though still fighting with stones or with stakes hardened in the fire. (And so a development is traced up to the wars of nations and the invention of artillery.)

At all events, man's struggle with the beasts in the Age of Zeus was hardly equal. We have learned this from Plato's *Statesman*. In the *Protagoras*, we learn more of the details. According to the apologue there put into the mouth of the Sophist Protagoras, in the beginning Epimetheus gave to the lower animals all the advantages: (1) the means of self-protection—swiftness or strength, natural armament or wings or size, (2) protection against the elements—hair and thick skins as bed and clothing, hooves for shoes, and (3) food readily accessible—grass, roots, and other animals; but man was left 'naked and unshod, without bed or arms of defense.' He was, however, rescued by Prometheus' gift of the mechanical arts and Zeus's gift of the social virtues, reverence and justice. This is the first, or nearly the first, appearance of an animal theme that would surpass all others in usefulness—would at all events be endlessly harped upon—in the philosophical and literary tradition of the West. In its underlying

---

[82]*LB* 2.955A–956B. Erasmus himself twice quotes from the Ovidian passage; his dependence on Plutarch's *De Esu* is pointed out by Yvonne Remy and René Dumil-Marquebreucq in their edition of the *Bellum*, p. 34, n. 2.

motive, to define the place of man in nature in comparison with the other animals, it is as lively today as ever. But our concern with it here is limited, since it is primarily a theme of the literature *de dignitate hominis*, and only infrequently enters the literature *de pace*.

Plato's assignment of this theme to the Sophist Protagoras, together with the fact that it is reflected earlier in Xenophon's *Memorabilia* and *Cyropaedia*, has led to the inference that it was organized by the Sophists in the discussion of Nature versus Convention.[83] In the *Memorabilia*, Socrates already gives the counterarguments for the superiority of man—his possession of upright stature, adaptable hands, speech, reason (γνώμη): he is a god in comparison with the animals—arguments that would be constantly reiterated, and on which Plato's 'mechanical arts, reverence, and justice' read like a *variatio*.[84] Aristotle is also interested in this topic from the point of view of man's superiority.[85] In a form unfavorable to man, it is reflected in several surviving fragments of the New Comedy—for example, Philemon, fragm. 88: 'Man is the most wretched of animals . . . to the others Earth freely gives their daily bread . . .'; Menander, fragm. 534: 'The animals are most blessed, and more intelligent than we . . . they have only the evils that Nature gives them, we invent others of our own.'[86] In this form, unfavorable to man, the topic was useful to the Cynics as a point against human pretensions, especially athletic pretensions.[87] But the arena in which the superiority of the animals became a veritable shuttlecock was that of the controversy between Stoics and Epicureans concerning the existence

[83]The theme has been much studied, though perhaps never in a thoroughly comprehensive manner. The best treatment is still S. O. Dickermann's dissertation, *De Argumentis quibusdam apud Xenophontem, Platonem, Aristotelem obviis e structura hominis et animalium petitis* (Halle, 1909); but essential also are Karl Gronau, *Poseidonius und die jüdisch-christliche Genesisexegese* (Leipzig, 1909). See also Eduard Norden, "In Varronis Saturas Menippeas," *Jahrbücher für klassische Philologie*, Suppl. 18 (Leipzig, 1892), 298–306; G. A. Gerhard, "Cercidaea," *Wiener Studien*, 37 (1915), 23, and his *Phoinix von Kolophon* (Leipzig, 1909), pp. 48–54; W. Nestle, *Die Vorsokratiker* (Jena, 1922), 119, 29; Lovejoy-Boas, Ch. 13, 'The Superiority of the Animals.' For the Renaissance and later periods, see George Boas, *The Happy Beast in French Thought of the Seventeenth Century* (Baltimore, 1933).

[84]Xonophon, *Mem.* 1.4.11–12 (cf. 4.3.10 and *Cyr.* 2.3.9–10). Dickermann, *De argumentis*, pp. 92–101, has a useful list of passages on 'upright stature.' Gelli, *Circe*, 8th Dialogue, 1.10.

[85]See especially *De Part. An.* 687[a-b] (hands); *Pol.* 1253[a] (speech; sense of justice), 1332[b]5 (reason).

[86]In all, Philemon, fragms. 88, 89, 93; Menander, fragms. 223, 534, turn on the superior fortune of the beasts (collected in Lovejoy-Boas, pp. 393–96), though not strictly in the terms of the theme here contemplated. They are preserved by Stobaeus, Menander 223 in *Flor.* 107, *De illis qui indigne miseri sunt*, the others in *Flor.* 98, *De Vita*.

[87]Norden, "In Varronis Saturas," 303–6; cf. below, p. 250.

of divine Providence.[88] Indeed some such context is already implied by the passage we have just noticed in Xenophon's *Memorabilia*. Marvelously as the animals are adapted to live in nature, said the Stoics, man equipped with Reason (and with hands and speech) is better adapted than they; he has them in his dominion, and, erect and looking upward to the heavens, he is a little lower than the gods.[89] If some animals in some ways are better adapted than we, that too is intended for our benefit. Our sheep are born already shod, says Epictetus, so that we may be spared the trouble of finding shoes for them.[90] But the case for the providential arrangement of the world in man's favor is not so complete that the opposite view could not be defended. There is a fish, the *uranoscopus*, says Galen, that has its head so fixed that it has to look at the heavens whether it wants to or not.[91] It was easy to infer from the better adaptation of the animals that the world was created for their sake at least as much as for the sake of man.[92] As for the divine gift of reason, says the Academic Cotta in Cicero's *De natura deorum*, consider the use Medea made of it: rascality, then, must also be the gift of Providence; Providence would have done well to withhold so disastrous a boon.[93] But it was the Epicureans who made the most impressive use of this theme in opposing *providentia*. Indeed the phrase that recurs in so many versions: 'Nature, a mother to the beasts, but a stepmother to man . . . ,' has been tentatively ascribed to Epicurus himself.[94] And best-known

[88]Norden, p. 306, believed that it was used, in the unfavorable sense, by the Stoics against the Peripatetic doctrine of external goods, and again by the Academics against Stoic *providentia*; but the evidence is indirect and uncertain.

[89]E.g., Cicero, *DND* Book II, esp. Ch. 56ff., 140ff.; Seneca, *De Ben.* 2.29; Quintilian, *Inst. Orat.* 2.16.13; and others.

[90]*Discourses* 1.16, *De Providentia*; cf. Cicero, *DND* 2.63, 158ff.

[91]*De Usu part.* 3.3. Compare Montaigne, *Essais* 2.12, p. 201.

[92]Plato, *Laws* 903C; Seneca, *Epist.* 73.6–7; Philo, *De Opif. mundi* 13; Cicero, *DND* 2.53.133; Celsus in Origen, *Contra Celsum* 4.74, 4–5: οὐδὲν μᾶλλον ἀνθρώπων ἢ τῶν ἀλόγων ζῴων ἕνεκεν γέγονε τὰ πάντα (all was created no more for man than for the irrational animals).

[93]*DND* 3.26.67ff.; 3.30.75; 3.27.69. The last passage is quoted by Montaigne, *Essais* 2.12, p. 204. The Stoic answer (cf. Seneca, *Epist.* 90.24.46) is that an instructed and purified reason will right the wrongs of perverse reason; but Cotta anticipates this point by saying that few or none (as the Stoics admitted) possess this *bona ratio*, and the proof of Providence fails if we imagine that Providence works only for a few exceptional persons.

[94]This is no more than a guess of Norden's ("In Varronis Saturas," p. 436), approved by Gerhard, "Cercidaea" p. 23. The phrase first occurs in Cicero, in Augustine, *Contr. Jul. Pelag.* 4.12 (60), and in Philo, *De Posteritate Caini* 162. Philo ascribes it to τοῖς δοκιμωτάτοις πάλαι λογίων (The most approved of the learned men of former days [Loeb trans. F. H. Colson and G. H. Whitaker]), a phrase suggesting that he at least did not associate it with the Epicureans.

of all statements of the theme are those of Lucretius[95] and Pliny;
for Pliny's version is essentially Epicurean, though starting out from
a Stoic sentiment. It is summarized here, since it is the chief source
of this theme in the Renaissance:[96]

> We begin with man, for whose sake Nature appears to have created
> all other things—but at a cruel price, so that it is hard to say whether
> she has been more a kind parent or a harsh stepmother to him. First,
> man alone she drapes in borrowed resources, while on the rest she be-
> stows coverings—shells, bark, spines, hides, fur, bristles, hair, down,
> feathers, scales, fleeces. Man alone on the day of his birth she casts away
> naked on the naked ground to burst at once into wailing and weep-
> ing—the animal that is to lord it over all the rest; and he initiates his
> life with punishment because of the one offense of being born. Alas the
> folly of those who think that from these beginnings they were bred to
> proud estate! And at the beginning he is like a four-footed animal.
> When does man begin to walk? to speak? Then his diseases—and the
> cures. All other creatures know their own nature, some using speed,
> some flight, some swimming, whereas man knows nothing save by edu-
> cation—nothing, that is, by instinct except to weep. He alone has grief,
> luxury, ambition, avarice. In fine, while all other animals live worthily
> within their species—lions do not attack lions—man has most of his
> evils from his fellow man.

Even in the matter of Reason, though the animals are deficient in
'extrinsic' reason (speech), they are generally allowed some degree
of intrinsic reason.[97] In his amusing dialogue *On the Animals' Use of
Reason*, Plutarch endows them with both kinds: Gryllus, trans-

[95]*De rer. nat.* 5.222–34:

> Tum porro puer, ut saevis proiectus ab undis
> navita, nudus humi iacet, infans, indigus omni
> vitali auxilio, cum primum in luminis oras
> nixibus ex alvo matris natura profudit,
> vagituque locum lugubri complet, ut aecumst
> cui tantum in vita restet transire malorum.
> At variae crescunt pecudes armenta feraeque
> nec crepitacillis opus est nec cuiquam adhibendast
> almae nutricis blanda atque infracta loquella
> nec varias quaerunt vestes pro tempore caeli,
> denique non armis opus est, non moenibus altis,
> qui sua tutentur, quando omnibus omnia large
> tellus ipsa parit naturaque daedala rerum.

[96]*HN* 7, *Praef.*, résumé from H. Rackman, trans. (Loeb).
[97]Alcmaeon, Diels, ed. (5th ed.) 24.1[a]; Sextus Empiricus, *Pyrrh. Hyp.* 1.62–78; Por-
phyry, *De Abstin.* 3.2–9. See Max Pohlenz, 'Tierische und menschliche Intelligenz bei
Poseidonius,' *Hermes*, 76 (1941), 1–13.

formed by Circe into a pig, rejects Odysseus' plea that he consent to return to human shape and cogently argues that animals are superior to man in happiness and virtue.

Nevertheless it was the Stoic view that prevailed—or perhaps one should say that the form in which the topic existed in popular philosophy was in agreement with the Stoic view.[98] Having much in common with the Old Testament view, it is found everywhere in early Christian literature—for example, in Minucius Felix, in commentaries on Genesis, and above all in the special treatises on the creation and status of man, which in any case owe much to Stoic arguments for Providence.[99] Yet the Epicurean view did not die all at once. The Celsus whose *Alethes logos* is answered by Origen may not have been an Epicurean, but he seems to have developed this argument at great length, saying boldly that the animals are dearer to God—not merely to Nature—than man is.[100] Indeed it is not unchristian, perhaps not unstoic, to dwell on the miseries of man's external condition, as Gregory Nazianzen does in a striking poem founded on our topic:[101]

> What was I born? What am I? What shall I be ere long? . . . Our pride is in vain—if we were only what the many think we are, and if at life's end we were to have nothing more. The calf on issuing from the womb already frisks and feeds. . . . The dappled fawn, slipping from its mother's belly, sets its foot by hers, and at three years bears the yoke. . . . Bears, boars, lions, tigers, pards, bristle at once and leap on the huntsman. . . . Earth gives them sustenance freely, and houses them. . . . They die easily; they do not mourn their dead. But wretched man, vilely engendered and born in pain, is reared with endless toils. . . . (Gregory details the woes of mankind from cradle to grave; but concludes that man is not only body but soul, the breath of God, and in this is great, even an angel: the Cross is his refuge from envy.)

[98]Versified in Phaedrus, *Fabl.* App. 2; Anacreontic 24, Φύσις κέρατα ταύροις [Nature gave horns to bulls]; ps.-Phocylides 125–28. All these give man 'reason.'

[99]It prevails in the Middle Ages; see, e.g., Migne, *PL* Index 2.61, references under 'Homo animalibus per rationem praestat.' Minucius Felix, *Octavius* 17.10; Basil, *Hom. IX in Hex.* (Migne, *PG* 29.192); Marius Victor (Migne, *PL* 61. 945); Gregory of Nyssa, *De Hom. opificio* 7; Nemesius, *De Nat. Hom.* 1; Theodoretus, *De Provid.* 4 (Migne, *PG* 83.613); ps.-Basil, *De Hom. Struct.* 1.7 (Migne, *PG* 30.17); Lactantius, *De Opific. Dei* 2–3. St. Basil is the prime source of the Renaissance hexaemeral poems (see Robbins, *Hex. Lit.* Chs. 4 and 5).

[100]Origen, *Contra Celsum* 4.74–99. See Henry Chadwick, "Origen, Celsus, and the Stoa," *Journal of Theological Studies* 48 (1947), 36–39, on this subject, and Chadwick's translation of Origen, *C. Cels.* (Cambridge, 1953), Introd., on the question whether Celsus was an Epicurean.

[101]*Carm.* 1.2.15, 'On the worthlessness of the outer man' (Migne, *PG* 37.766).

When in the Renaissance the patristic treatises *de opificio hominis* find their successors in treatises *de dignitate hominis*, this theme of the *grandeurs et misères* of the human condition vis-à-vis the animals is still found in place. Already indeed in the thirteenth century, it occupies a chapter in the ever-popular *De miseriis* of Innocent III.[102] In reply to Innocent's pessimistic view (which we can hardly in this connection call Epicurean) Giannozzo Manetti expands upon the topic in his *De Dignitate et excellentia hominis* (1452) to exalt the special powers of man endowed with reason.[103] The Platonists, led by Ficino, celebrate the freedom of the human soul in contrast to the animals, who are bound by necessity.[104] Pico takes the same line in his *Oratio de dignitate hominis*.[105] Like Pico, Folengo in his *Caos del Triperuno* declares that it is through the liberal arts that man may regain his heavenly origin, though the animals, who do not have to learn, may seem the favorites of Nature.[106] Man is a second god.[107] If we do encounter pessimists who praise the condition of

[102]Lotharii Cardinalis (Innocentii III) *De miseria humane conditionis*, Michele Maccarrone, ed. (Lucani, 1955), 1.5 (pp. 12–13): 'Quid hic particulariter dixerim quibusdam, cum generaliter omnes sine scientia, sine verbo, sine virtute nascimur? Flebiles, debiles, imbecilles, parum a brutis distantes, immo minus in multis habentes: nam illa statim ut exorta sunt gradiuntur, nos autem non solum erecti pedibus non incedimus, verum etiam curvati manibus non reptamus.' This seems to reflect Pliny, and perhaps Lactantius (cf. below, n. 123).

[103]Giovanni Gentile, *Giordano Bruno e il pensiero del rinascimento* (Florence, 1920), pp. 158ff.

[104]*Theologiae Platonicae* 13.3, cited by Gentile, *Bruno*, p. 141. Here Ficino follows the Platonic *Axiochus* in noting that the animals lack art, or if they possess some one art, do not improve on it, whereas man is the inventor of many arts. Man's freedom is demonstrated in another way by Pietro Crinito, *De honesta disciplina* 13.1, who quotes Bardesanes from Eusebius (*Praep. Evang.* 6.10.1–6) to the effect that while the brutes are provided at birth with their appropriate food, man, with his reason, can enjoy a wider variety of diet. Cf. Pontano, *De prudentia* 3.2: 'The animals know what is good or bad for them, man investigates why this is so.' Other defenses of man in Pontano, *Urania* 1; Rhodiginus, *Lectiones antiquae* 3.10; Palingenius, *Zodiacus vitae* 5.235–75 (cf. 2.27ff. and 4.569ff.); J. C. Scaliger, *Poematum pars altera* (Heidelberg, 1600), p. 194, an epigram specifically rebuking Pliny; Joannes Lygaeus, poem *De corporis humani harmonia* in *DPG* 2.423–24.

[105]'Summam et admirandam hominis felicitatem! cui datum id habere quod optat, id esse quod velit. Bruta simul atque nascuntur id secum afferunt . . . a bulga matris quod possessura sunt.'

[106]*Opere italiane*, Umberto Renda, ed. (Bari, 1911), 1.194:

Indi Natura, per supplicio degno,
Men se gli mostra madre che noverca;
La quale ogni animal provvede contra
L'onte del tempo, dandogli sostegno.
Nasce pur l'uomo ignudo. . . .

[107]See, e.g., Campanella's poem "Della possenza de l'uomo" quoted by Gentile, *Bruno*, p. 127 (*Poesie*, ed. Gentile [Bari, 1915], p. 170). Cf. Du Bartas, *Sixième Jour* 440 (though not on our theme): God consults how 'Il doit d'un second Dieu former le

the animals above that of man, they tend to be frankly paradoxical, and to revoke what they have said before they are through.[108] Even Montaigne, who gives this theme of the superior equipment a sort of climax in his treatise on the dignity of man, after quoting the 'plaintes vulgaires' of Lucretius and Pliny, concludes with Seneca that man is 'ny au dessus, ny au dessoubs du reste,' having his own place in nature, and if he alone has the liberty of imagination to depict what is not present, whether true or false, the advantage costs him dear, being the source of his ills: vice, malady, irresolution, trouble, and despair.[109] On the whole, the Renaissance holds staunchly to the idea of man's superiority through Reason. G. B. Gelli in his famous *Circe*, elaborated from Plutarch's *Gryllus*, does not end as Plutarch does, but shows the Elephant, the most prudent of beasts, to be capable of seeing the point and glad to accept Ulysses' invitation to return to the shape of reasonable man.[110] Indeed in the eighteenth century, Pope is still paraphrasing Seneca upon this point in his *Essay on Man* (1.6):

> What would this Man? Now upward will he soar,
> A little less than angel, would be more;
> Now looking downward, just as grieved appears
> To want the strength of bulls, the fur of bears.
> Made for his use all creatures if he call,
> Say what their use, had he the pow'rs of all?
> Nature to these, without profusion, kind,
> The proper organs, proper powers assigned;
> Each seeming want compensated of course,
> Here with degree of swiftness, there of force;
> All in exact proportion to the state;

bastiment.' See also V. Rufner, "Homo secundus deus," *Philosophisches Jahrbuch*, 63 (1955), 248–91. Erasmus, *Bellum* 953A: 'Proinde Deus in hoc mundo velut simulacrum quoddam sui constituit hominem.' *Hamlet* 2.2.309.

[108]So Pierre Boaystuau, *Théâtre du monde* (1558) ed. of 1607, pp. 72ff., who paraphrases Pliny at great length. See Boas, *Happy Beast*, pp. 10–17, on the writers of paradox.

[109]*Apologie de Raimond Sebond* (*Essais* 2.12.168). Cf. Seneca, *Epist.* 90.18: 'Non fuit tam inimica Natura, ut cum omnibus aliis animalibus facilem actum vitae daret, homo solus non posset sine tot artibus vivere. . . . Ad parata nati sumus: nos omnia nobis difficilia facilium fastidio fecimus.'

[110]Plutarch's dialogue may be incomplete. Cf. Seneca, *De Ben.* 2.29: 'Vide quam iniqui sint divinorum munerum aestimatores. . . . Queruntur, quod non magnitudine corporum aequemus elephantos, . . . impetu tauros; quod solidior sit cutis beluis, . . . densior ursis. . . . Et cum quaedam ne coire quidem in idem natura patiatur, ut velocitatem corporum et vires, ex diversis ac dissidentibus bonis hominem non esse compositum, iniuriam vocant et negligentes nostri deos. . . . Vix sibi temperant quin eo usque impudentiae provehantur, ut naturam oderint, quod infra deos sumus.'

Nothing to add, and nothing to abate.
Each beast, each insect, happy in its own:
Is Heav'n unkind to man, and man alone?

Among the advantages of the animals, their superior equipment for war figures prominently in the ancient sources. The first point made in the apologue of Plato's *Protagoras* is their possession of natural defensive armor, while man is born unarmed and defenseless (ἄοπλος, γυμνός); and the counterargument for man is already made in Xenophon's *Cyropaedia*: men know by instinct (φύσει) to defend themselves with hand and sword, as well as bulls know by instinct to use their horns, or boars their tusks; man's wit and his hands produce a fighter better than any centaur.[111] Aristotle notes that, after all, man unlike the beasts does not fight continually,[112] and argues that the possession of natural instruments of defense is a point of inferiority in the animals; they cannot remove them: 'they have to wear their shoes to bed,' whereas man can adopt any weapon that suits the occasion; his hand is the equivalent of many weapons because it can grasp them all.[113] Generally, however, if the superiority of the animals is denied in this matter, a blanket reference to Reason suffices.[114] Man is defended as a better fighter than the animals, and this is in accordance with the tendency of this *topos* to lower or to raise the estimation of man. It is not used to discourage man from fighting. This is noticeable, since the topic is commonly used in propaganda against athleticism: you cannot rival the strength of a bull or the swiftness of a hare, why then pride yourself on athletic prowess?[115] But ancient peace propaganda, I believe, never says: since Nature has equipped the animals, and not men, with natural arms, men should leave fighting to them. Perhaps it was only too clear that man suffered from no lack in this respect. At

[111]*Cyr.* 2.3.1–10; 4.3.18.
[112]*Hist. An.* 9.1: 610ᵃ3.
[113]*De Part. An.* 687ᵃ⁻ᵇ. In *Pol.* 1253ᵃ33, he says briefly that man 'is equipped at birth with arms.'
[114]Not denied, of course, in 'Epicurean' versions—e.g., Lucretius 5.232; Plutarch's Gryllus argues that the beasts fight with more courage and decency than man (cf. Aelian, *De Nat. an.* 6.1). Denied with a general reference to 'reason', e.g., in Quintilian 7.4; Hierocles, *Eth. Elem. SVF*, von Arnim, p. 11; and, with the Aristotelian topic of 'detached' armor, in late writers: St. John Chrysostom, *Ad pop. Antioch.* 11.4 (Migne, *PG* 49.125); Gregory of Nyssa, *De hom. opif.* 7 (Migne, *PG* 44.141); Lactantius, *De opif. Dei* 2 (Migne, *PL* 7.15). Note that in Pliny's influential version quoted above, p. 246 it is not a question of arms at all, only of 'coverings' (*tegimenta*).
[115]Philo, *De Post. Caini* 46 (161); Cicero, *De Sen.* 9.27; Dio of Prusa, *Or.* 9.15–22; Seneca, *Epist.* 124.22–23; ps-Galen, *Protrept.* 9.13; and numerous texts collected by Norden, "In Varronis Saturas" 303–6.

most, there are traces of such a usage. The fifteenth satire of Juvenal, as we have noted, combines some of the terms of this animal theme with the theme of the peaceful kinds: Nature in giving man tears thereby gave him a kind heart (*mollissima corda*); by this and by his possession of reason, he is distinguished from the beasts; yet there is more peace among serpents than among men. If Juvenal follows Pliny in this combination of topics, he has drawn an implication that Pliny ignores. A similar note is struck, though very casually, by St. John Chrysostom in connection with the Aristotelian topic of 'natural' and 'detached' arms:[116]

> The brute beasts have weapons in their bodies—the bull horns, the boar tusks, the lion claws—but it is not in my body but outside of it that God has placed my weapons, showing thereby that man is a peaceable (tame) animal, and that occasion for the use of arms is not in my case ever-present. . . . He made them separate from my body in order that I might be free and at ease, and not have to carry them all the time. For we not only prevail over the animals in having a rational soul, we surpass them in body also, since God has given us . . . the kind of body that is likely to serve a rational soul.

With a Platonic phrase—'man a peaceable or tame animal' —injected into an Aristotelian topic,[117] St. John only just misses saying that man, lacking natural arms, is born for peace. Perhaps in some Hellenistic discussion of *philanthropia* the point had been made, since elsewhere we find the phrase accompanying the topic of the peaceful animal kinds.[118] Galen, however, in elaborating the same Aristotelian passage, employs the expression: 'Man, born for peace as well as for war, uses his hands to write laws, build altars and ships, play flute and lyre, handle chisel and fire-tongs and tools of all the other arts, and put down his thoughts in writing' (as well as for fighting).[119]

[116]*Ad pop. Antioch.* 11.4 (Migne, *PG* 49.125A).
[117]ἥμερον ζῷον ὁ ἄνθροπος; cf Plato, *Soph.* 222B: the sophist hunts tame animals, εἴπερ γέ ἐστιν ἄνθρωπος ἥμερον ζῷον; *Laws* 766A: ἄνθρωπος δὲ, ὥς φαμεν, ἥμερον (sc. ζῷον), but if not educated or badly educated, he beccomes ἀγριώτατον, ὅποσα φύσει γῆ (the most savage of earthly creatures).
[118]Libanius, *Dial.* 12.6, p. 537 in *Opera*, R. Foerster, ed., 12 vols. in 13 (Leipzig, 1903–27): 'Is not a man a tame animal in name only (ἥμερον μὲν τὸ ζῷον ἄχρι ῥήματος), but a wild animal in deeds? What lions make military expeditions against other lions? What war is there between animals of the same kind?' Compare, earlier, the elder Seneca, *Controv.* 2.1.10: 'nam neque feris inter se bella sunt, nec si forent, eadem hominem deceant, *placidum proximumque deo genus*.'
[119]*De Usu partium* 1.2.5. Εἰρηνικὸν δ'ὅμως καὶ πολιτικὸν (ζῷον) ἄνθρωπος χερσὶ καὶ νόμους ἐγράψατο καὶ βωμοὺς καὶ ἀγάλματα θεοῖς ἰδρύσατο καὶ ναῦν

When, therefore, we find the topic 'man designed for peace, the animals for war,' fully elaborated by Erasmus as the first major development of his *Dulce bellum inexpertis*, we must in all likelihood give him credit for a degree of originality. His stated intention is to paint first the portrait of Man and then the portrait of War, in order to show how incompatible they are. All these earlier parts of the *adagium* are constructed with extremely conscious rhetoric. His *ecphrasis* of Man appropriately turns on a *syncresis* of man and beast. Essentially, then, he employs the theme of the animal's superior armament just as the ancients did, to establish the status of man; but by shaping it to an argument for peace, he has given it a special and novel form. The long passage must be represented here by excerpts:[120]

> First, then, if one considers only the appearance and form of the human body, does he not immediately understand that Nature (or rather God) created this being not for war but for friendship? . . . For she equipped every one of the other living creatures with weapons of its own. She armed the charging bull with horns, the fierce lion with claws . . . she protected some with shells, others with hides, still others with scales. . . . She added to these a horrid and brutish appearance and savage eyes. . . . Man alone she brought forth naked, weak, delicate, and unarmed, with smooth skin and the tenderest of flesh. It would seem that none of his limbs could ever be fit for fighting and violence; but as for the other creatures, I would even say that almost as soon as they are born they are self-sufficient and able to preserve their lives; only man is so born that for a long time he is wholly dependent upon others. He cannot speak or walk or find food; he can only wail for help. . . . And again, she did not give him a hideous and savage appearance, as she did the rest, but one that is meek and gentle. . . . She gave him friendly eyes. . . . She gave him arms that curve to embrace. . . . To him alone she gave laughter . . . to him alone tears, the mark of mercy and pity. Moreover, she gave him a voice, not menacing and fearful like that of beasts, but friendly and soft.
>
> Nor was Nature content with these gifts: to him alone she gave the use of speech and reason, the gifts best suited to create goodwill. . . . She implanted a hatred of loneliness, a love of companionship. . . . She took care that what is most wholesome is also the sweetest, for what gives more joy than a friend? . . . On top of that she added an enthusiasm for the liberal arts. . . . For indeed neither kinship nor consanguinity binds souls together in closer and firmer ties of friendship than the

κατεσκευάσατο καὶ αὐλὸν καὶ λύραν καὶ σμίλην καὶ πυράγραν καὶ τἄλλα πάντα των τεχνῶν ὄργανα καὶ ὑπομνήματα δ'αὐτῶν τῆς θεωρίας ἐν γράμμασιν ὑπελίπετο.
[120]Trans. Martha Malamud.

sharing of noble pursuits. . . . And finally she endowed man with a
spark of the divine mind. . . . So God has set man as a sort of image of
himself in this world, so that some sort of earthly divinity should look
after the well-being of all. Even the beasts feel this, since we see that not
only the tame ones, but even leopards and lions and beasts more fierce
than these fly to man for help in times of great danger.

Since following this picture of Man and the contrasting picture of
War,[121] Erasmus introduces, with equal elaboration, the topic of
the animals at peace in their kinds (as above, p. 223), it may be that
the whole was suggested to him by Pliny, who also combines these
two topics. In the first paragraph, there are verbal echoes of Pliny
and Seneca.[122] Yet even here there are turns of phrase that are
found only in other versions of the theme.[123] Moreover, the lead-
ing thought, that Nature or God produced man for peace and
friendship and not for war, very likely comes from Juvenal, who had
furnished Erasmus with so much of his earlier *Oratio de pace et dis-
cordia*. But in the contrast between the ferine and human forms, the
details purporting to prove that man was born for friendship seem
to be Erasmus' own.[124] In the second paragraph, the gift of speech
and reason,[125] the love of companionship,[126] the pursuit of the lib-

[121]This owes nothing to the *ecphrasis* of War constructed for a similar purpose by
Aristides (above, p. 33).

[122]'genuisse naturam' = Pliny: 'videtur genuisse natura'; 'testis . . . corio . . .
cortice' = Pliny: 'testas, cortices, . . . coria'; 'solum hominem nudum pro-
duxit' = Pliny: 'hominem tantum nudum . . . abicit'; 'nec fari novit, nec ingredi, nec
cibum capere, vagitu lumen implorat opem' = Pliny: 'non fari, non ingredi, non
vesci, breviterque non aliud naturale sponte quam flere.' The extended list of animals
(mostly omitted above) may have been suggested by Seneca's list in *De Ben.* 2.29.1, and
'taurorum impetus' seems to echo Seneca's '(non aequamus) impetu tauros.' Pliny spe-
cifies no animals.

[123]E.g., 'caetera fere statim ut nata sunt, sibi sufficiunt.' Cf. Gregory Nazianzen,
Carm. 14: 'Ex quo matris elapsus sinu, primum effudi lachrymam, In quot et quantas
incursurus calamitates'; Lactantius, *De opif. Dei* 3.1: 'quae ut sunt edita ex utero, pro-
tinus in pedes suos erigi'; Innocent III, *De miser.* 5: 'illa, statim ut exorta sunt, gradi-
untur.' All refer to walking. But Pico, *Orat. de dig.*: 'Bruta simulatque nascuntur, id
sibi afferunt . . . quod possessura sunt.'

[124]Comparisons of this kind, often involving the adaptation of the human and ani-
mal form to their functions, are of course common—e.g., Plato, *Tim.* 91E–92; Aristo-
tle, *De Part. An.* 686ª24ff.; Cicero, *DND* 2.58ff.; and the various patristic treatises *de
opificio hominis* (cf. esp. Gregory of Nyssa, *De hom. opif.* 7–8, and Lactantius, *De opif.
Dei* 2); but even when the object is to show how man was made in the image of God, it
is Reason, not Love, that controls the form. Note that Erasmus fails to specify erect
stature, presumably as not to his purpose.

[125]'Extrinsic' and 'intrinsic' reason (above, p. 246). Compare Cicero, *DND* 2.59
(148): 'hac vi sermonis consolamur afflictos . . . hac cupiditates iracundiasque restu-
ingimus . . . haec a vita immani et fera segregavit' (close to Isocrates, *Nicocles* 5–6 and
Antid. 253–56).

[126]'Odium solitudinis, amorem sodalitatis': Cicero, *De off.* 1.4.12 (Lovejoy-Boas, p.

eral arts,[127] the divine spark, and man placed on earth as a kind of divinity to care for the rest of creation[128]—all are familiar topics in the literature *de dignitate hominis*. That even the wild beasts seek the protection of man in time of danger is a less common topic.[129]

In Ronsard's *Exhortation pour la Paix* we read (107–22):

> Ah malheureux humains, ne scauriez vous congnoistre
> Que la nature, helas, ne nous a point fait naistre
> Pour quereller ainsi, vous qui naissez tous nus
> Sans force et desarmez? les animaux cognus
> Par les grandes forets, dragons, lions, tigresses,
> Sont armez ou de griffe, ou d'escailles espaisses,
> Et sortant hors du ventre au profond d'un rocher,
> Desja naissent guerriers, et se paissent de chair,
> Les vaines de leur col noyrcissent de colere,
> Ja font mine de guerre, et ensuivent leur mere.
> Mais vous, humains, à qui, d'un seul petit couteau
> Ou d'une esguille fresle, on perseroit la peau,
> Les muscles et les nerfs, contre vostre nature
> Qui ne cherche que paix, allez à l'avanture
> Au milieu des cannons, obliant vos maisons,
> Enflez de trop d'orgueil ou de trop de raisons.

In view of the rarity of this theme in peace literature, and the emphasis with which Erasmus had brought it into such a context, there can be little doubt that its presence in Ronsard's poem goes back to the *Dulce bellum inexpertis*. There are verbal echoes: 'ne scauriez vous *congnoistre* / Que la nature . . . ne vous a point fait naistre / Pour quereller ainsi' renders '*intellecturus* est, naturam . . . animal hoc non bello sed amicitiae . . . genuisse'; and compare 'vous qui naissez tous *nus* / sans force et desarmez'* with 'solum hominem *nudum* produxit, *imbecillem*, tenerum, *inermen*,' though these terms are found in many

---

249); *De fin.* 2.14.45; Plato, *Laws* 3.678; Lucretius, *Der rer. nat.* 5.1019; Lactantius, *Div. Inst.* 6.10.18.

[127](See Migne, *PL* Index: *Rationis excellentia generaliter expressa*, Migne, *PL* 219.63.) John Chrysostom, *Ad. pop. Antioch.* (Migne, *PG* 49.125): man's superiority to the beasts is in his mind; Basil, *De Hom. Struct Orat.* I, (Migne, *PG* 30.11); Tertullian, *De Pallio* (Migne, *PL.* 2.1050); Augustine, *De ordine* (Migne, *PL* 32.1015).

[128]Cicero, *De fin.* 2.13.40, 'mortalem deum'; see above, n. 107.

[129]Virgil, *Georg.* 3.539–40: 'timidi dammae cerrique fugaces / nunc inter canes et circum tecta vagantur.' See Claude Colet in Hutton, *Essays*, p. 276: 'Dieu créa l'homme imbecille et tendre / A ce semblance et divine figure, / Pour faire bien à toute créature: / Ce qu'ont congnu les bestes brustes mesmes, / Qui se voyans estre en perils extremes, / Et ne pouvans plus trouver subterfuge, / Ont accouru à l'homme pour refuge.'

versions of the theme; and perhaps the development 'à qui, d'un seul petit couteau, . . . on perseroit le peau' may follow from the hint in 'mollissima carne, cute levi.'

But Ronsard does not habitually transcribe a whole passage from a single source. He knows when he is using a *locus communis* and often exerts himself to fill it out with expressions taken from more than one version.[130] The present passage is made into poetry by the addition of a number of picturesque phrases that are not taken from Erasmus. Thus the sentence, 'Et sortant hors du ventre . . . Ja font mine de guerre, et ensuivent leur mere,' which corresponds to Erasmus' sentence, 'caetera, fere statim ut nata sunt, sibi sufficiunt ad vitam tuendam,' abounds in such details. Ronsard may have created them *ex nihilo*, but if he did so the result is curiously similar to some lines in Gregory Nazianzen's poem on this topic:[131]

The dappled fawn, when it slips from the belly, at once puts its foot by its mother's foot (that is, runs at her side). . . . Bears, and the race of destructive boars, lions and swift tigers, and fierce panthers at once (at birth) bristle at the mane when they see a weapon—bristle, and leap at the hardy huntsman.

If we are only authorized in noting a parallel here,[132] we can point to a virtual translation in the line that interrupts, or at least suspends, the thought:

[130]I have remarked on this habit of Ronsard in *Essays*, p. 227.
[131]Above, p. 247 and n. 101. Gregory, *Carm.* 1.2.15, 11–18 (Migne, *PG* 37.766–67):

Νεβρὸς δ' αἰολόδερμος, ἐπὴν διὰ γαστρὸς ὀλισθῇ,
Αὐτίκα μητρὸς ἑῆς πὰρ ποδὶ θῆκε πόδα . . .
Ἄρκτοι δ', οὐλομένων τε συῶν γένος, ἠδὲ λέοντες,
Τίγρις τ' ἠνεμόεις, παρδαλίων τε μένος,
Αὐτίκα φρίξεν ἔθειραν ἐπὴν κε σίδηρον ἴδηται
φρίξεν, καὶ κρατεροὺς ἆλτ' ἐπὶ θηρολέτας.

A Latin translation of this poem by Aldus Manutius is included in his *Carmina Gregorii Nazianzeni* (Vol. 3 of *Poetae Christiani*) (Venice, 1504). I am indebted for this information to Sister Agnes Clare, Our Lady of the Lake College, San Antonio, Texas.
[132]Other parallels are Lucan 1.328–30:

Utque ferae tigres numquam posuere furorem,
Quas nemore Hyrcano *matrum dum lustra secuntur*,
Altus caesorum *pavit cruor* armentorum.

and Claudian, *Tert. Cons. Honorii* 77–82:

Ut leo quem fulvae matris spelunca tegebat . . .
uberibus solitum pasci, cum crescere sensit
ungue pedes et terga iubis et dentibus ora,
iam negat imbelles epulas et rupi relicta
Gaetulo comes ire patri stabulisque minari
aestuat et celsi tabo sordere iuvenci.

Les vaines de leur col noyrcissent de colere
Ora tument ira, nigrescunt sanguine venae
[Ovid, *Ars. Am.* 3.503][133]

Suitably to the events of 1558, Ronsard made the inclusive theme of his poetical declamation—expressed in the exordium and repeated in the peroration—that Christians ought not to make war on other Christians.[134] The theme itself brings him close to Erasmus; and it seems possible to detect other specific echoes of *Dulce bellum inexpertis* in the *Exhortation*.[135] In particular, like Erasmus, Ronsard a little later (157–70) draws a 'portrait' of War, though he does not call it so, ending with a 'cumulative' passage that may have been suggested by the cumulative passages in Erasmus.[136]

It might be thought that the popularity of Erasmus' *Bellum* would often have brought this theme of the well-equipped animals into the rhetorical peace poetry. Yet such is not the case—so firmly fixed is the theme in its traditional direction of determining the status of man. If the peace poet thinks of the animals, he tends to think of the traditional peace theme of the kindly species. Even in the prose literature, Erasmus' unusual invention seems to be reflected only in works immediately related to his.[137] Ronsard's *Exhortation*, however,

[133]This, oddly enough, is the line immediately following 'Candida pax homines, trux decet ira feras,' which we have noted as often quoted in peace literature, and as included in Mirandula's commonplace book under the topic 'De Bello' (above, n. 1). My impression is that Ronsard rather frequently borrows single lines; another example in this same poem is 'Qu' heureuse fut la gent qui vivoit sous Saturne' (147) from Tibullus 1.3.35: 'Quam bene Saturno vivebant rege.'

[134]See 'Rhetorical Doctrine and Some Poems of Ronsard,' in Hutton, *Essays*, pp. 291–310.

[135]Compare *Exhort.* 4–7: 'Et ne trampez vos dards dans le sang de vos freres, / que Christ . . . a rachetez . . . et nous a tous *conjoins*,' with *Bellum* 959C–D: 'Parricidium vocatur si frater occidit fratrem, at Christianus *conjunctior* Christiano quam ullus germanus germano'; and *Exhort.* 54–55: 'Et nos rois auront fait mourir cent mille hommes en vain / Au tour d'un froid *village*, ou d'une *pauvre ville*, / Ou d'un petit chateau *pour le rendre serville*,' with *Bellum* 959B: 'tantam hominum turbam educis in periculum ut *oppidum* aliquod evertas,' and 965A: 'ut unum aliquod *oppidulum* suae vindicent *ditioni*, totum imperium adducunt in extremum discrimen.'

[136]Erasmus has two such passages, one in the 'portrait' of War (953B–E), the other somewhat later (957E–958A). In the first, compare: 'congestae strages, undantes cruore campos, fluvios humano tinctos sanguine' with 'tant de monceaux de mors qui engressent les champs . . . les rouges flots de la Meuse'; and in the second passage, compare: 'simul atque belli saeva tempestas ingruerit, . . . civitates una procella subvertuntur, . . . silent leges, . . . nullum habet locum aequitas' with: 'par la cruelle guerre on renverse les villes, . . . L'equité ne fleurist, la justice n'a lieu.' These to be sure are commonplaces. The last line (170) of Ronsard's cumulation: 'Et d'un vice execrable on fait une vertu' may echo Virgil's cumulation at the end of the first *Georgic*: 'Quippe ubi fas versum atque nefas: tot bella per orbem.'

[137]E.g., Guillaume Aubert, *Oraison*, f.8ʳ.

is not quite unique in adopting this motif. One earlier poem offers itself that does the like, but a poem so close to Ronsard that some relationship is virtually certain. This is Antoine de Baïf's poem *Sur la Paix avec les Anglois* of 1549.[138] After summoning the people to rejoice and make holiday, Baïf declares that the Golden Age is about to be renewed under Henri II with the return of the goddess of Peace; he describes the Golden Age and curses those who first dug iron from the earth and forged weapons, opening the way for wars.[139] Under Henri these evils will cease:

> L'humaine gent aux bestes laissera
> Leur cruauté, entre soi retenant
> Celle douceur aux hommes convenant.
> Les animaux armez de leur nature
> Doivent aller contre toute droiture:
> Et nous humains, qui sans armes tous nus
> Sommes aux rais du clair Soleil venus,
> Devrions tous jours le repos meintenir,
> Comme n'ayans, voire dès la naissance,
> Que de la Paix seulement conoissance.
> Mais, ô forfait, nous estions entre nous
> Pires, qu'entre eux, les lions et les lous.

This rather colorless statement of the theme nevertheless owes its point of view and its occurrence in this context to Erasmus. The poem was Baïf's first sustained poetical effort, written when he was seventeen, and is chiefly notable for the praise of Ronsard, Du Bellay, and Mellin de St. Gelais (and Baïf himself) with which it ends.[140] There is every likelihood that Ronsard recalled it ten years later when writing his *Exhortation*, and it may have prompted him to turn to Erasmus. But more than once we have reason to suspect that in these years Ronsard's (hypothetical) commonplace book had materials in common with Baïf's.[141]

---

[138]Above, p. 91

[139]The Golden Age is described after Ovid, *Met.* 1.94ff., except that one trait ('Et sans avoir nulle atteinte mauvaise / Comme dormans ils mouroyent à leur aise') is from Hesiod, *Erga* 116.

[140]Baïf calls it 'des mes ecris le premier que jamais / Je mis au jour' (*A Monseigneur de Villequier*, *Euvres*, Marty-Laveaux, ed. 2.403). No doubt it was presented to the king, to whom it is addressed. Mathieu Augé-Chiquet, *La vie, les idées et l'œuvre de Jean Antoine de Baïf* (Paris, 1909), p. 56 n. 3, observes that Claude Binet apparently thought that this poem was published in 1552. So far as we know, however, it was first printed in Baïf's *Euvres* of 1573.

[141]It is perhaps not remarkable that the two poems in question have also in common the description of the Golden Age and that both, following Ovid, deplore the

Paul Laumonier long ago uncovered Ronsard's debt to the *Florilegium* of Stobaeus.[142] It seems not to have been noticed, however, that Baïf borrowed from the same collection, quite independently, two of the pieces imitated by Ronsard. These are two fragments of Menander already mentioned as embodying the theme of the superiority of the animals. Fragment 223 begins: 'If one of the gods should come to me and say: 'Crato, when you die, you will at once be reborn and will be whatever you wish, dog, sheep, goat, man, horse, for you must live twice—that is fated; choose what you wish,' I think I would instantly answer: 'Make me anything but a man, this animal alone has a hard time.' A good dog or horse, he continues, gets good treatment, but a good man is sure to be pushed aside by flatterers, sycophants, and the like. Ronsard takes only the first sentence for the opening of his elegy to Robert de la Haye published in 1560.[143] He then expands freely on the miseries of life, reverting more than once to the animal comparison, but concludes that just as some animals excel others in prudence and in this are equal to men, so some men excel others and resemble the gods: among these is La Haye, whose religious instruction has taught Ronsard to hope for eternal life and realize that 'rien de plus sainct que l'homme au monde ne peut naistre.'[144] Baïf, for his part, very faithfully paraphrases the whole of this fragment of Menander in a poem of unknown date *A Monsieur de Mauru.*[145] The role of the good man thrust aside by the unworthy is one in which he often casts himself.[146]

---

discovery of iron; but verbal expression too in one instance is close: Baïf, 'Maudit, par qui fut le fer deterré / Dans les boyaux de la terre enterré'; Ronsard, 'Que maudit soit celuy qui dechira la terre / Et dedans ses boyaux le fer y alla querre'; Ovid, *Met.* 1.138ff., 'itum est in viscera terrae . . . effodiuntur opes.' But Ronsard takes other details from the Ovidian passage that Baïf ignores.

[142]Laumonier, 1.xxxiii.

[143]Laumonier, 10.315. For 'one of the gods' (τις θεῶν), Ronsard substitutes 'la Parque,' presumably derived from εἱμαρμένον [that is fated] in v. 5 of the fragment.

[144]For vv. 71–75—

> Et mesme que le Ciel se monstre ami plus doux
> Et père plus benin aux animaux qu' à nous,
> Qui pleurons en naissant, et qui par le supplice
> D'estre au berceau liés (comme si ce fust vice
> De naistre dans ce monde) à vivre commenceons . . .

Laumonier should have referred not to Lucretius 5.222, but to Pliny; compare 'iacet manibus pedibusque devinctis flens . . . et a *supliciis* vitam auspicatur unam tantum ob culpam, *quia natum est*' (*H N* 7, *Praef.* 1, 3). For the comparison of animal to animal and man to man, see Plutarch, *Bruta animalia ratione uti sive Grylluo*, 992D. For the phrase, 'rien de plus sainct,' etc., cf. Ovid, *Met.* 1.76: 'Sanctius his animal.' 'To hope for eternal life . . .' see below, n. 148.

[145]*Euvres*, Marty-Laveaux, ed. 2.366. He renders 'one of the gods' by 'quelque Promethée.'

[146]Cf. Augé-Chiquet, pp. 150–55.

Baïf's *Vie des Chams*, also of unknown date, mostly consists of a long paraphrase of a part of the second *Georgic* of Virgil, celebrating the peace of rural life and its inspiration for the poet.[147] To this Virgilian passage Baïf has given his own meaning by appending an introduction of fifty-five lines on the miseries of human life. Such are man's troubles, he says, but if happiness is anywhere attainable, it is attainable in the *vie champêtre*. In this introductory section, man's woeful lot is contrasted with the better fortune of the beasts. Did Baïf not hope for a better life hereafter, he would blame 'la marâtre Nature' for placing him among mankind, and not among the well-armed animals:

> La Nature a doné dès leur naissance
> Aux animaux leur arme et leur defance:
> Les uns la corne, aucuns ont la vitesse,
> D'autres la patte, et d'autres s'on les blesse
> Frapent des pieds et devant et derriere,
> Aucuns dentuz d'une machoire fiere
> Claquent leurs dents.

He continues through the other items of the topic.[148] But far from concluding that man excels by the gift of Reason, Baïf turns the motif into an attack on Reason itself:

> *Nature non ne nous a pas fait étre*
> *Mieux fortunés pour nous avoir fait nétre*
> *De la raison ayans l'ame pourvuë,*
> *Que par trop cher elle nous a venduë.*
> Des animaux la race moins chetive
> Que n'est la nôtre (à son mal inventive
> De mille soins) autre soin ne se done
> Que l'apetit que sa nature, ou bone
> Ou bien mauvaise ainsi qu'elle est encline,
> Luy a doné: mais *la raison maline*
> Qui nous gouverne, outre ceux de la nature
> Dix mille maux encore nous procure.
> Nous faisons cas si quelcun eternuë,
> Pour un seul mot nous avons l'ame emuë,

---

[147]*Euvres* 2.36.

[148]If Baïf follows any single source here, it has escaped me. Pliny does not have the armed animals; Augé-Chiquet rightly refers the cause of the infant's tears 'montrant . . . que nous naissons pour vivre miserables'—to Lucretius 5.227: 'cui tantum in vita restet transire malorum.' The initial reservation: 'Si ce n'étoit qu'après cette mortelle / Nous attendons une vie eternelle,' may be illustrated by the poem of Gregory Nazianzen (above, p. 247); G. B. Gelli, *Capricci del Bottaio, Opere* (Milan, 1805) 2.19; the first sentence of Pontus de Tyard's *Le Solitaire premier*.

Un songe vain en dormant nous effraye,
Nous palissons du cry d'une Frezaye.
Les vains honeurs, les sottes bigotises,
De plus grands biens les palles convoitises,
L'ambition que rien ne ressasie,
Des sens troublez la fausse fantasie,
Et les rigueurs des loix qui nous étonnent,
Ce sont les maux que les homes se donnent
Par leur raison, outre ceux dont leur vie
De sa nature est troublée et suivie.
C'est tout malheur que la vie de l'home,
Que sa raison ronge mine et consome.

Here at the climax of Baïf's introduction we have what is in the main a translation of Menander, frag. 534, but a translation strongly controlled by Baïf's intention. He has enclosed it within lines of his own that emphasize the evils of Reason; he has put in 'reason' where no such word appears in the original; and has omitted it where it does occur in the statement that the animals have more reason than men.[149] His attitude is precisely that of the Academic Cotta in Cicero's *De natura deorum*. By contrast, nothing of this attitude appears in Ronsard's imitation of the same fragment in his *Odelette à Panjas* published in 1554. What he adds (at the beginning) is a reference to the peaceful animals; and in rising above Menander's comic style, he replaces the ass of the original (omitted by Baïf) with the more poetical ox:

De tous les animaux qui vivent sur la terre
L'homme est le plus chetif, car il se fait la guerre
Luimesmes à luimesme, et n'a dans son cerveau
Autre plus grand desir que d'estre son bourreau.
Regards, je te pri, le beuf qui d'un col morne
Traine pour nous nourrir le joug dessus la corne. . . .
Mais nous, pauvres chetifs, soit de jour ou de nuit,
Tousjours quelque tristesse épineuse nous suit,
Qui nous lime le cœur: si quelcun esternuë
Nous sommes courroussés: si quelcun par la ruë

[149]I borrow the translation of Menander, fragm. 534, from Lovejoy-Boas, p. 395: 'All the animals are most blessed and have much more intelligence (νοῦν ἔχοντα μᾶλλον . . . πολύ) than man. Look first at this ass. He is admittedly born under an unlucky star. No evil comes to him through himself, but whatsoever evils Nature has given him, these he has. But we, aside from the necessary evils, invent others by ourselves. We are pained if someone sneezes; if someone speaks ill, we are angry; if someone has a dream, we are frightened; if an owl hoots, we are terrified. Struggles, opinions, contests, laws, all these evils are added to those in nature.'

Passe plus grand que nous, nous tressuons d'ahan:
Si nous oyons crier de nuit quelque Chouan,
Nous herissons d'effroi: bref, à la race humaine
Tousjours de quelque part lui survient quelque peine,
Car il ne lui soufist de ses propres malheurs
Qu'elle a dès le berceau, mais elle en charche ailleurs:
La court, procés, l'amour, la rancoeur, la faintise,
L'ambition, l'honneur, l'ire, et la convoitise,
Et le sale appetit d'amonceler des biens
Sont les maus estrangers que l'homme adjouste aux siens.[150]

Again it is clear that neither French poet depends on the other, but it is likely that their common studies fixed their attention on precisely the same pieces in Stobaeus.[151]

The fact that Baïf as well as Ronsard made use of these two fragments of Menander gains at least a curious interest from the *Dialogues contre les nouveaux Academiciens* of Guy de Bruès, published in 1557. In these philosophical dialogues, in which the speakers are Ronsard, Baïf, Jean Nicot, and Guillaume Aubert, the Academic or sceptical view is maintained, as a paradox, by Baïf and Aubert, while the dogmatic and conservative view is allowed to triumph in the speeches of Ronsard and Nicot. In the first dialogue, 'Baïf' begins the argument (that we should live at the prompting of Nature, and not by our 'fantastic' opinions of right and wrong) by quoting the first sentence of Menander, fragm. 223:

L'autre jour apres avoir leu quelques vers d'un ancien poete Grec,[152] ou il disoit que si Jupiter [*sic*] luy eust donne a choisir lequel il eust mieux ayme estre, homme, ou quelque autre des animaux, il eust mieux ayme estre le plus miserable des animaux que d'estre homme.' 'Baïf' is inclined to agree, because the beasts 'estoient plus heureuses que les hommes, parce qu'elles ont la fruition libre de tous les plaisirs que na-

[150]Laumonier, 6.116. Laumonier notes the borrowing and observes that in the first line of the poem, 'Nous vivons, mon Panjas, une vie sans vie,' this common phrase may come from Philemon, fragm. 93: ἡμεῖς δ'ἀβίωτον ζῶμεν ἄνθρωποι βίον. Laumonier does not remark that Philemon, fragm. 88 (in the same chapter of Stobaeus) is also involved ('L'homme est le plus chetif' = πάντων ζῷον ἀθλιώτατον ἄνθρωπος). It is noteworthy that this poem is immediately preceded in Ronsard's *Bocage* of 1554 by his imitation, in *A Jan Nicot*, of the Anacreontic φύσις κέρατα ταύροις on the gifts of Nature to the animals.
[151]It would be hard to explain why Ronsard has given 'Si quelcun par la rue passe plus grand que nous' for ἂν εἴπῃ κακῶς, which Baïf correctly renders 'par un seul mot. . . .' Ronsard also omits the dream in the next line.
[152]Morphos, *Dialogues*, p. 95. The Greek original is identified by Morphos, who further compares later phrases in 'Baïf's' speech with Philemon, fragm. 93 and Menander, fragm. 534.

ture leur presente, sans qu'aucune trouve mauvais ce que l'autre faict, comme nous faisons pour la fantasticque opinion que nous avons conçeüe des choses honnestes et deshonnestes, du vice et de la vertu: au moien de quoy nous sommes assugetiz à une infinité de loix qui nous font vivre miserables; car sans telles sottes opinions, toutes choses seroient indifferentes, san que personne fust condamne pour aucun forfaict, ny reprins pour aucune faute.'

And implying that the beasts who live by nature are peaceful in their kinds, he quotes the first four verses given above from Ronsard's *Odelette à Panjas* (Menander, fragm. 534). Thus, as a poet, 'Baïf' starts the discussion with poetry; 'Aubert,' as becomes a lawyer and orator, similarly opens the argument of the second dialogue (that the law, based on our shifting notions of right and wrong, is worthless) with a sustained rhetorical panegyric of the animals—mostly a series of apostrophes with anaphora: 'Vous n'avez aucunes lois. . . . Vous n'avez jamais pensé les moiens de faire la guerre les uns contre les autres. . . . Vous n'avez jamais entretenu des advocats.'[153]

We might infer that Bruès wrote from knowledge in making Baïf show familiarity with Menander, frag. 223, in 1557, and also that he did him no wrong in attributing to him a bias toward scepticism. These inferences may be just; but meanwhile we remain ignorant of the dates of Baïf's *Vie des Chams* and his poem to Mauru. Both may well be later than 1557.[154] Certainly Ronsard's elegy to Robert de la Haye is later than the *Dialogues*.[155] It begins with the same first sentence of Menander, fragm. 223, that Bruès gives to 'Baïf' (though Ronsard clearly knows the original) and embodies an attitude not far from that of the *Dialogues*: the animals are better off than we, who suffer chiefly from our Reason (and this part of the poem is clearly what interests the poet); but La Haye's ethical and religious counsel has saved Ronsard from his passions and from despair (145–48). The poem passes, somewhat abruptly, from a sceptical to a Stoic and

[153]Morphos, *Dialogues*, pp. 185–86. The argument is allowed to die out as irrelevant (p. 197) but recurs (*Dial.* 3., p. 258).

[154]Morphos, *Dialogues*, pp. 72; 81–82, says ideas expressed by 'Baïf' in the *Dialogues* are not representative of the poet, who was not 'inclined to philosophical speculations.' Neither his previous nor subsequent works, according to Morphos, reflect Bruès' ideas. Nicolas de Neuville, to whom the *Vie des Chams* was dedicated, was Seigneur de Villeroy. His father had been *secrétaire des finances,* and the charge came to Neuville in 1559 when he was twenty-four. He kept it for nearly half a century, honored by successive sovereigns. See P. Lévis-Mirepois, *Les Guerres de Religion* (Paris, 1950), pp. 179–81. It is perhaps unlikely that Baïf dedicated the poem to Neuville before 1559.

[155]Published in 1560, it contains (v. 141) a reference to the death of Henri II in July 1559.

religious attitude. The lines disparaging Reason (31–80) may be compared with those quoted above from Baïf's *Vie des Chams*:

> De tous les animaux le plus lourd animal,
> C'est l'homme, le subject d'infortune et de mal.
> Toutesfois à l'ouir discrettement parler
> Vous diriés que soubdain au ciel il doit voller,
> Tant il faict en parlant de la beste entendue,
> Ignorant que les dieux luy ont trop cher vendue
> Cette pauvre raison, qui malheureux le fait,
> D'autant que par sus tous il s'estime parfaict.
> Cette pauvre raison le conduict à la guerre, . . .
> Luy apprent les mestiers dont il n'avoit besoing,
> Et comme d'un poinçon l'aiguillonne de soing:
> Et pour trop raisonner miserable il demeure,
> Sans se pouvoir garder qu'à la fin il ne meure:
> Au contraire les cerfs qui n'ont point de raison,
> Les poissons, les oiseaux, sont sans comparaison
> Trop plus heureux que nous, qui sans soing et sans peine
> Errent de tous costez où le plaisir les meine:
> Ils boivent de l'eau clere, et se paissent du fruict
> Que nostre mere grand d'elle-mesme a produict.

Pliny perhaps is still in the background; his version of the topic also turns on the contrast between human pretensions and human weakness. But his phrase, Nature exacts 'a high price' for her benefits, has been distorted to mean 'a high price' for Reason—Baïf: 'que par trop cher elle nous a vendue'; Ronsard: 'que les dieux luy ont trop cher vendue'; and Montaigne (calling it 'imagination,' but meaning the same): 'un advantage que luy est bien cher vendu.'[156] Montaigne's attitude in the *Apologie* has with good cause been carried back to the circle of Bruès.[157] Man dislikes to be counted among the animals, preferring to hear himself called a second God— 'tant nous sommes plus jaloux de nostre interest que de celuy de nostre Createur.'[158] And Ronsard similarly concludes this part of his elegy with the thought that if we would but realize that we have no wings to fly up to heaven, we would live 'contans de la terre, et

[156]Earlier in the *Apologie*, Montaigne with some irony places reason among our 'imaginary' goods, while the animals are assigned the 'essential' goods, 'peace, security, innocence, health' (2.12.184).
[157]Morphos, *Dialogues*, p. 81; Boas, *Happy Beast*, p. 45.
[158]*Essais* 2.12.209. After this time, the disparagement of human reason becomes rather closely attached to the theme of the well-equipped animals; see the writers cited by Boas, *Happy Beast*: Estienne Pasquier, *Lettres* 10.1 (p. 53); Pierre Charron, *De la Sagesse* 1.8 (p. 59); Mme Deshoulières, *Les Moutons* and *La Solitude* (pp. 147–52).

des traces humaines' (77–83). Man, who now 'se fait la guerre luimesmes à luimesme,' might thus recapture some of the peace of the peaceful animals or of the Golden Age, for 'cette pauvre raison le conduict a la guerre,' into which we enter (*Exhort.* 122)

Enflez de trop d'orgueil ou de trop de raisons.

Encomium Pacis: Topics

The absence of any true cult of Eirene or Pax-Concordia in antiquity left the praises of peace, when sung at all, as by Bacchylides and Aristophanes, unconventionalized and without the ordered topics of a true hymn. For the Roman poets, peace was a subject associated with praise of the Empire and the Emperor—as in Horace, *Carm.* 4.5; it is impossible to list all the Horatian echoes—and the topics for the commendation of peace, though now sufficiently conventionalized, were not—at least in the extant literature—organized as an encomium of Peace herself. The nearest we get to this is Tibullus 1.10, which does indeed seem to reflect a hymn to Peace. In prose, as we have noted, the case is otherwise, and a rhetorical scheme for the encomium of peace existed, with topics on the whole different from the poets' topics. The rhetoricians' topics are derived from the philosophical treatises (Stoic), the poet's from the earlier poets and from the symbols and cult of the empire. The case remained much the same under Christianity, prose discourses such as that of St. Augustine (*De civ. D.* 19) deriving from the philosophical-rhetorical tradition, poetical expressions about peace, in hymns for example, more from the poets and from the empire cult transferred to the Prince of Peace.

It is perhaps only with the Renaissance, when abounding national consciousness met with a renewal of ancient rhetoric (and the two are closely associated) that we find the topics for the praise of peace organized in a formal manner in poetry; for the Renaissance, though professing to admire the ejaculations of the *furor poeticus*, was rather too deeply schooled by logic and rhetoric ever to give way to it entirely. The recipe for an encomium as set out by Menander and Aphthonius was rather simple: after the exordium, give the honorable descent or derivation of your subject, detail his beneficial acts, and end with an invocation. This is practically the recipe for the ancient hymn, and Aphthonius notes that encomium and hymn differ only in that the hymn is addressed to a god. Thus, for example, in Milton's hymns to Melancholy and Cheerfulness he details their honorable birth, lists their effects, and ends with an invocation.

Ronsard was conscious of these rules (as well as being a close student of the form of actual hymns), and, for example, in *La Paix, au Roy* 49 announces his intention: 'D'une si belle Paix je veux chanter merveille,' after which words he begins with the cosmic beneficence of Peace in ordering the elements and comes down to the blessings of human and political peace. So also Baïf begins his *Hymne* (Marty-Laveaux 2.224), 'Ie veu louer la Paix, c'est la Paix que je chante,' and proceeds in the same way with Peace ordering the elements and eventually blessing mankind. Ronsard's *Exhortation* is a much more elaborate composition, but the last part is formally a hymn or encomium, though without *exordium* or genealogy, giving only beneficent acts and the final invocation.

195 La Paix premierement composa ce grand monde,
 La paix mist l'air, le feu, toute la terre, & l'onde
 En paisible amitié, & la paix querella
 Au Chaos le discord, & le chassa delà
 Pour accorder ce tout, la paix fonda les villes,
200 La paix fertilisa les campaignes sterilles
 La paix de soubs le joug fist mugir les toreaux,
 La paix dedans les prez fist sauter les troupeaux,
 La paix sur les coutaux tira droit à la ligne
 Les ordres arengez de la premiere vigne:
205 De raisins empamprez Bacche elle environna,
 Et le chef de Ceres de fourment couronna,
 Elle enfla tout le sein de la belle Pomonne
 D'abondance de fruitz que nous produit l'Autonne,
 Elle défaroucha de nos premiers Ayeux
210 Les cuers rudes & fiers, & les fist gracieux,
 Et d'un peuple vaguant es bois à la fortune
 Dedans les grans cités en fist une commune.
  Donc, Paix fille de Dieu, vueille toy souvenir,
 Si je t'invoque à gré, maintenant de venir
215 Rompre l'ire des Rois, & pour l'honneur de celle
 Que Jesus Christ a faitte au monde universelle
 Entre son Pere et nous, repousse de ta main

Appendix

Loing des peuples Chretiens, le Discord inhumain
Qui les tient acharnez, & veuilles de ta grace
A jamais nous aymer, & toute notre race.

So intent now is Ronsard on the topics of an encomium that he runs into a contradiction, as Laumonier notes, between what he says in vv. 209–12: 'Elle defaroucha . . . Et d'un peuple en fist une commune,' and what he had said in praise of primitive life in vv. 147–52: 'Qu' heureux fut le gent . . . erroit de toutes pars / Par les bois assuree, et du fruit de la terre / En commun se paissoit.' In his devotion to ancient commonplaces, the poet has run afoul of the ancient quarrel of 'soft' and 'hard' primitivism, or 'the Golden Age' and the 'Growth of Civilization'—one may take two views of living on acorns, but hardly in the same poem.[1]

In the present essay, however, our purpose is not to study the rhetorical arrangement, but the substance of these poems, and in the remainder of this section we shall look at a number of the common topoi and their background in literature.

1. *Peace among the Elements.* This first and greatest among the common topics we shall not attempt to discuss in detail here, since we have studied it in connection with Ronsard's *Ode de la Paix* (above, Ch. VII), where it plays a major role. Laumonier rightly enough refers to the *Ode* in his notes on *Exhortation* 199. One or two observations must suffice. This is a topic of the ancient philosophical and rhetorical tradition about peace, and not at all a topic of the ancient poetical tradition of the praise of peace.[2] In the prose tradition, it duly appears in Erasmus' *Bellum* and *Querela*, and in the *Oratio . . . de pace* of Louis Le Roy. In the Renaissance Latin poems that we have noticed, this topic does not yet appear, and so far as my collections go (which may not be very far), Ronsard's splendid *Ode* of 1550 is the first poem on peace to include it. However that may be, it becomes at this time one of the regular topics. Du Bellay includes it in his *Discours sur la Trefve* of 1555:[3]

> J'irois avec Ascrée en Parnasse songer
> Cent mille inventions pour blasmer la Discorde,

[1]See Lovejoy-Boas, pp. 7ff.
[2]For the topic, see Fuchs, *Augustin*, Index, s.v. 'Elements,' 'Weltall.' For my distinction above, note that the topic of the ordering of the elements does of course appear in ancient poetry and may be described as *concordia* and even *pax*, and Pax may even be its agent (Ovid, *Met.* 1.25); but in the poets the intention and the context are always concerned with the nature of the cosmos and not with the nature of Peace.
[3]*Œuvres poétiques*, Henri Chamard, ed., 6.13.190–97.

Et louer ceste-la qui les Princes accorde,
La Paix fille de Dieu, nourrice des humains,
Qui forma ce grand Tout, et de ses propres mains
Debrouilla le Caos, ou d'une horrible guerre
Ensemble combattoient le feu, l'onde, la terre,
Et cest autre element qui nous faict respirer.

In the *Exhortation* (above) it is succinctly stated; in *La Paix, au Roy*
53ff. it is extended in a fairly close paraphrase of Ovid *Met.* 1.5–30
(as noted by Laumonier). Baïf, as aforesaid, elaborates it in his
Hymne de la Paix. Belleau also places it first among the *beneficia*:

Ie te salue, ô Repos eternel,
De l'univers l'alliance première,
Qui debrouille la confuse matière, . . .
Et suspendis de main industrieuse
La pesanteur des plus Elemens.

2. *Discord*. The opponent of Peace or Concordia is Discordia, and
the opposition between them may be viewed either transcendentally
or on the human plane. When the ancients describe the universe as
a *concordia discors* (that is, a 'warring peace'), they generally, though
not always, leave the impression that the tension amounts to a har-
mony that will last and that demands our admiration. My impression
is that the Renaissance poets dwell more than the ancients on Discor-
dia and fear it more. The idea is frequent in Ronsard, who is con-
scious of 'la tendance de l'Univers à toujours glisser vers l'anarchie,'
and that 'son harmonieuse ordonnance n'est jamais définitivement
acquis, mais toujours conquise par les vertus providentielles de
Dieu.'[4] In Ronsard's *Ode* 78, 'l'horrible Dieu de violence' (Discord)
has like Peace a place beside the throne of God (a difficult concept!),
but in *Paix* 75–76, 'Elle fist ataches à cent chaines de fer / Le mal-
heureux Discord aux abysmes d'Enfer,' where Discord recalls Satan,
and this is the usual concept (cf. Belleau, *Chant pastoral*, 'C'est toy
[Paix] qui tiens en cent chaisnes d'airain / L'Inimitié, le Discord et la
Guerre.' Buttet, *Oeuvres* 2.127: 'Lors Bellone en aspre furie, / . . .
Aux grands abimes des enfers, / Trebuchant, pour jamais descend.'
Grévin, *Chant de Ioie*, sta. 20: 'chasse l'orgueilleuse Eryne Eryne,' and
sta. 29; 'Puisse tu mener Bellone / Captifve.' Discord appears as War
on the human plane. The chaining of Discord or War is often an
echo of Virgil, *Aen.* 1.293ff.:

[4]Albert-Marie Schmidt, *La Poésie scientifique*, pp. 86–87.

Appendix

dirae ferro et compagibus artis
claudentur Belli portae; Furor impius intus
saeva sedens super arma et centum vinctus aënis
post tergum nodis fremet horridus ore cruento.

Cf. Calpurnius 1.47–50:

Post tergum Bellona manus spoliataque telis
In sua vesanos torquebit viscera morsus . . .
Omnia Tartareo subigentur carcere bella
Immergentque caput tenebris.

So Zanchi, *Hymnus*, sub fin.:

Sub te ferratos belli Concordia postes
Effringet. . . .
Ipsa sinu scissaque gemens Discordia palla
Cocyti stagna alta petet violentaque bella
Involuetque Chao atque Erebi pallentibus umbris.

The Renaissance poets seem to have little direct memory of the triumph of Pax over Discordia in Prudentius' *Psychomachia*, where Discordia, like Pax/Concordia also has her 'Comites'—Metus, Labor, Vis, Scelus, Fraus (*Psych.* 604ff.). Frequently Discordia, with her synonymous companions, figures in the triumphal processions of Peace. Graphaeus (*DPB* 2.496) lists her among the 'Comites' of Mars, and, 2.498, describes her captive: '*Discordia*, vinctis / A tergo manibus, per terram in pulvere plantis / Antrorsum versis trahitur gemebunda, furorem / Antiquium eructans.' Cf. J. Secundus, *De pace Cameraci*: 'Ergo, age Pauperies . . . Fames . . . Cura Luctusque . . . Mors, / Ite per extremas gentes . . . ;' and again: 'I procul . . . Mars ferrea Ditis ad umbras. / Aufer . . . Furias . . . / Te Bellona . . . teque hinc Discordia demens / Proripe . . . et Ira.' Ronsard, *Chant de liesse* 25–28: 'Tu [Henri II] as lié de cent chaines de fer / Le cruel Mars aux abysmes d'enfer, / Et la Discorde, Enyon, et Bellone / Par ton moyn n'offencent plus personne.'

3. *Peace, the daughter of God.* In *Exhort.* 213, Ronsard invokes 'Paix fille de Dieu,' as also in *Paix*, 237–38: Dieu . . . Paix sa fille vous donne,' and 247: 'O Paix fille de Dieu.' In Belleau's *Chant* 1–2 the expression is redoubled: 'Ie te salue, ô Paix fille de Dieu, / Fille de Dieu.' Des Autels, *Paix venue*, sig. D: Jupiter addresses her: 'fille m'amie . . . ma chère fille Paix;' later, sig. E2, she is 'O fille de Themis' (her birth from Themis by Jupiter at beginning of poem).

Buttet *Ode, Œuvres* 2.122, begins with this phrase: 'Fille de Dieu, des peuples mère' (cf. 2.129: 'La grande fille de Themis'). Du Bellay already has the phrase in his *Discours* of 1555 *(De pace inter principes Christianos ineunda)* where Chamard refers to Marot, *Cantique de la Chrestienté* (1538): 'Paix la belle, humble fille de Dieu.' Jean de La Taille, *Remonstrance (Œuv.*2.xvii): 'O grand Dieu, . . . Envoye-nous, O Sire, / Ta fille qui est paix.' Compare also *Epitre . . . touchant l'armée du Roy en Heynaut* (Marot, *Œuvres,* Jannet 1.145): 'la tressacrée fille de Jesus-Christ, nommée Paix.' But as we have seen, Alain Chartier already ascribes this parentage to Peace: 'Paix eureuse fille du Dieu des dieux.'[5] Possibly Marot may have taken the phrase from Alain Chartier, and the Latin poets have taken it from Marot; but more probably wider search would find it in common use. It belongs, in fact, to the theological aspects of peace. Cornelius Graphaeus, in his poem on the Peace of Aigues-Mortes (above, p. 86), has the precise Latin equivalent; God says to Pax: 'Surge age, Nata,' and later, 'Oscula dat Natae.'[6] Cesarini[7] later (1623): 'Pax ardor Superum, Coeli mitissima proles.' Hence Antoine de Baïf, reflecting on the peace of the universe as equivalent to (Empedoclean) Love, varies the expression to 'La fille d'Amitié.'[8] The Pléiade were well aware that in Hesiod (*Theog.* 902) Eirene is the daughter of Zeus: Εὐνομίην τε Δίκην τε καὶ Εἰρήνην τεθαλυῖαν, but it is unlikely that this knowledge affected their use of a phrase that came to them in the mediaeval tradition clothed with philosophical and theological meaning. The Son of God is also Peace. But more of these topics in another place.

4. *Peace Descends from Heaven.* Whether called the daughter of God or not, her natural abode is in heaven, whence the poets entreat her to descend. This topic has philosophical and theological implications as well. It also means that she has withdrawn thither, as we shall see below. Eustache Deschamps (*Œuvres* 4.118): 'Dieu envoya la paix du ciel en terre / Quant il tramist son fils pour les humains.' Marot, *Cantique* (*Œuvres* 2.105): 'Approche toy, Charles, . . . Approche toy, Françoys, . . . pour tirer Paix, la tant desirée, Du ciel tràshault, là où s'est retirée.' This parallel with Aristophanes' Peace, who has also withdrawn to heaven, and is to be brought down by the peace hero Trygaeus, seems close, but is probably accidental. When

[5]Above, p. 64. Cf. Nesson's answering description of Guerre as 'engendré du felon Lucifer.'
[6]*DPB* 2.481–82.
[7]*CPI.* 3.9.
[8]*L'Hymne de la Paix* in *Euvres* 2.224 and 225.

in Ronsard's *Ode* (1550), Peace withdraws to heaven, it is in recompense for her work as Creator; and similarly in *Paix*, 77–78, after chaining Discord: 'Puis au throne de Dieu, . . . Alla prendre sa place, où elle se repose.' With the modern poets the theological sense is always near at hand. Zanchi begins:

> O quae Coelicum sedes, quae lucida templa
> Prima tenes, prima ante omnes fulgentia cernis
> Ora Dei, totoque nites pulcherrima coelo
> Huc aditum, Pax alma, feras . . .

Cf. Secundus, *De pace Cameraci*: 'Prodit ab astrifero, tandem, optissima coelo, / Laureola placidos Pax redimita comas;' Graphàeus (*DPB* 2.479): 'Optatam Genitor Pacem demittit Olympo'; Capilupi: 'revocastis alto ab / Aethere Pacem; Alma Pax . . . veniens Olympo;' Coquillart, *Ballade* (Le Roux de Lincy, *Chants* 1.402): 'Du ciel sont cheutes ces plaisantes images.' La Taille, *Remonstrance* (*Œuvres* 2.xix), of Henri II: 'Il avoit bien du ciel en naissant amenée / La Paix.' Buttet (*Œuvres* 2.122) recognizes that Peace has left the world: 'Puis au ciel, en majesté grand, / T'allas près de ton père assoir' (cf. Ronsard, *Ode* of 1550, 1.75–76); and hence constantly entreats her to descend: 'Partant du ciel . . . Lance ta grand' force' (2.126), and 'Descend, descend, ô paix heureuse' (2.130).

5. *Saturnian Themes.* Thus Peace is in heaven because she withdrew thither (with Dike and Astraea) at the end of the Golden Age (the first age in Hesiod, *Erga* 110–25), having in that bright dawn prevailed among mankind; so Marot: 'là où s'est retirée.' Buttet (2.124), introduces perhaps a novel idea: that if war continues, heaven will destroy us and 'douera un siècle nouveau' (cf. Ronsard, *Exhort.* below [Mother Earth angry]). Des Autels, *Paix venue*, sig. E3: 'Tu fais en ces beaux jours finir l'age de fer, / Ramenant la vertu au monde que tu dores: / Pour faire voir le temps Saturnien encores.' Pujol, *De pace* sig. A2 and also sig. C: 'O quanto melius Saturno rege tenente / Vivebant homines,' and so on. We have discussed Saturnian themes in the Renaissance peace poems above, Ch. VI.

6. *The Companions of Peace.* Peace is always in company, since Hesiod, with Eunomia and Dike. She is entreated to bring along with her a number of companions whose personalities express the gifts expected from her. The Greek Eirene is regularly accompanied by Ploutos the god of wealth, whose nurse she is said to be; but this god is lacking to the Roman poets whom the Renaissance mainly follows. These poets also place Astraea among the companions of

Peace, presumably on the basis of Virgil, *Ecl.* 4.6: 'Iam redit et Virgo, redeunt Saturnia regna.'[9] A conspectus of these *comites* may be had from the following quotations: Virgil, *Aen.* 2.292: 'cana Fides et Vesta, Remo cum fratre Quirinus / iura dabunt;' Horace, *Carm. saec.* 57–60: 'Iam Fides et Pax et Honor Pudorque / Priscis et neclecta redire Virtus / Audet, apparetque beata pleno / Copia cornu;' *Carm.* 4.5.18–19: 'Nutrit rura Ceres almaque Faustitas;' Petronius, *Carm. de bel. civ.* 229ff: 'Pax, Fides, Iustitia, Concordia;' Juvenal, 1.116: 'Pax, Fides, Victoria, Concordia;' Martial, 12.6: 'Recta Fides, hilaris Clementia, cauta Potestas iam redeunt;' Claudian, *In Ruf.* 1.51–53: 'En aurea nascitur aetas / en proles antiqua redit, Concordia, Virtus / cumque Fide Pietas alta cervice vagantur.'

The Renaissance poets follow suit, with some tendency to extend the list. Secundus, *De pace Cameraci*: 'Sunt comites . . . Astraea . . . incorrupta Fides . . . et vos Pierii turba novena chori . . . Phoebus . . . Mercurio coecus cum duce Plutus adest'—here for once actually alluding to the blind Wealth of Aristophanes' *Plutus*. Secundus also includes Amor. Torrentius, *DPB* 4.438: 'Tuque alma Pallas . . . Bacche . . . Ceresque, Nymphae . . . Satyri'; Marot, *Cantique* (2.107) also invokes Pallas. Zanchi (*CPI* 11.427) mentions Concordia, Ceres, Liber, and Pomona, and adds: 'Te Pax Pietas, te cana Fides, Astraeaque virgo . . . comitantur.' Ronsard, *Exhort.* 205–7 mentions Bacchus, Ceres, and Pomona, though not precisely as companions; Belleau, *Chant* 3: 'La belle Astrée, et Themis la chenue'; Baïf, *Hymne* (2.225): 'Et Ceres et Bacchus et Palès et Pomone / Font que parmy les chams grand planté foisone . . . / Et le gentil Amour.' André (*DPG* 1.69): 'Mox honor et Cereri prior et reddetur Iaccho.' Cesarini (*CPI* 3.9): 'Quaecumque . . . felici Copia cornu / It comes . . . Ceres / Te sequitur Bacchus.' Des Autels, *Paix venue* (sig. D): Astrée, Graces, Concorde, Amalthée, and two Hymenées, called (sig. E2) 'ta compagnie.'

7. *Nature Flourishes.* As one of the Horae, Eirene κουροτρόφος shares in the character of a vegetation deity, and is often associated with Demeter and Dionysus, and Pax with her cornucopia retains this power; where she comes, the hillsides are clothed with vines and the plains with corn, and from the Golden Age she brings with her a breath of its *Ver perpetuum*. This spontaneous effect of her approach is something more than the association of peace with agricultural

[9]Aratus, *Phaen.* 96 identifies Astraea with Hesiod's Dike, who quits mankind at the end of the first Age (*Erga* 110–25); cf. Virgil, *Georg.* 2.473 and Ovid, *Fasti* 1.249, where she is Justitia. Martianus Capella 2.174, identifies Astraea with Themis and Eryone (as does Belleau, *Chant*, 3).

Appendix

plenty (see below No. 8), and allies her also with Aphrodite, under whose feet, too, the earth bursts into bloom. Yet the concepts merge, and divine spontaneity is coupled with the simple fact that in peace there is opportunity for farming in such expressions as that of Tibullus (1.10.45–47): 'Pax arva colit . . . Pax aluit vites et sucos condidit uvae,' and in Ronsard's imitation (*Exhort.* 200–208): 'La paix fertilisa les campaignes stériles, . . . Elle enfle tout le sein de la belle Pomonne / D'abondance de fruitz.' Her purely divine effect is like that of the sun. So Horace (*Carm.* 4.5.6–8) sees the approach of the peace hero Augustus: 'Lucem redde tuae, dux bone, patriae: / Instar veris enim voltus ubi tuos / Adfulsit populo, gratior it dies / Et soles melius nitent.'[10]

The Renaissance poets, responding to the mediaeval tradition of Natura, take even more readily to this concept. Mantuan: 'Gramina pace virent . . .' Buttet (2.128: 'Puis l'abondance prospere / Commence des thresors verser / A la tout-engendrante mere.' Capilupi (*De pace*, sta. 3): 'Cuncta sed jam te redeunte rident, / Cuncta mutantur, viret ipsa tellus, / Enitent fontes fluvii, lacusque / Et salis undae. Tu, velut sol aetheris, refulges.' Des Autels, *Paix venue*, sig. E2: 'Tu fais en arrivant reverdir les forests, / Les roses et les lis, le thim, la marjoleine / Naissent à ta venue.' So Torrentius (*DPB* 4.439), of the approach of Pax and her comites: 'Aprica laeti visite pascua; / Ut vestra tellus numina sentiat / Et summa dehinc frugum novarum / Copia fertilitate mira.' Hence these poets easily assimilate Peace in this function to the Venus of Lucretius, and do so justly, since this goddess already has the character of the Stoic Physis or Natura, fostering spontaneous growth, and as Empedoclean Love wins her counterpart, Strife, to peace: 'Alma Venus . . . quae terras frugiferentis concelebras . . . te, dea, te fugiunt venti, te nubila caeli / adventumque tuum . . . tibi suavis daedala tellus / summittit flores, tibi rident aequore ponti / . . . aeriae primum volucres . . . perculsae corda tua vi; / inde ferae pecudes persultant pabula laeta . . . / effice ut interea fera moenera militiai / per maria ac terras omnis sopita quiescant, / nam tu sola potes tranquilla pace iuvare / mortalis.' So Zanchi, of Peace (*CPI* 11.427): 'Adventuque tuo laetanti daedala tellus / E gremio iam fundit opes.' And Ronsard (*Paix*, 178–83) of the approach of Peace: 'Et tout qui habite / D'écaillé dans la mere, . . . / Tout ce qui vit en terre, et les legers oiseau, / . . . Sont tous remplis

[10]Cf. Capilupi, sta. 4: 'Tu [Peace], velut sol aetheris, refulges'; Belleau (1.189): 'Le clair Soleil . . . / Nous monstre . . . / Le grand plaisir qu'il reçoit de te [Peace] voir;' Andre (*DPG* 1.69): 'Omnia rident; / Sol quoque, tam nitida qui lustrat lampade terras.'

d'amour, et par luy s'entretiennent.'[11] Belleau (*Chant de la Paix*, p. 189–90): 'Donc que lon voye, à ton heureux retour, / Rire les champs, verdoyer les campagnes, / Le ciel sans nue . . . Et qu'en marchant à l'ombre de tes pas / Le sein fecond de la terre florisse / . . . Et le doux miel pleuve tousjours làbas / . . . Si que le ciel et la terre engrossée / Soit à iamais d'un eternel printemps.' Béreau, *Ecl. X* (*Œuvres* p. 86): 'La nature, voiez, plus joieuse met hors / De tous ses cabinets ses plus riches trésors / . . . Oiseletz par les bois ceci chantent et crient, / Sauvages animaux en sautent et en rient . . . toute chose à l'envy, qui prend sa nourriture / Dessus la terre mere, et dedans la closture / Des navigables eaux, . . . / S'esjouist du bon heur qu'est ceste paix donnant.' Elie André (*DPG* 1.69): 'Omnia recta vigent passim, passim omnia rident; / Sol quoque tam nitida qui lustrat lampade terras. / Ipsae adeo volucres dulci nunc aëra cantu / Permulcent.' Cesarini (*CPI* 3.9): 'Quaecumque ingrederis felici Copia cornu / It comes,' [etc., cf. Horace]. Though Lucretius seems in this topic to be the chief influence, a Saturnian strain is also sometimes heard, mediated by Virgil's fourth *Eclogue*. The effects described by Béreau above make him hope 'qu'en usage / Quelque traces bien tost du Saturnien age / Doibvent recommencer sous le regne puissant / D'Henry . . . / Encores de leur gré produyront les campagnes / Le froment nourricier, encores des montagnes / Heureux fleuves de laict et de vin couleront, / Et les chesnes encor le roux miel sueront' (Cf. Virgil, *Ecl.* 4.28–30).

8. *Celebrations and Revels.* We turn from the divine nature of Peace to her beneficent effects on mankind. When she comes, first of all there are celebrations. This topic is in all the poems. Already for Bacchylides (above, Ch. V), peace is a time when the streets are thronged with lovely banquets and the hymns to youth are blazing, and Euripides looks for 'the songs of lovely choirs and garlanded revels.' Such celebrations are enacted by the choir in Aristophanes' *Acharnians* and by Trygaeus and his friends in the *Peace*. 'When peace comes,' says Dio Chrysostom (*Or.* 38.19), 'we wear garlands, make sacrifices, and hold high holidays' (ἐπειδὰν εἰρήνη γένηται, καὶ στεφανούμεθα καὶ θύομεν καὶ ἑορτάζομεν). For the Roman such revelry is less spontaneous, but officially acknowledged in secular games or in the Pacalia (Ovid, *Fasti* 1.709–22). No literary tradition, however, is needed for this topic. Jean Regnier (Ed. Droz p. 73): 'Ilz dansoient / Et chantoient / Et rioient.' Marot, *Cantique* (2.107): 'Que

[11]So already, *Ode de la Paix* 314–18 (Laumonier 3.24): 'Les bestes sentent ta puissance / Alechés de ton doux amer; / De l'air la vagabonde troupe / T'obeist, et celle qui coupe / Le plus creus ventre de la mer.'

sur le soir l'un et l'autre pays / Reluyre tout de beaulx feux de liesse, / Pour le retour de Paix, noble déesse.' Graphaeus' whole *Gratulatio* is an immense Pompa (*DPB* 2.480): 'Se totum in lusus et publica gaudia mundus / Solvat et insolitas sonet undiique plausibus aether.' (2.499ff.) 'Ita domum laeti et chara cum coniuge, charis / cum natis, cum vicinis, hanc . . . celebrate diem / . . . primum Baccho spumantia ponam / Pocula . . . / Ad Pacis numeros potabo strenuus amplos / (quamquam inconsuetus, quamquam natura repugnet / Me namque haud fecit gracilis natura bibacem) . . .' Ronsard, *Ode* 341ff: 'En lieu du fer outrageus, . . . Tu nous rameines les jeus, / Le bel, et l'amour des Dames'; *Paix* 173–74: 'On chante, on saute, on rid par les belles preries, / On fait tournois, festins, masques, et mommeries'; cf. *Chant de liesse* 35–90; Buttet (*Œuvres* 2.128): 'Haut au ciel montent feux de joie / . . . Toute l'Europe . . . / Déborde en triomphes'; Grévin, *Chant de Ioie* sta. 17–18: music, bonfires, marriages, love. Béreau (*Œuvres* p. 85): 'Jeux, dances et festins . . . en village, / Et non plus de canons;' Baïf, *Hymne* (*Euvres* 2.225): 'Sous l'ombrage lon voit s'egaïer en la dance,' and so on; André (*DPG* 1.69): 'Mollia succedunt duris convivia pugnis.' Ronsard, *Paix*, 63–64: 'On n'oit plus les canons horriblement tonner, / Mais la lyre et le luth doucement resonner.'[12] Béreau (p. 84): 'La France . . . pour la trompette / Repandra le flageol et la douce musette'; (p. 85): 'De musique on oira resonner le village, Et non plus de canons qui souloient étonner / Tout le monde.' The popular poet emphasizes this topic; Guillaume Coquillart: 'Que tous nous deux sont au jour d'uy muez / En joyes et chants, en plaisirs et en jeu, / Par ces troys dames lesquelles cy voyez: / C'est France et Flandre et la Paix entre deux.'[13] Anon., in a dialogue between La Paix and La France (1578): 'Sus, bon temps, qu'on se resveille, / Il 'nest plus temps de dormir, / Qu'on reveille la bouteille / Qui nous fait tant resjouir.' Drinking is a regular σημεῖον of the revels of Peace. So Horace, *Carm.* 4.5.31: 'Hinc ad vina redit,' and 37–40: 'Longas o utinam, dux bone, ferias / Praestes Hesperiae!' dicimus integro / Sicci mane die, dicimus uvidi, / Cum sol Oceano subest.' Torrentius (*DPB* 4.439): 'qua [corona] cinctus, inter vina sodalium / Nulli molestus . . . / Possem aureae cantare pacis / Multa bona.' It remained for Malherbe to give this topic classical expression in an immortal strophe:[14]

[12]Ovid, *Fasti*, 1.716: 'Canteturque fera nil nisi pompa tuba.'
[13]*Ballade quand on cria la paix à Reims* (1482), Le Roux de Lincy, *Chants* 1.402.
[14]*Ode a la Reine mere du Roy, sur les heureux succez de sa regence* (1611). In *Les Poésies*, ed. J. Lavand (Paris, 1936), 1.83, sta. xi, p. 87.

C'est en paix que toutes choses
Succedent selon nos desirs:
Comme au printemps naissent les roses,
En la paix naissent les plaisirs;
Elle met les pompes aux villes,
Donne aux champs les moissons fertilles,
Et de la majesté des lois
Appuyent les pouvoirs suprêmes,
Fait demeurer les diadèmes
Ferme sur la teste des Rois.

9. *Laws and Good Customs Restored.* Malherbe, in the lines just quoted, has not only bestowed a classical phrasing upon the topics of peace, but has classically selected the central topics—'plaisirs' and 'pompes,' 'moissons,' and 'la majesté des lois.' This last, which he significantly associates with the security of kings, is par excellence a topic of the Roman poets of the *pax Romana.* To be sure, the Greek poets know the theme—Stobaeus, Aristophanes, Isocrates—and all goes back to Hesiod's association of Dike, Eunomia, and Eirene.

But the restoration of peace, of law, and of good *mores* was exactly the program of Augustus and exactly answered to the deepest ideals of the Roman character.[15] The Roman poets supporting Augustus' reforms, and those who followed, never forgot the lesson. Augustus' work is summed up neatly in a passage of Velleius Paterculus (2.89): 'Revocata pax, sopitus ubique armorum furor, restituta vis legibus, indiciis auctoritas, . . . prisca illa et antiqua rei publicae forma renovata, rediit cultus agris, sacris honos, securitas hominibus; certa cuique rerum suarum possessio.' Horace, in the poem to Augustus which we quote so often (*Carm.* 4.5.22): 'Mos et lex maculosum edomuit nefas, / Laudantur simili prole puerperae, / Culpam poena premit comes.' So Ovid, *Met.* 15.832–34: 'Pace data terris animum ad civilia vertet / *iura* suum *leges*que feret iustissimus auctor / exemploque suo *mores* reget.' Later, the early hopes of Nero's reign evoke similar expressions from Calpurnius Siculus (*Ecl.* 1.70–73): 'Nec vacuos . . . fasces et inane tribunal / Accipiet consul; sed legibus omne reductis / Ius aderit moremque fori vultumque priorem / Reddet.' On Roman coins of the empire the figure of Pax is hardly distinguishable from that of Justitia. We have noted the emphasis given to this topic for Christian writers by certain biblical passages, notably *Isa.* 32.17, 'Justitiae opus pax,' and Ps. 85.11: 'Justitia et pax

---

[15]'Leges, iura und pax bilden die Einheit der römischen Kultur,' Hans Christ, *Die römische Weltherrschaft,* p. 112. I have profited from Christ's wealth of quotations.

osculatae sunt.' Cassiodorus, *Var.* 1.1: [Tranquillitas] mores excolit.' Rufinus, *De bono pacis* 2.18, 'Pax producit rempublicam . . . condit leges.'

With the modern poets it begins early. Chartier: 'Justice y gardoye . . . Les bons soustenoye, Honneur maintenoye.' Mantuan (291ᵛ): 'Pax aperit iuris iustitiaeque forum,' and 'mores priscae simplicitatis habet.' But, though Erasmus notes of peace 'vigent leges' (*Bellum* 957E) the topic is not expanded by most of our modern Latin poets. Vida (above, Ch. V) remarks on the cessation of vices: 'Simul quiescent furta,' and so on; Graphaeus (*DPB* 2.484) places Libertas, Quies, Iustitia, and Virtus in the triumphal procession of Peace; and finally Cesarini gives the topic full expression (3.9): 'Fas graditur tecum, tibi rident oppida et urbes; / Tu maculosa gravi crimina lege domas. / Justitiam solio pulsam tu reddis eburno: / Illius horrendas instruis ense manus.' The vernacular poets, however, do not forget it. Buttet (*Œuvres* 2.129): 'La justice à tes pieds s'incline'; Ronsard, *Paix*, 147–48: 'La gravité se montre avecques la vertu, / Et par la sainte loy le vice est abatu.' Belleau, *Chant*, p. 190: 'C'est toy qui fais que les bourgs et les villes / Courbent le chef sous le joug de la loy.' Béreau, *Œuvres*, p. 85: 'Le juge vaquera au faict de la police, / Et remettera sus les loix et la justice.' Baïf, *Hymne* (2.225): 'la vertu se nourrit, / le vice est amorty.' Grévin, *Chant*, sta. 25: 'Qu'il [the king] voie souz son empire / Un iustice reluire / avec la saincte Loi / De nostre crestienne foi.' Passerat, *Hymne* (1.98): 'Tu as fondé des lois les antiques cités.'

10. *Divine Cult Restored.* Bacchylides already appears to associate an enriched cult of the gods with the coming of peace. Aristophanes, *Peace* 416 and ff. For Horace (*Carm.* 3.6.1–4) the restoration of the temples is a necessary expiation of the civil wars. Velleius, 2.89 notes the restoration of 'sacris honos.' Calpurnius, *Ecl.* 1.67: 'Pacis opus docuit [Numa] iussitque silentibus armis / Inter sacra tubas, non inter bella, sonare.' The fifteenth-century poets know this topic from the mediaeval religious tradition. Charles d'Orléans, *Prière*, sta. 3., laments that in war the church services are in abeyance; Alain Chartier, *Lay*, notes that in peace 'La foy augmentoye . . .' and in peace 'Les Prestres chantoient'; and Jean Regnier similarly remarks as a sign of peace: 'Les prestres messes chantoient.' The topic is not conspicuous in the Renaissance poets; perhaps as not wholly suited to their antique style, or perhaps as unreal, since religious services are generally not in abeyance during war. Mantuan (291ᵛ): 'Sacris altaria flammis, / Atque tepescentes suscitat igne focos.' Buttet (*Œuvres* 2.128): 'Les temples saints on voie orner,' and 'Le prestre dedans

son église.' André gives the topic an antique turn (*DPG* p. 69): 'Ipse sacrae mystes incumbit purior arae,' where 'purior' perhaps refers to our topic 24 below. Graphaeus sees Religio following Lex in the pomp of Peace (*DPB* 2.489): 'Et sacra Relligio, candenti in veste decora, / Flammantem dextra gladium, clypeumque sinistra / Gestans'—but there is no suggestion of restoration.

11. *Literature and Art*. Euripides (above, Ch. V) already associates literature with peace. In Horace (*Carm.* 3.4.36−40), the Muses refresh Augustus when he has restored his war-weary soldiers to civilian life and seeks to end his labors. Cassiodorus, *Var.* 1.1.: '[Tranquillitas] est enim bonarum artium decora mater.' Rufinus, *De bono pacis* 2.18: 'Pax . . . alit artes.' For Alain Chartier, in peace 'Science y mettoye,' while 'Clercz estudioient,' and similarly Jean Regnier says that in peace 'Les sciences que acqueriez / A grant honneur vous menoient.' Erasmus: 'Efflorescunt honestissimarum disciplinarum studia, eruditur juventus.' Mantuan (291ᵛ): 'Ingenuae redeunt artes, Academica florent / Ocia, Castaliae sollicitantur aquae.' Zanchi (11.427): 'Ingenuae florent artes atque otia dia, / Et divina pii meditantur carmina vates.' Marot, *Ballade* (2.73): 'Ma plume lors aura cause et loysir / Pour du loyer quelque beau lay escrire.' Graphaeus (*DPB* 2.480): 'Redivivae rursus et Artes'; and in the triumph of Pax, the Muses, the Arts, and Industria immediately precede Pax herself (2.493). Torrentius (*DPB* 4.438): 'Gaudete, Musae, Vester adest honos.' André (*DPG* 1.69): 'Doctae etiam sacrum repetunt Helicona sorores.' Ronsard, *Paix*, 146: 'Les Muses et les ars fleurissent par les villes.' Baïf, *Hymne* (2/225): 'Les arts sont en honneur.' Passerat, *Hymne* (1.98): 'Tu maintiens et accrois les Universités.'

12. *Commerce is Resumed*. That merchants may once more cross the borders, and especially the seas, is, with the resumption of agriculture, a most persistent topic in the encomium pacis. It appears in Euripides, *Supp.* 201−13 and plays a conspicuous role in Aristophanes; for example, *Acharnians*, *Peace*, and *Plutus*. Later Greek comic writers continued to use the topic. It was also a topic of the 'Praises of Athens,' appearing, for example, in Pericles' *Funeral Oration* (Thucydides 2.35−46). And it thus also became a topic of the 'Praises of Rome' and the Pax Romana. For the Renaissance poets, perhaps the most influential fact is its inclusion in the praise of Augustus in *Carm.* 4.5.19: 'Pacatum volitant per mare navitae' (cf. Propertius 3.11.71−2; Ovid, *Fasti* 1.68). It is still important for Prudentius (*C. Symm.* 2.612−14): 'Distantes regione plagae, divisaque ponto / Littora, conveniunt nunc per vadimonia ad unum / Et commune forum, nunc per commercia et artes / Ad coetum celebrem.' A curious

feature of this topic is the fact that it is in direct contradiction to the 'Saturnian' theme, that sailing was a first sign of evil and a falling away from primeval peace. But even Manilius' description of this evil (1.87–88)—'Et vagus in caecum penetravit navita pontum, / fecit et ignotis itiner commercia terris'—is sometimes echoed in the Renaissance poems in a good sense.

The fifteenth-century French poets know the topic, but come upon it not from the ancient literary tradition, but from life, or rather from their mediaeval rhetorical process of enumerating the classes of society affected by peace. So Chartier: 'Les marchans gaignoient, / Nobles voyageoit, / Clercz estudioient'; Charles d'Orléans; Jean Regnier. Vida, perhaps from life, thrusts it into his imitation of Stobaeus' Greek poets, who omit it: 'Tu merce transmarina opes parantibus / Voto invocaris publico'. Mantuan (291ᵛ): 'Pax vehit Eoas peregrina per aequora merces: / Et steriles ponti non sinit esse vias;' later, Mercatura appears in the train of Pax, and is described at length: 'Auroque gemmisque nitens . . . / Barbarico de more habitu vestita, . . . / Centum (mirabile) linguas / Centeno ore sonans . . . / Mercatura.' Capilupi, sta. 6: 'Puppe mercator liquidis per undas / Aequoris currit gravis aere et auro: / Nec tamen praedo ferus ullus illi / Se obvius offert.' Zanchi (*CPI* 11.427): 'Iam caerula Tethys / Mittit inexhaustas utroque a littore merces.' Anon. in *Chants historiques* 2.122 (an. 1538): 'Marchantz yront, jeunes et vieux, en marchandise jour et nuict . . . Marchantz de France et de Bretagne, / Allez tous sur mer hardiment, / En Portugal et en Espagne' (cf. ibid. 2.123). Ronsard, *Paix*, 149ff: 'Les navires sans peur dans les havres abondent, / Avec les estrangers les estrangers s'accordent.' Baïf, *Hymne* (2.225): 'Lors sans peur de domage, / De meurdre et de danger le marchand fait voyage.' Béreau (*Œuvres* p. 84): 'Le nocher voguera sa navire chargée / Seurement par la mer Oceane et Egée, / Conduisant le marchant qui, avaricieux,[16] / Aux Indes cherchera les lingos precieux.' Belleau, who often shows the most imagination in renewing these commonplaces (*Chant*, p. 190): 'C'est toy, c'est toy qui fais parler les ports / Divers langage, et qui permets encore / Que l'Espagnol, le Barbare et le More / Puissent surgir seurement à nos bords.' Grévin, *Chant*, sta. 14–15: 'Au lieu de mener armées / Dessus les plaines sallées, . . . Les marchans pourront sans crainte / Voiager, et sans contrainte / Trafiquer à l'etranger,' and so on. Anon. in *Chants* 2.569 (an. 1575): 'Que les chemins puissent estre / Abandonnez des mechans, / Pour en seureté se mettre / Tous voyageurs et

[16]Note the 'Saturnian' disapproval in 'avaricieux.'

marchands.' P. Thomas (*Poemata* p. 149): 'Nauta cum tutis mare per profundum / Mercibus ibit, . . .' Cesarini (*CPI* 3.9): 'Pacatum hinc volitant mutandis mercibus aequor, / Nec timet a nigris nauta pericla Notis.'

13. *Agriculture; Peaceful Labor.* We have already considered the theme of agriculture and country life in connection with the Saturnian themes with which this aspect of peace is shot through, especially in the Roman poets (above, Ch. VI). Here we may repeat the statement that, for the peace topic, this sentimentalized view is neither original nor basic. Quite simply, the *securitas* of peacetime displays itself in renewed industry and unravaged crops. This is what the Greek poets, as represented by the Stobaeus fragments and by Aristophanes, are thinking about. Nor are the Roman poets altogether obsessed by the dream of the Golden Age. At least, this aspect is not overt in Horace, *Carm. Saec.* 29–32, or *Carm.* 4.5.29–32, so often echoed: 'Condit quisque diem collibus in suis, / Et vitem viduas ducit ad arbores; / Hinc ad vina redit laetus et alteris / Te (sc. Caesarem) mensis adhibet deum,' nor always overt in Tibullus, for example, 1.10.45ff: 'Interea Pax arva colat; Pax candida primum duxit araturos sub iuga curva boves; Pax aluit vites,' and so on. This last passage is taken over by Ronsard, *Exhort.* 200–204: 'La paix fertilisa les campaignes steriles, / La paix de soubs la joug fist mougir les toreaux.'[17] The similar development in *Paix*, 141–44 is the poet's own variation: 'Adonques en repos,' and so on. Peace in Nero's time was anticipated by Calpurnius (*Ecl.* 1.37–41) thus: 'Licet omni vagetur / Securo custode pecus nocturnaque pastor / Claudere fraxinea nolit praesaepia crate, / Non tamen insidias praedator ovilibus ullas / Afferet aut laxis abiget iumenta capistris.' Baïf, *Hymne* (2.225), perhaps accidentally, finds a similar thought: 'Alors le laboureur au labeur prend plaisir / Quand le champ non ingrat répond à son desir. / L'ennemy fourageur son bestial n'emmene, / Et pillant ne ravit le doux fruit de sa pène.' Mantuan: 'Pax Cererem campis et mitem collibus uvam / Reddit, et armoso dividit arva bove.' Pontano's *Exultatio ob factam pacem* (above, Ch. III) is wholly elaborated on the two topics of country life and domestic joy; for example, 'Pax Cererem redditque agris, redditque Lyaeum.' Here again the Renaissance poet gives classical content to a topic that the mediaeval poet had already found simply by running through the classes of society. So Jean Regnier (Droz ed. p. 74): 'Les laboureux labouroient, / Ils couppoient / Et rompoient / Acertoient / Les boys.' Buttet may ac-

[17]But the next line, 'La paix dedans les prez fist sauter les troupeaux,' seems to echo Lucretius 1.15: '(inde ferae) pecudes persultant pabula laeta.'

Appendix

tually echo the other French tradition (*Œuvres*, 2.128): 'Rende à chacun ce qui est sien: / Le prestre dedans son église, / La noble l'autrui ne cherchant, / Le marchant en sa marchandise, / Le laboureur soit à son champ.' And the Renaissance poets also sometimes apply directly to experience; cf. Graphaeus (*DPB* 2.480): 'Attollat caput . . . *Industria*, sanctus emergat *Labor*.' And so apparently Béreau (*Œuvres*, pp. 84–85): 'Le laboureur ira . . . au marché porter maint gras frommage, / Le poullet, le chevreau, sans par toute saison / Qu'un gendarme cruel sacage sa maison,' and 'Le manouvrier fera retentir sa boutique / De mainte chansonette.' But following tradition, the poets mostly refer this *securitas* to farming; Zanchi (*CPI* 11.427): 'Vinitor et mites decerpit collibus uvas; / Et foetus Pomona novos foecunda ministrat.' Mantuan (f.291ᵛ): 'Pax facit innocuos saltus nemorumque recessus.' Graphaeus (*DPB* 2.480): 'Arator / In campos redeat securus'; Thomas: 'humum . . . vacui timoris / Rusticus curvo subigent aratro.'

14. *Peaceful Slumber.* Bacchylides (above, Ch. V) already recalls that in peace his 'eyelids are not despoiled of the honied slumber that soothes the heart.' For Tibullus (1.10.9–10) it is a topic of the Golden Age before greed created war: 'somnumque petebat / securus varias dux gregis inter oves.' Capilupi (sta. 7) reiterates: 'Jam capit tutus requiem colonus / Paupere in tecto.' Ronsard, *Paix*, 145: 'Le peuple à l'aise dort, les citez sont tranquilles.' Béreau, *Œuvres*, p. 85: 'De nuict nous dormirons avecques assurance / en noz lictz, et de jour sous les ombrages frais. Belleau, as we expect, translates the topic into a charming 'image': 'Dans sa moisson, la main sur la faucille.'

15. *The Spider and the Ploughshare.* No figure for peace is more persistent than that of the cobwebbed armor unless it be that of the swords beaten into ploughshares; and the two are often found in combination. For the cobwebbed armor, Bacchylides is our first witness (above, Ch. V)—'in iron-bound *shields* are the looms of busy spiders' (ἐν δὲ σιδαροδέτοις / Πόρπαξιν αἰθᾶν ἀραχνᾶν ἱστοὶ πέλονται)—if, indeed he is not its inventor. Most likely he is, since Plutarch (*Numa* 20) quotes him and this suggests the poem was still famous. Euripides follows suit (*Erechtheus* above, Ch. V), with the *spear* laid up for the spider to weave its web about (κείσθω δόρυ μοι μίτον ἀμφιπλέκειν ἀράχνᾳ). This is, of course, only a specially graphic manner of saying that in peace weapons are hung up in idleness, a thought which Euripides immediately repeats in another form, 'hanging my Thracian shield in the pillared shrine of Athena,' and which Aristophanes (*Acharnians* 279) gives as 'the shield shall be

hung up in the chimney-smoke (ἡ δ'ἀσπὶς ἐν τῷ φεψάλῳ κρεμήσεται). As for the spider, not only Euripides but Sophocles had used the figure (frag. 286): πάντα δ'ἐρίθων ἀραχνᾶν βρίθει. Theocritus repeats it (16.96–97): 'May the spiders stretch their fine webs over the armor' (ἀράχνια δ'εἰς ὅπλ' ἀράχναι / λεπτὰ διαστήσαιντο).[18]

The beating of swords into ploughshares is not known as a commonplace in Greek. The modern poet may always be supposed to have in mind Isaiah 2.4., together with the opposite sentiment of Virgil, *Georg.* 1.508: 'Et curvae rigidum falces conflantur in ensem'—which indeed may be Virgil's reversal of a sentiment like that of Isaiah. Ovid follows Virgil's lead (*Fasti* 1.697–99): 'Bella diu tenuere viros; erat aptior ensis / vomere, cedebat taurus arator equo, / sarcula cessabant, versique in pila ligones, / *factaque de rastri pondere cassis erat.*'

Similar to the cobwebs again is the rust or filth—*robigo* or *situs* (the latter meaning idleness, rust, and filth, and including cobwebs)—which may in war affect agricultural tools and in peace may affect weapons. The Flamen in Ovid (*Fasti* 4.923–30) bids Robigo spare the crops and attack weapons of war: 'utilius gladios et tela nocentia carpes; / nil opus est illis; otia mundus agit.' Let the ploughshares shine, and *situs* stain weapons: 'Sarcula nunc durusque bidens et vomer aduncus, / ruris opes, niteant; inquinet arma situs.' And Ovid may echo Tibullus 1.10.45: 'Pace bidens vomerque nitent, et tristia duri militis in tenebris occupat arma situs.'[19]

In the Renaissance Latin poems on peace, the sword beaten into the ploughshare (Virgil controlled by Isaiah) prevails. Secundus, *De pace Cameraci*: 'At vos in falces gladii nunc ite recurvas / Atque aciem in flavas vertite frugis opes. / Quique prius rigidae clypeus decusserat hastas / Nunc habilis paleas ventilet ille leves. / Et modo quae pressit fugientia lancea terga, / Scindat frugiferum vomer aduncus humum.' Graphaeus (*DPB* 2.480): 'In falces redeant fractis mucronibus hastae, / E gladio incurvus confletur vomer!' (again, p. 494). Elie André (*DPG* 1.69): 'In curvas rigidus falces conflabitur ensis.' Torrentius (*DPB* 4.439) thinks of war, 'Dum ruris instrumenta saevos / In gladios clypeosque belli / Vertebat usus.'

But the *situs*-theme is not forgotten. Capilupi (sta. 8): 'Militum jam

[18]A. C. Pearson, *The Fragments of Sophocles* (Amsterdam, 1963), vol. 1, note p. 210, lists other places where this expression occurs.

[19]Silius Italicus, 7.533–35, turns this sentiment round: 'quoniam data copia, longum / Detergete situm ferro multoque cruore / Exsatiate, viri, plenos robiginis enses.' Cf. Horace, *Serm.* 2.1.43: 'Ut pereat positum robigine telum, / nec quicquam noceat cupido mihi pacis.'

jam galeas et ensis / Occupat turpis situs: at renidet / Trita falx usu
assiduo; atque leve / Splendet aratrum.' Cesarini (*CPI* 3.9) echoes
Ovid: 'Sarcula pace vigent, rubigo amplectitur hastas: / cedit ruri-
colis gloria bubus equi.' And Paul Thomas (*Poemata*, p. 149) joins the
two themes as does Tibullus: 'funestique situ perenni / Langueant
enses, abeantve curvae / Falces in usum.'

The spider seems only to be known to the Greek tradition, the
ploughshare to the Roman. The Renaissance, fulfilling its task even
in this small detail, unites the two, or can choose between them.
Thus Béreau (*Œuvres* p. 85) recalls only *situs*: 'Le harnois inutil en
un coing *moisera*, / Au croc reposera et la mace et la lance'; and Ron-
sard chooses only this motif in his *Chant de liesse* 21–24: 'Tu [Henri
II] a changé tes guerriers estendars / En oliviers: le fer de tes
souldars, / Qu'avoit si bien affillé la querelle, / S'est emoussée des-
soubs la paix nouvelle;' while Jean de La Taille, *Remonstrance* (2.xviii,
ed. Maulde) knows only the spider: 'Qu'ils [gendarmes] s'en aillent
chez eux, leur lance et leur harnois, / . . . appendre encontre les
parois, / Afin que l'araignée y fasse son ouvrage.'

Vida (above, Ch. V), with the cobwebs of Bacchylides and Euri-
pides before him and the Roman and Hebrew ploughshare im-
pressed on his memory, seems to be the first plainly to join the two
motifs, though possibly *situs* in Tibullus and Ovid had a similar in-
tent. Vida: 'Videamque pendentes acervos arduis / Scutorum fila
quos obduxerint / Nigra vetusto in pulvere / ensesque rurus ferreas-
que cuspides / in vomerem conflarier.' Ronsard, *Exhort.* 185–92
gives us the same combination:

> Au croq vos morryons pour jamais soyent liez,
> Autour desquelz l'araigne en fillant de ses piedz
> Y ourdisse ses retz, et que dedans vos targes
> Les ouvrieres du miel y deposent leurs charges:
> Reforgez pour jamais le bout de vostre estoc,
> Le bout de vostre pique en la pointe d'un soc,
> Vos lances desormais en vouges soyent trempées,
> Et en faux desormais courbez moi vos espées.

Some relation must exist between this elaborate passage and the cor-
responding one in Belleau's *Chant de la Paix* (1.191). Marcel Ray-
mond (*Influence* 1.177) is undoubtedly right in saying Ronsard is
Belleau's source. Here is Belleau:

> Donque à fin qui jamais n'esperions
> Guerre ici bas, que l'estendart fleurisse

En verds rameaux, et que l'araigne ourdisse
Sa fine trame es vuides morions:
Que des brassarts et des corps de cuirasse
Le fer s'allonge en la pointe d'un soc:
Le coutelas, la pistolle, et la masse
Dans le fourreau se moisissent au croc.

Perhaps we may note that it is not, as formerly, in shields or spears that the spider is to work, but in empty helmets. Ronsard's graphic touch 'en fillant de ses piedz' has at least a parallel in Aristophanes, *Frogs* 1314: εἰλίσσετε δακτύλοις φάλαγγες. Belleau's 'fine trame' recalls Theocritus' ἀράχνια λεπτά. Ronsard, like the Latin poets, reverses Virgil in his last line.

But while the spider works in the helmet, another creature in Ronsard, the bee, works in the shield. This bee is from Alciati's *Emblem* 177, *Ex bello Pax*, which must take its place among the important Renaissance poems on peace, as introducing a widespread figure:

En galea intrepidus quam miles gesserat, et quae
Saepius hostili sparsa cruore fuit:
Parta pace apibus tenuis concessit in usum
Alveoli, atque favos grataque mella gerit.
Arma procul iaceant: fas sit tunc sumere bellum,
Quando aliter pacis non potes arte frui.[20]

Ronsard has shifted the bees from helmet to shield in his *Exhortation*, but in the *XXIII Inscriptions* some months later he naturally reverts to Alciati in an 'emblem' *Pour la Paix*[21]: 'Des morions *l'abeille* soit compaigne: / Pendent rouillez les coutelas guerriers: / Dans les harnois tousjours file *l'araigne*/ Et les lauriers deviennent oliviers.' Alciati's *Emblem* itself had more influence in spreading this image for peace about the literature of Europe than had Ronsard's verse, but we may safely see Ronsard behind the lines that end Amadis Jamyn's *Prière pour la Paix, faicte pour reciter en une Comedie*:[22]

L'Abeille puisse au creux de leur[23] cuiraces
Faire son miel: l'Araigne ses filaces:

[20]The only source even plausibly suggested for Alciati's fancy is a Greek epigram by Philippos (AP 6.236), in which bees make their hive in the abandoned enemy ships at Actium.

[21]Meanwhile, in *La Paix*, 257–62, he temporarily forgot the bee: 'Pends nos armes au croc . . . Et que le coutelas . . . , / Pendu d'une couraye au fourreau soit rouillé, / Et que le corselet au plancher se moisisse, / Et l'araigne à jamais ses fillets y ourdisse.'

[22]*Œuvres poétiques* (1575), f. 67ʳ.

[23]The nobles of France.

Que plus Bellonne on n'entende crier,
Que le poignard, que la trenchante espée
Soit en faucille et en faulx destrempée
Et l'Olivier triomphe du Laurier.

16. *Love.* Peace is also a time for love, and Amor tends to be included among the *comites* of Pax. There is also a special line of love elegies either comparing and contrasting Love and War (Propertius 3.5, Ovid *Amores* 1.9), or declaring that the poet of love will have nothing to do with warfare (Propertius 3.4, Tibullus 1.3). A variation is imagining the lover actually gone forth to war, as in Joannes Secundus, *Eleg.* 2.11 *Ad Carolum Catzium.* To the encomium of peace, however, belong rather the more incidental passages such as Tibullus 1.10.53: 'Sed Veneris tunc bella calent,' and so on, where love is thought of as one of the *signa* of peace. The topic comes naturally to the mediaeval love poet, and Charles d'Orléans, in running over the classes of society from prelates down, somewhat surprisingly ends with lovers where we should expect laborers: 'Priez, amans, qui boulez en liesse / Servir Amour, car guerre par rudesse / Vous destourbe de vos dames hanter.' Mantuan (291ᵛ): 'Sine pace . . . nullus amor.' Secundus brings this as his climax: 'Pro dura galea roseis ornate corollis / Tempora, proque tubis sumite plectra manu. / Bellaque lascivis nocturna movete puellis, . . .' Pontano (*CPI* 7.457): 'Iam facilis jam laeta choros per prata Voluptas / Ducit ut optatus rura revisit Amor.' In Navagero's *Damon* (72ff.), the shepherd in peace may love the shepherdess; and the same bucolic motif occurs to Béreau (*Œuvres* p. 84): 'Desormais le berger, dispos, gaillard, joieux, / Entretiendra d'amour la bergére aux beaux yeux; Faisant bruire son nom dans les forestz prochaines.' So Ronsard, *Paix* 153–58: 'Venus avec son filz . . . / Errent parmi le peuple, et aux jeunes plaisirs / Des combas amoureux chatouillent noz desirs: / Amour comme une flamme entre dans noz courages, / . . . il joinct les mariages.' Compare Belleau, *Chant* (1.190): 'Par toy lon fait tournois et mariages, / Par toy Venus allume noz courages / D'un feu secret,' and so on. Passerat (*Poésies* 1.92) reminds us that the topic belongs to Lucretius' proem: 'Mars . . . vaincu d'amour . . . s'endort au gyron de la belle Cyprine.'

17. *Marriages; Domestic Joys.* Ronsard and Belleau, prompted perhaps by the events of 1559, have completed love with marriages. Though ostensibly speaking only in general, Elie André virtually describes how the royal marriages of that year came about—through War and Policy (*DPG* 1.69): 'Mollia succedunt duris convivia pugnis, / *Mars laetus primus Pallasque parant Hymenaeos.*' Here reality met the

literary tradition, for from of old the poets had praised peace as 'delighting in children' (Euripides) and 'bestowing weddings' (Philemon); it is not merely from comic 'form' that Aristophanes' *Peace* ends with a marriage. Cassiodorus *Var.* 1.11: Peace multiplies mankind; so Rufinus *De bono pacis*: 'Pax implet urbem, multiplicat sobolem.'

Pontano's *Exultatio ob factam pacem* is taken up wholly by the topics of rural peace and domestic peace; for example, 'Huc propera mecum huc uxor amata veni.' Children: Mantuan (291ᵛ): 'Pax hominum genetrix;' 'Pax aperit thalamos hymenaeaque carmina cantat.'

Virtually all the poems of 1559 mention among joys the marriages of Elizabeth of France and Philip and Marguerite and the Duke of Savoy.

As a reversal of the horrors of war (below, no. 22), we sometimes find the motif, 'husbands need not be torn from their wives'—so Vida, adding to the Greek poets: 'Juvenemque vellentis ab conjugis / Gremio, metu inspersum genas,' and Capilupi: 'Nulla flens uxor revocat maritum, / Signa dum Martis sequitur, nec ulla / Filium mater mediis in armis / Deflet ademptum' (cf. Horace, *Carm.* 1.1.24–25: 'bellaque matribus detestata'). More positive joys are suggested by Tibullus 1.10.39–42: 'Quin potius laudandus hic est quem prole parata / occupat in parva pigra senecta casa! / Ipse suas sectatur oves, at filius agnos, / et calidam fesso comparat uxor aquam.' This passage, as Laumonier duly notes, is copied by Ronsard in *Exhort.* 171—'N'aymeriez vous pas mieux, ô soldats magnanimes, / . . . Bien vivre en vos maisons sans armes, et avoir / Femme tresbelle et chaste entre vos bras, et voir / Vos enfans se jouer au tour de la tetins / Vous pendilles au col d'une main infantine, / Vous frisoter la barbe, ou tordre les cheveux, / Vous appeller papa, vous faire mille jeux, / que de vivre en un camp . . . ; / Et pres de ses parents mourir bien ancien, / Que d'avoir pour sepulchre un estomac d'un chien?' Ronsard has replaced the pastoral vignette of Tibullus with a domestic scene of his own.

In *La Paix, au Roy* 221–28, this topic is interestingly applied to Henri II: 'Il vaudroit beaucoup mieux, vous qui venez sur l'age / Ja grison, gouverner vostre Royal menage, / Vostre femme pudique, et voz nobles Enfans / Qu'acquerir par danger des lauriers triomphans: / Il vaudroit beaucoup mieux joyeusement bien vivre, / Ou batir vostre Louvre, ou lire dans un livre.' The last phrase probably only accidentally recalls Euripides' wish for peace and a chance to read.

18. *Old Age vs. Short Life.* In peace the expectation of life is longer,

in war death comes early—μετὰ δ'ἡσυχίας πολίῳ γήρᾳ συνοικοίην, said Euripides (Erechtheus): 'in peace may I dwell with grizzled age.' Rufinus, *De bono pacis* 2.18: 'Pax . . . canitiem condecorat senectutis.' The Renaissance poets who use this theme generally follow Tibullus 1.10.33–44: 'Quis furor est atram bellis arcessere Mortem? / imminet et tacito clam venit illa pede. / Non seges est infra, non vinea culta, sed audax Cerberus et Stygiae navita turpis aquae. / . . . quin potius laudandus hic est quem prole parata / occupat in parva pigra senecta casa . . . Sic ego sim, liceatque caput candescere canis, / temporis et prisci facta referre senem.' Ronsard already imitates this passage, as Laumonier notes, in *Les Armes* 87–102:[24] 'Pourquoi chetifs humains, avés vous tant d'envie / A grande cous de canons d'acoursir vostre vie? / Vous mourés assés tost.' In *Exhort.* 81–86: 'Quelle fureur vous tient de vous entretuer, / Et de cent millions qui vivent en ce temps, / Un a peine vient-il au terme de cent ans.' To his reference to Tibullus 1.10.33–34, the editor might well have added, for the last two lines, the well-known words of Xerxes in Herodotus: Ἐσῆλθε γάρ με λογισάμενον κατοικτῖραι ὡς βραχὺς εἴη ὁ πᾶς ἀνθρώπινος βίος, εἰ τούτων γε ἐόντων τοσούτων οὐδεὶς ἐς ἕκαστον ἔτος περιέσται. Baïf, *Hymne* (2.227), perhaps recalls *Les Armes*: 'Et quel plaisir prens-tu, race frelle chetive, / De te hâter la mort, qui jamais n'est tardive?'

19. *Symbols of Peace.* The olive spray, the wheat spike, the cornucopia; the laurel, the palm, the caduceus; even the infant Ploutos, represented Peace in the iconography, as we have seen (above, Ch. I) on Roman coins, and (Ch. VI) in Renaissance funerary sculptures. Hans Christ, *Die römische Weltherrschaft*, p. 106, notes that Eirene with cornucopia was Greek, with the laurel, the Roman Pax Victoria.

While the Renaissance poets made liberal use of these motifs and symbols, they seem to have summoned the Peace of fertility and abundance more often than the bèarer of palm and scepter. Thus, Alain de Lille (Migne, *PL* 210–502:

> Virginis in dextra, foliorum crine comatus,
> Flora tenens, fructus expectans, *ramus olivae pubescit.*

Prudentius (*Psych.* 687) gives the olive branch to Concordia. Secundus, *De pace Cameraci*: 'Pax altera caerulea ramum pertendit *olivae* . . . *fruges.*' Vida 74: 'Cinctus *olea* canum caput.' Zanchi, *CPI* 11.428:

---

[24]Laumonier 6.209; but in the development Ronsard also thinks of the parallel passage in Tibullus 1.3.65ff., from which he later took the theme of the sonnet *Quand vous serez bien vielle.*

'Te Romana nurus . . . sertaque comas viridantis *olivae*.' Ronsard, *Liesse* 21–22: '*estendars En oliviers*.' Henardus Gamerius, *DPB* 2.441: 'ramus frondentis *olivae* / Quem Noa.' Grévin, sta. 6, will plait a 'couronne / De verd olivier' for peace. Some poets combine the two motifs: Marot, *Œuvres* 2.106: 'Paix descendra, portant en main *l'olive* / *Laurier* en teste.' Graphaeus, *DPB* p. 484: 'ramus frondentis *olivae* / *lauri* folia . . . / *palmae*.'

But the laurel and the palm appear rather infrequently in the Renaissance poets. They prefer the cornucopia. Passerat *Poésies*, 1.98: 'Tu tiens un espy meur en ta main fortunée / fruits d'Automne, corne d'abondance / fleur de Nectar . . . laict [the last is Saturnian]. Des Autels, *Paix venue* sig. E2: 'O Paix . . . couronée d'olive et des fruits de Ceres.' Grévin, sta. 7: 'le cor d'abondance.' Buttet (*Œuvres* 1.125): 'Empoigne la corne abondante, / Mais de l'arbre où tant tu te plais / Orne ta trouppe triumphante.' Cesarini (*CPI* 3.9): 'Quaecumque . . . felici Copia cornu / It comes . . . Ceres / Te sequitur Bacchus.' Copia and Ceres are named among the comites of Peace also by Torrentius, Zanchi, Ronsard (*Exhort.* 205–7), Baïf, *Hymne* 2.225. See above, No. 6.

20. *The Perils of Peace*. The words *pax perpetua* involve a very bold hope, but one that mankind is loath to relinquish. Meanwhile, experience suggests that War and Peace proceed in alternation, if not in rhythm, and that just as the *aurea aetas* may recur, so also, alas, it departs: 'erunt etiam altera bella / atque iterum ad Troiam magnus mittetur Achilles' (Virgil *Ecl.* 4.35–36). 'Peior est bello timor ipse belli' (Seneca, *Thyestes* 572). Naturally this topic is not very prominent in the encomia of peace that we are considering, yet it is present in a note of anxiety that sounds more than once. Ronsard, *Paix*, 45–48: 'Il faut bien qu'on la [Paix] garde, / Ceux qui la gardent bien, le haut Dieu les regarde, / Et ne regarde point un Roy, de qui la main / Toujours trempe son glaive au pauvre sang humain.' And warmongers are cursed in ll. 263–68. So Baïf, *Hymne* (2.228): 'O Rois pensés à vous: et puis que Dieu vous done / La beau don de la Paix, chacun de vous s'adone / A l'aimer et garder. Qui premier l'enfreindra, / Qu'il tombe à la mercy du Roy qu'il assaudra,' and so on. Such are the feelings when peace is proclaimed at the end of a war. For a time, no 'incident' can provoke hostilities. Then we forget, and grow bolder. Peace itself may seem dull: Marot, *Cantique* (2.105): 'Si vous la [paix] fuyez, / Elle dira que serez ennuyez / De voz repos, et que portez envie / A la doulceur de vostre heureuse vie.' That, of course, was addressed to the kings and warlike nobles of 1538.

But peace has actual defects; Juvenal 6.292–93: 'Nunc patimur

longae pacis mala, saevior armis / Luxuria incubuit victumque ulcis-
citur orbem.' Amid the vices of peace we recall the virtues of war.
These verses of Juvenal were never forgotten: 'gravissima est
sententia et a multis decantata,' says a scholiast. Military writers nat-
urally emphasize the risk of unpreparedness when this 'longae se-
curitas pacis homines . . . ad delectationem otii . . . transduxit' (Veg-
etius, *De re mil.* 1.28), and conclude: 'Igitur qui desiderat pacem,
praeparet bellum' (ibid. 3 Praef.). Petrarch chooses to take this line
in *De remediis utriusque fortunae* 1.105–6 in *Opera*, pp. 88–89.

In the sixteenth century the cycle of war and peace became a dra-
matic theme, though rather on the popular level and seldom recog-
nized by the humanist poets. Marot (*Œuvres* 1.146) writing in Octo-
ber 1521 from the army in Hainault to Marguerite Duchess of
Alençon, quotes from a comedy by Minfant: 'Ainsi, bienheureuse
Princesse, esperons nous le non assez soudaine Venue de Paix, qui
toutesfoys peult finalement revenir en despit de guerre cruelle,
comme tesmoigne Minfant en sa comedie de *Fatalle Destinée*, disant:

> Paix engendre prosperité,
> De Prosperité vient Richesse,
> De Richesse Orgueil, Volupté,
> D'Orgeuil Contention sans cesse,
> Contention la guerre adresse,
> La Guerre engendre Povreté,
> La Povreté Humilité,
> D'Humilité revient la Paix,
> Ainsi retournent humains faicts.'

These verses represent the rhetorical device of 'climax,' as taught in
the mediaeval arts of poetry or rhetoric. They are not, however,
Minfant's personal invention, but are adapted from the *Roman de la
Rose*, 9517–9664 (ed. Langlois).[25]

I have not attempted to follow further the fortunes of this topic in
French poetry; it does not figure in the peace poems we are study-
ing. On the other hand, it enjoyed some success in England, where,
for example, it forms the whole idea of the play *Histriomastix*. I bor-
row from Richard Simpson's edition of this drama the following al-
lusions:[26] George Puttenham, *Arte of English Poesie* (1589), Book III,
Of Ornament, under 'Clymax,' quotes 'Ihean de Mehune': 'Peace
makes plentie, plentie makes pride' and so on. Quite possibly it is

[25][I am indebted to Professor Alice Colby-Hall for this reference. R.G.]
[26]Richard Simpson, *The School of Shakespeare* (New York, 1878), 2.87–89.

from Puttenham that the later English examples, including *Histrio-mastix*, derive. Simon Harward, *Solace for the Soldier and Sailor* (1592): 'Peace hath increased plenty, plenty hath wrought pride, pride hath hatched disdain, and disdain hath brought forth such strifes and debates, such suits of law, such quarrellings and contentions, as never were heard of in any age before us.'

21. *Origin of War.* The encomium of peace regularly demands a comparison (*syncrasis*) of peace and war, and such a comparison involves topics of the vituperation of war, which correspond to those of the encomium (below, No. 22). First of these topics is the derivation, or metaphorically the parentage of war; for example, Nesson answers Chartier's 'Paix . . . fille du dieu des dieux' by 'guerre . . . / Engendrée du felon Lucifer.' Since Ronsard's *Exhortation* exhibits a novel treatment of this topic, a special discussion of it is to be found in Chapter VII above.

The ambition of kings is a constant topic with Erasmus in both the *Dulce bellum inexpertis* and the *Querela pacis*. Thus in 965A: 'quamquam his temporibus omne fere bellum *è titulis* . . . et ex Principum ambitiosis foederibus, dum ut unum aliquod oppidulum suae vindicent ditioni, totum imperium adducunt in extremum periculum.' Des Autels, *Paix venue*, is explicit on this point: war comes from Ate stirring dissension and then Alecto is released on mankind: God is punishing men or their princes:

> L'arc de vengeance il [Jupiter] bande alors sur les provinces
> Pour leur propres pechez, ou pour ceus de leurs princes.

22. *Horrors of War.* As the encomium details the benefits of the object of praise, the *vituperatio* details the misdeeds of the object of blame. Our poems on peace regularly include a section on the horrors of war, introduced either simply to contrast with the state of peace or to give the background of the present moment of joy. The passage of Pindar which Erasmus took as his text, Γλυκὺ δὲ πόλεμος ἀπείροισιν, *Dulce bellum inexpertis*, may have had a context of this sort. Horace, *Carm.* 4.5.17–20, 'Nullis polluitur casta domus stupris,' glances at the topic. Mantuan, like Erasmus, uses the theme in a *comparatio* of war and peace (f.291ʳ): 'Bella necant homines, faciunt sine honoribus Aras / Urbis et agrorum depopulantur opes . . . / Pax coeleste bonum,' and so on. Erasmus, *Bellum* 953B–E, offers a rhetorically accumulated 'simulacrum' of war: 'barbarae cohortes . . . formidabilem armorum crepitum . . . congestas strages, undantes

cruore campos . . . protentas passim segetes, exustas villas, incensos pagos, abacta pecora, constupratas virgines, tractos in captivitatem senes, . . .' And later (957C–958A), and in *Querela* (627E), he elaborates a *comparatio* of war and peace. In *Bellum* war is thus described (we have given the description of Peace above, p. 53):

> Abiguntur armenta, proteruntur segetes, trucidantur agricolae, exuruntur villae, tot seculis instructae florentissimae civitates, una procella subvertuntur. . . . Civium opes ad exsecrandos latrones ac sicarios transferuntur. Moerent domus metu, luctu, et querimoniis, lamentis complentur omnia. Frigent artes opificum . . . Virginum aut nullae aut tristes et funestae nuptiae. Desolatae matrones . . . Silent leges . . . nullum habet locum aequitas . . . Religio ludibrio est. . . . Corrumpitur omni vitiorum genere juventus: damnant longaevitatem suam luctuosi senes. Nullus honos honestis litterarum studiis.

The first part of Navagero's *Damon* details the miseries of the shepherds in war (see above, p. 77). Vida: in peace, 'Quiescunt furta, caedes, vulnera, strages, ruinae, incendia, orbitates, liberorum stupra, crebrique raptus virginum.' Marot, *Ballade* (2.72): 'Famine vient . . . / Soubs terre voy gentilz hommes gesir;' and cf. *Cantique* (2.106); Capilupi: 'Cades, / queis adhuc agri recalent cruenti.' Buttet (2.123): A! las! . . . / Le cruel Mars l'univers monde . . . / Les cités, aux tonnans allarmes, / Rompant le saint honneur des loix / En grand effroi sautent aux armes; Des troupes les horribles voix / Noncent par tout ouverte guerre.'

Ronsard, *Paix*, 121–35: 'Toutes mechancetez aux soldas sont permises . . . les eglises . . . Le docte et l'ignorant . . . sans egard à la crainte des lois . . . jeune pucelle . . . enfant . . . Les viellars . . . la peste et la maigre famine'; cf. *Liesse* 35–55. Elie André (*DPG* 1.168): 'Scilicet horrendo passim quassata fragore.' Des Autels, *Paix venue*, Sig. C2: 'villes, pucelles, enfans, epouses.' Baïf, *Hymne* (2.226–27), 'O la pitié de voir la flamme qui saccage / Devorant sans mercy les maisons d'un vilage! . . . le pauvre citoyen . . . les meres desolées . . . la campagne fertile faite un hideux desert . . . un horrible carnage . . . voir de sang les ruisseaux.' Civil war has its special horrors, detailed with the more general ones in La Taille's *Remonstrance*, in Passerat's *Hymne*, and, after Horace, who naturally supplies a model on this topic, in Paul Thomas's *Ode* of 1586: 'Urbibus foedas dedimus ruinas, / Civico passim fluvios cruore / Fecimus, sacras manibus profanis / Vertimus aedes.' Ronsard's treatment of the theme in his *Exhortation* is a model of *communia dicendi* (163–70):

[291]

Par la cruelle guerre on renverse les villes
On deprave les loix divine et civilles
On brule les autelz, et les temples de Dieu
L'equité ne fleurist, la justice n'a lieu
Les maisons de leurs biens demeurent despouilées
Les viellards sont occis, les filles violées,
Le pauvre laboureur du sien est devestu,
Et d'un vice execrable on fait une vertue.[27]

23. *Abi bellum cruentum.* The exorcism of War, sending him across the frontier to vex, if he must, other peoples is doubtless primitive, but throughout historical times (see above, Chs. I, IV) has had a practical meaning in the sense that, if we must fight, let us turn our forces against a common external foe and cease from internecine strife, whether we are Greek states (Isocrates), Rome torn by Civil War (Horace, *Carm.* 1.2.21–24, *Epode* 7.16), mediaeval Europe tossed between empire and papacy (Bernard of Clairvaux),[28] or Renaissance Europe torn by royal or national aspirations. The pattern places the common enemy in the East—Persia, the Parthian, the Saracen, the Turk. The Renaissance poets think of the Turk, but are likely to express themselves in the terms of the Roman poets and demand that Mars return to 'Thrace' (Mars was a Thracian god) or be despatched to vex 'the Scythians' or 'the Parthians.'

The Roman poets' praises are for War already gone from *pacatam terram.* Horace (*Carm.* 4.5.25–28, and *Carm. Saec.* 53–56) offers a variation on the theme: the Parthians, Scythians, Germany, Ireland, Hibernians, Albanians, and Indians are declared to be no longer formidable, or themselves to be fearful, since Rome is strong under Augustus. And this turn is imitated by Capilupi, sta. 11: 'Pace quis iam composita timebit / Amplius Thracum celeres sagittas;' cf. Horace, *Carm.* 4.5.25: 'Quis Parthum paveat, quis gelidum Scythen.' But Capilupi goes on to say that now the kings have the resources and men for other purposes: 'Quae modo invicti posuistis arma, / rursus andantes, capite; atque in hostem / Nominis nostri et fidei secundo vertite Marte.'

The Renaissance poets tend to an exorcism of the comites of War (see 'Discord' above): Vida (p. 26): 'Tui simul Mars hauserit pedis sonum / Facessit hinc celerrimus; / Simul quiescent facta,' and so on. Secundus: *De pace Cameraci,* 'Ergo, age Pauperies . . . Fames . . . Cura, Luctusque . . . Mors, / Ite per extremas gentes, atque ite per

[27]Cf. Baïf (2.227), 'faisant de vertu vice.'
[28][My thanks for this reference to Professor James John. R.G.]

undas, / Nulla ubi quam rabidis sint loca trita feris.' Zanchi (p. 428): 'Ipsa . . . Discordia . . . / Cocyti stagna alta petet.' Graphaeus (p. 480): 'Eia, / Tristis abest; Metus, longe Terrorque Pavorque / . . . facessant.'

A combination of these topics (mention of Scyths, Medes, plus 'begone') is applied to the Turks: Ronsard, *Exhort.* 60; *Paix* 253–56: 'Chasse, je te supply, la guerre et les querelles / Bien loing du bord Chrestien de sus les Infidelles, / Turcs, Parthes, Mammelus, Scythes, et Sarrasins, / Et sur ceux qui du Nil sont les proches voisins;' *Liesse* 29–33: 'La mort, le sang, et le meurtre . . . Par ton moyen sont allé voyr les Scythes, / Loin de l'Europe.' Belleau (*Œuvres* 1.191): 'Et s'il restoit encor . . . / de rancoeur quelque trace, / A coups de pié pousse-le dans la Thrace, / Ou sur le chef des Scythes, et des Turcs.' Béreau (*Œuvres* p. 86): 'J'ay veu en songe Mars, tout debout sur la croppe / Du plus hault Appenin, dire adieu à l'Europe, / Et de là fendre l'air vers les champs Asians, / D'où ne puisse il en ça revenir de mille ans.' Baïf, *Hymne* (2.229): 'Dieu veuille detourner la discorde mortelle / D'entre les rois chrestiens sur le peuple infidelle.' André (*DPG* 1.69): 'Non fremitus posthac, non ulla placebit Erinnys, / Europa nisi quae cogat discedere Parthum.' La Taille (*Remonstrance*) (2.xx–xxi): 'Déa, se desirez tant vostre jeune vaillance / esprouver à la guerre, / . . . je vous mene, . . . / A des combats plus saincts, contre les Infidelles.' Jamyn, *A Vénus pour la Paix* (*Œuvres* f. 70ʳ): 'Pry-le [Mars] s'en retourner aux montagnes de Thrace; / qu'il laisse nostre France en un siècle de Paix.' Anon. (1578), *Chants* 2.371: 'Adieu, guerre, va hors de France, / Et nous serons hors de souffrance.' Cesarini (*CPI* 3.9): 'Quod si tantus amor caedis corda aspera pulsat, / . . . Thrax vocat . . . / Vos pia busta vocant foedo calcata tyranno, / Inque Palestinis sacra litata jugis, / In Scythicas,' and so on.

24. *The Peace Hero.* A few of the poems under consideration, even though occasional in origin, are conceived as encomia of peace in general. Such are the poems of Vida and Mantuan. But for the most part, the Renaissance poets follow the lead of the Roman poets (Virgil, Horace, Calpurnius, Claudian, Optatianus) in attaching their praises of peace to the person of the bringer of peace, who is generally the monarch in whose name the treaty in question has been made. An important difference, however, should be noted. The Roman poets generally represent the *benefacta* of peace as owing to the coming of the peace hero himself, whereas the Renaissance poets personify Peace and attach the *benefacta* to her, praising the hero only as the one who has made her coming possible. The reason for

the change is no doubt the underlying Christian thought that Christ alone is the Prince of Peace and is indeed Peace. To identify any contemporary prince with Peace would therefore be unthinkable. On the other hand, Peace herself in these poems is not identified with Christ—not even when, as in Ronsard's *Ode* of 1550, she is represented as creating the world; she is a personified virtue of God, not 'appropriated' to any person of the Trinity; she is one of the Divine Names, in the sense of the Areopagite. These, however, are implications; actually the power of the Latin language forces these poets to treat Peace like a figure of ancient mythology. As for the peace hero, the modern ruler may have 'divine rights' but is not deified. Even in this respect, however, literary imitation had little difficulty. Though Horace might (*Carm.* 4.5) represent Augustus as peace, the usual thought was that the prince ruled second to God (*Carm.* 3.1.56), and the theory of kingship urged him to 'imitate' God; successful imitation would result in apotheosis after the pattern of benefactors such as Hercules: 'Ille deum vitam accipiet divisque videbit / permixtos heroas et ipse videbitur illis, / pacatumque reget patriis virtutibus orbem' (Virgil, *Ecl.* 4.15–17); 'Hac arte Pollux et vagus Hercules / Enisus arces attigit ignes, / Quos inter Augustus recumbens / Purpureo bibet ore nectar' (Horace, *Carm.* 3.3.9–12). The Renaissance poet can repeat these very words, or nearly, in the sense that the good ruler, the εἰρηνόποιος, will like any good Christian be rewarded with immortality in heaven.

For a detailed discussion of the peace hero in Renaissance poetry see Chapter VI above.

25. *Final Prayer.* Those poets who remember that they are writing an encomium of a divinity, and that such encomia are properly hymns, tend to include this feature, which may thus almost be used to distinguish the types of poem that we have to do with. Charles d'Orléans (who presumably did not know this classical rule) makes his whole poem a prayer, but in another tradition; and such poems, wholly prayer, may be written at any time—for example, Jamyn, *A Vénus pour la Paix.* Encomia or Hymns ending with a short prayer are the following: Ronsard's *Exhort.* 213f: 'Donc, Paix fille de Dieu . . . Donne nous, . . . Donne nous.' Zanchi, Baïf, and Passerat entitle their poems *Hymnus pacis aeternae* or *Hymne de la Paix.* Of these, Zanchi has no special invocation at the end; Baïf ends with a prayer to God to guide the kings aright; and Passerat with a prayer in more technical form, to Peace (*Poésies* p. 99): 'Ie te prie, ô deesse, apporte les moyens / De desarmer du tout les mutins citoyens.' Others worth notice: Vida 'O Diva largitrix bonorum . . . Opulenta salve . . . Et nos

tuo vultu bea.' Graphaeus *DPB* 502: 'Quam cupidis animis et voto ardente precamur, / Durare aeternum . . . '; Grévin, *Chant* sta. 27–29: 'Et toi des peuples la mere / Alma Paix . . . '; Buttet, *Œuvres*, 2.130: 'O celeste . . . Antique reine des humains, / Oi comme chacun te demande, / T'addressant la voix et les mains.'

Index of Names

Alain de Lille, 44, 287; *Anticlaudianus*, 41–42, 182n, 206; *De planctu Naturae*, 42, 287n

Alciati, Emblem no. 177, 284; Emblem no. 178, 106n

Alcuin, *Moralia*, 40

Alençon, Duke of, 153, 154, 156

Alexander the Great, 26, 28

Allee, W. C., 227, 234n

André, Elie, 121n, 272, 274, 275, 276, 282, 285, 291, 292; *Carmen de Pace*, 121–22

Anonymous: *Adieu aux misères de la guerre*, 147, 155n, 166; *Advertissemens aux trois Estatz*, 154–155; *Cantique à Dieu*, 158; *Chant pastoral*, 162–63; *Chants historiques*, 279, 293; *Discours moral de la paix*, 120–21; *Echo parlant a la Paix*, 141; *Elegie*, 166; *Heracliti ad Democritum*, 122–23, 191n; *Hymne de la Guerre et de la Paix*, 160–61; *Hymne de la Paix*, 158; *Louanges de la Paix*, 139; *Ode sur la Trefve*, 161–62; *Resiouissance du peuple de France*, 166; *Resjouissance de la Paix*, 158

Antiphon, 24, 26; *Truth*, 24

Aquinas, St. Thomas: on animals, 235; on peace, 42

Aratus, 41, 90n, 116; *Phaenomena*, 117n, 175, 183n, 233n, 242, 272n

Aristides, Aelius, 32, 33, 46, 200n

Aristophanes: idea of peace in, 23, 276, 280; plays, 23, 170, 171, 173, 224, 278, 284; *Peace*, 23, 272, 273, 274, 277, 286

Aristotle, 25, 27; on animals, 226n, 230n, 239n, 244, 250, 251; in Middle Ages, 48; physical thought, 200, 215

Arius, 34

Arrian, 26n

Aubert, Guillaume, 127; in philosophical dialogue, 261–64; *Oraison de la Paix*, 127–29

Augustine, St.: on animals, 234n, 235; cosmic views of, 29, 23; *De civitate Dei*, 37–38, 199n, 203, 222; quotations from, 69

Augustus, Ara Pacis, 29; as peace hero, 31, 183, 190, 273, 276, 294; as harbinger of Christ, 34

Bacchylides, 22, 170, 274, 277, 281

Baïf, Jean-Antoine de: in philosophical dialogue, 261–64; and Ronsard, 151–53, 218–19, 258, 261; sources for, 218, 257–61; works: *Hymne de la Paix*, 151–53, 218–19, 268, 272, 275, 277, 278, 279, 280, 287, 288, 291, 292, 294; *A Monsieur de Mauru*, 258; *Sur la Paix*, 91, 110; *Vie des Chams*, 259–60

Bainton, Roland, 23n, 36n, 39n, 53n

Belleau, Remy; influence of, 111, 163n, 194; works: *Bergerie*, 110; *Chant pastoral de la Paix*, 109–10, 147, 191–92, 268, 269, 274, 277, 281, 283–84, 285, 292

Béreau, Jacques, 275, 277, 279, 281, 285, 292; *Complainte de France*, 138, 141, 227n; *Eglogue* X, 111, 192–93, 194, 274; *Sur la Paix faicte entre les François*, 141

Berenger de la Tour d'Albenas, *Cantique*, 142

Bernard of Clairvaux, 42–43, 292

Bernard Sylvestris, 205n, 206n

Index

Bez, Fernand de, *Esjouissance aux Chrestiens,* 140, 141
Boccaccio, Giovanni, *Dialoghi d'amore,* 208–9
Boethius, *Consolation of Philosophy,* 48n, 183, 184
Boileau, 230
Bruès, Guy de, *Dialogues,* 261–64
Bugnyon, Philibert, *De la Paix,* 155
Butler, Sir Geoffrey, 49
Buttet, Marc-Claude de: odes, 108–9; peace topics in, 268, 269, 271, 275, 277–78, 280–81, 288, 295; *Ode à la Paix,* 96–97, 108

Calpurnius, 19, 31, 183, 184, 269, 276, 277, 280
Calvin, John, 226n, 238, 239
Capilupi, Ippolito, 132; *De pace,* 131, 132, 271, 273, 279, 281, 282–83, 286, 291, 292
Caraffa, Oliviero, Cardinal, 75, 77, 124n, 188
Caraffa (Pope Paul IV), 124
Cardan, Jerome, 226n
Celsus, 245n, 247
Cephisodotus, statue of Peace, 23–24; *illust.* frontispiece
Cesarini, Virginio, 272, 274, 277, 280, 288, 293; *Ad Gregorium XV,* 78–79, 228
Charles V: conflict with Francis I, 82, 83, 84, 87; war with Henri II, 92–93; death, 94
Charles d'Orléans, 67–69, 277, 278, 285, 294
Chartier, Alain, 63, 65, 67, 216, 277, 278; peace themes in, 270, 277, 278, 279, 290; works: *Dialogus,* 64; *Epistola,* summary of, 63–64; *Lay de Paix,* 63, 64–65, 277
Chastellain, Georges, *Le Consile de Basle,* 69; *Le Dit de Verité,* 70; *Livre de Paix,* 69–70; *La Paix de Peronne,* 69
Chrysostom, St. John, 234n, 235n, 251
Cicero, 29; *De natura deorum,* 234n, 245, 260
Claudian, 185, 231
Clement of Rome, 36
Clichtove, Josse: influence of, 144; as source, 229; *De bello et pace opusculum,* 55, 56, 225–26
Collerye, Roger de, *Satyre,* 70n, 83n
Coquillart, Guillaume, 72, 275
Corrozet, Gilles, *Le Retour de la Paix,* 87–88, 119, 147
Coustau, Pierre, *Carmen de pace,* 123–24

Crucé, Emmerich, 59
Cusanus, Nicolas, 48–49, 56n, 63

Dante: *De monarchia,* 45; *Divina Commedia,* 44–45
d'Aubusson de la Maison-Neuve, Jean, *Colloque social,* 118–19
de Brach, Pierre, *Ode de la Paix,* 150–51
Delamare, Roger Bonnaud, *L'Idée de la paix,* 20
Des Autels, Guillaume: use of Greek sources, 174–79; works: *Eloge de la Paix,* 113, 178; *La Paix venue du ciel,* 114–16, 131, 174–78, 269, 271, 273, 279, 288, 290, 291; *Remonstrance au Peuple Françoys,* 113–14, 270
Deschamps, Eustache, 61–63, 270
Désiré, Artus, *Articles du Traicté,* 99–100
Dicaearchus, *Life of Greece,* 25, 234n, 241–42
Dio Chrysostom: cosmic view of, 203, 222, 223, 224; on kingship, 27n, 221n, orations on peace, 18, 32–33; on peace, 274
Dionysius the Areopagite, 38, 42, 203, 206
Dio of Prusa. *See* Dio Chrysostom
Dorat, Jean, 121, 194n; Latin version of Ronsard's *Exhortation,* 94; *Novem Cantica de Pace,* 147n
du Bartas, Guillaume, *Hymne de la Paix,* 156, 160, 239, 248n
Du Bellay, Joachim, 114; *Discours au Roy,* 111, 270; *Discours sur la Trefve,* 267–68; Latin poem on peace, 92; *Sur la Paix,* 108
Du Troncy, Benoît: description of peace celebrations, 101n, 102n, 103, 104, 105, 106, 116n
Du Verdier, Antoine, *Antitheses de la Paix,* 145; *Mysopolème,* 145

Empedocles, 24, 26, 233; Strife and Love in, 199, 201, 225, 273
Erasmus: animal theme in, 221, 221–25, 229, 243, 252–54; description of war, 290–91; influence of, 53, 55, 56, 82, 139, 144, 146, 256–57; in later poetry, 89, 128, 139; opposition to, 55; as source for Ronsard, 254–55, 256; source in Pindar, 22; topics in, 50–51, 54, 57, 71, 278; works: *Dulce bellum inexpertis,* 22, 50, 51–53, 136n, 139, 140n, 144, 223–24, 229, 243, 256, 290; *Institutio principis Christiani,* 51, 221;

Index

Index

Velleius Paterculus, 276, 277

Vida, Girolamo, *To Peace*, 171–74, 179, 277, 283, 286, 287, 291, 292, 293

Villon, François, *Le Dit de la naissance Marie*, 70n

Virgil, 28, 31; adaptations and imitations, 44, 110, 126, 163n, 189–90, 259; influence, 77, 190, 191, 193, 194; works: *Aeneid*, 29, 190, 210, 268, 272; *Eclogues*, 28, 31, 183, 184, 189, 190, 193, 232, 233, 234, 272, 274, 288; *Georgics*, 29, 31, 183, 185, 190, 194, 226n, 233, 259, 280

Xenophon, 22; man vs. animals, 244, 245, 250

Zanchi, Basilio, *Hymnus pacis aeternae*, 90, 190–91; concluding prayer, 294; peace topics, 269, 271, 272, 273, 278, 279, 281, 288, 292

Index of Subjects

Index

LIBRARY OF CONGRESS CATALOGING IN PUBLICATION DATA

Hutton, James, 1902–1980
 Themes of peace in Renaissance poetry.

 Includes index.
 1. European poetry—Renaissance, 1450–1600—History and criticism. 2.
Peace in literature. I. Guerlac, Rita. II. Title
PN1181.H884   1984   809.1'9358   84-7631
ISBN 0-8014-1613-2 (alk. paper)